LEGACY OF

dissent

40 YEARS OF WRITING
FROM *DISSENT* MAGAZINE

Edited by Nicolaus Mills
With an Introduction by Mitchell Cohen
Preface by Michael Walzer

A TOUCHSTONE BOOK

Published by Simon & Schuster
New York   London   Toronto   Sydney   Tokyo   Singapore

TOUCHSTONE
Rockefeller Center
1230 Avenue of the Americas
New York, New York 10020

TOUCHSTONE and colophon are
registered trademarks of Simon & Schuster Inc.

Designed by Irving Perkins Associates, Inc.
Manufactured in the United States of America

1   3   5   7   9   10   8   6   4   2

Library of Congress Cataloging-in-Publication Data

Legacy of *Dissent:* 40 years of writing from *Dissent* magazine/edited by Nicolaus
Mills; with an introduction by Mitchell Cohen; preface by Michael Walzer.
p.   cm.
"A Touchstone book."
1. Socialism. 2. Social problems. I. Mills, Nicolaus. II. *Dissent.*
HX15.L44 1994   94–28088
335—dc20   CIP

ISBN 0-671-88879-X

In memory of Irving Howe

Contents

III. Culture and Society

IV. Race

V. Feminism

Preface

◆

MICHAEL WALZER

Michael Walzer is co-editor of *Dissent*. He began writing for *Dissent* while a student at Brandeis University, where he studied with Irving Howe and Lewis Coser. Since 1980 he has been a member of the faculty at the Institute for Advanced Study, Princeton. His books include *Just and Unjust Wars, Spheres of Justice*, and *Company of Critics*.

Dissent is a magazine for people who know how to worry. Founded and sustained for forty years by editors and writers with strong democratic-socialist convictions who had, so to speak, lost their Marxist footing, it has steadfastly avoided the flat assurances of the old, ideologically driven Left. *Dissent*'s radicalism has never been scientific. No one in its pages has claimed to possess the single sure remedy for the sociological equivalents of hair loss, anemia, cancer, and the common cold. Its writers have developed a new version of the "union of theory and practice," joining moral commitment and political criticism, the two directed simultaneously against the conventional wisdom of the intelligentsia and the tyrannical rule of established elites in both the state and the economy.

I don't mean to suggest that *Dissent* has been without enthusiasm. But this enthusiasm has always been concrete—a celebration of men and women on the ground, in the "real world," fighting for civil rights, demanding democratic government, laying claim to a more equal share of opportunities, resources, powers. The articles and essays collected in this book record a continuous effort to locate these men and women, to understand what they are doing, to honor their struggle, and to offer them practical advice and honest criticism. What is missing here, and deliberately so, is any attempt to tell them what they must do, assign them a theoretical task or a world-historical role.

From its first issue, *Dissent*'s relation to the future has been one of hope, not prediction. Over the years, the reiterated message of the editors has gone something like this: "We have a vision of a better society (not the one and only best society), but we don't know with any certainty how to achieve it or who its agents are or what historical stages we must pass through to get there or exactly what its institutional structures will be like. All these things we have to argue about. Our vision is democratic and egalitarian, and so our arguments must be accessible to the widest possible public, undogmatic, open to contradiction, respectful of difference. We will not avoid polemical sharpness (as readers will quickly realize), but we renounce sectarian splits and excommunications. *Dissent* must not only express, but also incorporate dissidence."

So it has. The range of disagreement has been wide, its limits set only by the democratic commitments of the editors: the magazine has not published apologies for tyrants, even for tyrants masquerading as leftists, and it has consistently avoided the various forms of intellectual arrogance, the disdain for ordinary men and women who fail to live up to the expectations of high theory. With regard to every other question of political order, economic arrangements, and cultural values, writers have ranged freely, unconstrained by anything like a party line. In a sense, the "crisis of the left," supposedly brought about by the collapse of communism, has been anticipated in *Dissent* for forty years. Not that the specific character of the crisis was foreseen, but rather that the issues it has brought forward—statism, democracy, equality, nationalism, markets, welfare—have been the stuff of debate among dissenters from the beginning.

What has kept the debate going for so long is a democratic-socialist vision. If the magazine has been worried, it has also been stubborn. The point of it all, of politics and criticism alike, is a society more egalitarian, more cooperative, and more democratic, whose citizens are more engaged with one another and more active and decisive in shaping their common life. "More" means more than now: it is a relative, not an absolute measure—"a world more attractive" than this one.

The guiding spirit of the magazine over the years was Irving Howe, who did not live to see its fortieth birthday. This book is dedicated to him. But he did not work alone. The writers whose pieces are collected here are all contributors—in the strong sense of that word: unpaid volunteers, who shared the vision and the worries. The magazine is their collective effort, and the fact that it is celebrated here is no sign that the effort is nearing its end. It is as necessary today as it was in the dim years of the middle 1950s.

Introduction

The Road to Dissent: Some Prehistory

◆

MITCHELL COHEN

Mitchell Cohen is co-editor of *Dissent* and professor of political science at Bernard Baruch College and the Graduate School of the City University of New York. In 1993–94 he was a National Endowment for the Humanities Fellow at the Institute for Advanced Studies, Princeton. His books include *The Wager of Lucien Goldmann: Tragedy, Dialectics and a Hidden God, Zion and the State: Nation, Class and the Shaping of Modern Israel,* and (as editor) *Rebels and Reactionaries: An Anthology of Great Political Stories.*

When *Dissent* was born, in the winter of 1954, the cold war, more than anything else, shaped how Americans viewed the world. The Korean War had just ended; McCarthyism was still potent; Dwight Eisenhower had become president, marking the end of twenty years of liberal Democratic occupancy of the White House; and Joseph Stalin's death, in March 1953, had closed one of the ugliest chapters in human history, a quarter century during which, in the name of "socialism," a country was industrialized by means of extraordinary brutality.

Indeed, for most Americans, the very word "socialism" was (as it still is) identified with the Kremlin's late dictator—an identification applauded by both communists and right-wingers. Many intellectuals who had been on the left were fleeing their past, anxiously making peace with American prosperity, often through embracing an anti-communism blind to everything save East-West confrontation. It was not the most auspicious moment for a new journal to appear under the editorship of impassioned anti-Stalinists who nonetheless insisted, as Lewis Coser and Irving Howe did in *Dissent*'s second issue, that "socialism is the image of our desire."

In founding *Dissent,* a stubborn group of radical intellectuals decided to maintain intellectual radicalism, to step out of step—to dissent from the intellectual moment. They were vexed by the rightward
drift in the intellectual world, all while they were more and more restless with dogmatism and sectarianism in the American left. They denied to Stalinist and right-winger alike the definition of "socialism."

Yet, looking back at *Dissent*'s early years, one is struck not only by its
editors' dogged fidelity to socialist values but equally by their refusal
to allow that fidelity to become dogmatism. On one hand, socialism—by which they meant the extension of democracy throughout
all dimensions of life, economic and social as well as political—remained for them the best hope for a fair society, for an America in
which the word "justice" truly meant something. On the other hand,
they recognized that "the idea of socialism [had] itself to be treated
as problematic rather than as a fixed piety," as Howe, *Dissent*'s moving
spirit for its first four decades, later wrote. The socialist idea was "no
longer young, no longer innocent."

The early 1950s represented a juncture in which the New York intellectuals—products of the 1930s—were deradicalizing as the American left was unraveling. In these developments, and in resistance to
them, one finds the sources of *Dissent.* New York had been the center
of intellectual radicalism since before World War I, when Greenwich
Village bohemianism cross-pollinated with the nascent American socialist movement, then in its sole period of ascendance. The spirit of
the times was expressed by the mixture of political and cultural radicalism in journals like *The Masses* and *Seven Arts* and in the writings
and activities of Floyd Dell, Van Wyck Brooks, Emma Goldman, John
Reed, Max Eastman, and Randolph Bourne, among others.* That
spirit was dissolved by World War I and the Russian Revolution. Opposition to the war undid *The Masses* and *Seven Arts,* and by the end of
the decade, the American Socialist Party, which had received more
than nine hundred thousand votes in the 1912 presidential elections,
was shattered. Its leader, the remarkable Eugene V. Debs, was in
prison for his antiwar stance, and supporters of the Bolsheviks split
the party. The American Communist Party was to be the chief rival of

*Here, and throughout this introduction, my historical account draws from James
Gilbert's *Writer and Partisans: A History of Literary Radicalism in America* (Columbia
University Press, 1992); Irving Howe, *A Margin of Hope* (Harcourt Brace Jovanovich,
1982); Irving Howe, "Introduction," *25 Years of Dissent* (Methuen, 1979); and Maurice
Isserman's *If I Had a Hammer: The Death of the Old Left and the Birth of the New Left* (Ba-
sic Books, 1987).

the socialists when, a decade later, they again gathered some force under the leadership of Norman Thomas.

The 1930s posed substantial challenges to intellectuals on the left. Franklin Roosevelt's New Deal, combining government activism and the rudiments of a welfare state, seemed to carry out, at least in part, socialist tenets (Yes!—but on a stretcher, declared Norman Thomas). Above all, there was a new atmosphere of possibilities, of men and women energized for change, of new forces—unions, especially—on the move. Across the Atlantic, however, there were other, ominous developments. Hitler and Mussolini were in power, and soon Spain was submerged in civil war. Stalin was purging opponents (some real, some imagined), a process culminating in the Moscow Trials of 1936–38. Communists twisted and turned, trying to remain consistent with—and trying to excuse—the Kremlin's dizzying changes of policy. In the late 1920s, at Moscow's behest, Communist parties throughout the world had denounced socialists and social democrats as "social fascists." By the mid-1930s, however, Communists championed "Popular Fronts" of all "Democratic Forces"—now including both liberals and former "social fascists"—to face the threat of the real fascists. In the cultural realm, American communists, once advocates of "proletarian literature"—the realistic depiction of the situation of workers—now championed literature that espoused liberal and democratic themes (including "Americanism")—a literary Popular Front. In either case, revolution in cultural and literary forms—which in the early twentieth century meant modernism—was anathema to them.

This was the setting in which the "New York Intellectuals"—it is Howe's term—took shape, especially around *Partisan Review. PR* emerged in the late 1930s as the independent voice of political and cultural radicalism, upholding an anti-Stalinist left-wing politics and valuing the achievements of literary modernism. Initially it advocated an independent Marxism and many in its orbit were attracted to Leon Trotsky, the exiled Bolshevik who was a foe (and finally a victim) of Stalin. They were contemptuous not only of communist political apologetics and cultural simplicities, but of the Popular Front and liberals who embraced it. Politically speaking, Stalin's murderous deceit was there to be seen for whoever had eyes (the Moscow Trials deeply affected the New York intellectuals). And as far as communist literary dogma was concerned—it was absurd to reduce the poetry of T. S. Eliot (for one example) to its function (or nonfunction) in the political and social worlds.

Political intellectuals and cultural creators had to be granted their own space; one might say that in *PR* radical politics and literary modernism were united under one roof, but with separate bedrooms. It was a liberating move, if only because the Stalinist marriage of politics and literature was always at the expense of the latter. But in their (justified) reaction against Stalinism, *PR* intellectuals sometimes lost political perspective. Consider the following, an editor's response to criticisms of *PR* for its publication of Eliot: "It is coming to be something of a revolutionary act simply to print serious creative writing." These words appeared in the November–December 1941 issue, on the eve of Pearl Harbor—to which one could hardly respond with poetry.

In the late 1940s, with Hitler's defeat and the advent of the Cold War, *PR* moved increasingly away from a critical perspective on America. If, in 1940, political radicalism and literary modernism were cohabitants, a decade later one party had moved out—or had been moved out. In 1947, after the journal published a symposium on "The Future of Socialism," Irving Howe, then a Trotskyist-oriented political activist and aspiring literary critic, wrote to the managing editor about how "one-sided" the list of contributors was—most had abandoned any sort of socialist commitments.

In fact, less and less was left in left-wing anti-Stalinism; it was steadily displaced by a simplistic anticommunism. In this sense *PR*, along with magazines such as *Commentary* and *The New Leader,* served as midwives of neoconservatism. In *Partisans and Writers,* his history of *Partisan Review,* James Gilbert notes that *PR*, from the 1930s on, was marked by hostility to liberals; first because they weren't revolutionary enough, later because they weren't sufficiently anti-Soviet. One *PR* editor, William Phillips, in a letter to Arthur Koestler in October 1946, wrote that "the Left must not permit the struggle against Stalinism to be appropriated by the Right." Certainly he was right, but, rather than refusing such permission, many New York intellectuals moved to the right themselves. Eventually only the independent anti-Stalinist left was without an intellectual home—in a country notable for its dislike of both intellectuals and the left.

Here is where a second strand enters the story. Throughout its history, sectarianism has plagued the American—and not only the American—left. Irving Howe, together with some of his close associates in founding *Dissent,* knew a great deal about it. They had been sectarians, deeply immersed in a Trotskyist-oriented movement, and by the early 1950s were looking for a way out.

The Russian Revolution of 1917 lent Bolshevism and Communist parties prestige and captured the imagination of many radicals around the globe. However distant Lenin's ideas were from those of Marx, Moscow provided success and faith, even if the latter was doctored up as science. But the very idea of a vanguard party embodying "the science of society" lends itself to sectarianism: the party becomes the sole repository of truth, and everyone else becomes witch doctors.

By the 1930s the Soviet project presented an immense problem to all thinking intellectuals of the left—those, that is, who had not been bewitched by Stalinism. For many attached to the initial Leninist project—or what they conceived to be the initial project—Trotsky, the absent defendant at the Moscow Trials, incarnated Bolshevism unbetrayed. But soon enough—by the time of his murder in Mexico by a Stalinist agent in 1940—Trotsky's followers in the West splintered. Their dispute, though it might appear at first glance to have been yet another sectarian squabble, was of great importance. It helped to generate an idea that became enormously influential throughout the intellectual and academic world, in the U.S. and abroad: the idea that the Soviet Union represented a novelty in political history, a "totalitarian" regime.

On one side were those who followed Trotsky's line: the U.S.S.R. was a "degenerated workers' state," but a workers' state nonetheless, because of its nationalized economy. What was required, therefore, was a political—though not socioeconomic—revolution to overthrow the Stalinist bureaucracy. On the other side were those who thought the "old man" was wrong: the U.S.S.R., they contended, was neither a socialist nor a degenerated workers' state. On the contrary, it was something else, something new—"bureaucratic collectivist" and totalitarian in nature—which had to be opposed no less than capitalism. Within American Trotskyism, this latter position was articulated especially by Max Shachtman. Similar themes appeared in the writings of James Burnham and Dwight Macdonald.

Shachtman's Workers' Party, founded in 1940 (it later became the Independent Socialist League), sought to be both anti-Stalinist and faithful to Bolshevism. It was a small, intense, and committed band dominated by a clever, pugnacious, and forceful personality. Several of *Dissent*'s founders—Howe, Stanley Plastrik, Emmanuel Geltman— were leading activists in its ranks who, by the early 1950s, found its politics too rigid and its horizons too limited. They yearned for a more open American radicalism, one that retained a sharp critical edge but which spoke to American life, and not in the language of Russian revolutionaries. As Irving Howe wrote in his memoir *A Mar-*

gin of Hope, "those of us who rebelled against sect claustrophobia still wanted to keep some of the ideas and values that had propelled us into the sects in the first place." This would lead them, eventually, away from Trotskyism to the democratic-socialist/social-democratic politics for which *Dissent* became known.

Howe had, for a period, worked for *Politics,* a journal which, under the editorship of the maverick essayist Dwight Macdonald, had sought to revive an open-minded, independent radicalism. It was a short-lived but remarkable effort, and its demise left a real void—one that must have been particularly evident when a symposium appeared in *PR* in 1952 entitled "Our Country and Our Culture." In it an array of leading intellectuals, many of them ex-radicals, declared that they had "adjusted." Nowadays, its editorial preface attested, most intellectuals and writers "want very much to be part of American life." Two years later—just when the first issue of *Dissent* was about to appear—a powerful riposte appeared in *PR* entitled "This Age of Conformity." This article, a critical evaluation of the situation of the American intellectual, was written by Irving Howe. Its premise was simple: an intellectual's task was to maintain a critical edge and not to adjust to society.

Intellectuals, he warned, tend toward grandiosity. Nothing exemplified this more than Joseph Schumpeter's contention that capitalism would finally be undone not by economics (as Marx thought) but by its inability to command loyalty: it created neurotic intellectuals who in turn project utopian dreams that threaten the very capitalist system that made them possible. Howe protested: this theme—it was to become a favorite among neoconservatives—ignores the fact that intellectuals were actually being integrated into the system to an unprecedented degree. Western society needed them for ideological purposes and to provide for the burgeoning culture industry.

Moreover, bohemia, whose rise accompanied the most vibrant moments in intellectual life, had disintegrated as the setting for intellectual activities shifted to institutions, especially academic ones created by the rapid expansion of higher education. Intellectuals were becoming comfortable; their willingness to be iconoclastic, to be critical, to stand alone, was being undermined. The problem was not simply conservatism, but conformism: "let the zeitgeist give them a jog and they will be radical, all too radical," Howe wrote. In such an age, "the whole idea of the intellectual vocation—the idea of a life dedicated to values that cannot possibly be realized in a commercial civilization"—was threatened, and "it is this rather than the abandonment of a particular program which constitutes our rout." Several decades before, wealth was on the defensive and the intellect self-assured; now intellect lay prostrate before power and affluence and "a whining genteel chauvinism is spreading among intellectuals."

Irving Howe recognized that, due to the danger posed by Stalinism, political options had been limited for intellectuals. Yet, though this "may require temporary expedients in the area of power such as would have seemed compromising some years ago . . . there is no reason why it should lead us to become partisans of bourgeois society, which is itself . . . heavily responsible for the Stalinist victories. . . ." If compromises had to be made to survive in this world, the question became whether such compromises were undertaken with open eyes. Conformism, Howe maintained as well, had permeated the literary world, where among critics there seemed to be "a transparent lack of interest in represented experience." The "uneasy but fruitful union" between radicalism and culture, between "the critical consciousness and the political conscience, between the avant-garde of letters and the independent left of politics," once represented by *PR*, had been broken, with the literary avant-garde declining and American radicalism remaining little more than an idea.

Howe continued this argument in "Stevenson and the Intellectuals" in the first issue of *Dissent*—a journal which, one might say, aimed to promote an independent American radicalism in an age of conformity. A crucial link between the two articles is their understanding of liberalism and its relation to the left. Howe, in later years, often referred to himself as a "liberal socialist." He believed that the egalitarian drive of socialism had to be bound inseparably to liberalism's most fruitful notions, such as tolerance and individual rights. But this bond also had to incorporate a critique of the myths, failures, and insufficiencies of liberalism.

Thus Howe was at odds with the relentless antiliberal posture of *PR* and, later, of the neoconservatives. He criticized liberals from the left—"liberalism's then dominant position in America contributed heavily to our intellectual conformity"—but he also wanted liberals as allies in changing America. A renewed American radicalism would have to "acknowledge not only its break from, but its roots in, the American liberal tradition."

So, when he wrote on "Stevenson and the Intellectuals," Howe began by saying—albeit with discomfort—that he favored reviving the left within the framework of the Democratic Party. (After the 1960s this became the strategy of the successor organizations to the Socialist Party—the Democratic Socialist Organizing Committee and later the Democratic Socialists of America, both led by Michael Harrington, Howe's longtime colleague and a member of the *Dissent* editorial board.) Yet, if the left was to work within a major party—that is, if it was going to engage the American mainstream—an essential question remained the terms of engagement. Consequently, while Howe suggested a strategy of working within the Democratic Party, he also analyzed and acutely criticized liberal intellectuals who were "bewitched" by Adlai Stevenson—a man who had supported the Smith Act, who managed in a speech to equate "anti-Southernism" with "anti-Negroism," and who was "the first of the liberal candidates in the post-Wilson era who made no effort to align himself with the plebeian tradition."

Of course Howe recognized that politics entailed, more than occasionally, doing some unpalatable things. The task was to fashion a practical politics that was equally a politics of integrity. So, when he declared that "the whole failure of recent liberalism has been precisely its inability to distinguish between expediency within the framework of principle and expediency that undermines and rots any principle," he was not only speaking as a critic of liberals and conformism, he was marking parameters for a nonsectarian democratic left engaged with, but not mindlessly celebrating, the American mainstream.

He took the symposium—or much of it—on "Our Country and Our Culture" in *PR* to be just such a hollow celebration. The premier journal for independent radicals—the only one with broad intellectual appeal—was no longer radical, leaving an intellectual void. Howe believed also that many intellectuals had failed to respond forcefully to McCarthyism. Moreover, McCarthyism had made it difficult for voices on the left—including what remained of the anti-Stalinist left—to be heard. And there seemed to be no appealing organizational home for independent radicals; their options for practical political engagement were limited. "When intellectuals can do nothing else," Howe later wrote, "they start a magazine."

In the early 1950s Howe was teaching literature at Brandeis University. With him was Lewis Coser, a sociologist who had fled Hitler and had written for a variety of American intellectual journals. It was Coser who proposed that they initiate a new magazine to be called *Dissent*. Howe and Coser asked Meyer Schapiro, the eminent art critic, to join them, and a meeting was called in New York. A small sum was raised—with the help of Joseph Buttinger, an exiled Austrian social democrat—and *Dissent* was launched. Its aim was to provide a forum in which a democratic and egalitarian American politics could be articulated—a forum and a politics unafraid of controversial ideas and ready to oppose, from the left, what was wrong in the United States, but also any regime masking oppression with left-wing language. In contrast to *PR*'s literary concerns, and despite its frequent coverage of cultural issues, *Dissent*'s preoccupations were primarily political.

And they still are. Of course, a great deal has changed. Since *Dissent* was founded, America has experienced the civil-rights movement, Vietnam, the ascent and fall of the New Left, the rise of feminism, Watergate, the Reaganite carnival of selfishness, and the disintegration of the Soviet Union. All these were reflected and dissected in its pages. Most recently the collapse of communism, one of the great moments of modern history, was applauded in *Dissent* both for its intrinsic value—the end of dictatorships—and because it freed the left of an albatross. Yet it is perhaps better to say that it only began to free the left, for the consequences of communism's violent abduction of the socialist idea will be with us for a long time. Frankly, we may never be rid of them fully.

But there always was an alternative—the combination of democratic radicalism and self-critical idealism that gave birth to and animated *Dissent* magazine for forty years. And that is what the reader will discover in this anthology.

Social Visions

Images of Socialism
1954

◆

LEWIS COSER AND IRVING HOWE

Irving Howe (1920–1993) was *Dissent*'s principal editor and guiding spirit from the magazine's formation until his death thirty-nine years later. A National Book Award winner and a MacArthur Fellow, he was a prolific essayist and critic for six decades. His books include biographies of Sherwood Anderson, William Faulkner, and Thomas Hardy, *Politics and the Novel, World of Our Fathers, Socialism and America,* and an autobiography, *A Margin of Hope.*

Lewis Coser, a past president of the American Sociological Association, is one of the founding editors of *Dissent*. His books include *The Functions of Social Conflict,* and, with Irving Howe, *The American Communist Party: A Critical History.*

"God," said Tolstoy, "is the name of my desire." This remarkable sentence could haunt one a lifetime, it reverberates in so many directions. Tolstoy may have intended partial assent to the idea that, life being insupportable without some straining toward "transcendence," a belief in God is a psychological necessity. But he must also have wanted to turn this rationalist criticism into a definition of his faith. He must have meant that precisely because his holiest desires met in the vision of God he was enabled to cope with the quite unholy realities of human existence. That God should be seen as the symbolic objectification of his desire thus became both a glorification of God and a strengthening of man, a stake in the future and a radical criticism of the present.

Without sanctioning the facile identification that is frequently made between religion and socialist politics, we should like to twist Tolstoy's remark to our own ends: *socialism is the name of our desire.* And not merely in the sense that it is a vision which, for many people throughout the world, provides moral sustenance, but also in the sense that it is a vision which objectifies and gives urgency to their criticism of the human condition in our time. It is the name of our desire because the desire arises from a conflict with, and an extension from, the world that is; nor could the desire survive in any meaningful way were it not for this complex relationship to the world that is.

At so late and unhappy a moment, however, can one still specify what the vision of socialism means or should mean? Is the idea of utopia itself still a tolerable one?

I

The impulse to imagine "the good society" probably coincides with human history, and the manner of constructing it—to invert what exists—is an element binding together all pre-Marxist utopias. These dreamers and system-makers have one thing in common: their desire to storm history.

The growth of the modern utopian idea accompanies the slow formation of the centralized state in Europe. Its imagery is rationalistic, far removed from the ecstatic visions that accompany the religiously inspired rebellions agitating feudal society in its last moments. As the traditional patchwork of autonomous social institutions in Western Europe was replaced, in the interests of efficiency, by an increasingly centralized system of rule, men began to conceive of a society that would drive this tendency to its conclusion and be governed completely by rationality. But not only the increasing rationality of political power inspired the thinking of social philosophers; they were stirred by the growth of a new, bourgeois style of life that emphasized calculation, foresight, and efficiency, and made regularity of work an almost religious obligation.

As soon as men began to look at the state as "a work of art," as "an artificial man, created for the protection and salvation of the natural man" (Hobbes, *Leviathan*), it took but one more step to imagine that the "work of art" could be rendered perfect through foresight and will. Thomas Campanella, a rebellious Calabrian monk of the seventeenth century, conceived in his *City of the Sun* of such a perfect work of art. In Campanella's utopia, unquestionably designed from the most idealistic of motives, one sees the traits of many pre-Marxist utopias. Salvation is *imposed*, delivered from above; there is an all-powerful ruler called the Great Metaphysicus (surely no more absurd than the Beloved Leader); only one book exists in the City of the Sun, which may be taken as an economical image of modern practice: naturally, a book called Wisdom. Sexual relations are organized by state administrators "according to philosophical rules," the race being "managed for the good of the commonwealth and not of private individuals. . . ." Education is conceived along entirely rationalist lines, and indeed it must be, for Campanella felt that the Great Metaphysicus, as he forces perfection upon history, has to deal with recalcitrant materials: the people, he writes in a sentence that betrays both his bias and his pathos, is "a beast with a muddy brain."

And here we come upon a key to utopian thought: the galling sense of a chasm between the scheme and the subjects, between the plan, ready and perfect, and the people, mute and indifferent. (Poor Fourier, the salesman with Phalanxes in his belfry, comes home daily at noon, to wait for the one capitalist, he needs no more than one, who will finance utopia.) Intellectuals who cannot shape history try to rape it, either through actual violence, like the Russian terrorists, or imagined violence, the sudden seizure of history by a utopian claw. In his City of the Sun Campanella decrees—the utopian never hesitates to decree—that those sentenced to death for crimes against the God-head, liberty, and the higher magistrates are to be rationally enlightened, before execution, by special functionaries, so that in the end they will acquiesce in their own condemnation. Let no one say history is unforeseen.

Two centuries after Campanella, Etienne Cabet, a disciple of Robert Owen and Saint-Simon, envisaged the revolutionary dictatorship of Icar, an enlightened ruler who refuses to stay in power longer than is necessary for establishing the new society; he no doubt means it to wither away. Meanwhile, Icaria has only one newspaper, and the republic has "revised all useful books which showed imperfections and it has burned all those which we judged dangerous and useless."

The point need not be overstressed. The utopians were not—or not merely—the unconscious authoritarians that malicious critics have made them out to be. No doubt, some did harbor strong streaks of authoritarian feeling which they vicariously released through utopian images; but this is far from the whole story. Robert Owen wanted a free cooperative society. Decentralization is stressed in Morelly's utopia, "Floating Islands." The phalanxes of Fourier are to function without any central authority, and if there must be one, it should be located as far from France as possible, certainly no nearer than Constantinople.

But it is not merely a question of desirable visions. In the most far-fetched and mad fantasies of the utopian there are embedded brilliant insights. The same Fourier who envisaged the transformation of brine into an agreeable liquid, and the replacement of lion and sharks by mildly domestic "anti-lions" and "anti-sharks," also writes with the deepest understanding of the need for both the highest specialization of labor in modern society and the greatest variety and alternation of labor in order to overcome the monotony of specialization. Puzzling over the perennial teaser set before socialists—"Who'll do the dirty work?"—Fourier comes up with the shrewd psychological observation that it is children who most enjoy dirt and . . .

The authoritarian element we find in the utopians is due far less to psychological malaise or power-hunger (most of them were genuinely good people) than to the sense of desperation that frequently lies beneath the surface of their fantasying. All pre-Marxist utopian thinking tends to be ahistorical, to see neither possibility nor need for relating the image of the good society to the actual workings of society, as it is. For Fourier it is simply a matter of discovering the "plan" of God, the ordained social order that in realizing God's will ensure man's happiness. (Socialism for Fourier is indeed the name of his desire—but in a very different sense from that which we urge!) The imagined construction of utopia occurs *outside* the order or flux of history: it comes through fiat. Once utopia is established, history grinds to a standstill and the rule of rationality replaces the conflict of class or, as the utopians might have preferred to say, the conflict of passions. In his "Socialism, Utopian and Scientific" Friedrich Engels describes this process with both sympathy and shrewdness:

> Society presented nothing but wrongs; to remove these was the task of reason. It was necessary, then, to *impose this upon society from without* by propaganda and, whenever possible, by the example of model experiments. These new social systems were foredoomed as utopian; the more completely they were worked out in detail, the more they could not avoid drifting off into pure phantasies. . . .

We can leave it to the literary small fry to solemnly quibble over these phantasies, which today only make us smile, and to crow over the superiority of their own bald reasoning, as compared with such 'in-san-

ity.' As for us, we delight in the stupendously great thoughts and germs
of thought that everywhere break out through their phantastic covering. . . . [Emphasis added.]

Given the desire to impose utopia upon an indifferent history, a
desire which derives, in the main, from a deep sense of alienation
from the flow of history, it follows logically enough that the utopians
should for the most part think in terms of elite politics. Auguste
Comte specifies that, in the "State of Positive Science," society is to be
ruled by an elite of intellectuals. The utopia to be inaugurated by the
sudden triumph of reason over the vagaries and twists of history—
what other recourse could a lonely, isolated utopian have but the
elite, the small core of intellect that, like himself, controls and
guides? Saint-Simon, living in the afterglow of the French Revolution,
begins to perceive the mechanics of class relations and the appearance for the first time in modern history of the masses as a decisive
force. But in the main our generalization holds: reformers who lack
some organic relationship with major historical movements must almost always be tempted into a more or less benevolent theory of a ruling elite.

II

Utopia without egalitarianism, utopia dominated by an aristocracy of
mind, must quickly degenerate into a vision of useful slavery. Hence,
the importance of Marx's idea that socialism is to be brought about,
in the first instance, by the activities of a major segment of the population, the workers. Having placed the drive toward utopia not beyond but squarely—perhaps a little too squarely—within the course
of history, and having found in the proletariat that active "realizing"
force which the utopians could nowhere discern on the social horizon, Marx was enabled to avoid the two major difficulties of his predecessors: ahistoricism and the elite theory. He had, to be sure,
difficulties of his own, but not these.

Marx was the first of the major socialist figures who saw the possibility of linking the utopian desire with the actual development of social life. By studying capitalism both as an "ideal" structure and a
"real" dynamic, Marx found the sources of revolt within the self-ex-
panding and self-destroying rhythms of the economy itself. The
utopians had desired a revolt against history but they could conduct

it, so to speak, only from the space-platform of the imaginary future; Marx gave new power to the revolt against history by locating it, "scientifically," within history.

The development of technology, he concluded, made possible a society in which men could "realize" their humanity, if only because the brutalizing burden of fatigue, that sheer physical exhaustion from which the great masses of men had never been free, could now for the first time be removed. This was the historic option offered mankind by the Industrial Revolution, as it is now being offered again by the Atomic Revolution. Conceivably, though only conceivably, a society might have been established at any point in historical time which followed an equalitarian distribution of goods; but there would have been neither goods nor leisure enough to dispense with the need for a struggle over their distribution; which means bureaucracy, police, an oppressive state; and in sum, the destruction of equalitarianism. Now, after the Industrial Revolution, the machine might do for all humanity what the slaves had done for the Greek patriciate.

Marx was one of the first political thinkers to see that both industrialism and "the mass society" were here to stay, that all social schemes which ignored or tried to controvert this fact were not merely irrelevant, they weren't even interesting. It is true, of course, that he did not foresee—he could not—a good many consequences of this tremendous historical fact. He did not foresee that "mass culture" together with social atomization (Durkheim's *anomie*) would set off strong tendencies of demoralization working in opposition to those tendencies that made for disciplined cohesion in the working class. He did not foresee that the rise of totalitarianism might present mankind with choices and problems that went beyond the capitalist/socialist formulation. He did not foresee that the nature of leisure would become, even under capitalism, as great a social and cultural problem as the nature of work. He did not foresee that industrialism would create problems which, while not necessarily insoluble, are likely to survive the span of capitalism. But what he did foresee was crucial: that the great decisions of history would now be made in a mass society; that the "stage" upon which this struggle would take place had suddenly, dramatically been widened far beyond its previous dimensions.

And when Marx declared the proletariat to be the active social force that could lead the transition to socialism, he was neither sentimentalizing the lowly nor smuggling in a theory of the elite, as many of his critics have suggested. Anyone who has read the chapter in *Capital* on the Working Day or Engels's book on the conditions of the English workers knows that they measured the degradation of the workers to an extent precluding sentimentality. As for the idea of the proletariat as an elite, Marx made no special claim for its virtue or intelligence, which is the traditional mode of justifying an elite; he merely analyzed its peculiar *position* in society, as the class most driven by the workings of capitalism to both discipline and rebellion, the class that, come what may, utopia or barbarism, would always remain propertyless.

There is another indication that Marx did not mean to favor an elite theory by his special "placing" of the proletariat. His theory of "increasing misery"—be it right, wrong, or vulgarized—implied that the proletariat would soon include the overwhelming bulk of the population. The transition to socialism, far from being assigned to a "natural" elite or a power group, was seen by Marx as the task of the vast "proletarianized" majority. Correct or not, this was a fundamentally democratic point of view.

Concerned as he was with the mechanics of class power, the "laws of motion" of the existing society, and the strategy of social change, Marx paid very little attention to the description of socialism. The few remarks to be found in his early work and in such a later book as *The Critique of the Gotha Program* are mainly teasers, formulations so brief as to be cryptic, which did not prevent his disciples from making them into dogmas. An interesting division of labor took place. Marx's predecessors, those whom he called the "utopian socialists," had devoted themselves to summoning pictures of the ideal future, perhaps in lieu of activity in the detested present; Marx, partly as a reaction to their brilliant daydreaming, decided to focus on an analysis of those elements in the present that made possible a strategy for reaching the ideal future. And in the meantime, why worry about the face of the future, why create absurd blueprints? As a response to Fourier, Saint-Simon, and Owen there was much good sense in this attitude; given the state of the European labor movements in the mid-nineteenth century it was indispensable to turn toward practical problems of national life (Germany) and class organization (England). But the Marxist movement, perhaps unavoidably, paid a price for this emphasis.

As the movement grew, the image of socialism kept becoming hazier and hazier, and soon the haziness came to seem a condition of perfection. The "revisionist" social democrat Eduard Bernstein could write that the goal is nothing, the movement everything; as if a means could be intelligently chosen without an end in view! In his *State and Revolution* Lenin, with far greater fullness than Marx, sketched a vision of socialism profoundly democratic, in which the mass of humanity would break out of its dumbness, so that cooks could become Cabinet ministers, and even the "bourgeois principle of equality" would give way to the true freedom of nonmeasurement: "from each according to his ability and to each according to his need." But this democratic vision did not sufficiently affect his immediate views of political activity, so that in his crucial pamphlet *Will the Bolsheviks Retain State Power?*, written in 1917, Lenin, as if to brush aside the traditional Marxist view that the socialist transformation requires a far greater popular base than any previous social change, could say that "After the 1905 Revolution Russia was ruled by 130,000 landowners. . . . And yet we are told that Russia will not be able to be governed by the 240,000 members of the Bolshevik Party—governing in the interests of the poor and against the rich."

What happened was that the vision of socialism—would it not be better to say the *problem* of socialism?—grew blurred in the minds of many Marxists because they were too ready to entrust it to History. The fetishistic use of the word "scientific," than which nothing could provide a greater sense of assurance, gave the Marxist movement a feeling that it had finally penetrated to the essence of History, and found there once and for all its true meaning. The result was often a deification of History: what God had been to Fourier, History became to many Marxists—a certain force leading to a certain goal. And if indeed the goal was certain, or likely enough to be taken as certain, there was no need to draw up a fanciful blueprint, the future would take care of itself and require no advice from us. True enough, in a way. But the point that soon came to be forgotten was that it is we, in the present, who need the image of the future, not those who may live in it. And the consequence of failing to imagine creatively the face of socialism—which is not at all the same as an absurd effort to paint it in detail—was that it tended to lapse into a conventional and lifeless "perfection."

III

Perfection, in that image of socialism held by many Marxists—the image, that is, which emerged at the level of implicit belief—was one of a society in which tension, conflict, and failure had largely disap-

peared. It would be easy enough to comb the work of the major Marxists in order to prove this statement, but we prefer to appeal to common experience, to our own knowledge and memories as well as to
the knowledge and memories of others. In the socialist movement
one did not worry about the society one wanted: innumerable and, indeed, inconceivable subjects were discussed but almost never the idea
of socialism itself, for History, Strategy and The Party (how easily the
three melted into one!) had eliminated that need. Socialism was the
Future—and sometimes a future made curiously respectable, the middle-class values that the radicals had violently rejected now being rein-
stated, unwittingly, in their vision of the good society. There could
hardly be a need to reply to those critics who wondered how some of
the perennial human problems could be solved under socialism: one
knew they would be. In effect, the vision of socialism had a way of declining into a regressive infantile fantasy, a fantasy of protection.

Our criticism is not that the Marxist movement held to a vision of
utopia: that it did so was entirely to its credit, a life without some glim-
mer of a redeeming future being a life cut off from the distinctively
human. Our complaint is rather that the vision of utopia grew slack
and static. Sometimes it degenerated into what William Morris called
"the cockney dream" by which efficiency becomes a universal solvent
for all human problems; sometimes it slipped off, beyond human
reach, to the equally repulsive vision of a society in which men become rational titans as well behaved and tedious as Swift's
Houhynhnms. Only occasionally was socialism envisaged as a society
with its own rhythm of growth and tension, change and conflict.

Marx's contribution to human thought is immense, but, except for
some cryptic if pregnant phrases, neither he nor his disciples have
told us very much about the society in behalf of which they called
men into battle. This is not quite so fatal a criticism as it might seem,
since what probably mattered most was that Marxism stirred millions
of previously dormant people into historical action, gave expression
to their claims and yearnings, and lent a certain form to their desire
for a better life. But if we want sustained speculations on the shape of
this better life we have to turn to radical mavericks, to the anarchists
and libertarians, to the Guild Socialists. And to such a writer as Oscar
Wilde, whose *The Soul of Man Under Socialism* is a small masterpiece.
In his paradoxical and unsystematic way Wilde quickly comes to a
sense of what the desirable society might be like. The great advantage
of socialism, he writes, is that it "would relieve us from that sordid necessity of living for others which, in the present condition of things,

presses so hard upon almost everybody." By focusing upon "the un-healthy and exaggerated altruism" which capitalist society demands from people, and by showing how it saps individuality, Wilde arrives at the distinctive virtue of socialism: that it will make possible what he calls Individualism.

IV

We do not wish to succumb to that which we criticize. Blueprints, elaborate schemes do not interest us. But we think it may be useful to suggest some of the qualities that can make the image of socialism a serious and mature goal, as well as some of the difficulties in that goal:

- Socialism is not the end of human history, as the deeply held identification of it with perfection must mean. There is no total fulfillment, nor is there an "end to time." History is a process which throws up new problems, new conflicts, new questions; and socialism, being within history, cannot be expected to solve all these problems or, for that matter, to raise humanity at every point above the level of achievement of previous societies. As Engels remarked, there is no final synthesis, only continued clash. What socialists want is simply to do away with those sources of conflict which are the cause of material deprivation and which, in turn, help create psychological and moral suffering. Freedom may then mean that we can devote ourselves to the pursuit of more worthwhile causes of conflict. The hope for a conflictless society is reactionary, as is a reliance upon some abstract "historical force" that will conciliate all human strife.
- The aim of socialism is to create a society of cooperation, but not necessarily, or at least not universally, of harmony. Cooperation is compatible with conflict, is indeed inconceivable without conflict, while harmony implies a stasis.
- Even the "total abolition" of social classes, no small or easy thing, would not or need not mean the total abolition of social problems.
- In a socialist society there would remain a whole variety of human difficulties that could not easily be categorized as social or nonsocial; difficulties that might well result from the sheer friction between the human being and society, *any* society—from, say, the process of "socializing" those recalcitrant creatures

known as children. The mere existence of man is a difficulty, a problem, with birth, marriage, pain, and death being only among the more spectacular of his crises. To be sure, no intelligent radical has ever denied that *such* crises would last into a socialist society, but the point to be stressed is that, with the elimination of our major material troubles, these other problems might rise to a new urgency, so much so as to become *social* problems leading to new conflicts.

<h1 style="text-align:center">V</h1>

But social problems as we conceive of them today would also be present in a socialist society.

Traditionally, Marxists have lumped all the difficulties posed by critics and reality into that "transitional" state that is to guide, or bump, us from capitalism to socialism, while socialism itself they have seen as the society that would transcend these difficulties. This has made it a little too easy to justify some of the doings of the "transitional" society, while making it easier still to avoid considering—not what socialism *will* be like—but what our image of it should be. Without pretending to "solve" these social problems as they might exist under socialism, but intending to suggest a bias or predisposition, we list here a few of them:

1) BUREAUCRACY

Marxists have generally related the phenomenon of bureaucratism to social inequality and economic scarcity. Thus, they have seen the rise of bureaucracy in Leninist Russia as a consequence of trying to establish a workers' state in an isolated and backward country which lacked the economic prerequisites for building socialism. Given scarcity, there arises a policeman to supervise the distribution of goods; given the policeman, there will be an unjust distribution. Similarly, bureaucratic formations of a more limited kind are seen as parasitic elites which batten upon a social class yet, in some sense, "represent" it in political and economic conflicts. Thus, bureaucratism signifies a deformation, though not necessarily a destruction, of democratic processes.

This view of bureaucratism seems to us invaluable. Yet it would be an error to suppose that, because a class society is fertile ground for bureaucracy, a classless society would automatically be free of bureaucracy. There are other causes for this social deformation; and while in a socialist society these other causes might not be aggravated by economic inequality and the ethos of accumulation as they are under capitalism, they would very likely continue to operate. One need not accept Robert Michels's "Iron Law of Oligarchy" in order to see this. (Michels's theory is powerful but it tends to boomerang: anyone convinced by it that socialism is impossible will have a hard time resisting the idea that democracy is impossible.) Thus, the mere presence of equality of wealth in a society does not necessarily mean an equality of power or status: if Citizen A were more interested in the politics of his town or the functioning of his factory than Citizen B, he would probably accumulate more power and status; hence, the *possibility* of misusing them. (Socialists have often replied, But why should Citizen A want to misuse his power and status when there is no pressing economic motive for doing so? No one can answer this question definitively except by positing some theory of "human nature," which we do not propose to do; all we can urge is a certain wariness with regard to any theory which discounts in advance the possibility that noneconomic motives can lead to human troubles.) Then again, the problem of sheer size in economic and political units is likely to burden a socialist society as much as it burdens any other society; and large political or economic units, because they require an ever-increasing delegation of authority, often to "experts," obviously provide a setting in which bureaucracy can flourish. But most important of all is the sheer problem of representation, the fact that as soon as authority is delegated to a "representative" there must follow a loss of control and autonomy.

Certain institutional checks can, of course, be suggested for containing bureaucracy. The idea of a division of governmental powers, which many Marxists have dismissed as a bourgeois device for thwarting the popular will, would deserve careful attention in planning a socialist society, though one need not suppose that it would have to perpetuate those elements of present-day parliamentary structure which do in fact thwart the popular will. Similarly, the distinction made in English political theory, but neglected by Marxists, between democracy as an expression of popular sovereignty and democracy as a pattern of government in which the rights of minority groups are especially defended, needs to be taken seriously. In general, a society that is pluralist rather than unitary in emphasis, that recognizes the need for diversification of function rather than concentration of authority—this is the desired goal.

And here we have a good deal to learn from a neglected branch of the socialist movement, the Guild Socialists of England, who have given careful thought to these problems. G. D. H. Cole, for example, envisages the socialist society as one in which government policy is a resultant of an interplay among socioeconomic units that simultaneously cooperate and conflict. Cole also puts forward the provocative idea of "functional representation," somewhat similar to the original image of the Soviets. Because, he writes, "a human being, as an individual, is fundamentally incapable of being represented," a man should have "as many distinct, and separately exercised, votes, as he has distinct social purposes or interests," voting, that is, in his capacity of worker, consumer, artist, resident, etc.

But such proposals can hardly be expected to bulk very large unless they are made in a culture where the motives for private accumulation and the values sanctioning it have significantly diminished. If, as we believe, the goal of socialism is to create the kind of man who, to a measurable degree, ceases to be a manipulated object and becomes a motivated subject, then the growth of socialist consciousness must prove an important bulwark against bureaucracy. A society that stresses cooperation can undercut those prestige factors that make for bureaucracy; a society that accepts conflict, and provides a means for modulating it, will encourage those who combat bureaucracy.

2) PLANNING AND DECENTRALIZATION

Unavoidably, a great deal of traditional socialist thought has stressed economic centralization as a prerequisite for planning, especially in the "transitional" state between capitalism and socialism. Partly, this was an inheritance from the bourgeois revolution, which needed a centralized state; partly, it reflected the condition of technology in the nineteenth century, which required centralized units of production; partly, it is a consequence of the recent power of Leninism, which stressed centralism as a means of confronting the primitive chaos of the Russian economy but allowed it to become a dogma in countries where it had no necessary relevance. Whatever the historical validity of these emphases on centralism, they must now be abandoned. According to the famous economist Colin Clark, the new forms of energy permit an economical employment of small decentralized industrial units. Certainly, every impulse of democratic socialism favors such a tendency. For, if mass participation—by the workers, the citizens, the people as a whole—in the economic life of the society is to be meaningful, it must find its most immediate expression in relatively small economic units. Only in such small units is it possible for the nonexpert to exercise any real control.

From what we can learn about Stalinist "planning," we see that an economic plan does not work, it quickly breaks down, if arbitrarily imposed from above and hedged in with rigid specifications which allow for none of the flexibility, none of the economic play, that a democratic society requires. Social planning, if understood in democratic terms—and can there really be social planning, as distinct from economic regulation, without a democratic context?—requires only a loose guiding direction, a general pointer from above. The rest, the actual working out of variables, the arithmetic fulfillment of algebraic possibilities, must come from below, from the interaction, cooperation, and conflict of economic units participating in a democratic community.

All of this implies a considerable modification of the familiar socialist emphasis on nationalization of the means of production, increase of productivity, a master economic plan, etc.—a modification but not a total rejection. To be sure, socialism still presupposes the abolition of private property in the basic industries, but there is hardly a branch of the socialist movement, except the more petrified forms of Trotskyism, which places any high valuation on nationalization of industry *per se*. Almost all socialists now feel impelled to add that what matters is the use to which nationalization is put and the degree of democratic control present in the nationalized industries. But more important, the idea of nationalization requires still greater modification: there is no reason to envisage, even in a "transitional" society, that all basic industries need be owned by the state. The emphasis of the Guild Socialists upon separate Guilds of workers, owning and managing their own industries, summons no doubt a picture of possible struggles within and between industries; all the better! Guilds, cooperatives, call them what you will—these provide possible bulwarks against the monster Leviathan, the all-consuming state, which it is the sheerest fatuity to suppose would immediately cease being a threat to human liberty simply because "we" took it over. The presence of numerous political and economic units, living together in a tension of cooperation-and-conflict, seems the best "guarantee" that power will not accumulate in the hands of a managerial oligarchy—namely, that the process already far advanced in capitalist society will not continue into socialism. Such autonomous units, serving as buffers between government and people, would allow for various, even contradictory, kinds of expression in social life. The conflicts that might break out among them would be a healthy social regulator, for, while the suppression of conflict makes for an explosive accumulation of hostility, its normalization means that a society can be "sewn together" by noncumulative struggle between component groups. And even in terms of "efficiency," this may prove far more satisfactory than the bureaucratic state regulation of Stalinist Russia.

Only if an attempt is made to encompass the total personality of the individual into one or another group is conflict likely to lead to social breakdown. Only then would conflicts over relatively minor issues be elevated into "affairs of state." So long as the dogma of "total allegiance"—a dogma that has proved harmful in both its social-democratic and Leninist versions—is not enforced, so long as the individual is able to participate in a variety of groupings without having to commit himself totally to any of them, society will be able to absorb a constant series of conflicts.

Nor would the criterion of efficiency be of decisive importance in such a society. At the beginning of the construction of socialism, efficiency is urgently required in order to provide the material possibility for a life of security and freedom. But efficiency is needed in order, so to speak, to transcend efficiency.

Between the abstract norms of efficiency and the living needs of human beings there may always be a clash. To speak in grandiose terms, as some anarchists do, of Efficiency versus Democracy is not very valuable, since living experience always requires compromise and complication. All one can probably say is that socialists are not concerned with efficiency as such but with that type of efficiency which does not go counter to key socialist values. Under socialism there are likely to be many situations in which efficiency will be consciously sacrificed, and indeed one of the measures of the success of a socialist society would be precisely how far it could afford to discard the criterion of efficiency. This might be one of the more glorious ideas latent in Engels's description of socialism as a "reign of freedom."

These remarks are, of course, scrappy and incomplete, as we intend them to be, for their usefulness has a certain correlation with their incompleteness; but part of what we have been trying to say has been so well put by R. H. S. Crossman that we feel impelled to quote him:

> The planned economy and the centralization of power are no longer socialist objectives. They are developing all over the world as the Political Revolution [the concentration of state powers] and the process is accelerated by the prevalence of war economy. The main task of socialism today is to prevent the concentration of power in the hands of *ei-*

ther industrial management or the state bureaucracy—in brief, to distribute responsibility and so to enlarge freedom of choice. This task was not even begun by the Labour Government. On the contrary, in the nationalized industries old managements were preserved almost untouched. . . .

In a world organized in ever larger and more inhuman units, the task of socialism is to prevent managerial responsibility degenerating into privilege. This can only be achieved by increasing, even at the cost of "efficiency," the citizen's right to participate in the control not only of government and industry, but of the party for which he voted. . . . After all, it is not the pursuit of happiness but the enlargement of freedom which is socialism's highest aim.

3) WORK AND LEISURE

No Marxist concept has been more fruitful than that of "alienation." As used by Marx, it suggests the psychic price of living in a society where the worker's "deed becomes an alien power." The division of labor, he writes, makes the worker "a cripple . . . forcing him to develop some highly specialized dexterity at the cost of a world of productive impulses. . . ." The worker becomes estranged from his work, both as process and product; his major energies must be expended upon tasks that have no organic or creative function within his life; the impersonality of the social relationships enforced by capitalism, together with the sense of incoherence and discontinuity induced by the modern factory, goes far toward making the worker a dehumanized part of the productive process rather than an autonomous human being. It is not, of course, to be supposed that this is a description of a given factory; it is a "lead" by which to examine a given factory. This theory is the starting point of much speculation on the nature of modern work, as well as upon the social and psychological significance of the industrial city; and almost all the theorizing on "mass culture," not to mention many of the efforts to "engineer" human relations in the factory, implicitly acknowledge the relevance and power of Marx's idea.

But when Marx speaks of alienation and thereby implies the possibility of nonalienation, it is not always clear whether he has in mind some precapitalist society in which men were presumably not alienated or whether he employs it as a useful "fiction" derived by a process of abstraction from the observable state of society. If he means the former, he may occasionally be guilty of romanticizing, in common with many of his contemporaries, the life of precapitalist society; for most historians of feudalism and of that difficult-to-label era which spans the gap between feudalism and capitalism, strongly imply that the peasant and even the artisan was not quite the unalienated man that some intellectuals like to suppose. Nonetheless, as an analytical tool and a reference to future possibilities, the concept of alienation remains indispensable.

So long as capitalism, in one form or another, continues to exist, it will be difficult to determine to what degree it is the social setting and to what degree the industrial process that makes so much of factory work dehumanizing. That a great deal of this dehumanization is the result of a social structure which deprives many men of an active sense of participation or decision-making and tends to reduce them to the level of controlled objects, can hardly be doubted at so late a moment.

We may consequently suppose that, in a society where the democratic ethos had been reinforced politically and had made a significant seepage into economic life, the problem of alienation would be alleviated. But not solved.

In his *Critique of the Gotha Program* Marx speaks of the highest stage of the new society as one in which "the enslaving subordination of individuals in the division of labor has disappeared, and with it also the antagonism between mental and physical labor; labor has become not only a means of living, but itself the first necessity of life. . . ." Remembering that Marx set this as a *limit* toward which to strive and not as a condition likely to be present even during the beginning of socialism, let us then suppose that a society resembling this limit has been reached. The crippling effects of the division of labor are now largely eliminated because people are capable of doing a large variety of social tasks; the division between physical and mental labor has been largely eliminated because the level of education has been very much raised; and—we confess here to being uncertain as to Marx's meaning—labor has become "the first necessity of life." But even now the problem of *the nature of work* remains. Given every conceivable improvement in the social context of work; given a free and healthy society; given, in short, all the desiderata Marx lists—even then there remains the uncreativeness, the tedium, what frequently must seem the meaninglessness, of the jobs many people have to perform in the modern factory.

It may be said that in a socialist society people could live creatively in their leisure; no doubt. Or that people would have to do very little work because new forms of energy would be developed; quite likely. But then the problem would be for men to find an outlet for their "productive impulses" not in the way Marx envisaged but in another way, not in work but in leisure. Except for certain obviously satisfying occupations, and by this we do not mean only intellectual occupations, work might now become a minor part of human life. The problem is whether in any society it would now be possible to create—given our irrevocable commitment to industrialism—the kind of "whole man" Marx envisaged, the man, that is, who realizes himself through and by his work. Which is not to say that there wouldn't be plenty of room for improvement over the present human condition.

It is not as a speculation about factory life in a socialist society that this problem intrigues us, but rather as an entry into another problem about which Marx wrote very little: what we now call "mass culture." Socialists have traditionally assumed that a solution to economic problems would be followed by a tremendous flowering of culture; and this may happen, we do not know. But another possible outcome might be a population of which large parts were complacent and self-satisfied, so that, if hell is now conceived as a drawing room, utopia might soften into a suburb. In any case, we are hardly likely to feel as certain about the cultural consequences of social equality as Trotsky did when he wrote in *Literature and Revolution* that under socialism men might reach the level of Beethoven and Goethe. This seems implausibly romantic, since it is doubtful that the scarcity of Beethovens and Goethes can be related solely to social inequality; and what is more it does not even seem very desirable to have a society of Beethovens and Goethes.

Between the two extreme forecasts there is the more likely possibility that under socialism a great many people would inevitably engage in work which could not release "a world of productive impulses" but which would be brief and light enough to allow them a great deal of leisure. The true problem of socialism might then be to determine the nature, quality, and variety of leisure. Men, that is, would face the full and terrifying burden of human freedom, but they would be more prepared to shoulder it than ever before.

VI

"The past and present," wrote Pascal, "are our means; the future alone our end." Taken with the elasticity that Pascal intended—he surely did not mean to undervalue the immediacy of experience—this is a useful motto for what we have called utopian thinking, the imaginative capacity for conceiving of a society that is qualitatively better than our own yet no mere fantasy of static perfection.

Today, in an age of curdled realism, it is necessary to assert the utopian image. But this can be done meaningfully only if it is an image of social striving, tension, conflict; an image of a problem-creating and problem-solving society.

In his *Essay on Man* Ernst Cassirer has written almost all that remains to be said:

> A Utopia is not a portrait of the real world, or of the actual political or social order. It exists at no moment of time and at no point in space; it is a "nowhere." But just such a conception of a nowhere has stood the test and proved its strength in the development of the modern world. It follows from the nature and character of ethical thought that it can never condescend to accept the "given." The ethical world is never given; it is forever in the making.

Some time ago one could understandably make of socialism a consoling daydream. Now, when we live in the shadow of defeat, to retain, to will the image of socialism is a constant struggle for definition, almost an act of pain. But it is the kind of pain that makes creation possible.

The Choice of Comrades
1955

◆

IGNAZIO SILONE

Ignazio Silone (1901–1978) was one of Italy's leading novelists and essayists. A lifelong socialist and, for a time, a member of the Communist Party, he was an outspoken opponent of fascism. He was forced to live in exile from 1931 to 1944. His books include *Fontamara*, *Bread and Wine*, and *School for Dictators*.

The last forty years have witnessed the collapse of most of the great political social myths bequeathed to us by the nineteenth century. As a result, certain kinds of people who had relied on these myths as a compass find themselves in a state of spiritual vagueness and ambiguity that is still far from being clarified. This situation is one aspect of the general crisis of capitalism and anticapitalism. We are confronted with the need for reassessment, not only of the problem of human behavior but also of the greater question of the meaning of our existence. It is not a matter, be it said, even in its subsidiary aspects, of literary diversion. There will always be a number of perfectly respectable people who interpret in their own fashion, by their haircut or the way they knot their ties, the spirit of the age in which they live. For others, less fortunate, however, times of crisis may bring graver consequences. My concern in these pages is with them.

Suicide among writers in various countries during the past thirty years has reached an unparalleled figure. It seems to me that, however much they may differ outwardly, the majority of these episodes have a common source: what Nietzsche called the nihilism of modern times. The lives of writers are, I think, not less significant than the books they write. Whenever I happen to consider the sense of bewilderment, tedium, and disgust characteristic of our age, my mind turns not to the books of Heidegger, Jaspers, and Sartre but to the suicides of Essenin, Mayakovsky, Ernst Toller, Kurt Tucholsky, Stefan Zweig, Klaus Mann, Drieu La Rochelle, F. O. Mathiessen, Cesare Pavese, and other, lesser-known figures. What a flock of terrifying ghosts they seem, when one names them all together. Persecution, exile, isolation, poverty, illness, abnormality—one or the other of these external reasons has been suggested in each case to explain how a man of talent could have sought such a desperate end. But the last writings of these men before death, or their last confidences to their friends, are invariably a confession of anguish or despair at the effort and the futility of living.

These suicides are not to be easily explained away. To pin responsibility for them on anyone political regime would clearly be a misrepresentation, since we know that they occurred under widely differing regimes, in Russia, America, and Western Europe. Still less can we blame the pernicious influence of some pessimistic doctrine; Mayakovsky was the poet of victorious revolution, and the others, from Zweig to Pavese, were deeply rooted in the humanist or religious traditions of the society from which they came. (Indeed, one might well reverse the explanation and say it was precisely because they were not pessimistic enough, because they had banished *Angst* from their doctrine and their art, that some of them were to end by succumbing to it so miserably. Inhibition is more deadly than sincerity.)

The decadence of our age, however, had already begun prior to these tragic episodes. It has not merely engulfed a number of cultivated and hypersensitive individuals; it has invaded entire classes and institutions, not even sparing the people. Nietzsche was the first to define this decadence, calling it nihilism, as I said, and giving the word a new meaning that it has retained, a meaning different from that found in Turgenev's famous novel. Since then, wars and revolutions in constant succession have borne out Nietzsche's prophecy, making evident what in his day was still perhaps obscure.

Nihilism, as Nietzsche conceived it, is the identification of goodness, justice, and truth with self-interest. Nihilism is the conviction that belief and ideas are, ultimately, a mere façade with nothing real behind them, and that consequently only one thing really matters, really counts: success. It is nihilistic to sacrifice oneself for a cause in which one does not believe, while pretending to believe in it. It is nihilistic to exalt courage and heroism independently of the cause they serve, thus equating the martyr with the hired assassin. And so on.

◆

How did we come to this pass? The First World War is generally blamed as the cause and origin of the disaster; but would that war ever have broken out in the first place had the civilized world not already been in a state of crisis? The war merely demonstrated how frail were the myths of progress on which capitalist civilization was based. Even in the victorious countries, venerable institutions were subjected to such terrible ordeals that they began to totter like rotten scaffolding. And from them, skepticism and corruption spread and seeped downward to the very foundation of society. Traditional moral and religious values, rashly invoked to prop up the vested interests which were being threatened, were thereby compromised.

The authoritarian restoration which followed the war—first in Italy and the Balkans, later in Germany and elsewhere—was a remedy worse than the disease. How could conservatives ever have deluded themselves into thinking that political tyranny of any kind would eliminate nihilism? On the contrary, fascism in all its forms meant that nihilism was installed in power. The dictatorships strengthened the old instruments of coercion and created new ones, but they did not create a new moral order; indeed, with their atmosphere of fear and servility, they aggravated and exacerbated the general decadence. With the collapse of these regimes, the basic nihilism remained, buried deep in people's consciences.

And so in many ways we are back where we were, except that we are once again free to discuss the moral situation of man without having to make concessions to a false optimism, dissimulation not being a civic virtue in a democracy.

Political regimes may come and go, bad habits remain. The big difficulty is this: nihilism is not an ideology, it cannot be legislated about, it is not a subject for school curricula; it is a disease of the spirit which can be diagnosed only by those who are immune from it or have been cured of it, but to which most people are quite oblivious, since they think it corresponds to a perfectly natural mode of being. "That's how it has always been; that's how it will always be."

We are all familiar with the picture which post-Nietzschean and existentialist literature has drawn of the predicament of present-day man. It can be summarized as follows: all links between the existence and the being of man are broken; existence has no meaning beyond itself; what is human is reduced to mere vitality. Before commenting on what I consider the provisional and transient nature of this representation, I feel bound to state that in some respects I find it praiseworthy. I think sincerity is always to be admired, especially if it requires a certain amount of courage, for without sincerity neither morality nor art can exist. And, moreover, at the state to which things are now reduced, I as a writer see no other way, outside the freedom of art, of placing before the minds of men the problems which elude them, and of presenting them with a truer image of themselves than that which they see daily in the mirror. However, literature cannot take up permanent abode in a nihilist situation, and the only way out for it, I think, is to explore courageously the entire surface of this situation. Anyone undertaking to do so with absolute intellectual honesty and an uncorrupted heart should sooner or later be able to reach its farthest limit. At that point, one of two things will happen to him: either he will find the abyss of suicide yawning at his feet, or else he will rediscover some valid meaning in human existence. This is no abstract hypothesis, but the plain truth of what has happened to quite a number of people.

The examples are far from insignificant. Here I shall only mention two: the literary path of Ernst Jünger and that of Albert Camus. The German writer reached the farthest limit of nihilism in his famous message *Der Arbeiter.* In this description of a new type of proletarian, depersonalized and standardized, without heart, soul, or brain—a living robot—he depicted the protagonist of the transformation which is taking place in modern society. The greatest freedom of this human robot would consist in being mechanically employed in the series of civil and imperialist wars on which we have already embarked and which will dominate the coming centuries. "To sacrifice oneself for faith," wrote Ernst Jünger, "means to reach one's maximum, irrespective of whether that faith is true or false. The mere fact that men throw themselves into the fray, even though they are knotted up with a fear that no discipline and no love of country can dispel, makes them, like martyrs, bear witness to an ultra-human reality that is beyond and within them." The heroism of Jünger's proletarian robots would therefore be all the more sublime the remoter it was from the traditional human sphere and the more closely it resembled that of highly perfected machines. This was a final point beyond which it was impossible to advance. Ernst Jünger retreated from it in time, while Hitler was still in power. In his subsequent works, among which may be mentioned the pages on pain, the novel *Auf den Marmorklippen,* and the diary he kept during the invasion of France in the Second World War, his condemnation of nihilism is increasingly explicit and increasingly based on human motives.

The experience of Albert Camus is different but analogous. No reader of his books can fail to discern the sharp contrast dividing *Le Mythe de Sisyphe* and *L'Etranger* on the one hand, from *La Peste* and the book of essays entitled *L'Homme Révolté* on the other. Camus opens *Le Mythe de Sisyphe* with the concept of suicide, in order to distill from it an explanation of the meaning of life. He bluntly defines as absurd the reasons for living. "To die voluntarily," he writes, "implies that one has recognized, at least instinctively, the absurd nature of this habit, the absence of any serious reason for living, the senselessness of this daily agitation and the futility of suffering." To kill oneself means "simply to recognize that life is not worth the trouble." In compassion Camus finds the cure for this desolate sense of the absurd. "The world in which I live repels me," he wrote later, in *L'Homme Révolté*, "but I feel with its suffering inhabitants." In his novel *La Peste* the existence of the characters is presented, not as the impassive unfolding of arbitrary and meaningless facts, but as the compassionate encounter of human beings suffering and struggling against a common destiny.

At a certain point in *La Peste* one of the characters—Rieux, a doctor—meets a municipal clerk named Grand whose wife has just left him, with no ill-will on either side. "From a distance he looked at Grand, who was standing almost glued to a shop window full of roughly carved wooden toys. Tears were streaming down the cheeks of the old clerk. And those tears shook Rieux, because he understood them and could feel them in the dryness of his own throat. He could even remember the day when the poor fellow had got engaged to be married; he had seen him standing in front of a shop decked out for Christmas, with Jeanne bending towards him, telling him she was happy. No doubt but that Jeanne's fresh voice was echoing now to Grand across the distant years. Rieux knew what the old, weeping man was thinking of at that moment, and he too thought that without love this world of ours is a dead world, and that there always comes a time when, weary of the prisons of work and courage, one wants the face of another human being and a heart filled with the wonder of tenderness. . . . He felt Grand's unhappiness as his own, and something gnawed at his heart at that moment—the fierce anger that comes over one at the suffering which human beings have to endure." Even the revolt born of pity alone can restore meaning to life.

André Malraux presents a more remarkable case, because this French descendant of Nietzsche, through his progress from communism back to nationalism, gives the impression of having remained a

Nietzschean at heart all the time. The stormy curve of his life's journey does indeed seem the adventure of a "superman" seeking tests
and opportunities for his own dreams of glorification. Nevertheless,
it would be unjust to consider it as a superficial movie-hero affair. Between *La Tentation de l'Occident* and *La Psychologie de l'Art* there is more
than a change of scene. In 1926 Malraux was announcing the historical downfall of Europe, "this cemetery where only dead conquerors
sleep." The communist revolt of the colored peoples seemed to offer
him hope; but how ambiguous was his adherence to it. The virile
sense of a new brotherhood of man alternated, in the pages of *La
Condition Humaine,* with the intoxication of action for its own sake. In
Le Temps du Mépris, brotherhood was invoked more wholeheartedly,
as the last resort against nihilist desperation. It was an active sympathy, consecrated by the sacrifices which culminated in the act of an
unknown comrade who saved Kassner, the communist leader, from
Nazi torture. But did this member act on his own initiative or by order of the party machine? And can brotherhood be founded on anything but freedom and personal responsibility? "Economic servitude
is hard," old Alvear was to say in *L'Espoir,* "but if in order to destroy it
we are obliged to strengthen political or military or religious or police servitude, then what does it matter to me in comparison?" Revolutions, like trees, are to be judged by their fruits, and not by the
effort they cost.

I know that these are isolated examples, and that one or even two
swallows do not make a summer. Still, they do point to a path of salvation, a true way out of nihilism, which springs from a sure and inde-
structible element deep-rooted in man.

But to return to my point. The particular spiritual condition I wish
to discuss has affinities with the instances I have just mentioned.
However, it follows a different path and has a significance of its own.
For example, it never starts from philosophical or scientific conviction, but almost always from simple instinctive revolt against family or
social surroundings. One fine Sunday some of us stopped going to
Mass, not because Catholic dogma seemed to us, all of a sudden,
false, but because the people who went began to bore us and we were
drawn to the company of those who stayed away. A young man's revolt
against tradition is a frequent occurrence in every age and every
country, and his reasons are not always clear to the onlooker. According to circumstances, it can lead to the Foreign Legion, to common
crime, to a film career, to a monastery, or to political extremism.

What characterized our revolt was the choice of comrades. Outside our village church stood the landless peasants. It was not their psychology that we were drawn to: it was their plight. A choice once made, the rest, as experience shows, follows automatically. Without the slightest attempt at resistance—indeed, with the well-known fervor of neophytes—one accepts the language, symbols, organization, discipline, tactics, program, and doctrine of the party to which one's new comrades belong. It is hardly surprising that rarely should anything to be learned in the catechism and schoolbooks hinder one's docile acceptance of the new orthodoxy. Indeed, one does not even feel the need of refuting them, because all of that has become part of the world one has left behind. They are neither true nor false: they are "bourgeois," dead leaves. The choice is emotional, beyond logic. And the claim of the new orthodoxy, which one has accepted so completely, to be scientific and objective—that is not the least of the inconsistencies which you will vainly seek to force on the attention of the convert.

This is the rule. I have read a certain number of biographies of anarchists, socialists, communists, and fascists, and I am more or less familiar with the circumstances that led some of my acquaintances into political activity; so far I have found no exceptions to the pattern I have just described, and if any do exist, I think they are rare. We proclaim ourselves revolutionaries or conservatives for motives, often ill-defined, that are deep within us, and before choosing we are, unknown to ourselves, chosen. As for the new ideology, we learn that, usually, at the schools of the party to which we have already pledged allegiance by an act of faith. Altogether similar—and just as it should be—is the opposite process of abjurement. Ideology is now given the same tough treatment once meted out to the catechism and to patriotic stories. To speak in old-fashioned terms, the head, even in the process of relearning, is towed along by the heart—or, according to the health of the person in question, by the stomach.

There is one duty, however, that we cannot evade: to be aware of what is happening. What could the landless peasants of his southern-Italian village have meant to a young student, in the years immediately preceding the First World War, that he should embrace their cause? He was certainly not thinking of politics as a career. Besides, he as yet knew nothing of the proud Marxist prophecy acclaiming the proletariat as the legitimate heir of modern philosophy. Neither did he know that, after the Milanese revolution of 1848, Carlo Cattaneo had declared the cause of the proletariat to be indissolubly linked thenceforth with that of freedom, one destined to travel through the coming ages with the other, like horseman and rider. He had as yet heard nothing of Rosa Luxemburg's theory of the natural impulse to revolution of the working class, or of Lenin's theory of the forces which propel modern society on the path of progress. Nor did he know of Sorel or other prophets of the new Messiah. But if the new revolutionary theories of the historical mission of the proletariat had not yet reached that remote district of southern Italy, emigrants re- turned from America were already prompting the landless peasants to form their first resistance leagues. It is not to be wondered at that a young man already secretly disgusted with his surroundings, witness- ing this unaccustomed ferment, should undergo a profound change of heart and become convinced that, in an old, tired, decrepit, blasé society such as the one in which he lived, the poor represented the fi- nal refuge of life—something real, to which it would be wholesome to attach oneself.

Those were the declining years of an epoch in which a number of events had seemed to prove the myth about the liberating mission of the proletariat. The fascination of that myth spread far beyond the narrow limits of party politics. It was the great popular alternative to the nihilist decadence of Nietzsche's prophecy—the promise of a new earth and a new heaven. Morals, art, philosophy were all directly in- fluenced by it. And events seemed to indicate that Rosa Luxemburg was right. In those years one did not yet risk contradiction if one claimed that wherever a workers' organization was active, under whatever regime, in whatever climate or social conditions, despite its shortcomings it would move "naturally" toward freedom and re- newal. Indeed, a certain episode occurred around 1905 in Moscow which has remained a classic in the history of the workers' movement and seemed to have been created for the express purpose of proving even to skeptics how well founded was the theory of Rosa Luxemburg about the liberating impulse of the working class. The tsarist secret police, the Okhrana, decided to encourage the formation of a labor union in the hope of drawing underground agitators into it and ar- resting them. These, however, scented a trap and kept clear of it; but the labor union, despite its police origin, became of its own accord a revolutionary organization, so that the Okhrana was soon obliged to disband it.

Since then, as we all know, the myth of the liberating power of the proletariat has dissolved along with that other myth of the inevitability of progress. The recent examples of the Nazi labor unions, those of Salazar and Perón and, in a broader sense, all reformist and cooperative unions, have at last convinced of this even those who were reluctant to admit it on the sole grounds of the totalitarian degeneration of communism. Now, however, the decline of that myth must be obvious to anyone who takes the trouble to inform himself of the conditions prevailing in the world beyond his own backyard. It is no longer merely a question of a few privileged workers (the so-called "proletarian aristocracy" of the imperialist countries, made possible by the exploitation of colonial peoples); nor of the inferior groups on the margin of the productive process (the so-called lumpenproletariat); but of the normal working classes. Today an experiment such as the Okhrana made in 1905 would not necessarily be doomed to failure. For Marxists the moral to be drawn is clear: a similar way of living no longer determines an identical or analogous way of thinking. Class consciousness is no longer a natural product of class. Ever since this situation arose, ever since there ceased to exist a worldwide trend of the working classes to freedom, human life has acquired a new aspect, spiritually as well as politically. The workers' world is spiritually broken up. It is multiform. The horse of Carlo Cattaneo has thrown its rider and gone wild again. The worker, as we have seen and as we continue to see, can work for the most conflicting causes; he can be Blackshirt or partisan, executioner or victim, or simply, in rich and peaceful countries, a lazy philistine with no ideals, insured against unemployment, old age, illness, and also against the risk that the insurance company might go bankrupt. But generally, in poor countries, because of his relative political simplicity, he can still be the prey of extremists. He can still be Christ, taking on himself the sins of others; and he can also be Barabbas, an ignoble totalitarian. Barabbas, trampling on all that is most human in man. Either way he is a protagonist on the world stage. He is the *deus ex machina* of modern politics. It is futile to think that this fact can be abolished or that a democracy can maintain itself for very long, propped by police tribunals in the face of working-class opposition. The vital role of the workers in production, their numbers, their greater social compactness and homogeneity—the sum of these factors in every country gives them the decisive voice in politics. No other single element is so powerful. On it depends the freedom of mankind and much else. But since it is no longer class that decides, but conscience, we are back where we started.

◆

One need only look around one to see the state to which consciences have been reduced. Nihilism has spread from the upper classes over the entire surface of the social fabric: the epidemic has not spared the working-class districts. Today the nihilist cult of force and success is universal. And the widespread virtue that identifies History with the winning side, the ignoble cowardice that leads so many intellectuals to communism or to McCarthy—that too is nihilism. Are the dead, are the weak always in the wrong? Was Mazzini wrong? Was Trotsky wrong only because he was defeated? Were Gobetti and Matteotti wrong? And did Gramsci begin to be right only after April 1945? Will he cease to be right if the strength of his party declines? And is fear of the hydrogen bomb the fear of a stronger right, a right therefore more convincing than the others?

To the general feeling of personal insecurity which in our age has been engendered by the economic crisis and the intrusion of the state and politics into every field of human activity there corresponds the anxious search by individuals for some kind of security and protection in one or other of the political mass parties. This by no means excludes, incidentally, a double game with the opposing party, which might be the winner tomorrow. If ideological criticisms and moral campaigns cannot shake the compactness of the mass parties, if they leave the majority of their members indifferent, it is precisely for the reason already mentioned: those joining the mass parties out of inner ideological conviction are very few. And to the opportunism of individuals obsessed with their own security and that of their families, there is added the usurping tendency of collective organizations. Frankly, I cannot think of a single collective organization today which could be said to be untainted by the leprosy of nihilism. Group living, it would almost seem, creates the most favorable temperature for the incubation of its germs. Human stupidity is so monotonous. The deathly mechanism is always the same: every group or institution arises in defense of an ideal, with which it rapidly comes to identify itself and for which it finally substitutes itself altogether, proclaiming its own interests as the supreme value. "Whoever injures the Party is against History." The members of the group in question are unruffled by this procedure; in fact, they find it serves their purposes. The advantages are by no means negligible, because they are completely absolved from all personal responsibility. In the deplorable event of someone having a scruple, all he need do is bring his problem to the propaganda office. If the matter is delicate, the answer will be delivered to him at home. Few people realize that the tyranny of means over ends is the death of even the noblest ends. And it is a mere mystification to claim that the reduction of human beings to the status of instruments and raw materials can ever ensure human happiness.

There is no more melancholy image than that of the persecuted who in their turn become persecutors. Here I should like to recall the terrible letter which Simone Weil wrote to Georges Bernanos in the spring of 1938 about the Spanish Civil War. The Catholic-royalist writer's vehement indictment of the excesses of the Franco repression in Majorca is countered by the anguished confession of the young revolutionary intellectual, then a volunteer on the Republican side. The letter has been published only recently. It expresses a sensitive woman's horror at the useless massacres which accompanied these events. But she had witnessed something else that had made an even more painful impression on her than brute violence. A purer-hearted witness or a more exemplary circumstances would be hard to find.

"I have never seen," she writes, "either among the Spaniards or among the French who have come here to fight or to amuse themselves (the latter often being gloomy, harmless intellectuals) anyone who expressed, even in private conversation, repugnance or disgust for, or even only disapproval of, unnecessary bloodshed. You talk of fear. Yes, fear has played a part in these killings; but where I was I did not find that it played as large a part as you ascribe to it. Men to all appearances courageous, when dining with friends, would relate with a warm, comradely smile how they had killed priests or 'fascists'—a word of elastic meaning. I felt that whenever a certain group of human beings is relegated, by some temporal or spiritual authority, beyond the pale of those whose life has a price, then one finds it perfectly natural to kill such people. When one knows one can kill without risk or punishment or blame, one kills; or at least one smiles encouragingly at those who kill. If at first one happens to feel some revulsion, one hides it, stifles it, fearing to seem lacking in virility. There seems to be in this some impulse or intoxication which it is impossible to resist without a strength of mind which I am obliged to consider exceptional, since I have not found it in anyone. On the contrary, I have seen sober Frenchmen whom I had not previously despised—men who of their own accord would never have thought of killing anyone—plunging with obvious relish into that blood-soaked atmosphere. The very aim of the struggle is blotted out by an atmosphere of this kind. Because the aim can be formulated only in terms of the public good, the good of human beings; and human beings have no value." And the letter ends: "One sets out as a volunteer, with ideas of sacrifice, only to find oneself in a war of mercenaries, with a great deal of unnecessary cruelty thrown in."

Of course there will be people foolish enough to dismiss Simone Weil's letter as defeatist; but the defeat had preceded it, as an illness precedes its diagnosis. In this worldwide moral shipwreck, what scrap of driftwood can one clutch in order not to drown? Among the reflections of Simone Weil collected under the title *La Pesanteur et la Grâce,* we find this indirect answer, the validity of which goes far beyond politics: one must, she says, "always be ready to change sides with justice, that fugitive from the winning camp."

We have come a long way now from the very simple situation in which some of us revolted against our familiar surroundings and went over to the side of the proletariat. The proletariat of this world are no longer in agreement among themselves; they are no longer the incarnation of a myth, and if one were to follow them blindly and unconditionally one might find oneself where one least wants to be. The initial choice must now be followed by another. To judge men, it is no longer enough to see if they have callused hands: one must look into their eyes. There is no mistaking the look of Cain. Do we side with the inmates of the slave-labor camps or with their jailers? This dilemma we can no longer evade, because the executioners themselves are forcing it on us. Threateningly they demand: "Are you with us or against us?" We must call a spade a spade. We are certainly not going to sacrifice the poor to the cause of freedom, nor freedom to the poor, or rather to the usurping bureaucrats who have climbed on the shoulders of the poor. It is a matter of personal honor to keep faith with those who are being persecuted for their love of freedom and justice. This keeping faith is a better rule than any abstract plan or formula. In this age of ours, it is the real touchstone.

It should be apparent from the foregoing why humanism in general, literary or philosophical, means very little to us. Perhaps the time for it will come again, but at present we feel remote from the serenity and harmony it represents. To us it seems that the self-complacency of man implicit in humanism has scant foundation nowadays. Mankind today is in poor shape. Any portrait of modern man, if at all faithful to the original, cannot but be deformed, split, fragmentary—in a word, tragic.

This confession of humility does not cost us an effort, since we have no answers to the supreme questions about man's origins and his destiny. Frankly, these traditional problems do not even trouble us. We have stopped pondering the riddle of egg-or-chicken priority, for what is perhaps a very banal reason: we are not responsible for it, and whichever way things may originally have happened, it was not our fault. That is not the sort of problem that can give us sleepless nights. The problems that beset us are those of our present existence, of our responsibility as men of today. Only within these limits can we reach a true definition of ourselves.

This amounts to saying that we are not believers, we are not atheists, and still less are we skeptics. These labels, with their conventional implications, do not concern us. Anyone who tries to attach them to us will merely increase terminological confusion. A distaste for verbalism and facile consolations holds us back from more general statements. A proper awe of the transcendental prevents us from taking its name in vain and using it as a narcotic. And if we are not too proud to confess that there have been moments of anguish and solitude when our thoughts returned with piercing nostalgia to the tradition-bound order, the peace and security, of the home we knew in childhood, we are nevertheless obliged to add that love of truth has always ended by prevailing over considerations of personal convenience.

In situations where the premises of metaphysics and even of history are uncertain and open to question, the moral sense is forced to extend its scope, taking on the additional function of guide to knowledge. The pitfall of abstract and superficial moralism can be a real one, but only if the moral sense is operating on a *tabula rasa*. In reality, even beyond one's frontiers of awareness, one remains a creature of flesh and blood, a man of a certain region, a certain class, and a certain time. For our part, the vital resource which saves us from the extremist situation of nihilism can be easily identified: the same emotional charge which impelled us to our initial choice has not been exhausted by disillusionment. This is not an individual case. I am not using the pronoun "we" as a puffed-up form of the first person singular. Our number is an ever-welling legion: the legion of refugees from the International. There are really a great many, belonging to no church or political party, who now bear in secret these same burning stigmata.

Does anything at all remain to us? Yes, there are some unshakable certainties. To my way of feeling, they are Christian certainties. They appear to me so deeply immured in human existence as to be identified with it. Man disintegrates when they are denied.

This is too little to constitute a profession of faith, but it is enough for a declaration of trust. The trust is founded on something more stable and more universal than the mere compassion of Albert Camus. It is founded, in the last analysis, on the certainty that we human beings are free and responsible; that we feel the need of reaching out to touch the inmost reality of our fellow men; and that spiritual communion is possible. The fact that spiritual communion is possible— surely this is the irrefutable proof of human brotherhood? Furthermore, it contains a rule of life. Love of the oppressed is born from it as a corollary that the disillusionments of history—the love being of a disinterested nature—can never place in doubt. To be valid, it does not need success. With these certainties as a basis for existence, how can we resign ourselves to seeing man's noblest faculties stifled in so many human creatures born to poverty and wretchedness? How can we conceive of a moral life from which this fundamental concern is absent?

Need I add that this is not to be interpreted in political terms of power or tyranny? To use the oppressed as a stepping-stone to power and then betray them is undoubtedly the most wicked of all sacrileges, because of all human beings they are the most defenseless. Frankly we must confess that we have no panacea. There is no panacea for social evils. All we have—and it is a great deal—is this trust that makes it possible for us to go on living. We are forced to pick our steps beneath a sky that is, ideologically speaking, dark. The clear, ancient Mediterranean sky, once filled with shining constellations, is overcast; but this small circle of light that remains to us enables us at least to see here to place our feet for the next step.

This amounts to saying that the spiritual situation I have just described admits neither of defense nor of arrogance. Frankly, it is merely an expedient. It resembles a refugee encampment in no-man's-land, an exposed makeshift encampment. What do you think refugees do from morning to night? They spend most of their time telling one another the story of their lives. The stories are anything but amusing, but they tell them to one another, really, in an effort to make themselves understood.

As long as there remains determination to understand and to share one's understanding with others, perhaps we need not altogether despair.

Translated by Darina Silone

Roots of the Socialist Dilemma
1972

◆

ROBERT HEILBRONER

Robert Heilbroner is a member of the *Dissent* editorial board and Nor-
man Thomas Professor of Economics at the Graduate Faculty of the New
School for Social Research. He is a regular contributor to *The New
Yorker* and *The New York Review of Books*. His books include *The
Worldly Philosophers, Between Capitalism and Socialism,* and *Beyond
Boom and Crash.*

Socialism in our time is undergoing a crisis. It is not a crisis of existence, for our age has seen the arrival of socialism on a scale that surpasses the fondest hopes of socialists of the past generation. Indeed,
it is difficult to believe that thirty years ago socialism was to be found
in only one country, whose very survival appeared to be gravely
threatened. Today at least a third, possibly half, of the world's population lives under regimes that, however subject to political change, appear indissolubly wedded to socialism as an economic system. In the
retrospective glance of the future, ours will certainly be known as the
period in which socialism ceased to be a mere wish, a vague destina-
tion of history, and became a major part of current reality.

Nevertheless, when we look not to its outward manifestations of
success but to its inward state of mind, there is no doubt that socialism is in crisis. For among those individuals who are, so to speak, the
fathers of the socialist faith, there is a visible *crise de foi*. In the hectic
atmosphere of the newly founded socialist nations—China, Cuba,
Chile, the African socialist states—this crisis is submerged by the
struggle to install and manage a new form of society against immense
obstacles. But in the calmer setting of the Western world, where that
most subversive of all activities—reflection—is still rated or even encouraged, one discovers a pervasive unease.

Let me give a few examples of this unease. Less than ten years ago, Paul M. Sweezy, perhaps the leading American Marxian economist, declared that "The *differentia specifica* of socialism as compared with capitalism is public ownership of the means of production." Yet more recently Sweezy has admitted, "I no longer think this goes to the heart of the matter. But I have no neat formulas or definitions to replace it with."

Another critic, Gar Alperovitz, has spelled out the substance of Sweezy's doubts:

> Classical socialism has . . . usually resulted merely in state agencies running state industries in an authoritarian economy, leaving unfulfilled a host of such humanist ideals as freedom, democracy, equality and cooperation. . . . Perhaps most critical in human terms is state-socialism's dynamic tendency toward hierarchy and centralization, for this reduces individual and social responsibility, thereby destroying the basis both for freedom and for a practice and ethic of voluntary cooperation.

Perhaps Irving Howe has expressed the prevailing mood most vividly:

> The whole tragic experience of our century, I would submit, demonstrates this to be one of the few unalterable commandments of socialism: the participation of the workers, the masses of human beings, as self-conscious men preparing to enter the arena of history. Without that, or some qualified version of it, socialism is nothing but a mockery, a swindle of bureaucrats and intellectuals reaching out for power.

Thus, starting from many different vantage points, these critics concur that something is missing from the traditional definition of socialism as a society that can be characterized simply in terms of the public ownership of the means of production and the presence of planning. And the reason for the dissatisfaction is not difficult to discover. Our age has encountered with shocking force the problems inherent in two processes of world history—on the one hand, the cumulative addition to our technological capabilities; on the other, the relatively unchanged level of our social and political capabilities. We have faced, to a degree never before experienced in history, a wholly unequal contest between our ability to control the physical environment and thus to alter the setting of society, and our inability to control the political and social repercussions to which these environmental changes give rise.

Before this technological juggernaut, socialism as well as capitalism have found themselves virtually helpless. How to humanize production on a vast scale; how to organize enormous networks of collective effort without equally enormous networks of bureaucratic controls; how to spur incentive without catering to greed; how to adduce political participation without manipulation—these are problems that confront every advanced society and that have found solutions in none.

Thus the immediate crisis of socialism appears in a widespread uncertainty as to how to manage the societies that socialism will inherit or that it is fast at work building. Not surprisingly, nothing like unanimity marks the present socialist debate as to how to avoid the problems I have mentioned. Everywhere we find a chastened awareness that "planning" is a word far easier to pronounce than to spell out, but a debate still rages as to whether this requires more efficient centralization or a much greater degree of decentralization. So too there is general agreement that "democracy" is an indispensable condition for socialism, but nothing like agreement as to the limits of dissent to which a socialist citizen may go. In the same way, alienation is an ailment on which all socialists fasten their gaze, but whose prescribed remedies range from a return to the simplicities of small-scale communal life to the final liberation of labor through total mechanization. And, finally, it is surely grounds for rueful commentary that the two socialist nations that have consciously sought to curb the bureaucratic phenomenon—Yugoslavia and China—each regard the approach of the other as a betrayal of socialism.

◆

I do not call attention to the specter of unease that is haunting socialism in a mocking vein. On the contrary, I believe its present intellectual disarray to be a sign of strength, not of weakness. Now that socialism has ceased to be a mere wishful projection of history, it must come to grips with the disconcerting realities and paradoxes of life, and the price of this coming-to-grips is inevitably a mood of sobriety. The assurance and clarity that were appropriate for socialism at one stage of its career would only be evidence of its dogmatism or barrenness at another. I hope that the present temper of inquiry, self-doubt, and uncertainty does not give way prematurely to a set of intellectual convictions and institutional commitments that socialism (or any other social philosophy) is not in a position to afford.

Hence I shall say nothing more about the substance of the contem-

porary socialist unease insofar as it concerns the search for institutions. But my reticence is not only an admission that I do not know
how socialism should be structured. Rather, it reflects my belief that
the roots of the socialist crisis lie deeper than its current confusion
before the challenges of technology, bureaucracy, and democracy.
For behind the uncertainty with which socialism faces these problems
is a much more fundamental uncertainty of which socialists themselves are only gradually becoming aware. It is an uncertainty concerning the nature of the social existence to which socialism aspires.
Is the goal of socialism a society that will encourage the freest expression of individuality in art, in sexual and social relations, in political
thought and act? But does this not conflict with the vision of socialism as an organic society, one that applies the collective wisdom and
judgment of the community in establishing *norms* of behavior, *shared*
moral standards, a *unifying* vision of the good life? What are to be the
bounds of freedom? What are to be the standards of conduct?

Until socialists know the nature of the society they seek, it will be
difficult, perhaps impossible to determine the institutional means
best suited for the future. But that is not the only problem. Behind
the hesitation and ambivalence of its social visions are the conflicts in
its conceptions of the human being as an infinitely plastic creature,
capable of "making" himself without any boundaries or constraints
other than those he imposes on himself? If so, what boundaries
should he choose? Or is there an "essence" of man whose primordial
and persistent existence can be ignored only at the gravest peril? But
if there is such an essence, what is it? What constraints and boundaries does it ordain for men?

◆

Now, I cannot hope, in this brief space, to elucidate a problem of
such vast dimensions and ancient lineage as the question, What is
man? But perhaps I can add some measure of clarification to the
present socialist crisis by asking socialists about the problem in a *radical* way.

What is the "radical" approach to the question of human nature?
We get a first definition of the idea if we contrast it to what we usually
call the "conservative" view of man. As we ordinarily use both terms,
these two words express conflicting judgments regarding the political capabilities of man. Although there are many conservative
philosophies, all are marked by an explicit distrust of the motives and
capacities of men engaged in political action. In direct contrast, radi-

calism rests its faith precisely in the ability of men and women to put their motives and capabilities to effective and morally laudable political use.

We shall return later to the so-called conservative skepticism with regard to political behavior. What I want to examine now is the relevance of the radical faith itself to the crisis of socialism. For unless I am mistaken, much of the unease that underlies the socialist mood stems from the unexamined implications of what it takes to be the radical view of man.

◆

As a declaration of faith in the human capacity for self-direction, radicalism is, as we all know, a very modern idea, scarcely older than the great political revolutions of 1776 and 1789. At its core is the advocacy of an ever-expanding exercise of conscious control by the great masses of men over their individual and collective destinies—here is Irving Howe's entrance of the workers into history.

Although it was originally propounded as a political rather than economic ideal, it is from this declaration of faith in the self-governing potentialities of man that socialism draws its strength. For what is attractive to the radical mind in the conception of socialism is above all the idea that a socialist society is best suited for the active development of the human capacity for self-determination. That is why the radical embraces socialism boldly and eagerly, in contrast to the defensive posture so characteristic of the conservative, who chooses those institutions most likely to buffer and dampen the potentially dangerous proclivities of the political animal.

I stress this radical commitment to socialism as a vehicle for human self-direction for a very important purpose. It is here that socialism rests its case for the basic institutional changes it has traditionally sought—the replacement of private by public command over productive property and the disposition of output. However short these traditional aims may fall in bringing about the sufficient conditions for a "humanist" socialism, they are indeed necessary conditions if socialism is to achieve its radical aim of enlarging the area of human self-determination.

The issue is so important in the light of the present self-doubting mood of socialism that I must take a moment to review the argument in its support. Why does socialism insist on the public ownership of productive wealth? Essentially because it maintains that private ownership, under the dynamic conditions of capitalism, constitutes a direct barrier to the widest possible self-direction of man. A society in which less than 2 percent of all family units own some 80 percent of its corporate assets is, from the standpoint of a philosophy that seeks the widest possible individual autonomy, as anachronistic and indefensible as the societies of feudalism or antiquity, where tiny fractions of the population enjoyed the privileges of their social orders.

◆

It may well be, as bitter experience has shown, that socialism will destroy this form of privilege only to replace it with another. In lieu of the aristocracy of wealth, socialism may install an oligarchy of the party elite or of planners. Moreover, as our knowledge of Stalinist Russia makes clear, the gulf between the living conditions of these elites and the living conditions of the masses may be as great as that between the capitalist rich and the capitalist masses. Thus I do not maintain that socialism fulfills the radical prescription for self-determination by the mere act of expropriating the expropriators. But I do hold that the abolition of the privileges of wealth associated with capitalism nevertheless constitutes a necessary step for the realization of the socialist ideal.

This is so because noncapitalist forms of privilege, such as those of bureaucratic preferment or naked political or military power, even when they are more crushing than the privileges of wealth, are nonetheless more transparent and self-evident *as* privileges. By contrast, what is so inimical to the cause of autonomy within the structure of privileges peculiar to capitalism is that its prerogatives are veiled and masked by the ideology of the market system. No feudal lord, no Egyptian noble, no slaveowner was unaware of his privileged status, although he may not have felt in any way defensive about it. Neither was any serf, peasant, or slave deceived as to the brute realities of the class structure, although he may have resigned himself to it. But what is unique about capitalist society is that most men are unaware of the very presence of privilege within it. The rich congratulate themselves on the money they have "made." Moreover, much of the rest of society, including many of the poor, agree that the rich have earned their favored place because of the contribution "their" capital has made to production. In a word, men who are enthralled by the ideology of capitalism do not see, and cannot understand, the difference between the undeniable contribution made to production by the physical artifacts of capital, and the claims made on that production in the name of the private "ownership" of these artifacts. The socialist institution of public ownership, despite its immense problems of administration and bureaucracy, destroys this deep-seated mystique and thus makes possible an advance toward the radical goal of a society of men who understand and therefore command the conditions of their existence.

◆

Now let me advance a second argument in support of the traditional institutional definition of socialism—an argument that also stems from the radical commitment to individual and collective self-realization. This argument concerns the need to replace the market disposition of resources by a planning mechanism of some sort. Here also harsh experience has taught us that planning, as such, may not succeed in achieving this aim. Especially in its centralized form, planning has proved inimical to self-determination insofar as it has ignored the preferences by which men express their individuality or has manipulated those preferences as shamelessly as corporate capitalism at its worst. Thus, however useful centralized planning may be for forcing economic growth, once beyond the dire needs of an impoverished society, such planning is a dubious instrument of socialism measured by the criteria of radicalism itself.

Indeed, a telling attack can be mounted against the socialist embrace of planning by conservative economists who point out that the much-maligned market is actually a form of "planning" more conducive to individual autonomy than that of any central planning board. I do not quarrel with this contention but only propose to push the idea of "market planning" to its logical conclusion within the framework of a socialist society. It will then be seen that we can use the market as a planning mechanism for the attainment of radical goals, provided that we intervene at one critical juncture of the process, namely where incomes are set and demand is initially created. Thus planning may well concentrate on the critical determination of income levels, leaving the socialist factory managers thereafter to compete for the purchasing power whose original distribution has received a conscious social approval.

There may be other means of circumventing the bureaucratic incubus of central planning, but that is not my concern here. Rather, I wish only to make the point that the radical aim of systematically expanding the potentialities of all men requires some form of deliberate intervention into the determination and distribution of society's output. Until society has consciously answered the question of what is to be a "fair" allocation of the claims of each individual against the community, the radical goal of individual autonomy cannot be achieved.

These considerations make it clear, I trust, that I believe in the relevance and legitimacy of the now much-questioned institutional definition of socialism as a society in which the ownership of productive resources has been removed from private hands and in which rational planning has replaced the blind play of an unsupervised distribution of individual buying power. This declaration of faith should permit me to return to an examination of the radical philosophy itself. For, having declared my belief in the legitimacy of the basic institutions of socialism, I must now declare my further conviction that radicalism, insofar as it depends on a commitment to the limitless perfectibility of man, is an inadequate guide either for the construction of the society that those institutions must undergird, or for the definition of the nature of the human beings they must serve.

What is deficient in the radical view? Its most vulnerable aspect clearly lies in its initial premise: that man is perfectible and capable of moral improvement by conscious design. Essentially this is a premise beyond empirical demonstration. It is a statement of faith—as is also the contrary assertion that man possesses a propensity for evil that will express itself despite all efforts to repress or expunge it.

Yet, however open to question, this is not where I find the radical belief lacking. Whatever man's inherent capacity for evil, I feel reasonably secure in believing that the realized and overt expressions of that evil owe more to nurture than to nature. If one member of every pair of identical twins born in the ghetto and the suburbs could be switched at birth, as in fairy stories, does anyone doubt that the subsequent social histories of those twins would reflect their changed environments at least as much as their unchanged endowments?

It is possibly more difficult to retain a belief in the perfectibility of man if one looks to history, where mass murder has reached a kind of crescendo in the wars of the twentieth century. Yet I cannot even read the historical record in a wholly pessimistic frame of mind. There have been changes in human behavior in the Western world (where the effort to perfect man has been largely concentrated) whose importance we may overlook in our appalled recognition of the extent to which evil still flourishes. Slavery—a condition once taken for granted—has disappeared. Torture, not too long ago publicly offered for the delectation of the spectator, is now conducted in shame and secrecy. Mental illness is no longer the occasion for ridicule and punishment. Even war itself is now the object of a widespread moral revulsion to a far greater extent than ever in the past.

It would be fatuous to claim that the historical evidence is clearly on the side of radicalism. It is quite enough, however, to maintain that it does not contradict the belief in some degree of moral and social plasticity for man. To put it differently, I see no reason, based in history, to doubt that a society that devoted its full efforts to the cultivation of the moral, aesthetic, and intellectual capabilities of its people could elevate the prevailing level of social decency as much above present-day society as the level of Sweden is elevated above that of the Union of South Africa.

◆

What is the weakness of radicalism, then, if we accept its faith in the capacity for human improvement? The answer lies not in the idea of perfectibility as such but in certain human attributes to which the criterion of perfectibility does not apply and to which the radical creed therefore pays no heed. Since I have used the word "radicalism" to describe the idea of humanity that rests on perfectibility, let me, for the moment, use the word "conservative" to indicate these missing aspects of human experience.

I begin a discussion of these aspects by returning again to the wariness with regard to political behavior that I have already singled out as typically "conservative." Now, what is it that conservatives are wary about? To the radical it seems to be only a fear that the masses will throw off their habits of subservience and rise against their masters. But this is too easy a reading of the conservative view. For the conservative warnings apply equally to those at the top as well as to those at the bottom. This conservative caution goes beyond the obvious warnings with respect to the behavior of the political leaders of socialism. It is the thought that even men who have "everything" cannot be trusted to act well. Men are dangerous political animals because there is an inner core that remains beyond the reach of reason, deaf to the counsels of morality, indifferent to the best-intentioned policies.

In a word, the conservative sees that man, at the very center of his being, is "free" in the sense of being unpredictable and untamable; and that this freedom is not an attribute that is necessarily congenial with social order. It is thus a view of man at once more hopeful and more skeptical than that of the radical—more hopeful in its denial that men can be totally programmed, more skeptical in its denial that this unexpungeable individuality is an attribute that unfailingly redounds to the higher purposes of society.

◆

This is a view with profound relevance for the radical reconstruction of society. For it locates within man himself an imperative reason for a socialist commitment to the spontaneity and individuality of life. A recognition of an inviolable inner preserve of the personality informs the radical that, when he speaks of the "liberation" of the human spirit, he is not merely projecting an ideal of what man could or should be, but also acquiescing in a realization of what man *is*.

Such an acquiescence requires more than a pietistic affirmation for socialism. For the conception of an unreachable core of behavior comes squarely into conflict with the idea of the limitless perfectibility of man. To the extent that radicalism sees in every instance of human misbehavior—in every instance of criminality, laziness, amorality, political disaffection—a *social* fault, it erects a vision of man that invites an indefinite degree of social correction. But if the "conservative" conception is correct in emphasizing elements or layers of the personality that cannot be managed—or that can be invaded only at the cost of destroying the person—then socialism must reconsider its utopian image of what man can be. This involves the painful admission that perfectibility is a process that socialism does not want to press indefinitely. In the end, a socialist society must reconcile itself to an indeterminate space within which men can express their wishes and drives, *whether or not these conform to the ideals and goals of socialism itself.*

But it is not only with regard to freedom that socialism has something to learn from the "conservative" view of human nature. Perhaps even more important is the question that this view raises with respect to the collective morale, the sense of shared well-being that socialism also aims to achieve. Here the focus of attention turns away from the problem of individuality and spontaneity to the opposite question of the norms and values that socialism should incorporate.

Now, it is no more my intention to discuss the specific nature of these norms than it was to define the boundaries for the expression of the free human personality. In the present case, as in the former, I wish only to stress the relevance of the "conservative" view of man in locating a psychobiological base that may provide a more secure foundation for socialist thought than that offered by the radical faith in human perfectibility. For with regard to the problem of norms, as with that of individuality, it seems conservatism has something to say that is very different from the standard views of radicalism and of the utmost importance.

◆

The difference between the conservative and the radical view of norms derives from a difference in the perspective with which each views the drama of life. The radical views life as an epic, a quest, to be consummated in the future. The conservative views it as a process of reenactment, of renewal, to be justified in the present. And from this perspective the conservative again sounds warnings for the radical. Liberate man? By all means! But liberate him from what? From all that is personal as well as all that is selfish? From all that is ancient as well as all that is archaic? From all that is ritual as well as all that is rote? From everything nonrational as well as everything that is mistaken? From all faith as well as all fetishism?

These questions pose the crucial issue of what *kinds* of norms and values will best sustain a socialist society in the long run. To the radical, intent on perfecting man, norms tend to be hortatory and demanding. For the conservative, intent on reaffirming a persistent elemental nature in man, they tend to be supportive and reassuring. As such, these "conservative" norms have an unrecognized—perhaps a surprising—relevance for socialism. For I do not think it is merely a romantic yearning of our age that makes it discover in primitive cultures a wholeness and psychological security whose absence we feel so keenly in our own. The aim of a socialist society cannot be a return to primitivism, for that would totally conflict with its faith in the capacity of men to understand and order their own lives. But neither can its aim be the relentless pursuit of an ever-receding goal of perfection. In the end, socialism must seek to build a society that is at least as interested in the celebration and preservation of the timeless rules of cherished lifeways as in the continuous pioneering of ever-new modes of social existence.

It is with some misgiving that I offer these counsels as being relevant for socialism today. It will be said that the need for social change is so overwhelming, at home as well as abroad, that words such as these can only work harm by instilling doubts where there should be resolve—and that, for all the disclaimers one may make, conservatism remains and must always remain a view that favors complacency over indignation and that encourages passivity in the face of social evil.

I am aware of a grain of truth in these charges. I have entirely ignored the practical problems of achieving a socialism that combines the indispensable elements of economic structure we have discussed, along with the political and social essentials of a good society. During the long years in which that effort must be made, considerations such as mine may seem remote, almost diversionary. Yet even—or should I say especially—in the midst of the tactical decisions, uncertainties, and compromises that political struggle must bring, socialism needs some sense of its ultimate objectives, some philosophical counterpart of a magnetic North, past which its compass needle may swing but to which it will return.

The problem, however, is that socialists will not find such a lode-stone unless they formulate a surer conception of the human being than the one they now entertain. Thus, even in the throes of political turmoil, I ask whether it can be detrimental for the cause of socialism to consider and reconsider the nature of man. More than that, I press the question of whether socialism must not reflect on the limitations of the creed of perfectibility, or the elusive core of the individual, or the existential anxieties inextricable from life, as it seeks to build institutions in the name of man.

It is another matter when I turn to the second criticism and consider whether "conservatism" can ever be absorbed within and reconciled to the socialist faith. Here I confess to a certain discomfort. However purified of apologetics, there remains a tincture of regret in conservatism. Perhaps it is for that reason that radicalism and conservatism, like oil and water, can be shaken up together but cannot really blend.

But here too I have an answer that may save the day. For it is not really a conservative philosophy that I am recommending for socialism; indeed, that is why I have used quotation marks so often around the word "conservatism." Instead, what I have extracted from conservative thought are assumptions about the nature of man that are in themselves only the constitutive elements of a philosophy, socialist or conservative. And what is such a philosophy to be called if it is to be placed in the service of socialism? I have kept until the very end the proper word to describe a faith that includes a strong belief in the limited perfectibility of man and a recognition that man is more complex, obscure, and defiant than the idea of perfectibility alone suggests. The appropriate word for that faith is, of course, "radical," in its primary sense of "penetrating to the roots."

This is not a mere trick of words. What socialism needs now is a philosophy that searches for elemental moorings along with programmatic change. I do not know any other way to describe such an outlook, at once forward-looking and inward-looking, than to call it radical. More important, I believe that in such a truly radical view of man—a view that embraces both his potential and his condition, his possibilities and his requirements, his open-ended future and his never-discarded past—socialism may discover the guiding principle that it now lacks.

Markets and Plans
1989

◆

MICHAEL HARRINGTON

Michael Harrington (1928–1989) was a member of the *Dissent* editorial board and founder of the Democratic Socialists of America. He was professor of political science at Queens College. His book *The Other America* (1962) was crucial in inspiring the government's war on poverty during the 1960s. His other writing includes *The New American Poetry, The Long Distance Runner,* and *Socialism: Past and Future.*

China, one has been told since Deng Xiaoping's market-oriented reforms began in the late 1970s, is becoming capitalist. So is the Soviet Union under Gorbachev, similarly with Hungary, Angola, Vietnam, and all the other economies that were once centrally planned and have now introduced markets to achieve efficient production.

If this were simply one more example of a superficial journalistic dichotomy—either a society is planned and socialist or relies on markets and is capitalist—it would not be too bothersome. But it goes beyond that. Serious scholars employ this facile distinction. And there are not a few socialists who believe that tolerating markets may be a political necessity but still somehow represents a surrender of rectitude, compromising the basic vision.

The fact is that we cannot evaluate, or even describe, the workings of markets independently of the social structure in which they operate. The "free choice" of goods, jobs, or investments is one thing in a laissez-faire economy of extreme inequality; another in a monopoly or oligopoly system; still another in a democratic welfare state; and quite different in a communist dictatorship. And, under conditions that must be carefully specified, free choice—without quotation marks—would have a completely new, and potentially positive, significance in any foreseeable transition to a socialist society. General-

izations about the meanings of markets in the abstract are, then, all
suspect.

In a sense, the superficial dichotomy of plan and market, an abstraction par excellence, is the heir—usually unwitting—of a central
tradition in capitalist thought. In that perspective, there is an economic "human nature" that exists throughout history even if it is im-
perfectly developed in precapitalist societies. The stone tool of
paleolithic humanity is an embryonic form of capital, the precursor
of an automated factory. And a market is a market is a market. Thus
the announcement of "the emergence of capitalism" in China or the
Soviet Union is made triumphantly as a proof that the eternal verities
have again prevailed.

The point is not just to make a critique of a bad theory. It is to understand the very different relations between planning and markets
in various societies and to free the socialism of tomorrow from the assumption that a market in a social order of increasing equality and
popular democratic control is somehow as reprehensible as a market
that functions to provide shacks for the poor and mansions for the
rich.

Let me put my point paradoxically: only under socialism and democratic planning will it be possible for markets to serve the common good as Adam Smith thought they did under capitalism.

I am not proposing that the new socialism project a market utopia.
Far from it. In the advanced welfare states socialists have already removed critical areas of life from the market economy. In every one of
them, save the United States, basic health care is collectively financed
and provided without reference to income—and that process will,
and should, continue. And the actual functioning of some of the
most important contemporary markets—the capitalist world market
that integrates North and South, for instance—are viciously and completely at odds with the virtues still imputed to them. I insist that, in
the dimly foreseeable and utterly international future of, say, the next
fifty years, markets can be an important instrument of free choice
rather than of perverse maldistribution if they are reorganized within
a socialist context.

Ambivalence in the Marxist Tradition

It may seem strange that I begin an analysis of current and future
markets by going back to Marx. But, as Keynes said, the pragmatic,

no-nonsense proponents of the simplistic plan/market dichotomy often repeat abstractions that are more than a century old. Marx, I am afraid, is a major source of the contemporary confusion, not the least because he provides solid authority for contradictory positions. Even more to the point, a careful reading of *Das Kapital* yields, of all things, a Marxist methodology capable of grasping the positive potential of markets even as that book brilliantly denounces their functioning under laissez-faire.

At first glance there seems to be no ambiguity. It is, one would think, painfully obvious that Marx equated markets with capitalism and socialism with their abolition. The opening chapter of *Das Kapital* defines the "commodity" as the very basis of the capitalist system. And the commodity is, of course, not simply a useful good or service but a useful good or service that is produced to be sold on a market at a profit. Commodities, Marx argued, have existed ever since human beings, in the mists of time, went beyond subsistence production and began to make things to exchange with one another. But it is only with the rise of capitalism that commodity production—market production—becomes the dominant activity of an entire society. Isn't it inescapably clear, then, that the system is defined by markets?

Those markets, Marx continues, are pernicious. Where people produced for their own needs—in families, tribes, or self-contained communities—there was misery as a result of the low level of economic development and periodic hunger and famine when the harvest failed or the fishing gave out. But there were not such things as overproduction and underproduction, no economic breakdown that occurred because there was "too much" to be sold at a profit. It was only with the dominance of commodity production that poverty resulted from glut. At the same time that this market process regularly plunged masses into a social abyss, it enormously increased the wealth of the successful rich. Markets were, Marx held, engines of social inequality, reproducing elite domination as well as physical products.

So far, the attack on the market is straightforward and principled. But then, when he turns to his central theory of exploitation, Marx becomes more complex. In the calculated oversimplification of his basic analysis, which generations have mistaken for a flawed description of the real world, it was assumed that raw materials, machines, and finance were all exchanged according to their value and that sellers charged buyers a fair price. Where, then, was the source of profit? In the labor market. The workers sold their labor power like any other commodity. In theory, the resulting wage was the outcome of a bargain between equals, each of whom was "free" to deal with the other. In reality, this was a deal between unequals: between a wealthy buyer and a precarious seller trying to keep body and soul together. The content of the market agreement was, then, determined, not by markets *per se* but by the social conditions under which the markets operated.

So labor markets under capitalism, based on economic rather than political coercion, forced workers to "freely" sell their labor power at a fair value that produced more for the capitalist than it cost. But that opened up the possibility that, if one changed the circumstances under which the wage bargain was made, the market outcomes would be different. And in an analysis of a historic event of enormous importance for his theory, Marx went on to show that that eventuality had taken place.

◆

The discussion of the Ten-Hours Law, which legally limited the working day in Britain, occupies a central place in volume I of *Kapital* because it was the basis of a crucial distinction between "absolute" and "relative" surplus value. If one assumes that the worker produces enough to "pay back" his or her wage during only a portion of the working day, then an obvious way to increase profits is to extend that working day. That was the first capitalist strategy. As a result of this savage process, "every limit of morality and nature, of age and gender, of day and night, was destroyed." This was the drive for "absolute" surplus value.

But then, continues Marx, a number of things happened. The physical brutalization of the working class literally threatened its biological existence and thereby the future of the system itself. The landlords, still furious with the industrial capitalists for having abolished agricultural protectionism in order to cheapen the price of bread and thereby the subsistence wage, were willing to make common cause with the reformers and the workers and to join in a campaign to put a limit on the working day. The official economists predicted, of course, that such a move would destroy capitalism. In fact, Marx argued, it forced capital to seek more profits by increasing productivity, by working labor intelligently rather than working it to death. And one of the consequences of this political struggle was that capitalism now oriented itself toward "relative" surplus value, toward getting more out of each hour of work rather than simply extending the hours. This was one of the many reasons why it was superior—economically and even morally—to the brutal exploitation of the past.

What is relevant here is that Marx regarded the Ten-Hours Law—only a minimal humanization of the laissez-faire labor market—as nothing less than a "modest Magna Carta," as "the triumph of the political economy of the working class over the political economy of the middle class." A merely reformist change in the structure of the labor market could profoundly affect the very meaning of the market economy and even give rise to a new epoch in the history of capitalism. These texts provide clear warrant for the notion that, under the radically changed circumstances of a socialist-tending society, markets would have an utterly different meaning than under capitalist laissez-faire. Unfortunately, *Das Kapital* also provides solid reasons for arguing a contrary proposition: that socialism must totally dispense with markets. Small wonder that matters get confused.

Ironically, Marx gets into this contradiction in the process of once again making the point that markets do not have a fixed, immutable content. Indeed, under capitalism they inexorably tend to turn into their opposite: it is the "historic tendency" of competition to culminate in monopoly. At that point, Marx argued, the pursuit of private profit no longer motivates the capitalist to act as the greedy agent of progress by constantly revolutionizing the productivity of the entire society. Now, monopolists "fetter" production precisely because they can dictate to markets and are therefore no longer subjected to the discipline of efficiency. As the system falters, the working class, which needs more productivity in order to raise its own living standard, becomes the economically dynamic class.

This means many things. What is particularly relevant here is that socialism is defined as a monopoly—a democratic, socially conscious monopoly, but a monopoly nevertheless, a system without effective markets. As Radoslov Selucky, who brilliantly understands this contradiction, has put it, in this context, "Marx's economic concept of socialism consists of a single social-wide factory based on vertical [hierarchical] relations of superiority and subordination. . . ." This is the planned, marketless society with a vengeance. But at the very same time, Marx's "political concept of socialism consists of a free association of self-managed work and social communities based on horizontal relations of equality. Whoever accepts in full Marx's first concept has to give up the latter, and vice versa: they are mutually exclusive."

In short, even though Marx in one persona clearly rejected markets altogether, his methodology allows room for the assumption that the markets of a socialist future need not be anything like the markets of the capitalist past. And, much more important, his basic political values, his commitment to freedom and human emancipation, are simply at odds with the consequences that follow from his own analysis of socialism as a centrally planned society or a progressive monopoly. When Karl Kautsky concluded that in the good society workers would not have the right to change their jobs at will—because there would be no labor markets—he had solid grounding in Marx at the same time as he was contradicting the latter's vision of a truly free and communitarian association of the direct producers.

Piety about an ambiguous tradition should not, then, keep socialists from seeing that markets can, and must, play a role in the transition to a humane future. All one needs to do is to choose the libertarian Marx over the centralist Marx and then confront reality instead of texts.

How the Bolsheviks Coped, or Didn't

The first socialists to confront reality, in the sense of actually taking responsibility for the organization of an entire economy, were the Bolsheviks. And their experience, as the Soviet rehabilitation of Nikolai Bukharin in the 1980s testifies, is relevant to the present and future.

Indeed, the thesis that any reliance on markets is a sure sign of capitalism, so popular in the eighties with regard to China and the Soviet Union, first surfaced in the 1920s under Lenin's New Economic Policy (NEP). The antisocialist press gleefully reported that the Soviets were making the transition from communism to capitalism because they had turned to market forces, a judgment that proved to be spectacularly wrong and about as substantial then as it is now.

Bukharin was a champion of "socialism at a snail's pace," which would make use of market incentives. But Trotsky, who was then Bukharin's principle antagonist and the chief defender of "planning" as against "markets," also recognized that the latter had a critical role to play throughout the entire period of transition. Trotsky was ultimately committed to the vision of a planned society that would dispense with markets; but he was equally emphatic that, on the road to that final goal, it was necessary to have a sound currency to measure the market value of investment costs and consumer goods. Stalinist planning—a command economy operated bureau-cratically from a single center—was, he rightly thought, a political and economic disaster.

But before we turn to Trotsky's advocacy of markets, two of Bukharin's particularly illuminating insights in this area are worth re-membering.

In a 1924 polemic, Bukharin raised the problem of the "tendency toward monopoly" in Soviet society. That, he said, could indeed allow the state to get an extra profit without any effort at all. "But isn't the result of that the danger of parasitism and stagnation?" "Our eco-nomic administrators," he went on, "work for the proletariat, but they are not exempt from human weakness. They can doze off in a beatific quietude instead of being constantly concerned for progress toward communism." In order to keep up the pressure on the bureaucrats, Bukharin said, they must be driven to meet the needs of the people. That means the cheapest prices for the mass of consumers, which can only be delivered if the costs of production are kept to an absolute minimum. Efficiency was thus an imperative of the commitment to a higher living standard for all.

This theme—that the replacement for the capitalist profit motive was the drive to satisfy consumers—was shared by Preobrazhensky, Trotsky's economic theoretician, who differed with Bukharin only in being much more confident that it would be effective. Stalin, of course, did exactly the opposite of what Bukharin and Trotsky pro-posed, i.e., he cut consumption, turned the state into an absolute mo-nopolist that financed the industrialization of the society precisely by the super profits that could be derived thereby. The result was a sys-tem that by totalitarian pressure could effectively squeeze resources out of the masses of workers and peasants and an economy that, as Mikhail Gorbachev realized in the eighties, had all of the drawbacks that Marx—and Bukharin—had ascribed to capitalist monopoly. The Soviet state, rather than the international bourgeoisie, became a "fet-ter" on production and productivity. In the West there were comput-ers; in the East, the abacus.

In another essay, published in 1925, Bukharin speculated that in his final writings Lenin had broken with his theory that the road to socialism was along the path of state capitalism, i.e., the monopoly stage of capitalism. Lenin's remarks on the importance of coopera-tives, Bukharin said, "puts us in the presence of a program that is to-tally different [from the perspective of state capitalism]." He quotes Lenin: "Now we have the right to say that the *simple development of co-*

operatives . . . becomes identified for us *with the development of socialism itself.*" Did Lenin actually go that far? We will never know. But it is at least possible, and even plausible, that before he died the Bolshevik leader sensed the dangers of centralization in a command economy, what he called "a bureaucratic utopia."

About Trotsky we need not speculate. In a 1932 essay, "The Soviet Economy in Danger," he wrote,

> The innumerable living participants in the economy, state and private, collective and individual, must serve notice of their needs and of their relative strength not only through the statistical determinations of plan commissions but by the direct pressure of supply and demand. *The plan is checked and, to a considerable degree, realized through the market* [emphasis added]. . . . The blueprints produced by the departments must demonstrate their economic efficacy through commercial calculation.

And in his critique of the Stalinist planners in *The Revolution Betrayed,* Trotsky commented that

> the obedient professors managed to create an entire theory according to which the Soviet price, in contrast to the market price, has an exclusively planning or directive character. . . . The professors forgot to explain how you can "guide" a price without knowing real costs, and how you can estimate real costs if all prices express the will of the bureaucracy and not the amount of social labor expended. . . . [Socialist construction is unthinkable] without including in the planned system the direct personal interests of the producer and consumer, their egoism—which in its turn may reveal itself fruitfully only if it has in its service the customary reliable and flexible instrument, money.

There are two aspects to these statements by Trotsky and Bukharin. First, both the "left" and "right" Bolshevik critics of Stalin agreed that markets were an indispensable element in the transition to socialism (if not, to repeat, in the blessed "final state" of socialism itself). Without them, they argued, the system would become bureaucratic, wasteful, inefficient, and incapable of satisfying those basic human needs that were supposed to be the driving force, and the proof of the moral superiority, of the new economy. Second, Trotsky and Bukharin were right, as at least a portion of the present Soviet leadership has tacitly acknowledged (in Bukharin's case, the admission is even spoken aloud).

◆

Stalin settled the political argument by force and in the process liqui-
dated both Trotsky and Bukharin. He proceeded to a version of total
planning in which the omnipotent state swallowed up not just the
economy but the whole of society.

This does not mean that there were no markets under Stalin. Even
in the most extreme days of his rule, people bought consumer goods
with money. But the basic decisions with regard to work, production,
and consumption were taken by a centralized bureaucracy from on
high and almost all the institutions that might mediate between government and citizens were turned into "transmission belts" for official policy. In 1938 and 1940, for instance, it was decreed that
everyone would have a work book, that no one could leave a job on
pain of criminal punishment for "flitting" from post to post, that the
first offense of absenteeism would be punished by "forced labor at
the place of employment" (which involved a 25-percent cut in wages),
and the second offense by a mandatory jail sentence, and so on. This
draconian attack on the rights of workers was introduced at the initiative of "trade unions" reduced to organs of state discipline. And the
most severe rules were put in place, not under the siege conditions of
World War II, but during a period when Stalin was trusting in his deal
with Adolf Hitler.

The investment and production decisions were fixed according to
planned, quantitative targets, which facilitated both waste and
shoddy goods. If, a believable joke reported, a Soviet pin factory were
assigned a quota of so many tons of pins, it would turn out one, mon-
strously large and unusable pin; and if it were told to produce a certain number of pins, it would achieve the numerical goal with a
myriad of pins so thin that they were also useless. The collective farms
were required to deliver their crops to the state at less than their cost
of production. And consumption goods were manufactured, not in
response to demand, but according to a preset planners' decision,
which meant that waiting in line to buy items in short supply became
a major cause of squandered energy in the Soviet Union.

Yet this system, for all of its intolerable human and social costs,
"worked," i.e., it allowed the Soviets to create an industrial infrastructure in the space of a decade. Marx gave capitalism enormous credit
for having similarly raised the level of economic development by the
savagery of "primitive accumulation" and denounced the process as
morally vicious. But even leaving morality aside, this kind of "plan-

ning" was laying the groundwork for the economic crisis of the seventies and eighties.

It is possible to make the initial physical investments in modernization in a brutal way. The slave laborers of the Gulag could be, and were, driven to dig canals, because the productivity of a person with a pick or a shovel is not of great moment. That is what the Soviets now refer to as "extensive" growth and it corresponds to the period of "absolute surplus value" when capitalism thrived by working people to the edge of death. But the basis of a truly modern system, particularly in the age of automation and the computer, is "intensive" growth, an exponential increase in productivity that rests upon the facility of both human beings and machines. That requires a concern for the quality of work that slaves, or driven workers, will never exhibit. And even though the Soviet economy was significantly modified between Stalin's death in 1953 and Gorbachev's rise to power in the eighties, the institutional bias remained centralist, quantitative, "extensive," which all but guaranteed the declining growth rates of the last decade and a half.

In Stalin's day, however, there was little or no relief from bureaucratic commands backed up by a repressive state. It was this reality that gave rise to the theory of "totalitarianism," the idea that a totally controlled society without any real sources of internal opposition had actually come into existence. There was an attempt to mobilize the economy by a state that absorbed all of society into its dictatorial political system. In theorizing about this phenomenon, Hannah Arendt wrote in her influential *Origins of Totalitarianism* that "total domination succeeds to the extent that it succeeds in interrupting all channels of communication, those from person to person inside the four walls of privacy no less than the public ones which are safeguarded in democracies by freedom of speech and opinion." The aim, she said, was to make "every person incommunicado."

There were political consequences. If there was no possibility of internal change within the Stalinist empire, that made a hawkish cold-war policy of "liberation" all the more logical, since there was no hope that, as the original American "containment" theory of 1947–48 held, time and history would eventually soften Soviet policy. Arendt's book came out when Stalin was still alive, in 1951; a second edition, with an epilogue to deal with the anti-Stalinist rebellions in both Poland and Hungary in 1956, came out in 1958. Even then, Arendt was convinced that the Khrushchev reforms in the Soviet Union had already run their course, that the system was returning to type.

On a more superficial—even frivolous—level, Friedrich Hayek, normally a serious thinker, declared in *The Road to Serfdom* that the British Labour government of 1945 was a precursor of a totalitarian system. This was an attempt to make the case that Stalinism was an inherent tendency of any socialism, even a democratic socialism, a proposition refuted by every event that has occurred since it was first stated. Stalinism terrified its eternal enemies as well as its own people. Yet it turned out that opposition and criticism had not been abolished as Arendt thought. Hardly was the tyrant dead when some of the most repressive features of the regime were modified. In 1956, Khrushchev gave his famous speech in which he began to acknowledge the bloody historical record. Contrary to Arendt's 1958 speculation that the event was a momentary aberration, the anti-Stalin campaign was most marked between the Twenty-second Party Congress of 1961 and Khrushchev's downfall in 1964.

◆

The most dramatic break with Stalinist orthodoxy took place in China, not the Soviet Union, under the leadership of Deng Xiaoping.

Mao had turned on the Soviets as early as the late fifties. The "Great Leap" was a repudiation of the model of centralized command planning, of giant factories, and a celebration of the utopian potential of the people. But despite the utopian content of both the Great Leap and the Cultural Revolution (the latter directed against the evils of bureaucracy that Mao saw writ large in Soviet society), the mode of leadership was still quite Stalinist. That is, Mao believed that he could "write" on the Chinese people, whom he compared to a blank page. And from on high he engineered a revolution-from-below, a reality that became quite apparent in mid-1968, when Mao turned off the enthusiasm of the Red Guards, which he himself had originally decreed and relied on to enforce his will. Decisions were, in short, still taken on a political basis by small cliques—or by one man—and behind closed doors.

Mao died in 1976 and there was an interregnum that lasted until Deng took control in 1979. When that happened, the government decreed that individual peasant families, under the "household responsibility system," could—after paying their taxes, selling a quota of their output to the state, and meeting fees to the collective, which still owned the land—dispose of their surplus in any way they wanted. Industrial enterprises were made more autonomous and they, too, could decide how they used their surplus. Some radicals wanted to go further. They proposed to make the market, rather than the plan, the basis of the economy, to have "regulation" rather than control, and to significantly increase political pluralism.

In the wake of the 1979 changes, there were problems, and the moderates counterattacked the radicals. But in 1983 there was another period of reform, with enterprises given much more latitude to take initiatives on their own, a strengthening of the "household responsibility system," and a new emphasis on foreign trade. In the retail sector, markets became more and more important, capital markets were created, and some enterprises actually sold stock. At the end of 1984, the conservative columnist William Safire wrote in the *New York Times* that the biggest event of the year had been "the embrace of capitalism" by the Chinese Communist Party.

That assumed that markets *per se*, without any regard for their context and content, are always capitalist, an oversimplification that is not at all helpful in explaining what is going on in China. In the midst of the reforms, for instance, Deng at all times insisted on "four cardinal principles": Marxism-Leninism, Mao's thought, party leadership, and continuation of the existing state structure. In 1986, two years after Safire's discovery of "capitalism" in China, 68.7 percent of the industrial output came from the state sector, 29.2 percent from collectives, and 0.3 percent from private enterprises. In retail, the respective figures were 39.4 percent, 36.4 percent, and 23.9 percent, which did indeed mark a significant shift. But exactly how a stratified economy, run by a single party, which uses markets to forward its own planned policies, qualifies as "capitalist" is a mystery.

As John King Fairbank put it, "Anyone who concludes that Chinese agriculture, having seen the light and wanting to be more like us, has gone 'capitalist' is making a grievous error. The contract system [Fairbank's translation of the "household responsibility system"] must be seen as the latest phase of statecraft, how to organize the farmers in order to improve their welfare and strengthen the state." And a little later Fairbank writes, "the Deng reforms are not bringing Western-style capitalism to China, except for the state capitalism of corporations that make deals with foreigners, but rather they are bringing an expanded form of what might be called 'bureaucratic socialism'. . . . In other words, a modernization that elsewhere has generally produced a new middle class, in China seems likely to produce a local and mid-level leadership that remains essentially bureaucratic."

It is, at this writing, impossible to say how the economic reforms put into practice in the Soviet Union at the beginning of 1988 will change that society. Clearly, Gorbachev has decided to take seriously the need for "intensive growth," productivity, qualitative rather than quantitative measures of output, and the use of market criteria in investment policy. In a major report to the Party Central Committee in February 1986, for instance, the Soviet leader told his colleagues that "we must radically change the substance, organization and methods of the work of the financial and credit bodies. Their chief aim is not to exercise petty control over the work of enterprises but to *provide economic incentives and to consolidate money circulation and cost accounting, which is the best possible controller.*" (Emphasis added.)

That means a fundamental reorganization of the State Planning Committee, one of the most powerful bureaucracies in the society. It would also put the state in conflict with the least efficient enterprises, which would not be able to meet the requirements of profitability. And it opens up the possibility, in a society that, for all of its manifold faults, has prided itself on guaranteeing a job to every citizen (even if inefficiently), that unemployment, or at least firings, would become a necessary concomitant of market policies.

Dealing with that problem—putting market mechanisms at the service of social priorities rather than in command of the economy—is an area in which democratic socialists have contributions to make. But before turning to those specifics, it is important to locate the very possibility of a democratic-socialist dialogue with communist reformers in a much larger context.

◆

It may well be that the changes now taking place within the communist world define the beginnings of a new era in the relationship between democratic socialism and communism. The definitive split between those two ideologies occurred in the 1930s, when Stalin appropriated a socialist rationale to create a new, antisocialist system. The resulting hostility was not based on misunderstanding. It was the consequence of a real-world conflict between fundamentally different conceptions—and the actual practice—of how to organize, not simply society, but the world. And it was, of course, made all the more acute by the fact that most of the effective democratic-socialist parties in the world were European and supported the Atlantic Alliance in the cold war.

Indeed, that geographic dimension of the ideological quarrel was one of its most disturbing aspects, as Willy Brandt openly admitted when he became president of the Socialist International in 1976. Democratic socialism was "Western," largely confined to a European ghetto; communism was "Eastern" and a road of forced modernization for backward economies; and there was a nonaligned Third World, in which, in most cases, "socialism" had strong authoritarian tendencies.

The economic and structural sources of that ideological geography have not been abolished simply because communist reformers have changed their attitudes toward markets. China remains, for all of its material progress, a very poor country, subject to the vicious antisocialist constraints that Marx outlined well over a century ago. The Soviet Union is obviously at a higher economic stage but the institutional weight of its Stalinist history puts an enormous limit upon change. And it is, of course, true that in both the Soviet Union and China reform has come from concerned bureaucrats, none of whom propose mass democratic participation.

At the same time, the old-line Soviet conservatives, committed to defending the very structure of the state, are right: it is extremely difficult to segregate economic and political change, to embark on a course of liberalization in the one sphere without opening up the other. It is not an accident that *glasnost,* with all of its evident limitations, and *perestroika* were introduced together. For it is simply impossible to demand initiative and creativity from a labor force that, the moment it leaves the job, is not allowed to think aloud and to discuss freely. Does this mean that democratization will follow quickly and inevitably upon markets? Of course not.

Yet *possibilities* are opened up, not the least because no one knows where reform will lead. And that offers openings for democratic socialism that have not existed for more than half a century.

A particular example is relevant here. The adoption of market criteria of efficiency by communist reformers could, we have just seen, mean that workers will lose their jobs in inefficient plants. But doesn't that show that the communists are, willy-nilly, driven to accept the classic capitalist discipline, with its special cruelty toward those at the bottom? Not necessarily. For one of the most imaginative socialist attempts to deal with that problem—and one of the most creative illustrations of the use of markets within a planning framework—might become germane to the communist reformers. I refer to the Swedish active labor-market policies.

In the Light of European Socialism

At the very outset, it is necessary once again to acknowledge "Swedish exceptionalism," which, in the case of the active labor-market policy, is particularly strong. The point is not so much to examine a rich example of how socialists can combine elements of democratic planning and market efficiency. It is that mix which is relevant to a new international socialism which could make a contribution to democratization in the East.

As far back as the 1920s, the industrial unions of Sweden, the Swedish Labor Federation (LO), had declared their concern with the low-paid workers of the land and the forests. But it was not until 1936, with the metal workers taking an important role, that the notion of a "solidaristic wage policy" came to the fore, and only in 1951 was it decisively formulated. According to that concept, the unions would use their bargaining power to reduce the wage differentials within the working class by maximizing the gains for the lowest paid in negotiations with the employers.

There were a number of reasons for adopting this attitude and one of them had to do with a refusal to accept the verdict of the existing labor markets. Under "normal" capitalist circumstances, the employees of the most backward sectors would receive lower wages than those who worked for advanced, highly competitive companies. But the labor movement, the LO concluded, should favor the universalistic principle that there should be the same pay for the same expenditure of effort throughout the entire economy. And that meant that the unions should have a conscious policy of reshaping the outcomes of the labor market. This tactic was adopted on "trade-union," not feminist, grounds but it was one of the reasons why women in Sweden were to reach near parity with men. They benefited from a policy directed not to their gender but to the inferior position to which the "normal" workings of markets would have assigned them.

That policy was definitively adopted in 1951. Now, however, the economic environment was completely different from that of the thirties. Instead of mass unemployment and the danger of depression, there was full employment and the danger of inflation. How could the solidaristic wage policy, and all the other social goals of the unions, be made compatible with price stability? The answer was formulated by two union economists, Gosta Rehn and Rudolf Meidner, and it was taken up by the LO.

Ten years before the economist A. W. Phillips published his famous article on the relationship between joblessness and wages, the Swedish unions had identified what came to be known as the "Phillips Curve."* That was the theoretical basis in almost all of the Keynesian countries of the 1960s for the notion that there was an inevitable "trade-off" between full employment and price stability, something that Keynes himself believed and that Phillips had documented as a historical fact during a century of British experience. But the Swedish unions and socialists were not willing to accept periods of unemployment, even at relatively low levels, in order to deal with inflation and to make other social priorities possible.

As Meidner and his associate, Anna Hedborg, put the LO attitude in a retrospective of the early eighties, "The Phillips curve states propositions about certain economic relations under given institutional and economic policy assumptions. It is these assumptions that must be changed."

Prior to the adoption of the active labor-market policy, particularly in 1949–50, the Swedish unions had effectively experimented, like their counterparts throughout the West, with an "incomes policy" as a way of dealing with the problem. That is, the unions voluntarily accepted a two-year moratorium on wage increases and took much of the responsibility for dealing with inflation upon themselves. Relying on the "general" mechanisms of economic policy, it turned out to be a most fallible instrument of fighting even wage increases. For despite the moratorium there was an upward "wage drift." It was the result of local conditions, of piece workers making more money, of entire new categories of labor coming into the market, and other factors that escaped the macroeconomic net.

◆

Wage restraint also posed the incongruous issue of unions policing workers' demands rather than fighting for them. It also affected both the solidaristic wage policy and the efficiency of a national economy that was very much oriented toward competition on the world market. Ironically, the refusal to countenance low wages meant that marginal enterprises, which could survive in other economies, were subjected to particular pressure because they had the highest num-

---

*In "The Relation Between Unemployment and the Rate of Change of Money Wages in the United Kingdom, 1861–1972," Phillips argued that low unemployment led to higher wages and inflation, and joblessness to a downward pressure on wages.

ber of the underpaid. They could solve this problem either by becoming more productive—which would raise the efficiency level of the entire economy—or by going out of business. The Swedish socialists did not retreat in the presence of that last possibility of a plant shutdown (and the relevance to the Soviet problems of restructuring is, I assume, obvious). They proceeded to change the consequences of that market outcome by selective measures that saw to it that the workers would not suffer as a result of shutdowns or rationalization.

Local labor exchanges were created under the direction of a national Labor Market Board. A whole range of options was made available for dealing with the specific conditions of an enterprise or industry in a given area. There were job retraining, public-works employment, a sophisticated system of identifying new openings, aid to employers in creating new jobs, subsidies to cover the moving costs of those who had to go to a new region, and, in many ways, last and least, unemployment compensation. In 1979, for instance, the Swedes devoted only 10 percent of the labor-market funds to jobless benefits, compared with 31 percent for retraining, 13 percent for support to cooperating employers, and 45 percent for other measures to help the individual find new work. The goal was not to tolerate even subsidized joblessness, but to find useful work for every single citizen.

There is no reason to depict these policies as utopia in action. There were grave difficulties in the seventies and eighties because of the slowdown in Western growth, and a good part of the success of the socialists after their return to power in 1983 was the result of an old-fashioned competitive devaluation of the currency. But there were also new measures of public employment to deal with the specific problems of youth joblessness. However, I don't want to go into the actual workings of the system in any detail. I want instead to generalize from this rich experience to an overall socialist attitude toward the relationship between plan and markets.

How, it might be asked, can policies designed to defend workers against the impact of capitalist markets be used as a model for the socialist future? And isn't this objection reinforced by the fact that those policies were adopted as pragmatic, trade-union responses to a specific economic problem? In fact, a conception of the relationship between markets and plan is implicit in this Swedish history that could be quite relevant to the new socialism of the twenty-first century.

The positive aspect of Swedish policy was well stated by Jacques Attali in 1978, a time when he, and the entire French socialist movement, was quite critical of "mere" social-democratic solutions. Attali wrote that "plan and market are two inseparable sites of the encounter between the production of demand and supply: the plan participates in the creation of a market liberated from the logic of capital; the market transmits the collective demand elaborated under the plan to the enterprises." Translated into Swedish: the plan decommodifies the labor market and treats workers as human beings but it does so in response to signals from that labor market.

In putting these considerations in their larger context I will assume that the reality of the next half century or so will be nonutopian. Marx thought that ultimately there would be so much abundance that "economizing" would no longer be necessary; that, as Alec Nove put it, resources would be available at a zero price. As formulated in the anticipation of automation in Marx's *Grundrisse*, science applied to economic ends would so exponentially increase productivity that there would no longer be the possibility, much less the necessity, of measuring and compensating contributions to output in terms of hours of labor expended. At that point, "*the surplus labor* of the masses has ceased to be the precondition for the development of universal wealth and the *non-labor* of the few is no longer the precondition of the development of the universal power of the human brain."

Nove is quite right to reject this automated utopia as a guide to the formulation of socialist policy in the contemporary world. Whatever unimaginable potential there may be in technology, total abundance will not happen in the next fifty or even a hundred years, which means that it is irrelevant to even the most "long-run" planning. Yet I think Nove misses the possibilities of real-world approximations of that utopia. Hunger could be abolished in the next period even if scarcity cannot be, not least because the world already has the capacity to feed itself. And we must be sensitive, not simply to the material meaning of such a development, but to its moral capacity to transform "human nature" as well.

But for the world as a whole, economizing is clearly on the agenda for any time frame suitable to serious analysis. The question then is, how does one economize in socialist fashion? To answer that question we go back to some ABCs. In any dynamic society this side of total abundance, there must be, over the not-so-long run, a surplus from the productive system. Society cannot consume all that it creates in a year or a decade; it cannot eat its seed corn. At a minimum, there must be provision for depreciation and new investment. The necessity of such a surplus product takes the form of profit in, and only in, capitalism. It is only in that system that the surplus is the property of private individuals or corporations, which carry out the social function of depreciation and investment in order to maximize their own interest. In the Soviet Union under the Stalin model, for instance, there was a surplus product that was not assigned to a class of private capitalists, but rather was allocated by a class of bureaucrats who made sure, as Trotsky well put it, that the one thing the plan did not ignore was their own well-being.

◆

In a democratic-socialist society constrained by scarcity and committed to the global abolition of poverty, the surplus product would be socially and democratically allocated. And so long as the producers and/or the ecosphere are not violated in the process, such a society will, on grounds of solidarity and social justice, be as concerned with efficiency as is capitalism. That "efficiency" will be defined in a different way than under capitalism—to express social goals and not just private interest—is obvious. But there is still a moral, as well as an economic, necessity to minimize the human and material inputs in production—in the public sector as well as the private—in order to have a maximum surplus product for the work of justice.

Let me be specific on how this implies the use of both planning and market principles. It was, and is, one of the great accomplishments of European social democracy to have removed the minimum necessities of health care from market allocation. But in both Britain and Holland that accomplishment was under severe attack in the eighties. In part, that is because the socialization of health care does indeed increase demand as "ordinary" people want the kind of care once available only to the elite.

It is also true that the nonmarket sector can develop inefficiencies of its own. And that then opens it up to the attack of "privatizing" conservatives. In Margaret Thatcher's Britain, for instance, 10 percent of health care came under private health-insurance policies, and in the discussion of National Health in the eighties there were more than a few who wanted to extend the scope of for-profit care. Indeed, Thatcher tried to quintuple its role, and in many cases the assault on public health is being led by corporations from the socially backward United States. This threatens one of the greatest socialist triumphs over the "logic of capital."

When the National Health system was created by the 1945 Labour government, it was established as a *universal* entitlement. In part, this was an appropriately negative response to the means-testing of social programs in the depression; in part, it was the assertion of a basic socialist principle that medical care should be a right of the citizen, not of the poor citizen alone. With privatization, however, there is a tendency toward the "Americanization" of the entire system, i.e., toward the creation of two separate systems of medicine: a publicly financed one for those at the bottom and the middle of the income distribution; private financing—and superior care—for those at the top.

The private enterprise attack on socialist universality is, it should be noted, an inherent tendency of a society that is no longer entirely capitalist but certainly not yet socialist. Under such circumstances, private profit-makers will try to "cream" off the affluent functions in a given sector and graciously allow the state to socialize the remaining losses. That trend cannot be successfully combated simply by appealing to egalitarian value systems (although in Britain in the eighties, it is clear that there is enormous political support for National Health). The public sector has to respond to the private market attack—to markets—by controlling costs without sacrificing quality or the principle of universalism. In the mid-1980s, the Swedish socialists also addressed this issue. They have introduced reforms that seek to achieve private, market levels of efficiency in the public sector without compromising the basic commitment to services based on need.

Sometimes critically important ethical problems, which deserve to be dealt with in a calculus more humane than that of profit and loss, are involved. Medical technology now makes it possible to prolong a life of sorts for the very old if major, and rather expensive, investments are made in sophisticated technology. Is that a morally and socially sound use of resources? In *Setting Limits,* the bio-ethicist Daniel Callahan argues that, in the name of other health and social priorities, one cannot make such an open-ended commitment to maintain life without regard to cost. In Britain, he notes with approval, National Health has emphasized "improving quality of life through primary-care medicine and well-subsidized home care and institutional programs for the elderly rather than through life-ending acute-care medicine." In the United States, with its two-tier health structure, there has been a tendency to invest in the high-tech care of those who can pay for it.

So questions of efficiency—sometimes posed as profound choices relating to life and death—are important even in the nonmarket sector. They are also critical if the new socialism is to commit itself to decentralized forms of social ownership that open up new spaces for personal freedom and creativity as well as providing for the possibility of bottom-up control of the economy on a human scale.

Either, Alec Nove argues, there is a centralized and authoritarian plan for the allocation of resources, or there must be markets. There is, he asserted in a debate with a sophisticated "orthodox" Marxist, Ernest Mandel, no third possibility. Nove, I think, overstates this counterposition and Mandel projects a vision of democratic planning that is at least possible. The problem is, Mandel's model requires heroic consumers who would be willing to attend endless meetings in order to assure that they get exactly what they want. I am not sure that is feasible; I am quite sure it is not desirable. For one of the most effective arguments against socialism, as Oscar Wilde realized long ago, is that it would create a society with interminable meetings.

More broadly, Nove is right if one is serious about decentralized social ownership. What is the point of having a variety of forms of participatory control at the base—in nationalized industries, cooperatives, small private enterprises—if all of the critical decisions are to be made centrally? That would obviate one of the greatest gains that could come from that structure of ownership—namely, the encouragement of independence on the part of workers. For one of the sources of socialist productivity should be precisely that liberation of creativity, which is, under capitalism, smothered by the antagonistic relations on the shop floor.

◆

The French notion of "worker-self-managed socialism" *(socialisme autogestionaire)* was subverted by the events that caused the socialists to make a radical change of course while in government. But it has a relevance to the socialism of the future. And it is of some moment that all of the proponents of this approach understood that, if there is to be genuine grass-roots autonomy, then there must be a market space—modified by planning priorities, of course—in which the democratic enterprises are free to exercise their communal imagination and interact without supervision from above.

If, however, all decisions were taken by central planners, even if they were working under the instructions of the people, one would lose that new source of productivity. For the latter requires that the enterprise—private or public, large or small—have the possibility of coming up with new ideas and products. And that leads to what must

seem to be a very heretical thought for a socialist: that there must be
sources of individual and collective gain in this process.

Of course socialism will be marked by the expansion of nonmater-
ial incentives, by the degree to which people will strive for excellence
on social grounds or simply because it is its own reward. But so long
as there is scarcity and discretionary income, so long as there must be
a *social* concern with economizing inputs and therefore linking performance and success, just so long is there a necessity for material incentives. And that situation will most certainly obtain for the
foreseeable future. Obviously socialists will at the same time seek to
radically narrow the inequality characteristic of capitalist society,
which is not, as the system's defenders claim, a functional necessity
but a matter of ethos and legitimated greed.

But isn't it true that markets, even under optimum socialist conditions, inherently encourage self-seeking and even greed? That they
are antithetical to a society based on solidarity and cooperation?

The evidence is ambiguous. There is no doubt that, with the rise of
the mass standard of living in advanced capitalism in the West, millions have been liberated from the primordial struggle for necessities
and have freely chosen paths of culture, learning, and service. So we
might optimistically hope that rising levels of material satisfaction,
even if far short of abundance, will change human motivation and
make people impervious to the corruptions that have historically accompanied competition. But at the same time, we know that the
youth of the West in the sixties, sometimes proclaimed as a "postma-
terialist generation," were often as acquisitive as their elders, different only in what they coveted, not in coveting, disdaining suburban
comforts and exalting consumer electronics. Even more dispiriting,
not a few of these rebels became well-adjusted members of societies
with chronic poverty and unemployment.

Socialists should not passively wait to see how these ambiguities
turn out. The labor market can be consciously shaped so that there
are more opportunities for socially meaningful work that do not require heroic sacrifice. The prejudice for the private over the public
is, after all, an artifact of a system that carefully favors the former over
the latter. In other words, the psychological reaction to a socialist use
of markets is not a given, but a policy issue. At the same time, to repeat an earlier warning, there is no socialist market utopia. Making
self-interest—including collective self-interest—the instrument of
community purpose will be a contradictory, and even dangerous,
idea for the foreseeable future. It is also necessary.

The insightful—and heterodox—Yugoslavian Marxist, Svetozar Stojanovic, has made a most important point in this regard. On the one hand, he writes, worker self-management can lead to a "decentralized oligarchy," to an egoism, a sort of collective capitalism, of the democratic enterprise. In that case, the logic of capital takes on a communal form within the framework of the market. On the other hand, "self-management is not only threatened by statism, but also by a utopian image of human nature that leads to the naive expectation that self-managed groups produce rationally, without being challenged by competition. In a system without competition, solidarity turns into its opposite, into parasitism." The market is not a sufficient condition for the socialist functioning of self-management, but it is a necessary condition.

Integrate Stojanovic's point with the Swedish labor-market experience. One of the aims of the Swedish unions was, precisely, to counteract the market outcome according to which workers in advanced companies get higher wages than those in less successful industries. But at the same time, the Swedes did not abolish the labor-market mechanism itself; they restructured it to meet their priorities. In the case posed by Stojanovic, a similar solution would be appropriate: planned policies to see to it that the productivity of worker-managed enterprises would be, in some measure, shared by the society without abolishing the local incentives for productivity.

◆

So there must be room in the new socialism for initiative from the base, and one of the ways of encouraging that is precisely through markets that will reward—in the sense I have just defined—the most innovative producers. A cooperative should be motivated, say, to produce medical technologies that would make the nonprofit health sector more effective and free resources for other purposes; a hospital should be able to use its expertise to choose between medical technologies and to pick the one which most meets its needs. And this is particularly important, as Nove insists, in the area of capital goods where the "consumers" consist of other enterprises that must make a self-interested assessment of what they buy.

This means, as Jacques Attali suggests, that there must be room for failure in a socialist society. An incompetent cooperative or an ineffective management in a socialized industry wastes human skills and materials that could be put to a better social use and, as the Swedish socialists have understood within the context of capitalism, there must be socially acceptable ways of putting an end to such activities. The resulting "discipline" of markets must not be vicious, as it is now, where entire communities were sacrificed in Britain under Thatcher in order to make industry "lean" and competitive. But, particularly if one is serious about the commitment to abolish world poverty, there must be *a* discipline. Here the issue is not whether there are to be markets, but what kind of markets, with what kind of consequences.

That generalization applies to the area in which there is the most obvious case for socialist markets: consumer choice.

In the capitalist theory of "consumer sovereignty," it is the individual in the marketplace who dictates the patterns of production. In reality, monopoly capital produces that which will yield the largest profit, uses all the wiles of psychology and science to make sure that the consumer chooses what is good for the corporate bottom line, and will generate and satisfy pseudo-needs while desperate human needs—say for affordable housing in the decaying central cities of Britain in the eighties—are not met. Above all, under the consumer "democracy" of contemporary capitalism, the votes are determined by income and wealth, and the market is thus a mechanism for transmitting the desires of the privileged.

But, as Anthony Crosland suggested in *The Future of Socialism,* if there were a much more egalitarian society, *then, and only then,* would the essential virtue of markets really come into play. They would function as a decentralized and instantaneous device for registering the needs of people as determined by the people themselves. This they cannot do under contemporary capitalism, so that one of the basic socialist critiques of the prevailing system is that it systematically rigs and frustrates the free choice it claims as its greatest virtue. The new socialists can, and should, argue that their policies would lead to the liberation of markets from the manipulation to which they are subjected under capitalism.

In at least three areas, then—the efficiency of the nonmarket sector, the relations between decentralized democratic enterprises, and consumer choice—markets have an important role to play in the new socialism.

Markets are obviously not acceptable to socialists if they are seen as automatic and infallible mechanisms for making decisions behind the backs of those who are affected by them. That is indeed a profoundly capitalist notion and the new socialism should reject it out of hand. But within the context of a plan, markets could be, *for the first time,* an instrument for truly maximizing the freedom of choice of individuals and communities.

The aim, then, is a socialism that makes markets a tool of its nonmarket purposes. Socialists can argue that, in liberating markets from the capitalist context which frustrates their virtues, the visible hand can use the invisible hand for its own purposes.

Political
Arguments

A Day in the Life
of a Socialist Citizen
1968

◆

MICHAEL WALZER

Imagine a day in the life of a socialist citizen. He hunts in the morning, fishes in the afternoon, rears cattle in the evening, and plays the critic after dinner. Yet he is neither hunter, fisherman, herdsman, nor critic; tomorrow he may select another set of activities just as he pleases. This is the delightful portrait that Marx sketches in *The German Ideology* as part of a polemic against the division of labor. Socialists since have worried that it is not economically feasible; perhaps it isn't. But there is another difficulty that I want to consider: that is, the curiously apolitical character of the citizen Marx describes. Certain crucial features of socialist life have been omitted altogether.

In light of the recent discussions about participatory democracy, Marx's sketch needs to be elaborated. Before hunting in the morning, this unalienated man of the future is likely to attend a meeting of the Council on Animal Life, where he will be required to vote on important matters relating to the stocking of the forests. The meeting will probably not end much before noon, for among the many-sided citizens there will always be a lively interest even in highly technical problems. Immediately after lunch, a special session of the Fishermen's Council will be called to protest the maximum catch recently voted by the Regional Planning Commission. And the Marxist man will participate eagerly in these debates, even postponing a scheduled discussion of some contradictory theses on cattle-rearing. Indeed, he will probably love argument far better than hunting, fishing, *or* rearing cattle. The debates will go on so long that the citizens will have to rush through dinner in order to assume their roles as critics. Then off they will go to meetings of study groups, clubs, editorial boards, and political parties where criticism will be carried on long into the night.

Socialism, Oscar Wilde once wrote, would take too many evenings. This is, it seems to me, one of the most significant criticisms of socialist theory that has ever been made. The fanciful sketch above is only intended to suggest its possible truth. Socialism's great appeal is the prospect it holds out for the development of human capacities. An enormous growth of creative talent, a new and unprecedented variety of expression, a wild proliferation of sects, associations, schools, parties: this will be the flowering of the future society. But underlying this new individualism and exciting group life must be a broad, self-governing community of equal men. A powerful figure looms behind Marx's hunter, fisherman, herdsman, and critic: the busy citizen attending his endless meetings. "Society regulates the general production," Marx writes, "and thus makes it possible for me to do one thing today and another tomorrow. . . ." If society is not to become an alien and dangerous force, however, the citizens cannot accept its regulation and gratefully do what they please. They must participate in social regulation; they must be social men, organizing and planning their own fulfillment in spontaneous activity. The purpose of Wilde's objection is to suggest that just this self-regulation is incompatible with spontaneity, that the requirements of citizenship are incompatible with the freedom of hunter, fisherman, and so on.

Politics itself, of course, can be a spontaneous activity, freely chosen by those men and women who enjoy it and to whose talents a meeting is so much exercise. But this is very unlikely to be true of all men and women all the time—even if one were to admit what seems plausible enough: that political life is more intrinsic to human nature than is hunting and cattle-rearing or even (to drop Marx's rural imagery) art or music. "Too many evenings" is a shorthand phrase that describes something more than the sometimes tedious, sometimes exciting business of resolutions and debates. It suggests also that socialism and participatory democracy will depend upon, and hence require, an extraordinary willingness to attend meetings, and a public spirit and sense of responsibility that will make attendance dependable and activity consistent and sustained. None of this can rest for any long period of time or among any substantial group of men upon spontaneous interest. Nor does it seem possible that spontaneity will flourish above and beyond the routines of social regulation.

Self-government is a very demanding and time-consuming business, and when it is extended from political to economic and cultural life, and when the organs of government are decentralized so as to maximize participation, it will inevitably become more demanding still. Ultimately, it may well require almost continuous activity, and life will become a succession of meetings. When will there be time for the cultivation of personal creativity or the free association of like-minded friends? In the world of the meeting, when will there be time for the tête-à-tête.

I suppose there will always be time for the tête-à-tête. Men and women will secretly plan love affairs even while public business is being transacted. But Wilde's objection isn't silly. The idea of citizenship on the left has always been overwhelming, suggesting a positive frenzy of activity, and often involving the repression of all feelings except political ones. Its character can best be examined in the work of Jean Jacques Rousseau, from whom socialists and, more recently, New Leftists directly or indirectly inherited it. In order to guarantee public-spiritedness and political participation, and as a part of his critique of bourgeois egotism, Rousseau systematically denigrated the value of private life:

> The better the constitution of a state is, the more do public affairs encroach on private in the minds of the citizens. Private affairs are even of much less importance, because the aggregate of the common happiness furnishes a greater proportion of that of each individual, so that there is less for him to seek in particular cares.

Rousseau might well have written these lines out of a deep awareness that private life will not, in fact, bear the great weight that bourgeois society places upon it. We need, beyond our families and jobs, a public world where purposes are shared and cooperative activity is possible. More likely, however, he wrote them because he believed that cooperative activity could not be sustained unless private life were radically repressed, if not altogether eradicated. His citizen does not participate in social regulation as one part of a round of activities. Social regulation is his entire life. Rousseau develops his own critique of the division of labor by absorbing all human activities into the idea of citizenship: "Citizens," he wrote, "are neither lawyers, nor soldiers, nor priests by profession; they perform all these functions as a matter of duty." *As a matter of duty:* here is the key to the character of that patriotic, responsible, energetic man who has figured also in socialist thought, but always in the guise of a new man, freely exercising his human powers.

It is probably more realistic to see the citizen as the product of collective repression and self-discipline. He is, above all, *dutiful,* and this is only possible if he has triumphed over egotism and impulse in his own personality. He embodies what political theorists have called "republican virtue"—that means, he puts the common good, the success of the movement, the safety of the community, above his own delight or well-being, *always.* To symbolize his virtue, perhaps, he adopts an ascetic style and gives up every sort of self-decoration: he wears sansculottes or unpressed khakis. More important, he forgoes a conventional career for the profession of politics; he commits himself entirely. It is an act of the most extreme devotion. Now, how is such a man produced? What kind of conversion is necessary? Or what kind of rigorous training?

Rousseau set out to create virtuous citizens, and the means he chose are very old in the history of republicanism: an authoritarian family, a rigid sexual code, censorship of the arts, sumptuary laws, mutual surveillance, the systematic indoctrination of children. All these have been associated historically (at least until recent times) not with tyrannical but with republican regimes: Greece and Rome, the Swiss Protestant city-states, the first French republic. Tyrannies and oligarchies, Rousseau argued, might tolerate or even encourage license, for the effect of sexual indulgence, artistic freedom, extravagant self-decoration, and privacy itself was to corrupt men and turn them away from public life, leaving government to the few. Self-government requires self-control: it is one of the oldest arguments in the history of political thought.

But if that argument is true, it may mean that self-government also leaves government to the few. For, if we reject the discipline of Rousseau's republicanism (as we have, and for good reasons), then only those men and women will be activists who volunteer for action. How many will that be? How many of the people you and I know? How many ought they to be? Certainly no radical movement or socialist society is possible without those ever-ready participants, who "fly," as Rousseau said, "to the public assemblies."

Radicalism and socialism make political activity for the first time an option for all those who relish it and a duty—sometimes—even for those who don't. But what a suffocating sense of responsibility, what a plethora of virtue would be necessary to sustain the participation of everybody all the time! How exhausting it would be! Surely there is something to be said for the irresponsible nonparticipant and something also for the part-time activist, the half-virtuous man (and the most scorned among the militants), who appears and disappears, thinking of Marx and then of his dinner? The very least that can be said is that these people, unlike the poor, will always be with us.

We can assume that a great many citizens, in the best of societies, will do all they can to avoid what Mel Tumin has nicely called "the merciless masochism of community-minded and self-regulating men and women." While the necessary meetings go on and on, they will take long walks, play with their children, paint pictures, make love, and watch television. They will attend sometimes, when their interests are directly at stake or when they feel like it. But they won't make the full-scale commitment necessary for socialism or participatory democracy. How are these people to be represented at the meetings? What are their rights? These are not only problems of the future, when popular participation has finally been established as the core of political and economic life. They come up in every radical movement; they are the stuff of contemporary controversy.

Many people feel that they ought to join this or that political movement; they do join; they contribute time and energy—but unequally. Some make a full-time commitment; they work every minute; the movement becomes their whole life and they often come to disbelieve in the moral validity of life outside. Others are established outside, solidly or precariously; they snatch hours and sometimes days; they harry their families and skimp on their jobs, but yet cannot make it to every meeting. Still others attend no meetings at all; they work hard but occasionally; they show up, perhaps, at critical moments, then they are gone. These last two groups make up the majority of the people available to the movement (any movement), just as they will make up the majority of the citizens of any socialist society. Radical politics radically increases the amount and intensity of political participation, but it doesn't (and probably oughtn't to) break through the limits imposed on republican virtue by the inevitable pluralism of commitments, the terrible shortage of time, and the day-to-day hedonism of ordinary men and women.

Under these circumstances, words like "citizenship" and "participation" actually describe the enfranchisement of only a part, and not necessarily a large part, of the movement or the community. Participatory democracy means the sharing of power among the activists. Socialism means the rule of the men with the most evenings to spare. Both imply also an injunction to the others: Join us, come to the meetings, participate!

Sometimes young radicals sound very much like old Christians, demanding the severance of every tie for the sake of politics. "How many Christian women are there," John Calvin once wrote, "who are held captive by their children!" How many "community people" miss meetings because of their families! But there is nothing to be done. Ardent democrats have sometimes urged that citizens be legally required to vote: that is possible, though the device is not attractive. Requiring people to attend meetings, to join in discussions, to govern themselves: that is not possible, at least not in a free society. And if they do not govern themselves, they will, willy-nilly, be governed by their activist fellows. The apathetic, the occasional enthusiasts, the part-time workers: all of them will be ruled by full-timers, militants, and professionals.

But if only some citizens participate in political life, it is essential that they always remember and be regularly reminded that they are . . . only some. This isn't easy to arrange. The militant in the movement, for example, doesn't represent anybody; it is his great virtue that he is self-chosen, a volunteer. But since he sacrifices so much for his fellow men, he readily persuades himself that he is acting in their name. He takes their failure to put in an appearance only as a token of their oppression. He is certain he is their agent, or rather, the agent of their liberation.

He isn't in any simple sense wrong. The small numbers of participating citizens in the United States today, the widespread fearfulness, the sense of impotence and irrelevance: all these are signs of social sickness. Self-government is an important human function, an exercise of significant talents and energies, and the sense of power and responsibility it brings is enormously healthy. A certain amount of commitment and discipline, of not-quite-merciless masochism, is socially desirable, and efforts to evoke it are socially justifiable.

But many of the people who stay away from meetings do so for reasons that the militants don't understand or won't acknowledge. They stay away not because they are beaten, afraid, uneducated, lacking confidence and skills (though these are often important reasons), but because they have made other commitments; they have found ways to cope short of politics; they have created viable subcultures even in an oppressive world. They may lend passive support to the movement and help out occasionally, but they won't work, nor are their needs and aspirations in any sense embodied by the militants who will.

The militants represent themselves. If the movement is to be democratic, the others must *be represented*. The same thing will be true in any future socialist society: participatory democracy has to be paralleled by representative democracy. I'm not sure precisely how to adjust the two; I am sure that they have to be adjusted. Somehow power must be distributed, as it isn't today, to small groups of active and interested citizens, but these citizens must themselves be made responsible to a larger electorate. Nothing is more important than that responsibility; without it we will only get one or another sort of activist or *apparatchik* tyranny. And that we have already.

Nonparticipants have rights; it is one of the dangers of participatory democracy that it would fail to provide any effective protection for these rights. But nonparticipants also have functions; it is another danger that these would not be sufficiently valued. For many people in America today, politics is something to watch, an exciting spectacle, and there exists between the activists and the others something of the relation of actor and audience. Now, for any democrat this is an unsatisfactory relation. We rightly resent the way actors play upon and manipulate the feelings of their audiences. We dislike the aura of magic and mystification contrived at on stage. We would prefer politics to be like the new drama, with its alienation effects and audience participation. Fair enough.

But even the new drama requires its audience, and we ought not to forget that audiences can be critical as well as admiring, enlightened as well as mystified. More important, political actors, like actors in the theater, need the control and tension imposed by audiences, the knowledge that tomorrow the reviews will appear, tomorrow people will come or not come to watch their performance. Too often, of course, the reviews are favorable and the audiences come. That is because of the various sorts of collusion which presently develop between small and co-opted cliques of actors and critics. But in an entirely free society, there would be many more political actors and critics than ever before, and they would, presumably, be self-chosen. Not only the participants, but also the nonparticipants would come into their own. Alongside the democratic politics of shared work and perpetual activism, there would arise the open and leisurely culture of criticism, second-guessing, and burlesque.

It would be a mistake to underestimate the importance of all these, even if they aren't marked, as they generally won't be, by responsibility and virtue. They are far more important in the political arena than in the theater. For activists and professionals in the movement or the polity don't simply contrive effects; their work has more palpable results. Their policies touch us all in material ways, whether we go or don't go to the meetings. And those who don't go may well turn out to be more effective critics than those who do: no one who was one of its first-guessers can usefully second-guess a decision. That is why the best critics in a liberal society are men-out-of-office. In a radically democratic society they would be men who stay away from meetings, perhaps for months at a time, and only then discover that something outrageous has been perpetrated that must be mocked or protested. The proper response to such protests is not to tell the laggard citizens that they should have been active these past many months, not to nag them to do work that they don't enjoy and in any case won't do well, but to listen to what they have to say. After all, what would democratic politics be like without its kibitzers?

A Cheer for the Constitution
1987

◆

JOANNE BARKAN

Joanne Barkan is a member of the *Dissent* editorial board and author of
Visions of Emancipation: The Italian Workers' Movement Since 1945.
Her children's books include the award-winning *Anna Marie's Blanket*
and *Creatures That Glow.*

It's 1987. We're celebrating the two hundredth anniversary of the
drafting of the Constitution, and the Reagan administration has
done much to make the occasion relevant. With a fine sense of tim-
ing, it has gone public with the notion that the executive branch of
the government is above the law.

What's a president to do? Congress cut off aid to the Nicaraguan
contras, whom Reagan had been happily bankrolling for years. (The
"Reaganistas" see the contras as "freedom fighters"; most sensible
people see them as dominated by right-wing paramilitaries and free-
lance thugs trying to overthrow the Sandinista government.) The
White House simply shrugged off the law. It opened covert channels
and pumped tens of millions of dollars to the contras. The money
came from secret arms sales to Iran in exchange for that regime's
hushed-up help in bargaining for the release of American hostages in
Lebanon.

Political pundits aren't putting much emphasis on the constitutional connection in the Contragate scandal. We're more likely to
hear about "the dangers of crippling the presidency." (If we push the
investigations by Congress and the independent counsel too far, we'll
do permanent damage to an office that has already been weakened.)
We also hear a lot about "getting on with important business." (We'll
paralyze the government if this crisis isn't cut short.)

But what about permanent damage to the Constitution? And the issue of democracy? It's disturbing to see how small a portion of the media coverage of Contragate is devoted to the question of democratic government.

It's disturbing but not surprising. Those who argue the save-the-presidency and the let's-get-on-with-business lines actually have other concerns. The Republicans don't want the messy scandal to spill into the upcoming electoral season. The Democrats worry about being blamed for harassing a popular president and derailing the government. They also worry about being blamed for "losing Central America to the communists." They seem to be wrestling with any number of backlash nightmares.

◆

Then there are the conservatives in both parties who hope to limit the crisis and thereby salvage the substance of the administration's foreign policy. They would have the president acknowledge his little slip-up with the law, apologize in one of his shuffle-and-shucks routines, and then back to business as usual.

Finally, there are the foreign pundits and government officials abroad who go on at great length about American naïveté, puritan morality, and our immature propensity to self-flagellation. If we Americans were a bit older and wiser, we'd know that all governments engage in these *petites* improprieties. You can't stop the march of world history just because someone has violated a few little laws.

So when does a law become big enough to bother about? Where do we draw the line, saying that beyond this limit even a president must obey?

Obviously, no line can be drawn dividing the mandatory from the optional. In taking the oath of office, the president swears to preserve, protect, and defend the Constitution, and this includes executing the laws of the land. Unless the populace continues to see these obligations as inviolable and unless we can count on the constitutional separation of powers to provide a mechanism for investigating and prosecuting the abuse of power, government by law is jeopardized, and our democracy is undermined.

◆

No reasonable person claims that the Constitution is a perfect document. It's easy enough to argue that it's a bourgeois charter focused on property rights, a charter whose drafters included slaveholders.

Some critics would scrap the document altogether. They see it as a sorry anachronism and believe that what we really need is a constitutional convention that would start from scratch.

In preparation for this year's anniversary, a committee of some three hundred government and party officials, labor leaders, lawyers, and scholars undertook a five-year study of the Constitution. The committee issued its report in January and recommended some substantial changes, one of which would allow members of Congress to serve in the Cabinet and in other positions in the executive branch. Supporters of the proposal claim that it wouldn't affect the separation of powers *too much*. (Imagine the current investigations getting under way with several high-ranking senators also serving in the State and Defense Departments.)

It's doubtful that anything will come of this recommendation. But in mid-Contragate season, even the thought of tampering with the separation of powers can send a chill up the spine of a democrat. There's only a small arsenal of weapons available for the intermittent struggle against the imperial presidency. Not much more than a vigilant press, public sentiment, and the separation of powers stands between democratic government and the abuses of an administration that places itself above the law. So whatever guarantees do exist must be carefully safeguarded, and the best way to go about that is to push forward the toughest investigation possible.

◆

Two nagging questions remain. The first has to do with the focus of the Contragate investigation. Even if the various counsel and committees ferret out every violation of the law, is it possible that the content of Reagan's foreign policy could remain intact? Could we end up with technically legal versions of the same miserably immoral policies?

We could. Nothing in the Constitution prohibits the president or Congress from supporting murderous dictatorships around the world or exploiting the economies of destitute nations.

Replacing immoral policies with democratic and humane ones is the task of citizens and mass movements and public opinion—all those forces in society that put pressure on officials and policy shapers. The conclusion is straightforward. The malfeasance of the Reagan administration should be prosecuted to the fullest, but there's much to be done beyond Contragate.

The second question is more difficult to answer. Why did it take so long for the president's policies to create a scandal? The illegal mining of Nicaragua's harbors and illegal funding for the contras pre-ceded the revelation of arms sales to Iran, *and the Central America poli-cies were no secret.* Why is the furor so belated?

There are several possible explanations. Perhaps winning a major-ity in the 1986 Senate elections boosted Democratic confidence. Per-haps the media went after this story more aggressively because they felt duped by the administration's line of no arms to Iran and no ne-gotiations with terrorists.

Or maybe the administration simply went too far. A certain num-ber of illegal policies—even when combined with record-breaking levels of arrogance and incompetence—may still be "within bounds." But beyond that. . . . Finally, it's possible that there was enough pas-sive acceptance of the "Reagan doctrine" (support for anticommu-nist crusaders no matter what the circumstances) to allow the administration to carry on as it pleased in Central America. But the same anticommunist rationale did not apply in Iran, and so the scam exploded.

We know there should have been a major upheaval before now. And we're not sure we can count on this one being investigated to the fullest. The Democrats and Republicans will have more on their minds in the coming months than upholding the Constitution; the public could lose interest in the scandal or begin to feel that Mr. Nice Guy in the White House is getting a bum rap; or the media could de-cide that Contragate doesn't sell enough advertising time.

For the moment, however, the investigation is rolling along, and every day brings new revelations of the lawless dealings of an igno-minious presidency. There's even a chance that, during the course of the investigations, the assumptions underlying Reagan's foreign pol-icy will come into the debate. The imperfect mechanism that's meant to uncover the scoundrels and their misdeeds seems to be working.

So Happy Anniversary, old Constitution.

American Social Policy and the Ghetto Underclass

1988

◆

WILLIAM JULIUS WILSON

William Julius Wilson is the Lucy Flower Distinguished Service Professor of Sociology and Public Policy at the University of Chicago and a MacArthur Prize Fellow. His books include *The Truly Disadvantaged, The Declining Significance of Race,* and *Power, Racism, and Privilege.*

Why have the social conditions of the ghetto underclass deteriorated so rapidly in recent years? Racial discrimination is the most frequently invoked explanation, and it is undeniable that discrimination continues to aggravate the social and economic problems of poor blacks. But is discrimination really greater today than it was in 1948, when black unemployment was less than half of what it is now, and when the gap between black and white jobless rates was narrower?

As for the poor black family, it apparently began to fall apart not before but after the mid-twentieth century. Until publication in 1976 of Herbert Gutman's *The Black Family in Slavery and Freedom,* most scholars had believed otherwise. Stimulated by the acrimonious debate over the Moynihan report, Gutman produced data demonstrating that the black family was not significantly disrupted during slavery or even during the early years of the first migration to the urban North, beginning after the turn of the century. The problems of the modern black family, he implied, were associated with modern forces.

Those who cite discrimination as the root cause of poverty often fail to make a distinction between the effects of historic discrimination (i.e., discrimination prior to the mid-twentieth century) and the effects of contemporary discrimination. Thus they find it hard to explain why the economic position of the black underclass started to worsen soon after Congress enacted, and the White House began to enforce, the most sweeping civil-rights legislation since Reconstruction.

The point to be emphasized is that historic discrimination is more important than contemporary discrimination in understanding the plight of the ghetto underclass—that, in any event, there is more to the story than discrimination (of whichever kind). Historic discrimination certainly helped to create an impoverished urban black community in the first place. In *A Piece of the Pie: Black and White Immigrants Since 1880,* Stanley Lieberson shows how, in many areas of life, including the labor market, black newcomers from the rural South were far more severely discriminated against in Northern cities than were the new white immigrants from Southern, Central, and Eastern Europe. Skin color was part of the problem but it was not all of it.

In addition to the problem of historic discrimination, the black migration to New York, Philadelphia, Chicago, and other Northern cities—the continued replenishment of black populations there by poor newcomers—predictably skewed the age profile of the urban black community and kept it relatively young.

Age correlates with many things. For example, the higher the median age of a group, the higher its income; the lower the median age, the higher the unemployment rate and the higher the crime rate (more than half of those arrested in 1980 for violent and property crimes in American cities were under twenty-one). The younger a woman is, the more likely she is to bear a child out of wedlock, head up a new household, and depend on welfare. In short, part of what had gone awry in the ghetto was due to the sheer increase in the number of black youths.

The population explosion among minority youths occurred at a time when changes in the economy were beginning to pose serious problems for unskilled workers. Urban minorities have been particularly vulnerable to the structural economic changes of the past two decades: the shift from goods-producing to service-producing industries, the increasing polarization of the labor market into low-wage and high-wage sectors, innovations in technology, and the relocation of manufacturing industries out of the central cities.

Most unemployed blacks in the United States reside within the inner cities. Their situation, already more difficult than that of any other major ethnic group in the country, continues to worsen. Not only are there more blacks without jobs every year, men, especially young males, are dropping out of the labor force in record proportions. Also, more and more black youths, including many who are no longer in school, are obtaining no job experience at all.

◆

However, the growing problem of joblessness in the inner city exacerbates and is in turn partly created by the changing social composition of inner-city neighborhoods. These areas have undergone a major social transformation in the last several years as reflected not only in their increasing rates of social dislocation but also in the changing class structure of ghetto neighborhoods. In the 1940s, 1950s, and even the 1960s, lower-class, working-class, and middle-class black urban families all resided more or less in the same ghetto areas, albeit on different streets. Although black middle-class professionals today tend to be employed in mainstream occupations outside the black community and neither live nor frequently interact with ghetto residents, the black middle-class professionals of the 1940s and 1950s (doctors, lawyers, teachers, social workers, etc.), resided in the higher-income areas of the inner city, and serviced the ghetto community. The exodus of black middle-class professionals from the inner city has been increasingly accompanied by a movement of stable working-class blacks to higher-income neighborhoods in other parts of the city and to the suburbs. Confined by restrictive covenants to communities also inhabited by the urban black lower classes, the black working and middle classes in earlier years provided stability to inner-city neighborhoods and perpetuated and reinforced societal norms and values. In short, their very presence enhanced the social organization of ghetto communities. If strong norms and sanctions against aberrant behavior, a sense of community, and positive neighborhood identification are the essential features of social organization in urban areas, inner-city neighborhoods today suffer from a severe lack of social organization.

In contrast to previous years, today's ghetto residents represent almost exclusively the most disadvantaged segments of the urban black community—including those families who have experienced long-term spells of poverty and/or welfare dependency, individuals who lack training and skills and have either experienced periods of persistent unemployment or have dropped out of the labor force altogether, and individuals who are frequently involved in street criminal activity.

The significance of changes embodied in the social transformation of the inner city is perhaps best captured by the concepts "concentration effects" and "social buffer." The former refers to the constraints and opportunities associated with living in a neighborhood in which the population is overwhelmingly socially disadvantaged—constraints and opportunities that include the kinds of ecological niches that the residents of these communities occupy in terms of access to jobs, availability of marriageable partners, and exposure to conventional role models. The latter refers to the presence of a sufficient number of working- and middle-class professional families to absorb the shock or cushion the effect of uneven economic growth and periodic recessions on inner-city neighborhoods. The basic thesis is not that ghetto culture went unchecked following the removal of the higher-income family in the inner city, but that the removal of these families made it more difficult to sustain the basic institutions in the inner city (including churches, stores, schools, recreational facilities, etc.) in the face of prolonged joblessness. And as the basic institutions declined, the social organization of inner-city neighborhoods (defined here to include a sense of community, positive neighborhood identification, and explicit norms and sanctions against aberrant behavior) likewise declined.

◆

In underlining joblessness as an important aspect of inner-city social transformations, we are reminded that in the 1960s scholars readily attributed poor-black-family deterioration to problems of employment. Nonetheless, in the last several years, in the face of the overwhelming attention given to welfare as the major source of black-family breakup, concerns about the importance of joblessness have diminished, despite the existence of evidence strongly suggesting the need for renewed scholarly and public-policy attention to the relationship between the disintegration of poor black families and black male labor-market experiences.

Although changing social and cultural trends have often been said to explain some of the dynamic shifts in the structure of the family, they appear to have more relevance for changes in family structure among whites. And, contrary to popular opinion, there is little evidence to support the argument that welfare is the primary cause of family out-of-wedlock births, breakups, and female-headed households. Welfare does seem to have a modest effect on separation and divorce, particularly for white women, but recent evidence indicates that its total effect on the proportion of all female householders is small.

By contrast, the evidence for the influence of joblessness on family structure is much more conclusive. Research has demonstrated, for example, a connection between an encouraging economic situation and the early marriage of young people. In this connection, black women are more likely to delay marriage and less likely to remarry. Although black and white teenagers expect to become parents at about the same ages, black teenagers expect to marry at later ages. The black delay in marriage and the lower rate of remarriage, each associated with high percentages of out-of-wedlock births and female-headed households, can be directly tied to the employment status of black males. Indeed, black women, especially young black women, are confronting a shrinking pool of "marriageable" (that is, economically stable) men.

White women are not experiencing this problem. Our "male marriageable pool index" shows that the number of employed white men per hundred white women in different age categories has either remained roughly the same or has only slightly increased in the last two decades. There is little reason, therefore, to assume a connection between the recent growth of female-headed white families and patterns of white male employment. That the pool of "marriageable" white men has not decreased over the years is perhaps reflected in the earlier age of first marriage and the higher rate of remarriage among white women. It is therefore reasonable to hypothesize that the rise in rates of separation and divorce among whites is due mainly to the increased economic independence of white women and related social and cultural factors embodied in the feminist movement.

◆

The argument that the decline in the incidence of intact marriages among blacks is associated with the declining economic status of black men is further supported by an analysis of regional data on female headship and the "male marriageable pool." Whereas changes in the ratios of employed men to women among whites have been minimal for all regions of the country regardless of age from 1960 to 1980, the ratios among blacks have declined significantly in all regions except the West, with the greatest declines in the Northeast and North-Central regions of the country. On the basis of these trends, it would be expected that the growth in numbers of black female-headed households would occur most rapidly in the Northern regions, followed by the South and the West. Regional data on the "male marriageable pool index" support this conclusion, except for the larger-than-expected increase in black female-headed families in the West—a function of patterns of selective black migration to the West.

The sharp decline in the black "male marriageable pool" in the Northeast and North-Central regions is related to recent changes in the basic economic organization of American society. In the two Northern regions, the shift in economic activity from goods production to services has been associated with changes in the location of production, including an interregional movement of industry from the North to the South and West and, more important, a movement of certain industries out of the older central cities, where blacks are concentrated. Moreover, the shrinkage of the male marriageable pool for ages sixteen to twenty-four in the South from 1960 to 1980 is related to the mechanization of agriculture, which lowered substantially the demand for low-skilled agricultural labor, especially during the 1960s. For all these reasons, it is often necessary to go beyond the specific issue of current racial discrimination to understand factors that contribute directly to poor black joblessness and indirectly to related social problems such as family instability in the inner city. But this point has not been readily grasped by policymakers and civil-rights leaders.

The Limits of Race-Specific Public Policy

In the early 1960s there was no comprehensive civil rights bill, and Jim Crow segregation was still widespread in parts of the nation, particularly in the deep South. With the passage of the Civil Rights Act of 1964 there was considerable optimism that racial progress would ensue and that the principle of equality of individual rights (namely, that candidates for positions stratified in terms of prestige, power, or other social criteria ought to be judged solely on individual merit and therefore should not be discriminated against on the basis of racial origin) would be upheld.

Programs based solely on this principle are inadequate, however, to deal with the complex problems of race in America, because they are not designed to address the substantive inequality that exists at the time discrimination is eliminated.

On the other hand, the competitive resources developed by the *advantaged minority members*—resources that flow directly from the family stability, schooling, income, and peer groups that their parents have been able to provide—result in their benefiting disproportionately from policies that promote the rights of minority individuals by removing artificial barriers to valued positions.

Nevertheless, since 1970, government policy has tended to focus on formal programs designed and created both to prevent discrimination and to ensure that minorities are sufficiently represented in certain positions. This has resulted in a shift from the simple formal investigation and adjudication of complaints of racial discrimination to government-mandated affirmative-action programs to increase minority representation in public programs, employment, and education.

However, if minority members from the most advantaged families profit disproportionately from policies based on the principle of equality of individual opportunity, they also reap disproportionate benefits from policies of affirmative action based solely on their group membership. This is because advantaged minority members are likely to be disproportionately represented among those of their racial group most qualified for valued positions, such as college admissions, higher-paying jobs, and promotions. Thus, if policies of preferential treatment for such positions are developed in terms of racial-group membership rather than the real disadvantages suffered by individuals, then these policies will further improve the opportunities of the advantaged without necessarily addressing the problems of the truly disadvantaged, such as the ghetto underclass. The problems of the truly disadvantaged may require *nonracial* solutions such as full employment, balanced economic growth, and manpower training and education (tied to—not isolated from—these two economic conditions).

◆

It would be ideal if problems of the ghetto underclass could be adequately addressed by the combination of macroeconomic policy, labor-market strategies, and manpower training programs. However, in the foreseeable future employment alone will not necessarily lift a family out of poverty. Many families would still require income support and/or social service such as child care. A program of welfare reform is needed, therefore, to address the current problems of public assistance, including lack of provisions for poor two-parent families, inadequate levels of support, inequities between different states, and work disincentives. A national Aid to Families with Dependent Children (AFDC) benefit standard adjusted yearly for inflation is the most minimal required change. We might also give serious consideration to programs such as the Child Support Assurance Program developed by Irwin Garfinkel and colleagues at the Institute for Research on Poverty at the University of Wisconsin, Madison. This program, parts of which are currently in operation as a demonstration project in the state of Wisconsin, provides a guaranteed minimum benefit per child to single-parent families regardless of the income of the custodial parent. The state collects from the absent parent through wage-withholding a sum of money at a fixed rate and then makes regular payments to the custodial parent. If the absent parent is jobless or if his or her payment from withholdings is less than the minimum, the state makes up the difference. Since all absent parents regardless of income are required to participate in this program, it is far less stigmatizing than, say, public assistance. Moreover, preliminary evidence from Wisconsin suggests that this program carries little or no additional cost to the state.

Neither the Child Support Assurance Program under demonstration in Wisconsin nor the European family-allowances program is means-tested; that is, they are not targeted at a particular income group and therefore do not suffer the degree of stigmatization that plagues public-assistance programs such as AFDC. More important, such universal programs tend to draw more political support from the general public because they are available not only to the poor but to the working- and middle-class segments as well. Finally, the question of child care has to be addressed in any program designed to improve the employment prospects of women and men.

If the truly disadvantaged reaped disproportionate benefits from a child-support enforcement, child-allowance program, and child-care strategy, they would also benefit disproportionately from a program of balanced economic growth and tight labor-market policies, because of their greater vulnerability to swings in the business cycle and changes in economic organization, including the relocation of plants and the use of labor-saving technology. It would be shortsighted to conclude, therefore, that universal programs (i.e., programs not targeted at any particular group) are not designed to help address in a fundamental way some of the problems of the truly disadvantaged such as the ghetto underclass.

◆

By emphasizing universal programs as an effective way to address problems in the inner city created by historic racial subjugation, I am recommending a fundamental shift from the traditional race-specific approach of addressing such problems. It is true that problems of joblessness and related woes such as poverty, teenage pregnancies, out-of-wedlock births, female-headed families, and welfare dependency are, for reasons of historic racial oppression, disproportionately concentrated in the black community. And it is important to recognize the racial differences in rates of social dislocation so as not to obscure problems currently gripping the ghetto underclass. However, as discussed above, race-specific policies are often not designed to address fundamentally problems of the truly disadvantaged. Moreover, as also discussed above, both race-specific and targeted programs based on the principle of equality of life chances (often identified with a minority constituency) have difficulty sustaining widespread public support.

Does this mean that targeted programs of any kind would be necessarily excluded from a package highlighting universal programs of reform? On the contrary, as long as racial minorities are disproportionately concentrated in low-paying positions, antidiscrimination and affirmative-action programs will be needed even though they tend to benefit the more advantaged minority members. Moreover, as long as certain groups lack the training, skills, and education to compete effectively on the job market or move into newly created jobs, manpower training and education programs targeted at these groups will also be needed, even under a tight labor-market situation. For example, a program of adult education and training may be necessary for some ghetto-underclass males before they can either become oriented to or move into an expanded labor market. Finally, as long as some poor families are unable to work because of physical or other disabilities, public assistance would be needed even if the government adopted a program of welfare reform that included child-support enforcement and family-allowance provisions.

◆

For all these reasons, a comprehensive program of economic and social reform (highlighting macroeconomic policies to promote balanced economic growth and create a tight labor-market situation, a nationally oriented labor-market strategy, a child-support assurance program, a child-care strategy, and a family-allowance program) would have to include targeted programs, both means-tested and race-specific. However, the latter would be considered an offshoot of and indeed secondary to the universal programs. The important goal is to construct an economic-social reform program in such a way that the universal programs are seen as the dominant and most visible aspects by the general public. As the universal programs draw support from a wider population, the targeted programs included in the comprehensive reform package would be indirectly supported and protected. Accordingly, *the hidden agenda for liberal policymakers is to improve the life chances of truly disadvantaged groups such as the ghetto underclass by emphasizing programs to which the more advantaged groups of all races and class backgrounds can positively relate.*

I am reminded of Bayard Rustin's plea during the early 1960s that blacks ought to recognize the importance of fundamental economic reform (including a system of national economic planning along with new education, manpower, and public-works programs to help reach full employment) and the need for a broad-based political coalition to achieve it. And since an effective coalition will in part depend upon how the issues are defined, it is imperative that the political message underline the need for economic and social reforms that benefit all groups in the United States, not just poor minorities.

However, at this point, a program of economic reform is not one of the items currently under serious discussion in the national political arena. Indeed, discussions of reform seem to be limited to debates over the need for workfare programs for welfare recipients. In the 1970s the term "workfare" was narrowly used to capture the idea that welfare recipients should be required to work, even make-work if necessary, in exchange for receiving benefits. This idea was generally rejected by liberals and those in the welfare establishment. And no workfare program, even Governor Reagan's 1971 program, really got off the ground. However, by 1981 President Ronald Reagan was able to get congressional approval to include a provision in the 1981 budget allowing states to experiment with new employment approaches to welfare reform. These approaches represent the "new-style workfare." More specifically, whereas workfare in the 1970s was narrowly construed as "working off" one's welfare grant, the new-style workfare "takes the form of obligational state programs that involve an array of employment and training services and activities—job search, job training, education programs, and also community work experience."

According to Richard Nathan, "We make our greatest progress on social reform in the United States when liberals and conservatives find common ground. New-style workfare embodies both the caring commitment of liberals and the themes identified with conservative writers like Charles Murray, George Gilder, and Lawrence Mead." On the one hand, liberals can relate to new-style workfare because it creates short-term, entry-level positions very similar to the "CETA public service jobs we thought we had abolished in 1981"; it provides a convenient "political rationale and support for increased funding for education and training programs"; and it targets these programs at the most disadvantaged, thereby correcting the problem of "creaming" that is associated with other employment and training programs. On the other hand, conservatives can relate to new-style workfare because "it involves a strong commitment to reducing welfare dependency on the premise that dependency is bad for people, that it undermines their motivation to self-support and isolates and stigmatizes welfare recipients in a way that over a long period feeds into and accentuates the underclass mindset and condition."

◆

The combining of liberal and conservative approaches does not, of course, change the fact that the new-style workfare programs hardly represent a fundamental shift from the traditional approaches to poverty in America. Once again the focus is exclusively on individual characteristics—whether they are construed in terms of lack of training, of skills, or of education; or whether they are seen in terms of lack of motivation or other subjective traits. And once again the consequences of certain economic arrangements on disadvantaged populations in the United States are not considered in the formulation and implementation of social policy. Although new-style workfare is better than having no strategy at all to enhance employment experiences, it should be emphasized that the effectiveness of such programs ultimately depends upon the availability of jobs in a given area. Perhaps Robert D. Reischauer put it best when he stated:

> As long as the unemployment rate remains high in many regions of the country, members of the underclass are going to have a very difficult time competing successfully for the jobs that are available. No amount of remedial education, training, wage subsidy, or other embellishment will make them more attractive to prospective employers than experienced unemployed workers.

As Reischauer also appropriately emphasizes, with a weak economy, "even if the workfare program seems to be placing its clients successfully, these participants may simply be taking jobs away from others who are nearly as disadvantaged. A game of musical underclass will ensue as one group is temporarily helped, while another is pushed down into the underclass."

If new-style workfare will indeed represent a major policy thrust in the immediate future, I see little prospect for substantially alleviating inequality among poor minorities if it is not part of a more comprehensive program of economic and social reform that recognizes the dynamic interplay between societal organization and the behavior and life chances of individuals and groups—a program, in other words, that is designed both to enhance human-capital traits of poor minorities and to open up the opportunity structure in the broader society and economy to facilitate social mobility. The combination of economic and social welfare policies discussed in the previous section represents, from my point of view, such a program.

A Comprehensive Program

The problems of the ghetto underclass can be most meaningfully addressed by a comprehensive program that combines employment policies with social-welfare policies and that features universal as opposed to race- or group-specific strategies. On the one hand, this program highlights macroeconomic policy to generate a tight labor market and economic growth; fiscal and monetary policy, not only to stimulate noninflationary growth, but also to increase the competitiveness of American goods on both the domestic and international markets; and a national labor-market strategy to make the labor force more adaptable to changing economic opportunities. On the other hand, it highlights a child-support assurance program, a family-allowance program, and a child-care strategy.

I emphasize that although this program also would include targeted strategies—both means-tested and race-specific—they would be considered secondary to the universal programs, so that the latter are seen as the most visible and dominant aspects in the eyes of the general public. To the extent that the universal programs draw support from a wider population, the less visible targeted programs would be indirectly supported and protected. The hidden agenda for liberal policymakers is to enhance the chances in life for the ghetto underclass by emphasizing programs to which the more advantaged groups of all class and racial backgrounds can positively relate.

Before such programs can be seriously considered, however, the question of cost has to be addressed. The cost of programs to expand social and economic opportunity will be great, but it must be weighed against the economic and social costs of a do-nothing policy. As Levitan and Johnson have pointed out, "the most recent recession cost the nation an estimated $300 billion in lost income and production, and direct outlays for unemployment compensation totaled $30 billion in a single year. A policy that ignores the losses associated with slack labor markets and forced idleness inevitably will underinvest in the nation's labor force and future economic growth." Furthermore, the problem of annual budget deficits of almost $200 billion (driven mainly by the peacetime military buildup and the Reagan administration's tax cuts), and the need for restoring the federal tax base and adopting a more balanced set of budget priorities have to be tackled if we are to achieve significant progress on expanding opportunities.

In the final analysis, the pursuit of economic and social reform ultimately involves the question of political strategy. As the history of social provision so clearly demonstrates, universalistic political alliances, cemented by policies that provide benefits directly to wide segments of the population, are needed to work successfully for major reform. The recognition among minority leaders and liberal policymakers of the need to expand the War on Poverty and race-relations visions to confront the growing problems of inner-city social dislocations will provide, I believe, an important first step toward creating such an alliance.

Rooted Cosmopolitanism
1992

◆

MITCHELL COHEN

The resurgence of nationalism after the collapse of communism startled many observers in the West. What could have been more stark than the contrast between Western and Eastern Europe? As the European Community sought new modes of integration, nationalist virulence asserted itself in more than one of the previously communist lands. The bloody unraveling of Yugoslavia has been the most potent example, and the fear remains that the former Soviet Union could become Yugoslavia writ large. Evidently, Leninist and Stalinist dominion led neither to a withering away nor to the successful repression of national sentiments. (At the same time, Western European integration has proved to be a complicated matter, resisted in some quarters and accompanied by xenophobic outbursts in others.)

It is gradually becoming clear that nationalist aspirations were sometimes mistaken for democratic ambitions by Western observers of the momentous events between 1989 and 1991. Earlier, during the cold war, both theorists of totalitarianism and Stalinists, each for their own reasons, tried to convince us that ideology was redesigning in its own image every nook and cranny of—and brain cell in—Soviet-style societies. It is now evident how wrong they were, how much more complicated history has been. Much seems not to have been remade, but frozen or stunted or integrated and used by these regimes. National sentiment is one example, and it is a particularly thorny problem for the left.

The left, historically, never came adequately to grips with nationalism, and was often confounded by its intransigence. Consequently, its reemergence poses old quandaries anew. Marx's famous quip about modernity, that "all that's solid melts into air," would seem an appropriate metaphor for the last two years, save for one aspect of the modern world: national consciousness. Apart from circumstances in which nationalism served antiimperialist purposes, the left has tended to wishful anticipation of the dissipation of nations. For example, Eric Hobsbawm, one of the finest Marxist historians, wrote as recently as 1990: "The owl of Minerva, which brings wisdom, said Hegel, flies out at dusk. It is a good sign that it is now circling around nations and nationalism."

The left, habitually, advanced two linked assertions about nations: that they are products of history and not embodiments of timeless collective essences; and they should be regarded as epiphenomena, that is, as secondary (if often bothersome) matters. I generally agree with the first point but think the second misconceived. Considerable contemporary scholarship—not only of the left—addresses precisely these issues. Anthony Smith, in his thoughtful book *The Ethnic Origins of Nations* (1987), elucidates them neatly by means of a (Greek) ontological twist. He reminds us that Parmenides, the ancient Eleatic, proposed that "what is, is." He meant that change, "becoming," is illusion. A "Parmenidean" approach discerns in nations something inherent in human existence, something primordial that makes historical reappearances in varied guises yet that is in some way essential. The assumption is like that of Herder: nature creates nations. In contrast to Parmenides, Heraclitus of Epheus held that "all things are in a state of flux." A Heraclitian perspective on nations would emphasize their historicity. Nations, on this account, are a distinct product of modernity. They could not have come into being in earlier conditions, and will likely be transcended in the future. Thus Ernest Gellner, for instance, argues with characteristic erudition, in *Nations and Nationalism* (1983), that nations come of the transition from "agroliterate" to industrial societies, and Benedict Anderson, in *Imagined Communities* (1983), contends that, however subjectively ancient nationalists perceive their nations to be, they are objectively modern.

Smith seeks a middle ground between Parmenides and Heraclitus. He accepts the modernity of nations but traces their origins as far back as antiquity in what he calls *ethnie,* at whose core is a complex of myths and symbols tied to "the characteristic forms or styles and genres of certain historical configurations of peoples." All of them generate ethnocentrism, a sense of collective uniqueness and exclusivity that can be found, for example, in the oppositions between Greek and *barbaroi,* between Jews and pagan idolaters, in the self-conception of the Chinese as the Middle Kingdom, and in the Arab-Moslem notion of *Dar al-Islam.* In the West, an array of economic, political, and cultural transformations produced nations out of *ethnie.* So, rather than a break between premodernity and modernity, Smith perceives a political transformation leading from *ethnie* toward notions of common citizenship.

◆

The "collective uniqueness" of a social entity is a problematic notion for Marxism, which ascribed the most salient features of human reality to social class and conceived the future to be embodied in a *universal* class whose interests represented those of humanity as a whole. The proletariat's victory was to give birth to a classless society—the first truly universal society. Nations and nationalism had to be viewed as epiphenomena. In the socialist future, with human "prehistory" left behind, there would be a new social individual dwelling amid socialist humanity. Nothing would mediate between the individual and the human community writ large.

Marx was radically Heraclitian. However, one can find in his writings on nationalism at least two paradigms, as Shlomo Avineri notes. Before 1848 Marx believed that because of the universalizing tendencies of the capitalist market "national differences and antagonisms between peoples are daily more and more vanishing" (*The Communist Manifesto*). National cultural distinctions among workers were, objectively, secondary matters—at best. As Marx wrote in his unfinished critique of Friedrich List (1845), "The nationality of the worker is neither French, nor English, nor German, it is *labor, free slavery, self-huckstering.* His government is neither French nor English nor German, it is *capital.* His native air is neither French nor German nor English, it is factory air."

In Marx's post-1848 paradigm, nationalism tends to be a superstructural device employed by the bourgeoisie in its pursuit of expanding markets abroad and domestic mastery. In the first paradigm, the natural course of capitalist development ought to lead to the withering away of nationalism; in the second paradigm, nationalism is sustained by capitalists, distracting proletarians from their class interests and leading to the intensification of conflicts among nations.

Despite their divergences, the two paradigms are linked by Marx's insistence that "workers have no country." In both, nations and national cultures are viewed as historically created but, finally, as epiphenomena; Marx's ultimate vision is of a universal culture. It couldn't be otherwise if workers are the universal class, have no country, and breathe only factory air as their native air.

The difficulty is that this universal culture is something quite abstract. Here we may discern in Marx a problematic inheritance of Enlightenment rationalism. Now, few have been more incisive than Marx in criticizing bourgeois forms of abstract universalism, particularly concepts of the individual. He contrasted the Robinson Crusoe individual imagined by many capitalist ideologists with his own notion of "social individuals." In a trenchant passage in the *Grundrisse* he wrote:

> The more deeply we go back into history, the more does the individual appear as dependent, as belonging to a greater whole. . . . The human being is in the most literal sense a *zoon politikon* [political animal], not merely a gregarious animal, but an animal which can individuate itself only in the midst of society. Production by an isolated individual outside society . . . is as much of an absurdity as is the development of language without individuals living *together* and talking to each other.

In short, the self-created rugged individualist is an ideological fiction.

But Marx did not go far enough, and he thereby encouraged an abstract proletarian internationalism in place of abstract bourgeois universalism. Among other things, he should have said that individuals belong to greater wholes, not to a greater whole. Just as an individual is not an abstract entity, neither are the social realities through which one individuates oneself. The worker's native air may be factory air, and not French or German or English, but when the worker demands rights, it will be in French or German or English. By making a parallel between the producing and the speaking individual, Marx—unintentionally—implies the essential point. Societies are differentiated not only through productive relations but through language and culture, particularly national languages and cultures in the modern era. The most fruitful Marxist analyses of nationalism recognized just this. In *Die Nationalitätenfrage und die Sozialdemokratie* (1907) Otto Bauer argued that a nation is constituted by "common history as the effective cause, common culture and common descent as the means by which it produces its effects, a common language as the mediator of common culture, both its product and producer." Instead of proposing a classless society that would negate or homogenize national cultures, he advocated a federal socialist state that would provide national minorities with cultural autonomy on a "personal" (that is, nonterritorial) basis. Consequently, Bauer avoided the class reductionism that leads to an esperanto vision of socialist culture—a vision no less one-sided than that of nationalists who cannot see beyond their own tongues.

However, it is not true that all nationalists have had chauvinist views of the world and that all expressions of national sentiment represent particularist evil. For one example, a central current within the history of French socialism has been quite nationalist "when the nation in question represented the universal values of justice and progress" and antinationalist when "*la nation*" meant chauvinism and clericalism.* When Jean Jaurès rallied to the cause of the Dreyfusards, he refused to allow the right wing to be identified with "*la nation*," and concurrently demanded of the left that it make the French republic together with universal human values its cause. Any assault on human rights had to be its charge, not solely proletarian interests narrowly defined.

◆

Nationalists, like nationalisms, play different roles in different situations. As Avineri points out, in Marx's own day at least one socialist, Moses Hess, argued that nations should be conceived as mediators between the person and humanity. Hess, in response to Jew-hatred, espoused a socialist Jewish state as one link in an international chain of national redemptions. The title of his 1862 tract—*Rom und Jerusalem*—was not incidental, for Mazzini had made essentially the same arguments, though with republicanism in the place of Hess's socialism. Moreover, the apostle of Italian nationalism did not preach devotion to the nation alone but told his followers: "You are *men* before you are *citizens*." Like his Jewish counterpart, he saw the nation as a mediator between the individual and humanity; Mazzini and Hess both proposed their peoples' independence as sparks for universal liberation and not solely as particularist enterprises. The agenda was not just a flag but a pacific world of free nations. One may oppose their programs, find them bleary-eyed, ill-conceived, or historically deluded, but they cannot be classified as belligerent exclusivists. It is true that neither Hess nor Mazzini elaborated his ideas with the trenchancy of the author of *Capital*. Yet they grasped something that the more formidable mind did not.

To recognize the modernity of nations and to discard the notion that they incarnate timeless collective essences should not be translated simplistically into the proposition that nations and nationalism are nothing more than epiphenomena. Although it is incorrect to speak of "nations" before, roughly, the fifteenth and sixteenth centuries, and nationalism before the French Revolution, national cul-

---

*See K. Steven Vincent, *Between Marxism and Anarchism: Benoît Malon and French Reformist Socialism* (Berkeley: University of California Press, 1992), p. 116.

tures and national consciousness take on an autonomy beyond their origins. It is as historically spurious as it is politically hazardous to homogenize nationalist movements and sentiments.

Let's take a contemporary example. I think it incumbent upon the left—and everyone else—to speak out forcefully in behalf of the Kurds. Not just forcefully, but honestly, which is impossible apart from advancing Kurdish national aspirations. Kurds sometimes define their aspirations as autonomy (within Iraq or Turkey), sometimes as independence; social democracy is not their priority. Shall we tell them that Westerners will support them so that in a future era they can embody Western leftist ideas of universal humanity (whatever those are nowadays)? It is difficult to imagine a more condescending posture. And what should Kurds make of the part of the left that, preoccupied singularly by anti-imperialist indignation, draws attention to the Kurdish tragedy solely to indict American policy in the Gulf (as if Saddam Hussein would otherwise have been benevolent)? My point is simple: this is an oppressed nationality. Kurds are oppressed as Kurds and not as members of generalized categories. Their problem must be addressed in its specificity. Their national sentiments are legitimate, both intrinsically and as a response to oppression.

I do not mean to underestimate the murderous catastrophes wrought by nationalist fanaticism, especially in our century. (The Kurds themselves do not have entirely clean historical hands; should an independent Kurdistan arise, one would demand of it the same respect of minority rights Kurds should have been afforded in Iraq or Turkey.) Rather, I want to argue against conceiving nationalism as an either/or proposition: either all its forms to be condemned or all its expressions to be sanctioned. Both possibilities are inherently perilous. Michael Walzer has suggested what seems to me to be a sagacious alternative, that of domesticating nationalism's more dangerous impulses, seeking to integrate and counterbalance them within broader pluralistic frameworks. A useful historical model, as he notes, is religion, which, once a primary source of slaughter throughout Europe, was domesticated after its battered apostles reconciled themselves to multireligious societies and, consequently, to tolerance. I would add that this ultimately meant resigning themselves to an important principle, one that is key to such domestication and to which I will presently return, that of the legitimacy of plural loyalties and therefore difference.

◆

I employ the word "difference" with some hesitation, because it is now encumbered by faddish, often vacuous, usages. This baggage aside, "difference" is a vital historical and contemporary question in American and European societies. It has also been a longstanding problem for the left, rooted in that troublesome dimension of the left's Enlightenment heritage to which I alluded when discussing Marx. The friar tells Lessing's "Nathan the Wise": "You're a Christian soul! By God, a better Christian never lived." Nathan replies, "And well for us! For what makes me for you a Christian, makes yourself for me a Jew." A universal quality—reason—makes this identity of Christian and Jew possible. The tolerance suggested is based on equivalence, not acceptance of difference: the play is entitled *Nathan the Wise*, not *Nathan the Jew*. In later, left-wing versions, membership in the universal class became the solvent of differences, on the way to a universal, classless society.

Yet there are and will be "differences" not assimilable to sweeping universalist prescriptions. Although much of the left conceived the classless society as the melting pot of humanity, a striking alternative was formulated by an American radical not long before the U.S. entered World War I. It was a moment in which nativist prejudices against immigrants intensified considerably in this country. Many of these newcomers were stirred by European events, often asserting bonds to their "old countries." This begot huffy indignation, especially on the part of American Brahmins: why, these immigrants simply weren't becoming proper "Americans."

In his July 1916 essay, "Trans-national America," a young WASP named Randolph Bourne fashioned a remarkable retort. "As the unpleasant truth has come upon us that assimilation in this country was proceeding on lines very different from those we had marked out for it," he wrote, "we found ourselves inclined to blame those who were thwarting our prophecies. The truth became culpable." What was at stake was the relation between culture and democracy. "We act"— Bourne's "we" was dominant Anglo-America—"as if we want Americanization to take place only on our own terms, and not by the consent of the governed." Against the "thinly disguised panic which calls itself 'patriotism,' " he proposed celebrating as culturally invigorating the hyphen in Polish-American, Irish-American, Jewish-American, German-American, and so on. He went so far as to propose referring also to "English-Americans."

Instead of a melting pot, Bourne envisioned "trans-nationality." This was "a weaving back and forth with other lands, of many threads of all sizes and colors. Any movement which attempts to thwart the weaving, or to dye the fabric any one color or disentangle the threads of the strands, is false to this cosmopolitan vision." In a subsequent essay, Bourne argued that this thinking pointed toward "new concepts of the state, of nationality, of citizenship, of allegiance." Here we find a multidimensional conception of political society and human relations, one that implies an important democratic principle: the legitimacy of plural loyalties.

Perhaps I am not stretching the Austro-Marxists' purposes too far if I suggest that they too accepted this principle by championing a class politics aimed at fashioning a federal socialist republic in which there would be systems of both territorial representation and national linguistic cultural—personal—autonomy. This was at odds with the radical universalism of Marx or Luxemburg (and with the expectation that the state would wither away).

The Austro-Marxist position was expounded in a specific context: a debate inside a socialist movement within a multinational empire. One can also find a notion of plural loyalty articulated by the left within a national movement, with the use, notably, of metaphors like Bourne's—threads and cloth. In the late 1920s and early 1930s the growing dominance of the Labor-left within the Zionist movement was threatened by the right-wing "Revisionists" led by Vladimir Jabotinsky. The latter proclaimed himself a "pure" nationalist and denounced his adversaries as "*shaatnez*," a mixture of wool and cotton proscribed in Jewish garments by religious orthodoxy. The national raiment, in his formulation, had to be unsullied by foreign admixtures and universalistic notions such as socialism. David Ben-Gurion, then Labor's leader and later the first premier of Israel, proclaimed the very concept of *shaatnez* to be a deceit. A national movement without social conceptions was an abstraction, and Zionism, like any national movement, could be good or bad depending on the society it fashioned. He declared—changing the metaphor—that, unlike the right, the Zionist left stood not in one circle (that of nationalism) but in many circles, and "when we stand in two circles it isn't a question of standing in two separate areas, one moment in one and the next in another, but rather in what is common territory to both of them." He continued:

> In reality we don't stand within two circles alone, but within many circles—as citizens of Palestine we stand in the circle of the Land of Israel, as Jews we stand in the circle of a nation that aspires to its

homeland, as workers we stand in the circle of the working class, as sons of our generation we stand in the circle of modern history; our women comrades stand in the circle of the working women's movement in its struggle for liberation.

To stand in many circles is to accept the principle of plural loyalties. It must be readily conceded that subscribing to such a principle and practicing it are two different things. But for my purposes here, it is the theoretical point that is most salient, together with the fact that it has direct implications for concepts of citizenship. This was articulated with acuity by one of Ben-Gurion's colleagues, the American Labor Zionist thinker Hayim Greenberg, in his 1948 essay, "Patriotism and Plural Loyalties." Greenberg took the example of an Italian-speaking Swiss citizen. "He hardly knows himself how many different loyalties he harbors in various degrees." As a Swiss he owes fidelity to Switzerland; he is also a patriot of his canton. Whatever his "race," he feels a cultural and linguistic kinship to Italians in Italy. If he is Catholic he feels ties to Catholics around the world and in various regards accepts the "sovereignty" of the Vatican. Poor man should he become a UN official. And we should add: if he is a she, she may well have keen allegiances to the women's movement.

How shall we regard this individual? As a bundle of prospective betrayals? Or ought we accept, indeed value, the legitimacy of "pluralist-social relationships, attachments, sentiments and loyalties"? The true democrat, maintained Greenberg, will seek not to destroy but to harmonize such differences.

Which doesn't mean that they are easily harmonized. Plural dimensions of human identity often don't rest easily with each other, and sometimes not at all. Such discontents are the hobgoblins of what I'd call "unidevotionalists," those vigilant and anxious beings who are endlessly obsessed with litmus tests of absolute loyalty. Alas, their questions and answers, always so earnest, are ever easy. For them it is unimaginable that an individual might actually face moral dilemmas, might confront legitimate conflicts of fealty, might have to inquire of the rights and wrongs of contesting demands, might be compelled to assess the consequences of embracing this or that position. Unidevotionalists have their flag; they salute it; they legitimate only particularisms, usually just their own. Such onesideness—no less than that of abstract universalism—frustrates democratic pluralism, which demands refusal of singular answers (to borrow again from Walzer).

◆

It might seem that among today's advocates of multiculturalism a left has emerged that recognizes the problems I've been raising. Certainly, parallels to earlier discussions of national identity and culture can be found in the debates on multiculturalism. Yet I fear that too many votaries of multiculturalism have become unreflective celebrants of particularism, now that the working class has not fulfilled its universalizing mission. Missing is adequate meditation on the grounds of cultural diversity within a democratic society. Too often, the word "difference" is intoned indignantly without consideration of the "trans" of "trans-nationality," of the intersection of the hyphens Bourne—rightly—celebrated.

Bourne spoke of a cloth of many threads, but he still spoke of a cloth. If one asserts differences without conceptualizing the territory of multicultural exchange, one may reinvent just those particularist perils dreaded in nationalism by the historical left. In a world of resurgent nationalisms, and in an America debating multiculturalism, what is needed is the fashioning of a dialectical concept of *rooted* cosmopolitanism, which accepts a multiplicity of roots and branches and that rests on the legitimacy of plural loyalties, of standing in many circles, but with common ground.

The Rise of "Identity Politics"
1993

◆

TODD GITLIN

Todd Gitlin, a member of the *Dissent* editorial board, is professor of sociology at the University of California, Berkeley. His books include *Inside Prime Time, The Sixties,* and *The Murder of Albert Einstein.* "The Rise of 'Identity Politics' " is excerpted from "From Universality to Difference: Notes on the Fragmentation of the Idea of the Left," *Contention,* Winter 1993.

The rise of "identity politics" forms a convergence of a cultural style, a mode of logic, a badge of belonging, and a claim to insurgency. What began as an assertion of dignity, a recovery from exclusion and denigration, and a demand for representation, has also developed a hardening of its boundaries. The long-overdue opening of political initiative to minorities, women, gays, and others of the traditionally voiceless has developed its own methods of silencing.

At the extreme, in the academy but also outside, "genealogy" has become something of a universal solvent for universal ideas. Standards and traditions now are taken to be nothing more than the camouflage of interests. All claims to knowledge are presumed to be addressed from and to "subject positions," which, like the claims themselves, have been "constructed" or "invented" collectively by self-designated groups. Sooner or later, all disputes issue in propositions of the following sort: The central subject for understanding is the difference between X (for example, women, people of color) and Y (for example, white males). P is the case because my people, X, see it that way; if you don't agree with P, it is (or, more mildly, is probably) because you are a member of Y. And further: since X has been oppressed, or silenced, by Y—typically, white heterosexual males—justice requires that members of X, preferably (though not necessarily) adherents of P, be hired and promoted; and in the student body, in the curriculum, on the reading list, and at the conference, distinctly represented.

This is more than a way of thought. Identity politics is a form of self-understanding, an orientation toward the world, and a structure of feeling that is frequent in developed industrial societies. Identity politics presents itself as—and many young people experience it as—the most compelling remedy for anonymity in an impersonal world. This cluster of feelings seems to answer the questions, Who am I? Who is like me? Whom can I trust? Where do I belong?

But identity politics is more than a sensibility felt and lived by individuals. It is a search for comfort, an approach to community. The sense of membership is both a defense and an offense. It seems to overcome exclusion and silencing. Moreover, in a world where other people seem to have chosen up sides and, worse, where they approach you—even menace you—because you belong to a particular group, it seems a necessity to find or invent one's strength among one's people. From popular culture to government policy, the world has evidently assigned you a membership. Identity politics turns necessity to virtue.

But there is a hook: for all the talk about "the social construction of knowledge," identity politics in practice slides toward the premise that social groups have essential identities. At the outer limit, those who set out to explode a shrunken definition of humanity end by shrinking their definitions of blacks or women. In separatist theory, they must be, and have always been, all the same. After a genuflection to historical specificity, anatomy once again becomes destiny. This identity politics is already a tradition in its second generation, transmitted and retransmitted, institutionalized in jargons, mentors, gurus, conferences, associations, journals, departments, publishing subfields, bookstore sections, jokes, and, not incidentally, in affirmative action and the growing numbers of faculty and students identified and identifying themselves as "of color."

In this setting, identity politics promises a certain comfort. But what was, at first, an enclave where the silenced could find their voices tends now to harden into a self-enclosed world. In the academy, the pioneering work in the early 1970s toward making women's studies legitimate, bolstering labor studies, rethinking the damage done by slavery and the slaughter of the Indians, opening up the canon to hitherto silenced traditions—all this work was done by

scholars who had one foot in the civil-rights and antiwar movements
and who came to their specialties already bearing something of a universalist or cosmopolitan bent. But much of the succeeding work
tended to harden and narrow. Identity politics in the strict sense became an organizing principle among the academic cohorts who had
no political experience before the late 1960s—those now in their
twenties and early thirties. After the late 1960s, as race and gender
(and sometimes class) became the organizing categories by which
critical temperaments addressed the world in the humanities and social sciences, faculty people working this territory came to display the
confidence of an ascending class speaking predictably of "disruption," "subversion," "rupture," "contestation," "struggle for meaning."
The more their political life is confined to the library, the more aggressive their language.

But identity politics is not simply a product of the academic hot-
house. It also thrives in the society at large—in the media of the mass
and the margins alike, in schools and in street lore. Some students
carry the rhetoric of their particular group to campus with them.
Alert to slights, they cultivate a cultural marginality both defensive
and aggressive. Fights over appropriate language, over symbolic representation (whether in the form of syllabus or curriculum or faculty
or even cuisine), over affirmative action and musical styles and shares
of the public space are, to them, the core of "politics." Just as these cohorts have their clothes and their music, they have "their politics"—
the principal, even the only form of "politics" they know.

The specialists in difference may do their best to deny the fact that,
for a quarter of a century, they have been fighting over the English
department while the right held the White House as its private fief-
dom. But academic currents are not so insulated from the larger social world as parochial theory may presume. The legitimacy of racial
animus on a national scale, the boldness of right-wing politicians, the
profusion of straightforward race prejudice among students have all
made the academic left edgier and more offensive. Affirmative action
has been successful enough to create a critical mass of African Americans who feel simultaneously heartened, challenged, and marooned.
The symbolic burden they bear is enormous. In the absence of plausible prospects for fighting the impoverishment of the cities, unemployment, police brutality, crime, or any of the economic aspects of
the current immiserization, it is more convenient—certainly less
risky—to accuse a liberal professor of racism. Identity politics is intensified when antagonistic identities are fighting for their places

amid shrinking resources. The proliferation of identity politics leads to a turning inward, a grim and hermetic bravado celebrating victimization and stylized marginality.

◆

The thickening of identity politics is relative. We have to ask, Thickening compared with what? Compared with "universalism," "common culture," "the human condition," "liberality," "the Enlightenment project"—the contrary position wears different labels. I shall group them all (at Robert Jay Lifton's suggestion) under the heading of "commonality politics"—a frame of understanding and action that understands "difference" against the background of what is not different, what is shared among groups. This distinction is one of shadings, not absolutes, for differences are always thought and felt against a background of that which does not differ, and commonalities are always thought and felt in relation to differences. Still, the shadings are deeply felt, whence the intellectual polarization that shows up in debates about the complex of problems including the curriculum, diversity, and so on.

The point I wish to assert is that the thickening of identity politics is inseparable from a fragmentation of commonality politics. In large measure, things fell apart because the center could not hold. For, chronologically, the breakup of commonality politics predates the thickening of identity politics. The centrifugal surge, on campus and off, is the product of two intersecting histories. There is, obviously, the last quarter century of America's social and demographic upheavals. But these, in turn, have taken place within the longer history that snakes forward throughout the West since the revolutions of 1776, 1789, and 1848. Throughout this period and beyond, believers in a common humanity clustered around the two great progressive ideals: the liberal ideal enshrined in the Declaration of Independence and, later, in the Declaration of the Rights of Man and Citizen; and the radical ideal that crystallized as Marxism.

Such legitimacy as the left enjoyed in the West rested on its claim to a place in the story of universal human emancipation. Two hundred years of revolutionary tradition, whether liberal or radical, were predicated on the ideal of a universal humanity. The left addressed itself not to particular men and women but to all, in the name of their common standing. If the population at large was incapable, by itself, of seeing the world whole and acting in the general interest, some enlightened group took it upon itself to be the collective conscience, the Founding Fathers, the vanguard party. Even Marx, lyricist of the proletariat, ingeniously claimed that his favored class was destined to stand for, or become, all humanity. Nationalist revolutions—from 1848 to the present—were to be understood as tributaries to a common torrent, the grand surge of self-determination justified by the equivalent worth of all national expressions. Whether liberals or socialists, reformers or revolutionaries, the men and women of the left aimed to persuade their listeners to see their common interest as citizens of the largest world imaginable. *All* men were supposed to have been created equal, workingmen of *all* countries were supposed to unite. Historians of women are right to point out that the various founding fathers were not thinking of half the species; yet potentially inclusive language was in place. The power of the discourse of political rights was such that it could be generalized by extrapolation. Thus, within fifty years, women—grossly subordinated in the antislavery movement—were working up a politics based on their constituting half of a human race that had been decreed to share equal rights.

Marxism, in all its colorations, became the core of what may be called the idea of the left—the struggle to usher in and to represent common humanity. There exists, Marx asserts in his early writings, a universal identity: the human being as maker, realizing his "species being" in the course of transforming nature. With the audacity of a German idealist primed to think in first principles, Marx adapts from Hegel the idea that a "universal class" will give meaning to history—though not without help. To accomplish its mission, this class to end all classes requires a universal midwife: the revolutionary. To every particular circumstance and cause, the universal priesthood of communists is charged with bringing the glad tidings that History is the unfolding of Reason. The Communist Party, like God, has its center everywhere and nowhere. The proletariat is his nation. Like the émigré Marx, he is at home nowhere and everywhere, free to teach people of all nations that not a historical event or a struggle against oppression rises or falls which does not have its part to play in the great international transfiguration.

Such is the lyric of Marxism, the rhetoric that appealed to revolutionaries for a century after the death of the founding father. And therefore Marxism-Leninism, the universalist technology of revolution and rule later codified by Stalinists, is, if not the unshakable shadow of Enlightenment Marxism, at least its scion. Lenin's Bolshevik Party thrives on and requires this lineage, even if Lenin and Marx are not identical. Under Lenin, the party, this directive force that sees all and knows all and acts in the ostensibly general interest, becomes the incarnation of the Enlightenment's faith in the knowability of the human situation. Farther down a road already surveyed by Marx, Lenin makes intellectuals essential to the revolution, thereby securing the dominion of universal ideals.

From 1935 to 1939 and again during World War II, the Popular Front could even conjure a new commonality—a cobbled-together antifascist fusion. In the end, Marxists could always ask rhetorically, what was the alternative that promised universal justice, a single humanity? And so, partly by default, from one revision to the next, Marxism remained the pedigreed theoretical ensemble hovering over all left-wing thought. And yet, once the antifascist alliance was broken, the universalist promise of Marxism proceeded to unravel.

◆

From this point of view, the intellectual radicalism of the early sixties can be seen as a search for a substitute universalism. Having dismissed Marxism for what C. Wright Mills called its "labor metaphysic," the New Left tried to compose a surrogate universal. "The issues are interrelated" was the New Left's approach to a federation of single-issue groups—so that, for example, the peace, civil-rights, and civil-liberties movements needed to recognize that they had a common enemy, the "Dixiecrats" who choked off any liberal extension of the New Deal. More grandly, in a revival of Enlightenment universalism, Students for a Democratic Society's Port Huron Statement spoke self-consciously in the name of all humanity. The universal solvent for particular differences would be the principle that "decision-making of basic social consequence be carried on by public groupings": that is, participatory democracy. In theory, participatory democracy was available to all. In practice, it was tailored to students, young people collected at "knowledge factories" as the industrial proletariat had been collected at mills and mines; young people who were skilled in conversation, had time on their hands, and, uprooted from the diversities of their respective upbringings, were being encouraged to think of themselves as practitioners of reason. When the early New Left set out to find common ground with a like-minded constituency, it reached out to the impoverished—the Student Nonviolent Coordinating Committee to sharecroppers and SDS to the urban poor, who, by virtue of their marginality, might be imagined as forerunners of a universal democracy. If students and the poor were not saddled with "radical chains" in the system of production, at least they could be imagined with radical needs for political participation.

But the student movement's attempts at universalism broke down—both practically and intellectually. In fact, the ideal of participatory democracy was only secondary for the New Left. The passion that drove students—including Berkeley's Free Speech Movement—was the desire to support civil rights as part of a movement with a universalist design. The New Left was a movement-for-others searching for an ideology to transform it into a movement-for-itself, but participatory democracy was too ethereal an objective with which to bind an entire movement, let alone an entire society. Freedom as an endless meeting was only alluring to those who had the time and taste to go to meetings endlessly. The universalist impulse regressed. Enter, then, the varieties of Marxism by which universalist students could imagine either that they were entitled to lead a hypothetical proletariat (Progressive Labor's Stalinism) or that they themselves already prefigured a "new working class."

But these attempts at recomposing a sense of a unified revolutionary bloc were weak in comparison with centrifugal pressures. Such unity as had been felt by the civil-rights movement began to dissolve as soon as legal segregation was defeated. Blacks began to insist on black leadership, even exclusively black membership. Feminist stirrings were greeted with scorn by unreconstructed men. If white supremacy was unacceptable, neither could male supremacy be abided. One group after another demanded the recognition of difference and the protection of separate spheres for distinct groupings. This was more than an *idea,* because it was more than strictly intellectual; it was more a whole way of experiencing the world. Difference was now lived and felt more acutely than unity.

The crack-up of the universalist New Left was muted for a while by the exigencies of the Vietnam War and the commonalities of youth culture. If there seemed in the late 1960s to be one big movement, it was largely because there was one big war. But the divisions of race and then gender and sexual orientation proved far too deep to be overcome by any rhetoric of unification. The initiative and energy went into proliferation—feminist, gay, ethnic, environmentalist. The very language of collectivity came to be perceived by the new movements as a colonialist smothering—an ideology to rationalize white male domination. Thus, by the early 1970s, the goals of the student movement and the various left-wing insurgencies were increasingly subsumed under the categories of identity politics. Separatism became automatic. Now one did not imagine oneself belonging to a common enterprise; one belonged to a caucus.

But note: the late New Left politics of dispersion and separateness, not the early New Left politics of universalist aspiration, were the seed-ground of the young faculty who were to carry radical politics into the academy in the 1970s and 1980s. The founders of women's and black studies had a universalist base in either the Old or the New Left. But their recruits, born in the early or later 1950s, did not. By the time they arrived on campuses in the early seventies, identity politics was the norm. They had no direct memory of either a unified left or a successful left-of-center Democratic Party. In general, their experience of active politics was segmented. The defeat of the left was so obvious it was taken for granted. For these post-1960s activists, universalist traditions seemed empty.

The profusion of social agents took place throughout the society, but nowhere more vigorously than in the academy. Here, in black and ethnic studies, women's studies, gay and lesbian groupings, and so on, each movement could feel the exhilaration of group-based identity. Each felt it had a distinct world to win—first by establishing that its group had been suppressed and silenced; then by exhuming buried work and exploring forms of resistance; and, finally, by trying to rethink society, literature, and history from the respective vantages of the silenced, asking what the group and, indeed, the entire world would look like if those hitherto excluded were now included. And since the demands of identity politics were far more winnable in the university than elsewhere, the struggles of minorities multiplied. When academic conservatives resisted, they only confirmed the convictions of the marginal—that their embattled or not-yet-developing perspectives needed to be separately institutionalized. In the developing logic of identity-based movements, the world was all periphery and no center, or, if there was a center, it was their own. The mission of insurgents was to promote their own interests; for if they would not, who would?

From these endeavors flowed genuine achievements in the study of history and literature. Whole new areas of inquiry were opened up. Histories of the world and of America, of science and literature, are still reverberating from what can legitimately be called a revolution in knowledge. But as the hitherto excluded territories were institutionalized, the lingering aspiration for the universal subject was ceded. A good deal of the Cultural Left felt its way, even if half-jokingly, toward a weak unity based not so much on a universalist premise or ideal but rather on a common enemy—that notorious White Male. Beneath this, they had become, willy-nilly, pluralists, a fact frequently disguised by the rhetoric of revolution hanging over from the late sixties.

Soon, difference was being practiced, not just thought, at a deeper level than commonality. It was more salient, more vital, more present—all the more so in the 1980s, as practical struggles for university facilities, requirements, and so forth culminated in fights over increasingly scarce resources. For the participants in these late-sixties and post-sixties movements, the benefits of this pursuit were manifold—an experience of solidarity, a ready-made reservoir of recruits. Seen from outside as fragments in search of a whole, the zones of identity politics came to be experienced from within as worlds unto themselves. The political-intellectual experience of younger academics could be mapped onto other centrifugal dispositions in post-Vietnam America. Group self-definitions embedded in political experience merged with other historicist and centrifugal currents to form the core and the legitimacy of the multicultural surge, the fragments of the Cultural Left. The idea of a common America and the idea of a unitary Left, these two great legacies of the Enlightenment, hollowed out together.

Thus a curious reversal of left and right. In the nineteenth century, the right was the property of aristocracies who stood unabashedly for the privileges of the few. Today, the aspiring aristocrats of the academic right tend to speak the language of universals—canon, merit, reason, individual rights, transpolitical virtue. For its part, seized by the logic of identity politics, committed to pleasing its disparate constituencies, the academic left has lost interest in the commonalities that undergird its obsession with difference.

Culture and Society

The White Negro
1957
Superficial Reflections on the Hipster

◆

NORMAN MAILER

Norman Mailer has been one of America's leading novelists ever since the 1948 publication of his first novel, *The Naked and the Dead*. He has won both the Pulitzer Prize and the National Book Award. His other works include *Advertisements for Myself*, *Why Are We in Vietnam?*, *The Armies of the Night*, and *Of a Fire on the Moon*. He is a co-founder of *The Village Voice*.

Our search for the rebels of the generation led us to the hipster. The hipster is AN ENFANT TERRIBLE turned inside out. In character with his time, he is trying to get back at the conformists by lowing low. . . . You can't interview a hipster because his main goal is to keep out of a society which, he thinks, is trying to make everyone over in its own image. He takes marijuana because it supplies him with experiences that can't be shared with "squares." He may affect a broad-brimmed hat or a zoot suit, but usually he prefers to skulk unmarked. The hipster may be a jazz musician; he is rarely an artist, almost never a writer. He may earn his living as a petty criminal, a hobo, a carnival roustabout or a free-lance moving man in Greenwich Village, but some hipsters have found a safe refuge in the upper income brackets as television comics or movie actors. (The late James Dean, for one, was a hipster hero.) . . . It is tempting to describe the hipster in psychiatric terms as infantile, but the style of his infantilism is a sign of the times. He does not try to enforce his will on others, Napoleon-fashion, but contents himself with a magical omnipotence never disproved because never tested. . . . As the only extreme nonconformist of his generation, he exercises a powerful

if underground appeal for conformists, through newspaper accounts
of his delinquencies, his structureless jazz, and his emotive grunt
words.

"Born 1930: The Unlost Generation," by Caroline Bird
Harper's Bazaar, February 1957

Probably, we will never be able to determine the psychic havoc of the
concentration camps and the atom bomb upon the unconscious
mind of almost everyone alive in these years. For the first time in civilized history, perhaps for the first time in all of history, we have been
forced to live with the suppressed knowledge that the smallest facets
of our personality or the most minor projection of our ideas, or indeed the absence of ideas and the absence of personality could mean
equally well that we might still be doomed to die as a cipher in some
vast statistical operation in which our teeth would be counted, and
our hair would be saved, but our death itself would be unknown, un-
honored, and unremarked, a death which could not follow with dignity as a possible consequence to serious actions we had chosen, but
rather a death by *deus ex machina* in a gas chamber or a radioactive
city; and so if in the midst of civilization—that civilization founded
upon the Faustian urge to dominate nature by mastering time, mastering the links of social cause and effect—in the middle of an economic civilization founded upon the confidence that time could
indeed be subjected to our will, our psyche was subjected itself to the
intolerable anxiety that death being causeless, life was causeless as
well, and time deprived of cause and effect had come to a stop.

The Second World War presented a mirror to the human condition which blinded anyone who looked into it. For if tens of millions
were killed in concentration camps out of the inexorable agonies and
contractions of superstates founded upon the always insoluble contradictions of injustice, one was then obliged also to see that no matter how crippled and perverted an image of man was the society he
had created, it was nonetheless his creation, his collective creation
(at least his collective creation from the past) and if society was so
murderous, then who could ignore the most hideous questions about
his own nature?

Worse. One could hardly maintain the courage to be individual, to
speak with one's own voice, for the years in which one could compla-
cently accept oneself as part of an elite by being a radical were forever
gone. A man knew that when he dissented he gave a note upon his
life which could be called in any year of overt crisis. No wonder then

that these have been the years of conformity and depression. A stench of fear has come out of every pore of American life, and we suffer from a collective failure of nerve. The only courage, with rare exceptions, that we have been witness to, has been the isolated courage of isolated people.

II

It is on this bleak scene that a phenomenon has appeared: the American existentialist—the hipster, the man who knows that, if our collective condition is to live with instant death by atomic war, relatively quick death by the state as *l'univers concentrationnaire,* or with a slow death by conformity with every creative and rebellious instinct stifled (at what damage to the mind and the heart and the liver and the nerves no research foundation for cancer will discover in a hurry), if the fate of twentieth-century man is to live with death from adolescence to premature senescence, why then the only life-giving answer is to accept the terms of death, to live with death as immediate danger, to divorce oneself from society, to exist without roots, to set out on that uncharted journey into the rebellious imperatives of the self. In short, whether the life is criminal or not, the decision is to encourage the psychopath in oneself, to explore that domain of experience where security is boredom and therefore sickness, and one exists in the present, in that enormous present which is without past or future, memory or planned intention, the life where a man must go until he is beat, where he must gamble with his energies through all those small or large crises of courage and unforeseen situations which beset his day, where he must be with it or doomed not to swing. The unstated essence of Hip, its psychopathic brilliance, quivers with the knowledge that new kinds of victories increase one's power for new kinds of perception; and defeats, the wrong kind of defeats, attack the body and imprison one's energy until one is jailed in the prison air of other people's habits, other people's defeats, boredom, quiet desperation, and muted icy self-destroying race. One is Hip or one is Square (the alternative which each new generation coming into American life is beginning to feel), one is a rebel or one conforms, one is a frontiersman in the Wild West of American night life, or else a Square cell, trapped in the totalitarian issues of American society, doomed willy-nilly to conform if one is to succeed.

A totalitarian society makes enormous demands on the courage of men, and a partially totalitarian society makes even greater demands for the general anxiety is greater. Indeed if one is to be a man, almost any kind of unconventional action often takes disproportionate courage. So it is no accident that the source of Hip is the Negro for he has been living on the margin between totalitarianism and democracy for two centuries. But the presence of Hip as a working philosophy in the subworlds of American life is probably due to jazz, and its knifelike entrance into culture, its subtle but so penetrating influence on an avant-garde generation—that postwar generation of adventurers who (some consciously, some by osmosis) had absorbed the lessons of disillusionment and disgust of the Twenties, the Depression, and the War. Sharing a collective disbelief in the words of men who had too much money and controlled too many things, they knew almost as powerful a disbelief in the socially monolithic ideas of the single mate, the solid family, and the respectable love life. If the intellectual antecedents of this generation can be traced to such separate influences as D.H. Lawrence, Henry Miller, and Wilhelm Reich, the viable philosophy of Hemingway fits most of their facts: in a bad world, as he was to say over and over again (while taking time out from his parvenu snobbery and dedicated gourmandise), in a bad world there is no love nor mercy nor charity nor justice unless a man can keep his courage, and this indeed fitted some of the facts. What fitted the need of the adventurer even more precisely was Hemingway's categorical imperative that what made him feel good became therefore The Good.

So no wonder that in certain cities of America, in New York of course, and New Orleans, in Chicago and San Francisco and Los Angeles, in such American cities as Paris and Mexico, D.F., this particular part of a generation was attracted to what the Negro had to offer. In such places as Greenwich Village, a ménage-à-trois was completed—the bohemian and the juvenile delinquent came face-to-face with the Negro, and the hipster was a fact in American life. If marijuana was the wedding ring, the child was the language of Hip for its argot gave expression to abstract states of feeling which all could share, at least all who were Hip. And in this wedding of the white and the black it was the Negro who brought the cultural dowry. Any Negro who wishes to live must live with danger from his first day, and no experience can ever be casual to him, no Negro can saunter down a street with any real certainty that violence will not visit him on his walk. The cameos of security for the average white: mother and the home, job and the family, are not even a mockery to millions of Negroes; they are impossible. The Negro has the simplest of alternatives: live a life of constant humility or ever-threatening danger. In such a pass where paranoia is as vital to survival as blood, the Negro had stayed alive and begun to grow by following the need of his body where he could. Knowing in the cells of his existence that life was war, nothing but war, the Negro (all exceptions admitted) could rarely afford the sophisticated inhibitions of civilization, and so he kept for his survival the art of the primitive, he lived in the enormous present, he subsisted for his Saturday-night kicks, relinquishing the pleasures of the mind for the more obligatory pleasures of the body, and in his music he gave voice to the character and quality of his existence, to his rage and the infinite variations of joy, lust, languor, growl, cramp, pinch, scream, and despair of his orgasm. For jazz is orgasm, it is the music of orgasm, good orgasm and bad, and so it spoke across a nation, it had the communication of art even where it was watered, perverted, corrupted, and almost killed, it spoke in no matter what laundered popular way of instantaneous existential states to which some whites could respond, it was indeed a communication by art because it said, "I feel this, and now you do too."

So there was a new breed of adventurers, urban adventurers who drifted out at night looking for action with a black man's code to fit their facts. The hipster had absorbed the existentialist synapses of the Negro, and for practical purposes could be considered a white Negro.

To be an existentialist, one must be able to feel oneself—one must know one's desires, one's rages, one's anguish, one must be aware of the character of one's frustration and know what would satisfy it. The overcivilized man can be an existentialist only if it is chic, and deserts it quickly for the next chic. To be a real existentialist (Sartre admittedly to the contrary) one must be religious, one must have one's sense of the "purpose"—whatever the purpose may be—but a life which is directed by one's faith in the necessity of action is a life committed to the notion that the substratum of existence is the search, the end meaningful but mysterious; it is impossible to live such a life unless one's emotions provide their profound conviction. Only the French, alienated beyond alienation from their unconscious could welcome an existential philosophy without ever feeling it at all; indeed only a Frenchman by declaring that the unconscious did not exist could then proceed to explore the delicate involutions of consciousness, the microscopically sensuous and all-but-ineffable *frissons* of mental becoming, in order finally to create the theology of atheism and so submit that in a world of absurdities the existential absurdity is most coherent.

In the dialogue between the atheist and the mystic, the atheist is on the side of life, rational life, undialectical life—since he conceives of death as emptiness, he can, no matter how weary or despairing, wish for nothing but more life; his pride is that he does not transpose his weakness and spiritual fatigue into a romantic longing for death, for such appreciation of death is then all too capable of being elaborated by his imagination into a universe of meaningful structure and moral orchestration.

Yet this masculine argument can mean very little for the mystic. The mystic can accept the atheist's description of his weakness, he can agree that his mysticism was a response to despair. And yet . . . and yet his argument is that he, the mystic, is the one finally who has chosen to live with death, and so death is his experience and not the atheist's, and the atheist by eschewing the limitless dimensions of profound despair has rendered himself incapable to judge the experience. The real argument which the mystic must always advance is the very intensity of his private vision—his argument depends from the vision precisely because what was felt in the vision is so extraordinary that no rational argument, no hypotheses of "oceanic feelings" and certainly no skeptical reductions can explain away what has become for him the reality more real than the reality of closely reasoned logic. His inner experience of the possibilities within death is his logic. So, too, for the existentialist. And the psychopath. And the saint and the bullfighter and the lover. The common denominator for all of them is their burning consciousness of the present, exactly that incandescent consciousness which the possibilities within death has opened for them. There is a depth of desperation to the condition which enables one to remain in life only by engaging death, but the reward is their knowledge that what is happening at each instant of the electric present is good or bad for them, good or bad for their cause, their love, their action, their need.

It is this knowledge which provides the curious community of feeling in the world of the hipster, a muted cool religious revival to be sure, but the element which is exciting, disturbing, nightmarish perhaps, is that incompatibles have come to bed, the inner life and the violent life, the orgy and the dream of love, the desire to murder and the desire to create, a dialectical conception of existence with a lust for power, a dark, romantic, and yet undeniably dynamic view of existence for it sees every man and woman as moving individually through each moment of life forward into growth or backward into death.

III

It may be fruitful to consider the hipster a philosophical psychopath, a man interested not only in the dangerous imperatives of his psychopathy but in codifying, at least for himself, the suppositions on which his inner universe is constructed. By this premise the hipster is a psychopath, and yet not a psychopath but the negation of the psychopath for he possesses the narcissistic detachment of the philosopher, that absorption in the recessive nuances of one's own motive which is so alien to the unreasoning drive of the psychopath. In this country where new millions of psychopaths are developed each year, stamped with the mint of our contradictory popular culture (where sex is sin and yet sex is paradise), it is as if there has been room already for the development of the antithetical psychopath who extrapolates from his own condition, from the inner certainty that his rebellion is just, a radical vision of the universe which thus separates him from the general ignorance, reactionary prejudice, and self-doubt of the more conventional psychopath. Having converted his unconscious experience into much conscious knowledge, the hipster has shifted the focus of his desire from immediate gratification toward that wider passion for future power which is the mark of civilized man. Yet with an irreducible difference. For Hip is the sophistication of the wise primitive in a giant jungle, and so its appeal is still beyond the civilized man. If there are ten million Americans who are more or less psychopathic (and the figure is most modest), there are probably not more than one hundred thousand men and women who consciously see themselves as hipsters, but their importance is that they are an elite with the potential ruthlessness of an elite, and a language most adolescents can understand instinctively for the hipster's intense view of existence matches their experience and their desire to rebel.

Before one can say more about the hipster, there is obviously much to be said about the psychic state of the psychopath—or, clinically, the psychopathic personality. Now, for reasons which may be more curious than the similarity of the words, even many people with a psychoanalytic orientation often confuse the psychopath with the psychotic. Yet the terms are polar. The psychotic is legally insane, the psychopath is not; the psychotic is almost always incapable of discharging in physical acts the rage of his frustration, while the psychopath at his extreme is virtually as incapable of restraining his violence. The psychotic lives in so misty a world that what is happening at each moment of his life is not very real to him whereas the psychopath seldom knows any reality greater than the face, the voice, the being of the particular people among whom he may find himself at any moment. Sheldon and Eleanor Glueck describe him as follows:

> The psychopath . . . can be distinguished from the person sliding into or clambering out of a "true psychotic" state by the long tough persistence of his anti-social attitude and behaviour and the absence of hallucinations, delusions, manic flight of ideas, confusion, disorientation, and other dramatic signs of psychosis.

The late Robert Lindner, one of the few experts on the subject, in his book *Rebel Without a Cause—The Hypnoanalysis of a Criminal Psychopath* presented part of his definition in this way:

> . . . the psychopath is a rebel without a cause, an agitator without a slogan, a revolutionary without a program: in other words, his rebelliousness is aimed to achieve goals satisfactory to himself alone; he is incapable of exertions for the sake of others. All his efforts, hidden under no matter what disguise, represent investments designed to satisfy his immediate wishes and desires. . . . The psychopath, like the child, cannot delay the pleasures of gratification; and this trait is one of his underlying, universal characteristics. He cannot wait upon erotic gratification which convention demands should be preceded by the chase before the kill: he must rape. He cannot wait upon the development of prestige in society: his egoistic ambitions lead him to leap into headlines by daring performances. Like a red thread the predominance of this mechanism for immediate satisfaction runs through the history of every psychopath. It explains not only his behaviour but also the violent nature of his acts.

Yet even Lindner who was the most imaginative and most sympathetic of the psychoanalysts who have studied the psychopathic personality was not ready to project himself into the essential sympathy—which is that the psychopath may indeed be the perverted and dangerous front-runner of a new kind of personality which could become the central expression of human nature before the twentieth century is over. For the psychopath is better adapted to dominate those mutually contradictory inhibitions upon violence and love which civilization has exacted of us, and if it be remembered that not every psychopath is an extreme case, and that the condition of psychopathy is present in a host of people, including many politicians, professional soldiers, newspaper columnists, entertainers, artists, jazz musicians, call-girls, promiscuous homosexuals and half the executives of Hollywood, television, and advertising, it can be seen that there are aspects of psychopathy which already exert considerable cultural influence.

What characterizes almost every psychopath and part-psychopath is that they are trying to create a new nervous system for themselves. Generally we are obliged to act with a nervous system which has been formed from infancy, and which carries in the style of its circuits the very contradictions of our parents and our early milieu. Therefore, we are obliged, most of us, to meet the tempo of the present and the future with reflexes and rhythms which come from the past. It is not only the "dead weight of the institutions of the past" but indeed the inefficient and often antiquated nervous circuits of the past which strangle our potentiality for responding to new possibilities which might be exciting for our individual growth.

Through most of modern history, "sublimation" was possible: at the expense of expressing only a small portion of oneself, that small portion could be expressed intensely. But sublimation depends on a reasonable tempo to history. If the collective life of a generation has moved too quickly, the "past" by which particular men and women of that generation may function is not, let us say, thirty years old, but relatively a hundred or two hundred years old. And so the nervous system is overstressed beyond the possibility of such compromises as sublimation, especially since the stable middle-class values so prerequisite to sublimation have been virtually destroyed in our time, at least as nourishing values free of confusion or doubt. In such a crisis of accelerated historical tempo and deteriorated values, neurosis tends to be replaced by psychopathy, and the success of psychoanalysis (which even ten years ago gave promise of becoming a direct major force) diminishes because of its inbuilt and characteristic incapacity to handle patients more complex, more experienced, or more adventurous than the analyst himself. In practice, psychoanalysis has by now become all too often no more than a psychic blood-letting. The patient is not so much changed as aged, and the infantile fantasies which he is encouraged to express are condemned to exhaust themselves against the analyst's nonresponsive reactions. The result for all too many patients is a diminution, a "tranquilizing" of their most interesting qualities and vices. The patient is indeed not so much altered as worn out—less bad, less good, less bright, less willful, less destructive, less creative. He is thus able to conform to that contradictory and unbearable society which first created his neurosis. He can conform to what he loathes because he no longer has the passion to feel loathing so intensely.

The psychopath is notoriously difficult to analyze because the fundamental decision of his nature is to try to live the infantile fantasy, and in this decision (given the dreary alternative of psychoanalysis) there may be a certain instinctive wisdom. For there is a dialectic to changing one's nature, the dialectic which underlies all psychoanalytic method: it is the knowledge that if one is to change one's habits, one must go back to the source of their creation, and so the psychopath exploring backward along the road of the homosexual, the orgiast, the drug addict, the rapist, the robber, and the murderer seeks to find those violent parallels to the violent and often hopeless contradictions he knew as an infant and as a child. For if he has the courage to meet the parallel situation at the moment when he is ready, then he has a chance to act as he has never acted before, and in satisfying the frustration—if he can succeed—he may then pass by symbolic substitute through the locks of incest. In thus giving expression to the buried infant in himself, he can lessen the tension of those infantile desires and so free himself to remake a bit of his nervous system. Like the neurotic he is looking for the opportunity to grow up a second time, but the psychopath knows instinctively that to express a forbidden impulse actively is far more beneficial to him than merely to confess the desire in the safety of a doctor's room. The psychopath is inordinately ambitious, too ambitious ever to trade his warped brilliant conception of his possible victories in life for the grim if peaceful attrition of the analyst's couch. So his associational journey into the past is lived out in the theater of the present, and he exists for those charged situations where his senses are so alive that he can be aware actively (as the analysand is aware passively) of what his habits are, and how he can change them. The strength of the psychopath is that he knows (where most of us can only guess) what is good for him and what is bad for him at exactly those instants when an old crippling habit has become so attacked by experience that the potentiality exists to change it, to replace a negative and empty fear with an outward action, even if—and here I obey the logic of the extreme psychopath—even if the fear is of himself, and the action is to murder. The psychopath murders—if he has the courage—out of the necessity to purge his violence, for if he cannot empty his hatred then he cannot love, his being is frozen with implacable self-hatred for his cowardice. (It can of course be suggested that it takes little courage for two strong eighteen-year-old hoodlums, let us say, to beat in the brains of a candy-store keeper, and indeed the act—even by the logic of the psychopath—is not likely to prove very therapeutic for the victim is not an immediate equal. Still, courage of a sort is necessary, for one murders not only a weak fifty-year-old man but an institution as well, one violates private property, one enters into a new relation with the police and introduces a dangerous element into one's life. The hoodlum is therefore daring the unknown, and so no matter how brutal the act, it is not altogether cowardly.)

At bottom, the drama of the psychopath is that he seeks love. Not love as the search for a mate, but love as the search for an orgasm more apocalyptic than the one which preceded it. Orgasm is his therapy—he knows at the seed of his being that good orgasm opens his possibilities and bad orgasm imprisons him. But in this search, the psychopath becomes an embodiment of the extreme contradictions of the society which formed his character, and the apocalyptic orgasm often remains as remote as the Holy Grail, for there are clusters and nests and ambushes of violence in his own necessities and in the imperatives and retaliations of the men and women among whom he lives his life, so that even as he drains his hatred in one act or another, so the conditions of his life create it anew in him until the drama of his movements bears a sardonic resemblance to the frog who climbed a few feet in the well only to drop back again.

Yet there is this to be said for the search after the good orgasm: when one lives in a civilized world, and still can enjoy none of the cultural nectar of such a world because the paradoxes on which civilization is built demand that there remain a cultureless and alienated bottom of exploitable human material, then the logic of becoming a sexual outlaw (if one's psychological roots are bedded in the bottom) is that one has at least a running competitive chance to be physically healthy so long as one stays alive. It is therefore no accident that psychopath is most prevalent with the Negro. Hated from outside and therefore hating himself, the Negro was forced into the position of exploring all those moral wildernesses of civilized life which the Square automatically condemns as delinquent or evil or immature or morbid or self-destructive or corrupt. (Actually the terms have equal weight. Depending on the telescope of the cultural clique from which the Square surveys the universe, "evil" or "immature" are equally strong terms of condemnation.) But the Negro, not being privileged to gratify his self-esteem with the heady satisfactions of categorical condemnation, chose to move instead in that other direction where all situations are equally valid, and in the worst of perversion, promiscuity, pimpery, drug addiction, rape, razor-slash, bottle-break, what have you, the Negro discovered and elaborated a morality of the bottom, an ethical differentiation between the good and the bad in every human activity from the go-getter pimp (as opposed to the lazy one) to the relatively dependable pusher or prostitute. Add to this, the cunning of their language, the abstract ambiguous alternatives in which from the danger of their oppression they learned to speak ("Well, now, man, like I'm looking for a cat to turn me on . . ."), add even more the profound sensitivity of the Negro jazzman who was the cultural mentor of a people and it is not too difficult to believe that the language of Hip which evolved was an artful language, tested and shaped by an intense experience and therefore different in kind from white slang, as different as the special obscenity of the soldier which in its emphasis upon "ass" as the soul and "shit" as circum-stance, was able to express the existential states of the enlisted man. What makes Hip a special language is that it cannot really be taught—if one shares none of the experiences of elation and exhaus-tion which it is equipped to describe, then it seems merely arch or vulgar or irritating. It is a pictorial language, but pictorial like nonob-jective art, imbued with the dialectic of small but intense change, a language for the microcosm, in this case, man, for it takes the imme-diate experiences of any passing man and magnifies the dynamic of his movements, not specifically but abstractly so that he is seen more as a vector in a network of forces than as a static character in a crystal-lized field. (Which, latter, is the practical view of the snob.) For exam-ple, there is real difficulty in trying to find a Hip substitute for "stubborn." The best possibility I can come up with is: "That cat will never come off his groove, dad." But groove implies movement, nar-row movement but motion nonetheless. There is really no way to de-scribe someone who does not move at all. Even a creep does move—if at a pace exasperatingly more slow than the pace of the cool cats.

IV

Like children, hipsters are fighting for the sweet, and their language is a set of subtle indications of their success or failure in the competi-tion for pleasure. Unstated but obvious is the social sense that there is not nearly enough sweet for everyone. And so the sweet goes only to the victor, the best, the most, the man who knows the most about how to find his energy and how not to lose it. The emphasis is on energy because the psychopath and the hipster are nothing without it since they do not have the protection of a position or a class to rely on when they have overextended themselves. So the language of Hip is a language of energy, how it is found, how it is lost.

But let us see. I have jotted down perhaps a dozen words, the Hip perhaps most in use and most likely to last with the minimum of variation. The words are man, go, put down, make, beat, cool, swing, with it, crazy, dig, flip, creep, hip, square. They serve a variety of purposes, and the nuance of the voice uses the nuance of the situation to convey the subtle contextual difference. If the hipster moves through his night and through his life on a constant search with glimpses of Mecca in many a turn of his experience (Mecca being the apocalyptic orgasm) and if everyone in the civilized world is at least in some small degree a sexual cripple the hipster lives with the knowledge of how he is sexually crippled and where he is sexually alive, and the faces of experience which life presents to him each day are engaged, dismissed or avoided as his need directs and his lifemanship makes possible. For life is a contest between people in which the victor generally recuperates quickly and the loser takes long to mend, a perpetual competition of colliding explorers in which one must grow or else pay more for remaining the same (pay in sickness, or depression, or anguish for the lost opportunity), but pay or grow.

Therefore one finds words like go, and make it, and with it, and swing: "Go" with its sense that after hours or days or months or years of monotony, boredom, and depression one has finally had one's chance, one has amassed enough energy to meet an exciting opportunity with all one's present talents for the flip (up or down) and so one is ready to go, ready to gamble. Movement is always to be preferred to inaction. In motion a man has a chance, his body is warm, his instincts are quick, and when the crisis comes, whether of love or violence, he can make it, he can win, he can release a little more energy for himself since he hates himself a little less, he can make a little better nervous system, make it a little more possible to go again, to go faster next time and so make more and thus find more people with whom he can swing. For to swing is to communicate, is to convey the rhythms of one's own being to a lover, a friend, or an audience, and—equally necessary—be able to feel the rhythms of their response. To swing with the rhythms of another is to enrich oneself—the conception of the learning process as dug by Hip is that one cannot really learn until one contains within oneself the implicit rhythm of the subject or the person. As an example, I remember once hearing a Negro friend have an intellectual discussion at a party for half an hour with a white girl who was a few years out of college. The Negro literally could not read or write, but he had an extraordinary ear and a fine sense of mimicry. So as the girl spoke, he would detect the particular formal uncertainties in her argument, and in a pleasant (if slightly Southern) English accent, he would respond to one or another facet of her doubts. When she would finish what she felt was a particularly well-articulated idea, he would smile privately and say, "Other-direction . . . do you really believe in that?"

"Well . . . No," the girl would stammer, "now that you get down to it, there is something disgusting about it to me," and she would be off again for five more minutes.

Of course the Negro was not learning anything about the merits and demerits of the argument, but he was learning a great deal about a type of girl he had never met before, and that was what he wanted. Being unable to read or write, he could hardly be interested in ideas nearly as much as in lifemanship, and so he eschewed any attempt to obey the precision or lack of precision in the girl's language, and instead sensed her character (and the values of her social type) by swinging with the nuances of her voice.

So to swing is to be able to learn, and by learning take a step toward making it, toward creating. What is to be created is not nearly so important as the hipster's belief that when he really makes it, he will be able to turn his hand to anything, even to self-discipline. What he must do before that is find his courage at the moment of violence, or equally make it in the act of love, find a little more of himself, create a little more between his woman and himself, or indeed between his mate and himself (since many hipsters are bisexual), but paramount, imperative, is the necessity to make it because in making it, one is making the new habit, unearthing the new talent which the old frustration denied.

Whereas if you goof (the ugliest word in Hip), if you lapse back into being a frightened stupid child, or if you flip, if you lose your control, reveal the buried weaker more feminine part of your nature, then it is more difficult to swing the next time, your ear is less alive, your bad and energy-wasting habits are further confirmed, you are farther away from being with it. But to be with it is to have grace, is to be closer to the secrets of that inner unconscious life which will nourish you if you can hear it, for you are then nearer to that God which every hipster believes is located in the senses of his body, that trapped, mutilated, and nonetheless megalomaniacal God who is It, who is energy, life, sex, force, the Yoga's *prana,* the Reichian's orgone, Lawrence's "blood," Hemingway's "good," the Shavian life-force; "It"; God; not the God of the churches but the unachievable whisper of mystery within the sex, the paradise of limitless energy and perception just beyond the next wave of the next orgasm.

To which a cool cat might reply, "Crazy, man!"

Because, after all, what I have offered above is an hypothesis, no more, and there is not the hipster alive who is not absorbed in his own tumultuous hypotheses. Mine is interesting, mine is way out (on the avenue of the mystery along the road to "It") but still I am just one cat in a world of cool cats, and everything interesting is crazy, or at least so the Squares who do not know how to swing would say.

(And yet crazy is also the self-protective irony of the hipster. Living with questions and not with answers, he is so different in his isolation and in the far reach of his imagination from almost everyone with whom he deals in the outer world of the Square, and meets generally so much enmity, competition, and hatred in the world of Hip, that his isolation is always in danger of turning upon itself, and leaving him indeed just that, crazy.)

If, however, you agree with my hypothesis, if you as a cat are way out too, and we are in the same groove (the universe now being glimpsed as a series of ever-extending radii from the center) why then you say simply, "I dig," because neither knowledge nor imagination comes easily, it is buried in the pain of one's forgotten experience, and so one must work to find it, one must occasionally exhaust oneself by digging into the self in order to perceive the outside. And indeed it is essential to dig the most, for if you do not dig you lose your superiority over the Square, and so you are less likely to be cool (to be in control of a situation because you have swung where the Square has not, or because you have allowed to come to consciousness a pain, a guilt, a shame, or a desire which the other has not had the courage to face.) To be cool is to be equipped, and if you are equipped it is more difficult for the next cat who comes along to put you down. And of course one can hardly afford to be put down too often, or one is beat, one has lost one's confidence, one has lost one's will, one is impotent in the world of action and so closer to the demeaning flip of becoming a queer, or indeed closer to dying, and therefore it is even more difficult to recover enough energy to try to make it again, because once a cat is beat he has nothing to give, and no one is interested any longer in making it with him. This is the ter-

ror of the hipster—to be beat—because once the sweet of sex has de-
serted him, he still cannot give up the search. It is not granted to the
hipster to grow old gracefully—he has been captured too early by the
oldest dream of power, the gold fountain of Ponce de Leon, the fountain of youth where the gold is in the orgasm.

To be beat is therefore a flip, it is a situation beyond one's experience, impossible to anticipate—which indeed in the circular vocabulary of Hip is still another meaning for flip, but then I have given just
a few of the connotations of these words. Like most primitive vocabu-
laries each word is a prime symbol and serves a dozen or a hundred
functions of communication in the instinctive dialectic through
which the hipster perceives his experience, that dialectic of the instantaneous differentials of existence in which one is forever moving
forward into more or retreating into less.

V

It is impossible to conceive a new philosophy until one creates a new
language, but a new popular language (while it must implicitly con-
tain a new philosophy) does not necessarily present its philosophy
overtly. It can be asked, then, what really is unique in the life-view of
Hip which raises its argot above the passing verbal whimsies of the bohemian or the lumpenproletariat.

The answer would be in the psychopathic element of Hip, which
has almost no interest in viewing human nature, or better, in judging
human nature, from a set of standards conceived *a priori* to the experience, standards inherited from the past. Since Hip sees every answer as posing immediately a new alternative, a new question, its
emphasis is on complexity rather than simplicity (such complexity
that its language without the illumination of the voice and the articu-
lation of the face and body remains hopelessly incommunicative).
Given its emphasis on complexity, Hip abdicates from any conventional moral responsibility because it would argue that the results of
our actions are unforeseeable, and so we cannot know if we do good
or bad, we cannot even know (in the Joycean sense of the good and
the bad) whether unforeseeable, and so we cannot know if we do
good or bad, we cannot be certain that we have given them energy,
and indeed, if we could, there would still be no idea of what ultimately they would do with it.

Therefore, men are not seen as good or bad (that they are good-

and-bad is taken for granted) but rather each man is glimpsed as a collection of possibilities, some more possible than others (the view of character implicit in Hip) and some humans are considered more capable than others of reaching more possibilities within themselves in less time, provided, and this is the dynamic, provided the particular character can swing at the right time. And here arises the sense of context which differentiates Hip from a Square view of character. Hip sees the context as generally dominating the man, dominating him because his character is less significant than the context in which he must function. Since it is arbitrarily five times more demanding of one's energy to accomplish even an inconsequential action in an unfavorable context than a favorable one, man is then not only his character but his context, since the success or failure of an action in a given context reacts upon the character and therefore affects what the character will be in the next context. What dominates both character and context is the energy available at the moment of intense context.

Character being thus seen as perpetually ambivalent and dynamic enters then into an absolute relativity where there are no truths other than the isolated truths of what each observer feels at each instant of his existence. To take a perhaps unjustified metaphysical extrapolation, it is as if the universe which has usually existed conceptually as a Fact (even if the Fact were Berkeley's God) but a Fact which it was the aim of all science and philosophy to reveal, becomes instead a changing reality whose laws are remade at each instant by everything living, but most particularly man, man raised to a neomedieval summit where the truth is not what one has felt yesterday or what one expects to feel tomorrow but rather truth is no more nor less than what one feels at each instant in the perpetual climax of the present.

What is consequent therefore is the divorce of man from his values, the liberation of the self from the Super-Ego of society. The only Hip morality (but of course it is an ever-present morality) is to do what one feels whenever and wherever it is possible, and—this is how the war of the Hip and the Square begins—to be engaged in one primal battle: to open the limits of the possible for oneself, for oneself alone because that is one's need. Yet in widening the arena of the possible one widens it reciprocally for others as well, so that the nihilistic fulfillment of each man's desire contains its antithesis of human cooperation.

If the ethic reduces to Know Thyself and Be Thyself, what makes it radically different from Socratic moderation with its stern conservative respect for the experience of the past, is that the Hip ethic is immoderation, childlike in its adoration of the present (and indeed to respect the past means that one must also respect such ugly consequences of the past as the collective murders of the State). It is this adoration of the present which contains the affirmation of Hip, because its ultimate logic surpasses even the unforgettable solution of the Marquis de Sade to sex, private property, and the family, that all men and women have absolute but temporary rights over the bodies of all other men and women—the nihilism of Hip proposes as its final tendency that every social restraint and category be removed, and the affirmation implicit in the proposal is that man would then prove to be more creative than murderous and so would not destroy himself. Which is exactly what separates Hip from the authoritarian philosophies which now appeal to the conservative and liberal temper—what haunts the middle of the Twentieth Century is that faith in man has been lost, and the appeal of authority has been that it would restrain us from ourselves. Hip, which would return us to ourselves, at no matter what price in individual violence, is the affirmation of the barbarian for it requires a primitive passion about human nature to believe that individual acts of violence are always to be preferred to the collective violence of the State; it takes literal faith in the creative possibilities of the human being to envisage acts of violence as the catharsis which prepares growth.

Whether the hipster's desire for absolute sexual freedom contains any genuinely radical conception of a different world is of course another matter, and it is possible, since the hipster lives with his hatred, that many of them are the material for an elite of storm troopers ready to follow the first truly magnetic leader whose view of mass murder is phrased in a language which reaches their emotions. But given the desperation of his condition as a psychic outlaw, the hipster is equally a candidate for the most reactionary and most radical of movements, and so it is just as possible that many hipsters will come— if the crisis deepens—to a radical comprehension of the horror of society, for even as the radical has had his incommunicable dissent confirmed in his experience by precisely the frustration, the denied opportunities, and the bitter years which his ideas have cost him, so the sexual adventurer deflected from his goal by the implacable animosity of a society constructed to deny the sexual radical as well— may yet come to an equally bitter comprehension of the slow relentless inhumanity of the conservative power which controls him from without and from within. And in being so controlled, denied, and starved into the attrition of conformity, indeed the hipster may come to see that his condition is no more than an exaggeration of the human condition, and if he would be free, then everyone must be free. Yes, this is possible too, for the heart of Hip is its emphasis upon courage at the moment of crisis, and it is pleasant to think that courage contains within itself (as the explanation of its existence) some glimpse of the necessity of life to become more than it has been.

It is obviously not very possible to speculate with sharp focus on the future of the hipster. Certain possibilities must be evident, however, and the most central is that the organic growth of Hip depends on whether the Negro emerges as a dominating force in American life. Since the Negro knows more about the ugliness and danger of life than the White, it is probable that if the Negro can win his equality, he will possess a potential superiority, a superiority so feared that the fear itself has become the underground drama of domestic politics. Like all conservative political fear it is the fear of unforeseeable consequences, for the Negro's equality would tear a profound shift into the psychology, the sexuality, and the moral imagination of every White alive.

With this possible emergence of the Negro, Hip may erupt as a physically armed rebellion whose sexual impetus may rebound against the antisexual foundation of every organized power in America, and bring into the air such animosities, antipathies, and new conflicts of interest that the mean empty hypocrisies of mass conformity will no longer work. A time of violence, new hysteria, confusion, and rebellion will then be likely to replace the time of conformity. At that time, if the liberal should prove realistic in his belief that there is peaceful room for every tendency in American life, then Hip would end by being absorbed as a colorful figure in the tapestry. But if this is not the reality, and the economic, the social, the psychological, and finally the moral crises accompanying the rise of the Negro should prove insupportable, then a time is coming when every political guidepost will be gone, and millions of liberals will be faced with political dilemmas they have so far succeeded in evading, and with a view of human nature they do not wish to accept. To take the desegregation of the schools in the South as an example, it is quite likely that the reactionary sees the reality more closely than the liberal when he argues that the deeper issue is not desegregation but miscegenation. (As a radical I am of course facing in the opposite direction from the White Citizen's Councils—obviously I believe it is the absolute human right of the Negro to mate with the White, and matings there will un-

doubtedly be, for there will be Negro high-school boys brave enough
to chance their lives.) But for the average liberal whose mind has
been dulled by the committee-ish cant of the professional liberal,
miscegenation is not an issue, because he has been told that the Negro does not desire it. So, when it comes, miscegenation will be a terror, comparable perhaps to the derangement of the American
Communists when the icons to Stalin came tumbling down. The average American Communist held to the myth of Stalin for reasons
which had little to do with the political evidence and everything to do
with their psychic necessities. In this sense it is equally a psychic necessity for the liberal to believe that the Negro and even the reactionary Southern White are eventually and fundamentally people like
himself, capable of becoming good liberals too if only they can be
reached by good liberal reason. What the liberal cannot bear to admit
is the hatred beneath the skin of a society so unjust that the amount
of collective violence buried in the people is perhaps incapable of being contained, and therefore if one wants a better world one does
well to hold one's breath, for a worse world is bound to come first,
and the dilemma may well be this: given such hatred, it must either
vent itself nihilistically or become turned into the cold murderous
liquidations of the totalitarian state.

VI

No matter what its horrors the Twentieth Century is a vastly exciting
century for its tendency is to reduce all life to its ultimate alternatives.
One can well wonder if the last war of them all will be between the
blacks and the whites, or between the women and the men, or between the beautiful and the ugly, the pillagers and managers, or the
rebels and the regulators. Which of course is carrying speculation beyond the point where speculation is still serious, and yet despair at
the monotony and bleakness of the future has become so engrained
in the radical temper that the radical is in danger of abdicating from
all imagination. What a man feels is the impulse for his creative effort, and if an alien but nonetheless passionate instinct about the
meaning of life has come so unexpectedly from a virtually illiterate
people, come out of the most intense conditions of exploitation, cruelty, violence, frustration, and lust, and yet has succeeded as an instinct in keeping this tortured people alive, then it is perhaps possible
that the Negro holds more of the tail of the expanding elephant of

truth than the radical, and if this is so, the radical humanist could do worse than to brood upon the phenomenon. For if a revolutionary time should come again, there would be a crucial difference if someone had already delineated a neo-Marxian calculus aimed at comprehending every circuit and process of society from ukase to kiss as the communications of human energy—a calculus capable of translating the economic relations of man into his psychological relations and back again, his productive relations thereby embracing his sexual relations as well, until the crises of capitalism in the Twentieth Century would yet be understood as the unconscious adaptations of a society to solve its economic imbalance at the expense of a new mass psychological imbalance. It is almost beyond the imagination to conceive of a work in which the drama of human energy is engaged, and a theory of its social currents and dissipations, its imprisonments, expressions, and tragic wastes are fitted into some gigantic synthesis of human action where the body of Marxist thought, and particularly the epic grandeur of *Das Kapital* (that first of the major *psychologies* to approach the mystery of social cruelty so simply and practically as to say that we are a collective body of humans whose life-energy is wasted, displaced, and procedurally stolen as it passes from one of us to another)—where particularly the epic grandeur of *Das Kapital* would find its place in an even more Godlike view of human justice and injustice, in some more excruciating vision of those intimate and institutional processes which lead to our creations and disasters, our growth, our attrition, and our rebellion.

Growing Up Absurd
1960

◆

PAUL GOODMAN

Paul Goodman (1911–1972) was a prolific novelist and essayist, who in 1960, with the publication of *Growing Up Absurd,* a critique of American society, became identified with the youth culture of the sixties. His other books include *Compulsory Mis-Education, The Individual and Culture,* and, with his brother Percival Goodman, *Communitas: Means of Livelihood and Ways of Life.*

PART I: THE YOUNG

I

Growing up as a human being, a "human nature" assimilates a culture, just as other animals grow up in strength and habits in *their* appropriated environments, that complete their natures. Present-day sociologists and anthropologists don't talk much about this process, and not in this way. Among the most competent writers, there is not much mention of "human nature." Their diffidence makes scientific sense, for everything we observe, and, even more important, our way of observing it, is already culture and a pattern of culture. What is the sense of mentioning "human nature" if we can never observe it? The old-fashioned naïve thought, that primitive races or children are more natural, is discounted. And the classical anthropological question, What is Man?—"how like an angel, this quintessence of dust!"—is not now asked by anthropologists. Instead, they commence with a chapter on Physical Anthropology and then forget the whole topic and go on to Culture.

On this view, growing up is sometimes treated as if it were acculturation, the process of giving up one culture for another, the way a tribe of Indians takes on the culture of the whites: so the wild Baby-tribe gives up its mores and ideology, e.g., selfishness or magic-thinking or omnipotence, and joins the tribe of Society; it is "socialized." More frequently, however, the matter is left vague: we start with a *tabula rasa* and end up "socialized" and cultured. ("Becoming cultured" and "being adjusted to the social group" are taken almost as synonymous.) Either way, it follows that you can teach people anything; you can adapt them to anything if you use the right techniques of "socializing" or "communicating." The essence of "human nature" is to be pretty indefinitely malleable. "Man," as C. Wright Mills suggests, is what suits a particular type of society in a particular historical stage.

This fateful idea, invented from time to time by philosophers, seems finally to be empirically evident in the most recent decades. For instance, in our highly organized system of machine production and its corresponding social relations, the practice is, by "vocational guidance," to fit people wherever they are needed in the productive system; and whenever the products of the system need to be used up, the practice is, by advertising, to get people to consume them. This works. There is a man for every job and not many are left over, and the shelves are almost always cleared. Again, in the highly organized political industrial systems of Germany, Russia, and now China, it has been possible in a short time to condition great masses to perform as desired. Social-scientists observe that these are the facts, and they also devise theories and techniques to produce more facts like them, for the social-scientists too are part of the highly organized systems.

II

Astonishingly different, however, is the opinion of experts who deal with human facts in a more raw, less highly processed, state. Those who have to cope with people in small groups rather than statistically, and attending to *them* rather than to some systematic goal—parents and teachers, physicians and psychotherapists, policemen and wardens of jails, shop foremen and grievance-committees—all tend stubbornly to hold that there is a "human nature." You can't teach people some things or change them in some ways, and if you persist, you're in for trouble. Contrariwise, if you don't provide them with certain things, they'll fill the gaps with eccentric substitutes.

This is immediately evident when something goes wrong, for instance, when a child can't learn to read because he has not yet developed the muscular accommodation of his eyes; if you persist, he withdraws or becomes tricky. Such cases are clear-cut (they are "physical"). But the more important cases have the following form: the child *does* take on the cultural habit, e.g., early toilet-training, and indeed the whole corresponding pattern of culture, but there is a diminishing of force, grace, discrimination, intellect, feeling, in specific behaviors or even in his total behavior. He may become too obedient and lacking in initiative, or impractically careful and squeamish; he may develop "psychosomatic" ailments like constipation. Let me give an instance even earlier in life: an infant nurtured in an impersonal institution during the first six months, does not seem to develop abnormally; but if during the end of the first year and for some time thereafter he is not given personal care, he will later be in some ways emotionally cold and unreachable—either some function has failed to develop, or he has already blocked it out as too frustrated and painful. In such examples, the loss of force, grace, and feeling seems to be evidence that somehow the acquired cultural habits do not draw on unimpeded outgoing energy, they are against the grain, they do not fit the child's needs or appetites; *therefore* they have been ill-adapted and not assimilated.

That is, on this view we do not need to be able to say what "human nature" *is* in order to be able to say that some training is "against human nature" and you persist in it at your peril. Teachers and psychologists who deal practically with growing up and the blocks to growing up may never mention the word "human nature" (indeed, they are better off without too many *a priori* ideas), but they cling stubbornly to the presumption that at every stage there is a developing potentiality *not* yet cultured, and yet not blank, and that makes possible the taking on of culture. We must draw "it" out, offer "it" opportunities, not violate "it" except for unavoidable reasons. What "it" is, is not definite. It is what, when appealed to in the right circumstances, gives behavior that has force, grace, discrimination, intellect, feeling. This vagueness is of course quite sufficient for education, for education is an art. A good teacher feels his way, looking for response.

III

The concept of "human nature" has had a varied political history in modern times. If we trace it even roughly, we learn something about the present disagreement. In the eighteenth century, the Age of Reason and the early Romantic Movement, the emphasis was on "*human* nature" referring to man's naturally sympathetic sentiments, his communicative faculties, and inalienable dignity. (Immanuel Kant immortally thought up a philosophy to make these cohere.) Now this human nature was powerfully enlisted in revolutionary struggles against courts and classes, poverty and humiliation, and it began to invent progressive education. Human nature unmistakably demanded liberty, equality, and fraternity, and every man a philosopher and poet.

As an heir of the French Revolution, Karl Marx kept much of this concept. Sympathy appeared as solidarity. Dignity and intellect were perhaps still in the future. But he found an important new essential: man is a maker, he must use his productive nature or be miserable. This too involved a revolutionary program, to give back to man his tools.

During the course of the nineteenth century, however, "human nature" came to be associated with conservative and even reactionary politics. The later Romantics were historically minded and found man naturally conservative and not be uprooted. A few decades later, narrow interpretations of Darwin were being used to advance imperial and elite interests. (The emphasis was now on "*nature*"; the humanity became dubious.) It was during this latter period that the social-scientists began to be diffident about "human nature," for politically, they wanted fundamental social changes; and scientifically, it was evident that things were being called natural which were overwhelmingly cultural. Most of the social-scientists began to lay all their stress on institutionally organized reform. Nevertheless, scientifically trained anarchists like Kropotkin insisted that "human nature"—now become mutual-aiding, knightly, and craftsmanlike—was still on the side of revolution.

In our own century, especially since the twenties and thirties, the social-scientists have found another reason for diffidence: "human nature" implies "not social," referring to something prior to society, belonging to an isolated individual. They felt that too much importance was being assigned to Individual Psychology (they were reacting to Freud) and that this stood in the way of organizing people for political reform. It is on this view that growing up is now interpreted as a process of socializing some rather indefinite kind of animal, and "socializing" is used as a synonym for teaching him the culture.

IV

Let us now proceed more carefully, for we are approaching our present plight. *Is* "being socialized," no matter what the society, the same as growing up and assimilating human culture? The society to which one is socialized would have to be a remarkably finished product.

There are here three distinct concepts, which sometimes seem the same but sometimes very different: (1) society as the relations of human social animals, (2) the human culture carried by society, and (3) a particular society formed by its pattern of culture and institutions, and to which its members are socialized.

In ordinary, static circumstances, and especially when a dominant system in a society is riding high (as the organized system is with us), socializing to that society seems to provide all valuable culture, etc. But *as soon as we think of a fundamental social change,* we see that (1) at once "human nature" has been thwarted or insulted by the dominant system; (2) our notions of "human culture" at once broadens out to include ancient, exotic, and even primitive models as superior to the conventional standards (as, e.g., our disaffected groups lay store by the Japanese or the Samoans and Trobriand Islanders); and (3) "socialization" has been to a very limited kind of society. "Man" can no longer be defined as what suits the dominant system, when the dominant system apparently does not suit men.

A curious thing has occurred. Unlike most of their predecessors for a century and a half, most of our contemporary social-scientists are not interested in fundamental social change. To them, we have apparently reached the summit of institutional progress, and it only remains for the sociologists and applied-anthropologists to mop up the corners and iron out the kinks. Social-scientists are not attracted to the conflictual core of Freud's theory of human nature; a more optimistic theory is paid no attention at all. But they have hit on the theory I mentioned at the beginning: that you can adapt people to anything, if you use the right techniques. Our social-scientists have become so accustomed to the highly organized and by-and-large smoothly running society that they have begun to think that "social animal" means "harmoniously belonging." They do not like to think that fighting and dissenting are proper social functions, nor that rebelling or initiating fundamental change is a social function. Rather, if something does not run smoothly, they say it has been improperly socialized; there has been a failure in communication. The animal part is rarely mentioned at all; if it proves annoying, it too has been inadequately socialized.

Now, however, groups of boys and young men are disaffected from the dominant society. The young men are Angry and Beat. The boys are Juvenile Delinquents. These groups are not small and they will grow larger. Certainly they are suffering. Demonstrably they are not getting enough out of our wealth and civilization. They are not growing up to full capacity. They are failing to assimilate much of the culture. As predictable, most of the authorities and all of the public spokesmen explain it by saying there has been a failure of socialization. Background conditions have interrupted socialization, they must be improved. Not enough effort has been made to guarantee belonging, there must be better bait or punishment.

But perhaps there has *not* been a failure of communication. Perhaps the social message has been communicated clearly to the young men and is unacceptable.

I would therefore take the opposite tack and ask, "Socialization to what? to what dominant society and available culture?" And if this question is asked, we must at once ask the other question, "Is the harmonious organization to which they are inadequately socialized, perhaps against human nature, and *therefore* there is difficulty in growing up?" If this is so, their disaffection is profound and it will not be finally remediable by better techniques of socializing. Instead, there will have to be changes in our society and its culture, so as to meet the appetites and capacities of human nature, in order to grow up.

This brings me to another proposition about growing up, which is perhaps my main theme. *Growth, like any ongoing function, requires adequate objects in the environment* to meet the needs and capacities of the growing child, boy, youth, and young man, until he can better choose and make his own environment. It makes no difference whether the growth is normal or distorted, only real objects will finish the experience. (In psychotherapy one finds that many a stubborn symptom would vanish if there were a real change in the vocational and sexual opportunities so that the symptom is not needed.) It is here that the theory of belonging and socializing miserably breaks down. For it can be shown that with all the harmonious belonging and all the tidying up of background conditions that you please, our abundant society is at present simply deficient in many of the most elementary objective opportunities and worthwhile goals that could make growing up possible. It is lacking in enough man's work. It is lacking in honest public speech and taking people seriously. It is lacking in the opportunity to be useful. It thwarts aptitude and creates stupidity. It corrupts ingenuous patriotism. It abuses science. It corrupts the fine arts. It dampens animal ardor. It discourages the religious convictions of Justification and Vocation and it dims the sense that there is a Creation. It has no Honor. It has no Community.

Just look at that list. There is nothing in it that is surprising, in either the small letters or the capitals. I have nothing subtle or novel to say here; these are things that *everybody* knows. And nevertheless Governor Rockefeller of New York says, "We must give these young men a sense of belonging."

Thwarted, or starved, in the important objects proper to young capacities, the boys and young men naturally find or invent deviant objects for themselves; this is the beautiful shaping power of our human nature. Their choices and inventions are rarely charming, usually stupid, and often disastrous; we cannot expect average kids to deviate with genius. But on the other hand, the young men who conform to the dominant society are for the most part apathetic, disappointed, cynical, and wasted.

I would make little distinction in value between talking about middle-class youths being groomed for $10,000 "slots" in business and Madison Avenue, or underprivileged hoodlums fatalistically hurrying to a reformatory; or between hard-working young fathers and idle Beats with beards. For the salient thing is the sameness among them, the waste of humanity. In our society, bright lively children, with the potentiality for knowledge, noble ideals, honest effort, and some kind of worthwhile achievement, are transformed into useless and cynical bipeds, or decent young men trapped or early-resigned, whether in or out of the organized system. My purpose is a simple one: to show how it is desperately hard these days for an average child to grow up to be a man, for our present organized system of society does not want men. They are not safe. They do not suit.

Our public officials are now much concerned about the "waste of human resources," and they have appointed Dr. Conant to survey the high schools. But our officials are not serious. For the big causes of stupidity, of lack of initiative, and lack of honorable incentive, are glaring; yet they do not intend to notice or remedy these big causes. (This very avoidance of the real issues on the part of our public officials is, indeed, one of the big causes.) Our society cannot have it both ways: to maintain a conformist and ignoble system *and* to have skillful and spirited men to man that system with.

PART II: CLASS STRUCTURE

I

In our economy of abundance it is still subject to discussion whether or not there is as much poverty as there was in the thirties, when "one third of a nation was ill-housed, ill-clothed, ill-fed." Some say 20 percent are poverty-stricken, some as many as 40 percent. Nevertheless, all students would agree on two propositions: (1) The composition of the poor has immensely changed; it now consists mainly of racial and cultural minorities (including migrant farm labor); (2) And the economic relation of the poor to the system has importantly changed: simply, the earlier minorities, Irish, Jewish, Italian, Slavic, poured into an expanding economy that needed people; the new come into an expanding economy that does not need people. I would add another important difference: (3) The relation of the other classes to the poor has markedly changed. For example, many readers are no doubt surprised that there are so many poor and, reading about it, feel that it is a mere lag, a matter of mopping up, in our general productive advance. Everything looks pretty streamlined.

The income pyramid has changed in shape. It used to be that the most were the poor at the bottom and then, *evenly,* fewer and fewer at each level up to a few at the top. But the meaning of the economy of abundance is that there are now very many, perhaps even a bulge, at the lower-middle-income level. These are the people with semiprofessional and service jobs, the occupational category that has grown the most, and who get status-salaries; the skilled and semiskilled semimonopoly factory jobs, strongly unionized; the families where, in our artificially maintained nearly full employment, the man has two jobs or the woman also has a job; and families in newly industrialized areas in the South and Middle West. But conversely, the poorly paying unskilled jobs have diminished. It is here that simple automation (e.g., sweeping the floor in a factory) is allowed full development. Many categories are not unionized. Migratory farm labor, mostly Negro, usually is not covered by social insurance. By the connivance of union and management, Negroes and the new Spanish minorities are often rejected for apprenticeship. These poor groups, behindhand to begin with, get less schooling.

That is, the economy of abundance, the bulge in the pyramid, means also that those at the bottom tend to fall out of "society" altogether.

Consider it. There is a higher standard of living and more to conform to, in order to be "decent"; it is more expensive to be decently poor. Yet there is a tighter organization above that is harder to belong to, so that the standard is increasingly unattainable for the underprivileged. So far as economic and vocational causes, poverty and job-usefulness, are factors—and they are mighty important factors when they add up to being "out" of society—this is a sufficient explanation for juvenile delinquency. One need go no further. For in such hopeless conditions *any* grounds of family hostility, unusual childhood frustration, or a gang on the street, will tip the balance. The question is whether or not this structure is organic in our present system.

(Let me say at this point, however, that many of the humble jobs of the poor are precisely *not* useless, morally. Farm labor, janitoring, messenger, serving and dish-washing—these jobs resist remarkably well the imputation of uselessness made against the productive society as a whole. In the potency-ideology of teenage delinquents, of course, such jobs are contemptible and emasculating. But we shall see that they are important for the poverty-mystique of the more thoughtful of the Beat Generation.)

II

Recently I attended a conference (Student League for Industrial Democracy) where poverty was the theme. Eminent and earnest labor leaders spoke. As the day wore on I became more and more eerily disturbed at the difference in tone from such discussions in the thirties. At last I hit it: they were talking not political economy but philanthropy. Partly, maybe, this tone crept in because they were talking about our poor black and brown brothers. Mostly, however, it was because their attitude toward poverty is no longer part of their own fighting economy theory. As labor economists they do not have solidarity with *these* poor.

When poverty used to be discussed by the socialists (these same men younger), the theory was that in the capitalist system labor as a whole must be at the bottom and must become poorer, because of the falling return on investment and its pressure on wages, because of the concentration of ownership and control and the increase of inequality, and the periodic crises and unemployment. Therefore the fight against poverty was solidarity, it was the fight for the improvement of the whole system to give labor a better position. But now the rate of interest does not fall; the system cushions its crises; there is high employment or insurance. There is certainly a concentration of monopolistic control, but either inequality is less (that is debatable), or, certainly, workers on a fairly high standard don't much bother who has millions. Thus, nostalgic solidarity with poverty turns into philanthropy—and even exclusion, on issues where the poor are unassimilable into the abundant system.

One of the speakers, a portly labor leader, was asked whether the new pyramid did not resemble a middle-aged gentleman with a bulge beneath the middle.

I did not once hear the word "proletariat," and that made sense. For the word had been used, bitterly and nobly, in a different theory: "producers of offspring" paid by the iron law of wages just enough to reproduce labor. Our present poor are more like the ancient Roman proletariat, producers of offspring kept on a dole for political reasons. It was clear too why the word "do-gooder" has fallen into mild disrepute. It used to refer, like "muckraking," to quixotic attempts to reform the system; now it is diminishing suffering, accepting the system. (Muckraking, in turn, has become the protest of Angry Young Men. My own tone sounds like an Angry Middle-Aged Man, disappointed but not resigned.)

III

For those excluded from the high standard and its organization, it is becoming harder to maintain any American standard at all. It is characteristic of systems geared to high pay that it is hard to work for low pay. There are fewer such jobs; those there are, are without benefit of union and subject to grueling exploitation. Low pay generally means harder work under worse conditions. Prices are, of course, geared to the high standard; and the use of any commodity tends to be increasingly tied up with the use of many other commodities and services that cost money.

For instance, it is impossible to be poor and run a jalopy. The insurance costs three times as much as the car. The old car, which is safe at fifty miles per hour, is effectually barred from parkways made for cars at sixty-five miles per hour. The price of gasoline pays for the parkways. The price of repairs is geared to the new cars.

It costs money to have any job at all; transportation and lunches, presentable clothes and laundry, are priced for good wages.

Unless he is capable of a different, inventive, or community culture alto-gether, a poor person can afford little recreation; the popular culture is high-priced, and he gets the dregs of it. His poverty tends to degen-erate into stupidity. He cannot afford presentable shoes for the kids to go to school; they are ashamed and won't go. Thus, in Péguy's phrase, poverty becomes misery, and the poor belong to society less and less.

IV

There is little agreement in the sociology of delinquency. But one correlation that is generally agreed on is the following: Juvenile delin-quency, unlike adult crime, is more frequent in years of economic prosperity than in years of depression. Now this would seem to con-tradict the other, and rather *prima facie,* theory of poverty as the im-portant condition. The paradox is softened by pointing out that in prosperity there is more employment of women, there is more di-vorce, and there is more money to buy liquor and drugs. These fac-tors make sense, but let me raise some further considerations. First, there is the possibility that the prosperous, well-paying jobs do not fil-ter down evenly to the poorest groups, who tend much more to be unemployable altogether. This certainly seems to be our situation to-day. Second, in a high-standard economy, there is a great difference between having a little extra money and being accustomed to the well-paid standard. As our Manchester forefathers used to say, you do a disservice to the undeserving poor by giving them money, because they will get into trouble. Consider the concrete situation: Even if the parents are suddenly getting better pay, the young are getting merely a little extra spending-money, and this, in a society where there is sud-denly a lot of money, must work out as follows: (1) The underprivi-leged kids get around more and are exposed to the expensive glamour, but (2) this is precisely not attainable by them, unless they take short cuts. (3) Meantime, those who have the new money are more careless with it, they leave their cars unlocked, they buy sex. And (4) the spiteful feeling is increased, that those who are better off are squares, enemies, and fair victims of the gang. In boom-time, that is, there is effectually *more* exclusion than ordinarily.

During depression, contrariwise, there is more community be-cause many others are in the same boat. The street is occupied by kids used to other mores, to whom the gang values are pointless. This leads to friction, of course, but also to other friendships and other activities. But above all, as everybody knows who was unemployed during the Great Depression, it is easier to be decently poor when prices are low and the pressure to maintain appearances is diminished. Things get nearer to a human scale and life makes more sense. Likewise, at such times political activity is more common; it is educative and increases self-esteem in a worthwhile way.

This whole picture would be quite different if the underprivileged and somewhat unemployable families had a pretty secure income over a long period. They would then be members of society at least as consumers, and would eventually become as employable as the average. Such a device would at once diminish certain kinds of delinquency, e.g., thefts, malicious mischief, certain spiteful assaults, and maybe truancy. Simply to *subsidize* the poor might be the cheapest way of coping with juvenile delinquency. To reestablish in general what he calls the social balance, J. K. Galbraith proposes such a high longtime subsidy for all unemployed. He assures us that this would not be inflationary, and as the director of price controls for the OPA, he should know.

The popular bright idea to diminish delinquency is to penalize the parents; perhaps the effective method would be, rather, to give them more money to spend, a kind of prize!

V

At present, however, our society is settling for the first time in its history into a marked class system—with increasing mobility of persons but rigidifying of statuses and opportunities; less easy gradation and fewer unique "classless" positions.

At the bottom are those poor, "outside" of society. Next are those groups who are *in* the organized system of production: (1) Those who are "in" but-couldn't-care-less about the production and distribution, for instance factory-operatives. These are paid the lower-middle-income wages, say $4,000 to $6,000. They buy on credit and have to keep on the job to make both ends meet. If the work week is shortened to thirty hours, there is evidence that they get other part-time jobs to buy new refrigerators. (2) The next status who are "in" are the Organization Men proper, whose hours, thoughts, families, play, and peace of mind are dedicated to maintaining their positions in their particular firms and pushing upward there or in some other firm. Salary $7,500 to $20,000. It is this group of junior-executives, for instance, that we have compared to the juvenile delinquents for their safe conformity and competitive individuality. We shall see that another important trait in common is having no real activity but living by role-playing. (3) At the top, finally, are the nine hundred managers—figure of *Fortune* magazine—whose task is to minimize risk and maximize production, and sales. Also the fifty governors, the federal staff, heads of foundations, etc., etc.

It will be seen that these three statuses in the organized system (which includes bigger business, organized labor, entertainment, government, bigger educations, etc.) are engaged primarily in keeping the system itself running and slowly expanding. The most self-aware of its members are the intellectuals of the middle status, among the advertisers, and junior-executives; and they describe the system as the Rat Race.

But there is another large class, those who do not properly belong to the system and are not yet submerged into the poor "outside" of society: this is the vast herd of the old-fashioned, the eccentric, and criminal, the gifted, and serious, the men and women, the rentiers, the free-lances, the infants, and so forth. This motley collection has, of course, no style or culture, unlike the organization that has our familiar "functional" style and popular culture. Its fragmented members hover about the organizations in multifarious ways—running specialty-shops, trying to teach or give other professional services, robbing banks, landscape gardening, and so forth—but they find it hard to get along, for they do not know the approved techniques of promoting, getting foundation grants, protecting themselves by official unions, legally embezzling, and not blurting out the truth or weeping or laughing out of turn. They have no style at all, and it is understandable that neither they nor their usually rather irrelevant enterprises make much headway in the market, the universities, entertainment, politics, or labor. Besides, they often speak a minority language, English.

This is roughly the class structure of America in the middle of the twentieth century. It seems most functional to speak of three *classes,* the Poor, the Organization, and the Independents; and of three *statuses* within the dominant class, the Organization. Viz:

Organized System
   1. Workers
   2. Organization Men
   3. Managers
Poor
Independents

VI

Let us return now to our alert young man of average to good attainments and imagine him growing up in and *into* this arena. Most likely he will go to work for an Organization, in a factory or service job, manual or clerical, with the corresponding job attitude and way of life. But if he has been to college, he will likely be in the second class of the organization, in business-management, communications, sales, or technology, with *its* job attitude and way of life.

After a few years, many such young men will perceive that they are in a Rat Race. The young workers will perceive it as the work speeds up, the installment payments fall due, etc. The Organization Man will perceive it as competition, company pressure to conform, etc. Of these, most will race on but a few will balk and stop running. Now, what becomes of these few?

They are *not* likely to choose the other, motley, alternative of trying to remain in society independent of the organization. For their experience has been disillusioning. They have become hip. (We shall see later that this is a profoundly organizational attitude.) They *know* that the unorganized are up against it, for they have learned techniques of promotion and they don't think much, or much think, of other methods and kinds of results. But to be hip and cynical are not attitudes that prompt one to make a go on one's own. It is not surprising then that many of those who balk in the Rat Race will voluntarily choose the other remaining possibility, poverty "outside" society. (Whether they choose it or fall into it, comes to the same thing.) These, not boys but early-disillusioned, hip, and resigned young men are the Beat Generation. The organization they have quit may be the armed forces of a university they cannot compound with; these tend to be more naïve. Those who have had experience of working for a firm and making a pretty good living tend to be more cynical.

Naturally this cataclysmic transition, between being in and being "outside" society, does not occur without strong accompanying emotional moments—betrayals in love, beings, blow-ups against the boss, addiction to forbidden haunts and vices. But at this point let us stick to the social structuring of it.

VII

It is relevant to introduce our discussion of the Beat Generation in this context of present-day poverty because the present-day composition of the poor in America, Negroes, Puerto Ricans and Mexicans, migrant farm labor, with large urban juvenile delinquency, has been fateful for the particular culture of these young folks. Let us analyze the accidental and essential influences as an interesting example of acculturation.

Artists and bohemians have always gravitated to the bottom of the income pyramid. It is cheaper there. There is less timetable there. Life is simpler and more factual. These factors somewhat operate to-day too, but less so, because in some way it now costs more to be poor than modestly lower-middle, and in many of their tastes—e.g., clothes, cars, recreation, and even food—the poor are even more idi-otic than the average. So let us see what is particular in the cultural ef-fect of present-day poverty on present-day bohemians.

(1) The African and Spanish influence and a part of the migrant and delinquent influence on Beat culture is inevitable but accidental. Resigning, the Beats have chosen to be outside and the present poor happen to be those who, as unorganized minorities, *are* outside when they arrive. The poor might have been Chinese; the narcotics might have been different, or some other kick than narcotics altogether; the music might have been something else than *Negro* jazz; the jargon might not have had a Negro base; and perhaps there might have be less going on the road (but this ants-in-the-pants moving about is now pervasive anyway). Surely all of this will be denied by the Beat fellows; for if these aspects of their culture were not accidental, such bright and inventive fellows would already have made more out of them. The bongo drums and jazz, as they practice them, are childish in the light of their knowledge and abilities. The jazz-and-poetry is feeble compared even to the TV commercial jingles that they have turned away from. The jive language embarrasses their poetry. The style of the drugs remains crude and experimental. Much of the delinquency rouses guilt and fear in them, instead of defiant righteousness or calm philosophy (contrast the style and depth of Jean Genet with sim-ilar material).

(2) On the other hand, the *structural* characteristics of the present-day poor—those that did not especially belong to the poor of older bohemias—*are* essential in the culture of those who gravitate to these poor. These include: Out-casteness and being objects of prejudice. Giving up trying to explain to those who, often literally, do not speak the same language. Provocative exclusiveness and in-group loyalty. Fear of the cops. Economic and job uselessness. Courageously taking up or remaining with community substitutes rather than sinking in mere resignation (but this courage is common to many kinds of

poor). Exotic or at least not-standard-American arts and folkways, and awkwardness in the standard folkways.

These structural characteristics of the present-day poor are essential in Beat culture. As, contrariwise, are the organizational characteristics of being hip and convinced that society is a Rat Race. This combination, we shall see, mesmerizes them into behaving as though they were trapped in a Closed Room and must live on their own guts without environment.

(3) But finally, there are essential traits of Beat culture that go counter to the social traits of the poor whom they have chosen. This is the essential morality, that is acculturated least. One striking trait is nonconformism and tolerance in sexual and racial questions and behavior. The poor Negroes or Puerto Ricans may be exotic to the standard customs and prejudices, but they are all the more narrow about their own. (In the case of the delinquents, of course, this conformity is so extravagant as to be dangerous: they cannot inwardly tolerate anything that hints that their own image of perfection is questionable.) It is hard to be sure, but my impression is that other poor, who were at the bottom, but *in* society, were among the most tolerant. Hard knocks had taught them to live and let live; and they did not need to protect their repressions so much as an out-caste poor. In this respect the Beat are more like the old-fashioned poor, and this of course makes it easier and more profitable for them to be poor. This brings us to another striking difference. Despite having minority traditions of their own, our present poor are absolute sheep and suckers for the popular culture which they cannot afford, the movies, sharp clothes, and up to Cadillacs. Indeed, it is likely that the popular culture is aimed largely at them, as the lowest common denominator. I do not mean that this is not a reasonable compensation, like an Englishman's liquor and an Irishman's betting on the horses. Everybody has got to have something; so our poor people show off and feel big with the standard of living. But in these circumstances, it is immensely admirable that the Beat Generation has contrived a pattern of culture that, turning against the standard culture, costs very little and gives far livelier satisfaction. It is communally shared, in small groups. Much of it is hand-made, not canned. Some of it is communally improvised. We shall speak later about the limitations of this procedure and the weakness of its products; but the *fact* of it, of a culture that is communal and tending toward the creative, is so capital that it must have a future, and it is worthwhile to study its grounding and economy.

VIII

Let us look also at Beat economics, as an interesting sidelight on the American standard economy. The Beats have a mystique of voluntary poverty; but how to get along at all if one has dropped "outside" and has no incentive to work and "make good"?

In our times the distinction between case-poverty due to illness, life-accidents, or personality-defects, and class poverty, due to social defects, doesn't amount to much. For it could be asked: Why wasn't the accident insured? What social conditions formed such a careless personality? Or conversely: Doesn't the poor class have, economically, a personality defect? (Just as in the Protestant Ethic the poor had a theological defect; but of course it is also persistently true that "only the poor are saved.") Likewise, the old monastic concept of voluntary poverty is no longer much distinguishable from either case-poverty or class-poverty, for it happens that a person *cannot* continue the Rat Race—he gets sick—and he chooses out, to survive. Another man would like to be rich and famous but he *cannot* work otherwise than the work demands and this might not be marketable; so he could be said to choose poverty. In an organized system, all poor tend to be the same poor. (The same blurring of distinctions has occurred between "political" and "common" criminals. As society becomes more close-knit and total, a criminal act may well be a dumb political gesture, and political protest is certainly criminal in effect. So the anarchist philosopher refused to distinguish these and said, "As long as *one* of these is in jail, I am not free.")

It makes little difference, then, whether a young fellow chooses his lot or is cast among the poor; especially if, being there, he soon takes on habits which make it impossible for him, or unattractive to him, to belong to the system.

Suppose then, with pretty good awareness, our scarred young man is now confirmed poor. He must still face the problem of vocation and money. On these points the writers on the Beat Generation are confused. For one thing, they have a false notion that the kind of artistic activity that proliferates among the Beats is art, and gives the justification of art as a vocation. But it is not art but something else; and they do not behave as if they were justified by it.

The problem of money, again, seems simple, but it is not. In voluntary poverty the problem of money is to get enough to subsist. (Money is called "bread.") But how? In his book, *The Holy Barbarians*, Lawrence Lipton gives a considerable list of jobs that Beats take, generally temporarily, to get subsistence. The principle is that anything will do. A fellow might work in the organized system, e.g., dressing a window at Macy's; but, it is argued, he would not thereby be in the Rat Race because he just wants "bread" and will quit. Naturally Macy's didn't know this when they hired him; so he's using them, not they him. This might come to pretending to conform rather elaborately, for the system is total; e.g., a fellow will get the job if he shaves off his beard. Work is no different from shoplifting. One plays roles and is hip. (Money is now called "loot.") What is not understood in this form of reasoning is that playing roles and being hip in this way is very nearly the same as being an Organization Man, for the Organization Man doesn't mean it either.

Obviously the Holy Barbarian is here on shaky grounds. Getting his "loot," he is an exploiter of labor, but only a little bit. (The integral aim of useful man's-work is not mentioned by Lipton.)

Let me make a close analogy—so close that it is probably an identity—between the job in voluntary poverty and the service in wartime that a pacifist can agree to perform. Nearly any civilian job a man does advances the war. If he picks beans he replaces a farmer for the war-factory. Pacifists commonly have accepted jobs like attendant in a hospital (that is understaffed anyway). This is not a petty problem, for when the evil is general and close-knit, it is necessary to preserve one's own personal integrity, if only to influence the future when the emergency is past. Anyone who does not understand this, and the soul-searching and hair-splitting involved, will not understand ingenuous youth. (E.g., I myself am pretty easy with my "integrity" by now, and I would sign almost anything convenient; yet when I am a teacher, I cannot sign a loyalty oath if I am going to face a class of the young, for they count on me not to.)

Among some of the Beat, such a principle of integrity is clearly operating in the job-choice. To quote a paragraph earlier in this chapter: "many of the humble jobs of the poor are precisely *not* useless (or exploiting). Farm labor, hauling boxes, janitoring, serving and dishwashing, messenger—these resist remarkably well the imputation of uselessness (or exploitation) made against the productive society as a whole." These *are* preferred Beat jobs. For one thing, in them no questions are asked and no beards have to be shaved.

But on the other hand, such jobs, being hard and useful, are the most miserably exploited. (E.g., the hospital-workers who struck for a union so bravely last year were getting $34 a week. Migratory farmers might earn less than $900 a year, and the neighbors glad to see them leave.) All of the money is *in* the system. The wages are minimum, the price of subsistence is standard high; so a man loses his freedom, then never stops working. To have such a job is to be used and made a fool of by the system; and this is in itself dishonorable. This is the dilemma of voluntary poverty in our society: either to compromise one's integrity (but then why bother?) or to be abused and made a fool of.

Literary Radicalism in America
1985

◆

DAVID BROMWICH

David Bromwich is professor of English at Yale University and a member of the *Dissent* editorial board. He is the author of *Hazlitt: The Mind of a Critic*, *A Choice of Inheritance*, and *Politics by Other Means*.

Left-wing literary people talk more these days about criticism than about fiction or poetry or plays. The statement sounds too flat to be true, and it is fair to ask what "left-wing" signifies in the context. I am using it simply and I hope accurately to mean: people who in a better time would be doing political work. The criticism I have in mind is addressed to readers familiar with the current theoretical debates. It uses a political vocabulary ("undermining," "totalizing," "reification," "rupture," "bad faith") yet it has no implications for practical politics. The aim is not to interpret texts but to change them, and there the enterprise stops. Action means action with respect to texts. On occasions when one can sense other interests at work, the effect is very curious. In a polemical exchange, for instance, between a Marxist critic and a poststructuralist, one may know what sort of event is being staged; but, as one listens to the presentations, and compares the eloquence on both sides with its apparent subject, one sees that criticism is not the point at all. They are really arguing about something else—a social question of some kind—though neither knows it yet. Skeptics like to reply that the underground quality of such encounters is a sign of a hopeless cultural moment.

But the debates I mentioned have a more immediate cause. The language now spoken in literary theory is a language of the avant-garde. There is nothing surprising in this: every marginal movement in culture leads a second life in the history of criticism. What has changed is that the avant-garde has taken up residence in the academy. To be more precise, it has come to be identified with literary study in the universities, which once seemed a natural home for the academic view of art. An academy in the older sense existed for the purpose of inculcating received ideas and judgments. Now, with that function suspended, the avant-garde seems to be in force everywhere. It has become universal, and at the same time it has migrated inward. Much of this was foreseen by those who observed the progress of modern painting. The most acute descriptions of our situation were written more than a decade ago, by Harold Rosenberg, from a position sympathetic to the avant-garde but unhappy about the completeness of its acceptance. We have lately begun to get alternative descriptions from critics who speak for the homeless academy.

The *New Criterion* was launched two years ago as a monthly journal of the arts. Its editor, Hilton Kramer, and the regular contributors who set the tone are nonuniversity academicians. They present themselves as lonely and embattled figures. If their style is heavy, that is because their task is heavy. They are trying to invent cultural conservatism in America. In keeping with this aim, they satirize the universities, where the avant-garde is known to have taken cover; and yet, the tone of the attack is itself borrowed from the militant avant-garde, in the days before its triumph and assimilation. It is a pamphleteering manner, sometimes direct, sometimes ironic, always hectoring.

In this, the journal betrays a certain nostalgia. Its very name makes a similar point, for it honors as a precursor T. S. Eliot—founder of the old *Criterion,* but an avant-garde poet and critic before he became a Classicist, Royalist, Anglo-Catholic, and editor. "Tradition," Eliot wrote, "cannot be inherited"—not, that is, passed on like a correct opinion. "What happens," he added, "when a new work of art is created is something that happens simultaneously to all the works of art which preceded it." To believe this is not to deny the need in every culture for authority and deference. It gives the critic authority, indeed, to create new values, and not only to guard the values already in place. But the conservative wants to perform the latter function above all. He is guided in his judgments by a sequence of implicit equations: taste = inherited opinions = rules = norms (= social norms). His idea of culture is that it can be understood, and once understood it can be kept running smoothly by a team of impartial custodians.

Why does this sound strange to an American? Our daily habits of feeling seem to tell against it, and I think one reason is that the principle of self-trust, which we grew up believing, favors those who shake tradition in some way. We are still Emerson's disciples more or less, and he is a possible, though difficult, ally for a radical, as he cannot even begin to be for a conservative. O. W. Firkins wrote about this aspect of Emerson's appeal:

> His hunger was not greedy precisely because it was insatiable. Of two travellers, one, refusing to stop at the half-way house, pushes on to the large town which is his destination: he may stand for the average radical. The other, for whom the large town is itself a half-way house, whose destination is on the verge of the continent, stops contentedly at the first good lodging place: he may stand for Emerson. Both differ sharply from the man who stays at home.

Radicals are so little in evidence now that it is hard to know what an average radical would be. But when they reappear, in large enough numbers to think of travels like this, they will still be meeting Emersonian ideals along the way.

This essay is about the nature of those ideals, and I take it for granted that they are what we have to work with. A revisionist, whether in politics or culture, can no more exclude them than a speaker can exclude the perfect tenses, for they point to habits we still renew unquestioningly. If this is correct, the sort of criticism now emerging from the university avant-garde, as well as from the homeless academy, is in fact irrelevant to the growth of a new literature. These represent merely the latest efforts of exclusion—armed on one side with conventional skepticism, and on the other with conventional faith. Both attitudes retain the purity of assertions at the level of "as if." With no living tradition behind them, and an infinite vista of improvement ahead, they are free to enjoy the scandal of mimic wars. But the consequential debates in our culture have always taken place somewhere else, and the rival parties have agreed that words are acts that change our lives.

II

American literature is mostly the story of an avant-garde that did not stay at home. Many of its heroes come from two periods: in the nineteenth century, the twenty years leading up to the Civil War; and in the twentieth, the interval between the world wars. No single impulse unites such books as *The Scarlet Letter* and *The Sun Also Rises,* or even *Leaves of Grass* and *The Bridge.* But in the background of all these books has been an intellectual movement that could act as an incitement to their authors, and that saw itself as preparing the way for genius. The sort of figure who dominated such a movement used to be called a literary radical. I will use the phrase here because, provisionally, it helps to define Emerson. What he did was to describe, with sufficient plainness and sufficient profoundness, a condition of personal independence. And that was enough.

The great practical effect of Emerson's teaching was that it gave an idea of originality to a generation that included Whitman, Dickinson, Melville, along with others who seem minor talents only in that company. He accomplished this in a society where a shapeless conformity of opinion appeared to have taken hold forever. Indeed, if one tried to imagine an America free of Emerson's influence, the strictures of *Democracy in America* would turn into an accurate prophecy. As it is, they have come out looking *a priori* and shortsighted. Tocqueville simply did not bank on anyone like Emerson occurring.

This account may concede too much to the "great man" theory of history (in which, however, I believe). From another perspective Emerson was only the accidental success among many comparable types of the 1840s and 1850s. Evert Augustus Duyckinck, for example, and Cornelius Mathews, along with the critics, patrons, and entrepreneurs who made the subject of Perry Miller's *The Raven and the Whale,* set themselves up as New York's rivals to Concord, in the search for a native literature. They believed that they were looking for a home-grown epic to surpass Sir Walter Scott. What they wanted to foster, it seems clear in retrospect, was a gigantic second-rate literature, a sort of continuous collaborative American sublime, a high, flat, reliable, democratic achievement. It was not their fault that they could find nothing in that line big enough to satisfy their expectations. But when, from within their precincts, *Moby Dick* emerged, they were unequipped to appreciate it. The circumstance suggests that their ambition was essentially distinct from Emerson's. For the group around the first *Dial*—edited by Emerson and Margaret Fuller—formed an avant-garde in something like the modern sense. Other writers have noticed this, but the analogy has sometimes been called exotic, and I will try briefly to justify it.

An avant-garde differs from other societies for mutual promotion in only one way. It is willing to regard failure as a mark of election. It tells the artist, as Emerson told his young audience in "The American

Scholar": "If the single man plant himself indomitably on his instincts, and there abide, the huge world will come round to him." This was a good translation of Wordsworth's injunction to create the taste by which you are judged (grant *nothing* to the existing taste); and in the details of his practice, Emerson adopted the strategy of the Lake school in English poetry half a century before. He settled in a place unknown to letters, gathered significant neighbors around him, treated all his younger disciples as equals; and occasionally, instead of a Preface, he issued a Declaration. He is not quite a miracle, for he knew very well what he was doing. His glory was that he did it. The defect of many commentaries on Emerson—especially those written in the 1940s and '50s, from an effort to interpret the "American Renaissance"—is that they regard him altogether as a special case. Often, this is a result of valuing him as an encourager while underrating him as a writer. I believe it is more interesting to think of him as a *beginning:* someone, like Rousseau, whom others have to return to before they can start for themselves.

In what follows I try to sketch a recurring pattern for our literature since Emerson. I borrow Matthew Arnold's idea of antithetical "epochs": the epoch of expansion, in which great works are created; and the epoch of concentration, in which critical thinking advances and the impetus is given for expansion in the next age. This pattern of course leaves out a good deal, and I use it without any pretense of caution. Beginning, then, with Emerson, we have had an age of concentration and expansion close together; a second age of concentration in the early years of our century, with the criticism of Randolph Bourne, Van Wyck Brooks, and Waldo Frank; a second age of expansion, including Hemingway, Faulkner, Stevens, Frost, Hart Crane, Marianne Moore, Allen Tate, and William Carlos Williams, among others. What we see around us now, on the other hand, is probably not far different from the way things looked in 1885. The ages of contraction (to add a third term to Arnold's pair)—the age before Emerson's, the Gilded Age, ours—coincide with periods of retrenchment in politics. That is why the names Van Buren, Harrison, Tyler, Polk, Hayes, Garfield, Cleveland, McKinley, Nixon, Ford, Carter, Reagan make such a homogeneous list.

A change for the better usually happens like this. A small number of writers get together, agree that their culture has lost vitality, and decide to blame everything on its habitual arrangements, which they hold in contempt. If their analysis succeeds in fostering a literature that is powerful, the analysis and the literature stand doubly vindicated. But the important moment for a literary radical comes earlier, when he discovers that his analysis is widely shared; and the effect of such moments is to give fresh life to other radicals, who seek political remedies. There is a sense—better understood by historians than by critics—in which an Emerson makes room for a William Lloyd Garrison. What began as a program of literary revisionism thus works its way into all the channels of reform. One can see this in Emerson's writing, even when his subject is something as narrow as the use of meter in poetry:

> Great is the art,
> Great be the manners, of the bard.
> He shall not his brain encumber
> With the coil of rhythm and number;
> But, leaving rule and pale forethought,
> He shall aye climb
> For his rhyme.
> "Pass in, pass in," the angels say,
> "In to the upper doors,
> Nor count compartments of the floors,
> But mount to paradise
> By the stairway of surprise."

It is, on a narrow view, technical advice to poets about their craft. But there seems to me a nominal rather than a practical difference between this and his "Note to the Reader" of the *Dial*, written for the first issue in collaboration with Margaret Fuller:

> The spirit of the time is felt by every individual with some difference,— to each one casting its light upon the objects nearest to his temper and habits of thought. . . . In all its movements, it is peaceable, and in the very lowest marked with triumphant success. Of course, it rouses the opposition of all which it judges and condemns, but it is too confident in its tone to comprehend an objection, and so builds no outworks for possible defenses against contingent enemies. It has the step of Fate, and goes on existing like an oak or river, because it must.

The step of Fate and the stairway of surprise, the house without compartments and the fortress without outworks, offer variations on a single trope with a single moral: the power of individuals is equal to the power of fate.

Emerson's admirers, who liked his cunning, still heard the same sermon no matter what the text. It taught that a poem of 1,350 lines could be written proclaiming "oneself." Or it made the state appear as a contingent enemy to the man who would not pay taxes for an evil war. Responses like these have the terrible simplicity Emerson asked for but distrusted. He was, in consequence, the cruelest satirist of his own followers: he called Brook Farm "a perpetual picnic, a French Revolution in small, an Age of Reason in a patty-pan." Yet his warnings were directed against sects rather than causes, and in his 1851 address on the Fugitive Slave Law he told a Concord audience that it was "a law which every one of you will break on the earliest occasion." I quote these familiar judgments to show that his saying, "Whenever a man comes, there comes revolution," was merely an adequate description of the way his thinking had mattered in his own life. But his most solid effect may be seen in the lives of others who would have been free minds anyway, but were made bolder by his example. Margaret Fuller can stand for these; and, from an Emersonian point of view, I believe she had the better of her famous exchange with Carlyle, where she took a chance in speaking high-mindedly.

Fuller's "I accept the universe" meant that the universe was hers, to make of what she would (and change how she could). She was announcing her intention not to quit the contest, while acknowledging the conditions in which she was obliged to work. Carlyle, it seems, took her to be showing a polite condescension to the universe; and his reply, "By Gad, she'd better," was aimed at the paltriness of the human conceit that we have any choice in the matter. But, of course, we do have a choice. We can decide to risk everything for what we believe in, and there may be vastly different grounds of defense for such a move, even in thinkers as congenial as Emerson and Carlyle. Emerson's appeal, when he urged disobedience to the Fugitive Slave Law, was to a conscience that ought not to comply with the dictates of social expedience, or even the ultimate injunctions of social order. Carlyle's appeal, when he backed the South in the Civil War, was to an ideal duty, with fighting representatives in the actual world, who were to be honored as an active principle of order and the preservers of the spirit of a race. This is the light in which his witty reply must be read, and in this light it is honest enough, yet coarse and contemptible.

For we know what acceptances he had in view. In case we have forgotten, Emerson brings them all together in one sentence of a letter: "Carlyle is no idealist in opinions, but a protectionist in political economy, aristocrat in politics, epicure in diet, goes for murder, money, punishment by death, slavery, and all the petty abominations, tempering them with epigrams." Fuller knew most of this as well as

Emerson. And yet, after a meeting not much tempered with epigrams, she found a use for Carlyle, as he could not for her, and published an appreciation in the *New York Tribune:*

> His works are true, to blame and praise him, the Siegfried of England,
> great and powerful, if not quite invulnerable, and of a might rather to
> destroy evil than to legislate for good. At all events, he seems to be
> what destiny intended, and represents fully a certain side; so we make
> no remonstrance as to his being and proceeding for himself, though
> we sometimes must for us.

She speaks here on behalf of those who do want to legislate for
good—"we sometimes must for us." She is determined nevertheless to
build with such materials as the time affords, however intractable in
appearance. We can use Carlyle for his hatred of the laissez-faire system, though, to arrive at something better, we need to think beyond
his sense of "the duty to be intolerant."

The generosity of the verdict is Fuller's own, but it owes its confidence to Emerson's thought that genius is serviceable in spite of itself—that it cannot even be known, except as it assists the practical
ends of those who admire it. He wrote in "The Over-Soul":

> That which we are, we shall teach, not voluntarily but involuntarily.
> Thoughts come into our minds by avenues which we never left open,
> and thoughts go out of our minds through avenues which we never vol-
> untarily opened. Character teaches over our head.

So, once we have seen past the words of a writer, or the acts of a
leader, to the soul that produced them both, it turns out that we are
looking at something in ourselves. Emerson has more than one
name to describe what we recover then. But whatever he calls it, he
is sure that it has the power to alter traditions and laws as well as
customs and habits. He saw the extravagance of his claim, and
warned: "I unsettle all things." The tendency of his writing is to
break down the boundaries that separate literary invention from
the conduct of life.

III

Since Emerson, the project of literary radicalism has never been
isolable from an ambition to reform our social arrangements. At the

same time, it has resisted any steady collaboration with the short-term plans of reformers. It starts as a general hope, touching those who sympathize with movements outside literature, yet it ends in a general bewilderment. The strength of our individualism in culture appears to have been paid for by the eclecticism, the impatient or capricious energy, and above all the discontinuity of our radicalism in politics. The reason the balance works out this way is that, between cultural and political radicalism, the former adds up to the stronger tradition. Every American is born with a little of it. The pattern holds true to such an extent that some people have a special name for left-wing writers who think consistently about politics: they call them "European-style radicals." That label, if unfair, is at any rate intelligible, and we would be better off if it were not. But sometimes, the only way of changing an old story is to retell its happier episodes, in the hope that their atmosphere will invigorate. I turn accordingly from Emerson's group to their successors, the social critics whose work began in earnest about 1915.

In *America's Coming-of-Age,* Van Wyck Brooks argued that our official and popular cultures had taken opposite paths in the eighteenth century, and continued apart ever since, with results disabling for both. He allegorized the split by adopting the names "lowbrow" (for a writer like Franklin) and "highbrow" (for a writer like Edwards). The first type was marked chiefly by the instincts of gregarious self-advancement, the second chiefly by the duties of solitary speculation; and according to Brooks, they had joined only once, almost freakishly, in the writings of Whitman, whom he therefore called a "middlebrow." These types are cartoons. Yet they belong recognizably to a life we still know, where the literacy of our neighbors has nothing to do with their conversability. Liberals call the result pluralism, and think it the very stuff of democracy. Brooks, on the contrary, felt that, while capitalism thrived on such divisions, democracy grew weaker from them. Searching our tradition for a cause of the trouble, he came up with Emerson, whose thinking assured that we would remain content with our discrete virtues: for the lowbrow a vulgar gusto, for the highbrow an austere refinement. In short, the personal culture that Emerson invented had foreclosed the possibility of a common culture, even as it made ideals a redundancy for self-reliant men of action:

> The social ideal of Emerson . . . is a sort of composite of the philosopher, the mystic, the skeptic, the poet, the writer and the man of the

world. I wonder what passed through the mind of the American business man of Emerson's day when he heard all those phrases [of Emerson's], phrases so unrelated to the springs of action within himself. Did
he feel that his profound instincts had been touched and unified, did
he see opening before him the line of a distinguished career, lighted
up by a sudden dramatization of his own finest latent possibilities? Did
he not rather, with a degree of reason, say to himself: "These papers
will serve very well to improve my mind. I shall read them when I have
the time"? And did he not thereupon set to work accumulating all the
more dollars in order that he might have the more time to cultivate his
mind—in legal phrase—after the event?

Looked at from this side, Emerson has all the qualities of the typical baccalaureate sermon; and the baccalaureate sermon, as we know,
beautiful as it often is, has never been found inconveniently inconsistent with the facts and requirements of business life.

My argument thus far has been that Emerson is so expansive a friend
of revolt as to be favorable to no particular party. Brooks, however,
implies that this in effect makes him a valuable servant of the status
quo, which in America is itself expansionist. I believe that his interpretation is wrong; but it was sufficiently provoked. It reminds us of
Emerson's insistence, in a work like *The Conduct of Life,* that he be
taken at once as a detached aphorist and a guide to worldly advancement—part of his appeal that Melville captured in *Pierre,* with its portrait of Plotinus Plinlimmon, the half-inspired enthusiast with an eye
for the main chance. Yet Brooks, in a passage like this, was also reacting against the pragmatists, that is, against another school of Emerson's readers.

Brooks understood pragmatism as a decadent idealism that had betrayed genius in the name of practical power. He refers specifically to
James and Dewey, but otherwise leaves the charge unexplained, and I
can offer only a surmise about what he might have said. Emerson's
own thinking had been an idealist answer to the materialism he supposed was becoming the dominant philosophy of the age. His purpose was to give us back the world of our ideas, and hence of our
ideals and spiritual laws, as identical with the world of practice. He
meant this scrupulously: all the disposable materials of nature and
art, which he summed up as "commodity," were an outward realization of "Man thinking," a writing-it-large for the slow of wit. Now,
James and Dewey saw themselves as fighting the same battle, a little
further on. But idealism as they knew it was an exhausted orthodoxy
of a thoroughly antiempirical character. When, therefore, James

taught his readers to care for the "live option"—when Dewey rede-fined truth as "warranted assertibility"—they were seeking to make practical wisdom again coincide with the highest instincts of men and women. To act as if one's beliefs were part of a total drift that might some day carry everything with it, was to be *sound* on the only going definition of soundness. The life that these pragmatists wanted to en-courage was not mainly or even largely "business life."

Yet Brooks's analysis did not depend, after all, on a questioning of motives. Rather, he took it as simply demonstrable that the alliance suggested by pragmatism—between new successes of any kind and the creation of new truths—left radicals on a lower moral ground than before, in their contest with the heroes of industry and com-merce. All this remains implicit in Brooks's discussion. It became a conscious emphasis in the writings of Randolph Bourne, who had started as an admirer of the pragmatists. After Dewey lent his support to American participation in the war, Bourne published a record of his disenchantment, in an essay called "Twilight of Idols":

> To those of us who have taken Dewey's philosophy almost as our Amer-ican religion, it never occurred that values could be subordinated to technique. We were instrumentalists, but we had our private utopias so clearly before our minds that the means fell always into place as con-tributory. And Dewey, of course, always meant his philosophy, when taken as a philosophy of life, to start with values. But there was always that unhappy ambiguity in his doctrine as to just how values were cre-ated, and it became easier and easier to assume that just any growth was justified and almost any activity valuable so long as it achieved ends. The American, in living out this philosophy, has habitually con-fused results with product, and has been content with getting some-where without asking too closely whether it was the desirable place to get.

Earlier I quoted Emerson's disclaimer, "I unsettle all things"; and it is worth recalling here that his next words were: "No facts are to me sa-cred; none are profane; I simply experiment, an endless seeker with no Past at my back." For Bourne, this had become the voice of Ameri-can capitalism. It gave the master-clue to the workings of a state that was only healthy when at war.

On this analysis pragmatism, itself the offspring of idealism, was eventually converted to the uses of realism in the vulgar sense, which implies a hostility to all ideals. The hope before the war had been to fortify the individual in his plural relations with life, by representing his ability to shape it variously and inventively, from one situation to another. But a mistaking of product for results led the pragmatist (*we instrumentalists,* as Bourne puts it) to think well of those already employed in reshaping the world. This included the entrepreneurs of business and war. I do not want to enter into the merits of Bourne's view; but one thing about his argument is certainly attractive: it, too, is pragmatic. World War I was a disgraceful period in our intellectual life, and Bourne proposed to test radical ideas by the character they showed in surviving it. He had no stomach for truckling or compromise; in "The War and the Intellectuals" he wrote: "This realistic boast is so loud and sonorous that one wonders whether realism is always a stern and intelligent grappling with realities. May it not be a mere surrender to the actual, an abdication of the ideal through sheer fatigue from intellectual suspense?" About the same time, Brooks was writing a polemic against literary critics who pleaded for realism of a well-behaved sort.

Such critics exist at all times, and often speak on behalf of the imperative of the actual, or some similar phrase. The phrase always means, "Show us what is good about our society (we are so lost in it that occasionally we forget)." In *Letters and Leadership,* Brooks's immediate target was an assertion by W. D. Howells that "the more smiling aspects of life" are "the more American," and a request of novelists that they be faithful to our "well-to-do actualities." This thought has lately been echoed by Joseph Epstein in a review of two novels in *Commentary,* which concludes: "of plain pessimism . . . we have had quite enough. Let, please, the sun shine in." Brooks replied in 1918: "Could one ask for a more essential declaration of artistic bankruptcy than that? For what does it amount to, this declaration? It identifies the reality of the artist's vision with what is accepted as reality in the world about him." Artists, Brooks added, who do follow such advice "do not so much mature at all as externalize themselves in a world of externalities." One can expand this statement in a way that seems consistent with Brooks's intentions. An artist works from an internal life—thoughts, feelings, impressions—which he seeks to render external. There is no *thing* (at once diffuse and substantial) that the word "reality" helps to explain. There are only the available externalities. If we like some of them, we may call them actual; if we dislike others, we may call them pessimistic or less smiling. An artist is sometimes improved by a critic who shows how his work is careless or foppish. No artist has ever been improved by a critic who urges him to portray a certain kind of subject, or eliminate a certain mood.

IV

The legacy of Emerson, Fuller, James, Dewey, Bourne, and Brooks is what we still have to build on. A sustained effort to revise their style of cultural tolerance came in the 1930s and '40s, from the Eliotic-Trotskyist group around *Partisan Review*. These were critics who pointed to a recent past, and said: "The great thing is already there." They wrote with equal assurance as skeptical observers of American culture and as monumental historians of the European avant-garde. By this double emphasis, their work appeared to offer a new conception of intellectual freedom. The Emersonian sermon against public opinion is simple though hard to act upon. It tells us to stand apart from our society. The Eliotic-Trotskyist sermon against mass culture was less simple, and perhaps less hard to act upon. It told us to stand apart from one element of our culture. What, exactly, did the suggestion amount to?—for anyone, I mean, but especially for an American? We have to come at this a long way around. In his 1939 essay "Avant-Garde and Kitsch," Clement Greenberg imagined a Russian peasant after a long day's toil, offered him a choice of pictures to look at—on the one hand a battle scene by Repin, on the other a cubist abstraction by Picasso—and supposed he would prefer the Repin, on the ground that it was familiar. Repin's picture affords a "wealth of self-evident meanings" by which the peasant "recognizes and sees things in the way in which he recognizes and sees things outside of pictures—there is no discontinuity between art and life, no need to accept a convention." The notion of a familiarity that may be realized in the absence of any convention is of course very odd. Nevertheless, Greenberg, who in this may be taken to represent many others, made the following deductions from his reading of the hypothetical incident.

First, the taste for mass culture is instinctive in an industrial society. (The case of the peasant accidentally proves too much, by suggesting that it may be instinctive even in a state of nature.) Second, art alone has the task of modifying conventions; and the conventions themselves are defined formalistically: "the arts," as Greenberg said in another place, "have been hunted back to their mediums," and a work only exempts itself from mass culture by virtue of an emphatic concern with its medium. Third, in this situation—where art, if it is to be vital, is fated to be modernist, and the appeal of modernist works is confined to a few—the distance between the cultural and political avant-garde has widened irreparably.

The diagnosis turns on the assumption that avant-garde artists have the same superior indifference to mass culture as avant-garde critics, when in fact their attitude has more often been one of ambivalent fascination. But I suspect, for American readers, this weighs very little by comparison with a more local objection. Substitute a New England yeoman for the Russian peasant, and what happens to the fable? It is refuted by the miscellaneous power of his emblems and symbols. "In the political processions," Emerson observed, "Lowell goes in a loom, and Lynn in a shoe, and Salem in a ship." The arts do not disdain these things: "Some stars, lilies, leopards, a crescent, a lion, an eagle, or other figure which came into credit God knows how, on an old rag of bunting, blowing in the wind on a fort at the ends of the earth, shall make the blood tingle under the rudest or most conventional exterior." We can hardly know culture at all, except as just such a mixed entity.

So we easily stray across the boundaries that separate the exalted from the humble—categories that, with us, are always being revised for present purposes, and that a single sharp challenge may suffice to upset again. Nobody knew this better than Emerson, or kept it more constantly in mind. He sympathized with a new thought at the moment of its invention, and left others to plan its consolidation. In the arts he did without ideas of high and low. In religion, long before, he had moved from the doctrine of a visible church to that of a hidden personal divinity. His motive was a readiness to suffer inexpediences as the cost of fresh truths. Without something of the same sentiment, culture would cease to be a vivid abstraction, and turn into the sum of its institutional conquests. But "The Invisible Avant-Garde," which John Ashbery christened in an essay of that title, has always sustained a belief that culture is not identical with cultivation. The belief continues because the visible church takes many forms—a congregation, a board of censors, and an academy being only the most persistent.

Their successors appear to be "the media." But, writing in 1968, Ashbery saw all of these as contingent enemies, and remembered the example of Jackson Pollock in the late 1940s:

At that time I found the avant-garde very exciting, just as the young do today, but the difference was that in 1950 there was no sure proof of the existence of the avant-garde. To experiment was to have the feeling that one was poised on some outermost brink. In other words, if one wanted to depart, even moderately, from the norm, one was taking one's life—one's life as an artist—into one's hands. A painter like Pollock for instance was gambling everything on the fact that he *was* the greatest painter in America, for if he wasn't, he was nothing, and the drops would turn out to be random splashes from the brush of a careless housepainter. It must often have occurred to Pollock that there was just a possibility that he wasn't an artist at all, that he had spent his life "toiling up the wrong road to art," as Flaubert said of Zola. But this very real possibility is paradoxically just what makes the tremendous excitement of his work. It is a gamble against terrific odds. Most reckless things are beautiful in some way, and recklessness is what makes experimental art beautiful, just as religions are beautiful because of the strong possibility that they are founded on nothing.

The situation today, as Ashbery describes it, when the artist commonly finds himself "at the center of a cheering mob," is doubtless more enervating than in the heyday of the avant-garde, when an interval of decent neglect was still allowed. Yet the present mood is not less favorable to creation; it merely warrants a change of tactics, for the artist "must now bear in mind that *he,* not *it,* is the avant-garde." This I take to be what Emersonian critics from the first have been saying in other words.

I am aware that there is a strong and a weak version of my argument. In the strong version, we Americans are all potentially of the avant-garde. In the weak version, this turns out to be so because for us the avant-garde is only another name for radical individualism. I do not claim that political radicals ought to take satisfaction from the results as they stand. But it does seem possible to view them as a broken series of victories; they have too often been recounted as a single continuous defeat. The encouraging parts of the story, varied as they are, may seem to lack a moral about the uses of art. One reason is that art meant anything for Emerson—"beauty," "language," "discipline"— anything, that is, outside the world of commodity. He concluded every attempt to define it further with a pleasant but inscrutable compliment. And evidently, for an object with this range of meanings, we have to be content with a surmise as to its function. I have quoted some instances already, but saved the best for last. It comes from Kenneth Burke, whose career almost spans the period from Bourne's generation to mine, and who wrote more than fifty years ago in *Counter-Statement:* "An art may be of value purely through preventing a society from becoming too assertively, too hopelessly, itself."

With the Lower Depths
1991

◆

P A U L   B E R M A N

Paul Berman, a member of the *Dissent* editorial board and for many years a contributor to *The Village Voice,* is a writer for *The New Yorker, The New Republic, The New York Times Book Review,* and other journals.

In *The Bonfire of the Vanities,* Tom Wolfe devotes a single passage to the way historical memory influences a certain kind of modern liberal sensibility. Wolfe's Bronx assistant district attorney, Kramer, searching his political conscience, stumbles on the word "socialist" in the columns of *The Village Voice* (an enjoyable touch). And this word prompts a private rumination:

> Kramer had no interest in left-wing politics, and neither did his father. Yet in their house, when he was growing up, the word *socialist* had rebellious overtones. It was like *Zealot* and *Masada.* There was something Jewish about it. No matter how wrongheaded a socialist might be, no matter how cruel and vindictive, he possessed somewhere in his soul a spark of the light of God, of Yahweh.

Socialism leads to a contemplation of unions:

> His father was a would-be capitalist, a servant of capitalists in actual fact, who had never belonged to a labor union in his life and felt infinitely superior to those who did. Yet one night Senator Barry Goldwater had been on TV promoting a right-to-work bill, and his father had started growling and cursing in a way that would have made Joe Hill and the Wobblies look like labor mediators. Yes, the labor movement was truly religious, like Judaism itself. It was one of those things you believed in for all mankind and didn't care about for a second in your own life.

This isn't right. The father of someone like Assistant D.A. Kramer might have prattled on about Masada and God and indulged a religious streak, though probably not in words like these; and elsewhere in his inconsistent mind, he might have preached the evils of capitalism and the destiny of the proletariat. But the sacred and the socialist would probably not have mixed. Socialism among the New York Jews of a generation or two ago was not a liberation theology. It was secular, even antireligious.

Still, leaving aside the confusion over religious terminology, something is correct about Wolfe's picture. Conscience is a historical construction. In identifying the residue that old-fashioned New York socialism has left on someone like the not-too-principled assistant district attorney, in noticing that the mere shadow of a term like "socialism" arouses a kind of atavistic response in such a person, even if socialism's meaning has by now gotten tangled up in matters so extraneous as to reach all the way to religion—in noticing all this, Wolfe has observed something true and significant about liberal instincts in the present.

What is this half-remembered thing, the socialist shade from the past? Wolfe ascribes Kramer's sentiment to his father, but since even father "had no interest in left-wing politics," a reader might suppose that father's socialism, too, was merely half remembered and that, in the Kramer family, grandfather, the oppressed immigrant garment worker (taking a wild guess about Kramer family history), was socialism's truest tribune. Grandfather, we might suppose, did find himself now and then at left-wing meetings. Of course *The Bonfire of the Vanities* has no occasion to mention a grandfather and still less what was learned at the meetings. Yet to spell out the original Kramer family socialism is not so very difficult.

Grandfather—let us imagine—upheld essentially three doctrines, beginning with one about history. He felt that a more cooperative and egalitarian society than one based on sweatshop exploitation not only could be created but was, in fact, inevitable. His second belief was economic. He supposed that the vast working class was capable of forming its own economic system, that working people, either directly or through their leaders, could assume the management of production and distribution and do it more justly and more efficiently.

Finally, he subscribed to a set of moral values and instincts regarding society, a kind of moral sociology. He looked at other working people in all parts of the economy and the world, and his heart beat with sympathy and identification. Maybe his socialism tilted to the radical side. In that case, he looked downward, too, at people who were too oppressed and too wretched to be respectable workers like himself, at beggars and the utterly poor, and to some extent even at the people who had sunk into the criminal class—at prisoners and the pathetic lumpenproletariat who were the bane of his own existence. And for these people, too, he felt at least a flickering sympathy. He regarded the rich and powerful, not the very poor, as his enemies. He stood with and not against "the lower depths." The more abject and pathetic and defeated people were, the stronger was grandfather's conviction that socialist ideas of egalitarian cooperation and working-class productivity had a moral and not just historical or economic basis.

Now, grandfather's doctrines on history and economics have not been flatly disproved, and they have certainly not disappeared: but the sharpness of their contours has dropped away. Today no one seriously believes that an altogether new society is close at hand. The whole notion of an impending conflict between capitalism and socialism tends to obscure rather than clarify the actual alternatives in the modern predicament, which lean toward more capitalism or more socialism but not to a decisive historic choice between the two. Today we can imagine a greater concentration of power in the giant multinational corporations—or a greater democratic control over production and markets (instead of the outright nationalized economy dreamed of by state socialists of the past). We can picture a "South Africanization" of the work force based on unskilled labor and strict hierarchy—or a greater economic role for professionalism, pride-in-craft, decentralized management, worker participation, and other measures (instead of the direct seizure of the factories dreamed of by the old-time syndicalists).

We can imagine and even predict that choices like these will become unavoidable in the future, as the economy globalizes and advances, and that concepts of economic organization drawing on socialist inspirations will seem more relevant, not less, in the years to come. Yet socialist ideas in their modern form, lacking something of the old simplicity, do lack some of the old appeal, too. It's harder nowadays, in fact it's impossible, for a quick-witted comrade to stand on a crate with a flag and rouse a crowd of fellow wage slaves. That may explain why young Kramer takes "no interest" in left-wing politics.

What about grandfather's third doctrine, then, the moral sociology, the sympathy for fellow working people and even for the very poor and the oppressed? Wasn't this the old fundamentalism's most crucial feature of all? Has this idea, too, lost its contours, faded into the past? Does it, too, linger in the consciences of grandsons only as a half-forgotten tug on the conscience—"one of those things you believed in for all mankind and didn't care about for a second in your own life"?

◆

In a polemical essay that Wolfe has published in the brand-new edition of his novel, he takes up one aspect of this question, though by addressing issues that are literary and not socialist. He observes that the grand nineteenth-century novelists seized on the city as their subject, with its themes of rich and poor, extreme individuality, justice and injustice. Yet the life of cities (Wolfe argues) has not appealed to the greatest of the modern novelists, mostly because the elite intelligentsia looks down its nose at popular fictional studies of vast social themes and prefers topics that are more intimate and inaccessible. To the readers of Joyce and Bellow, Wolfe's point may seem hard to credit. Yet, as with his notion of Jewishness and socialism, perhaps something about it is not untrue. He quotes Lionel Trilling, who said that the great nineteenth-century novelists wrote studies of character as influenced by social class. In the same vein, it could be said that the great city novelists of the nineteenth century wrote studies of specific grand motives and emotions as influenced by the hubbub of city life. In the case of Dickens and Zola and many a lesser writer, the motives and emotions tended to be sympathy for the downtrodden. And hasn't *this* theme faded from the modern novel?

Wolfe pictures his own novel in the Zola tradition, but if Zola's social sympathies are kept in mind, *The Bonfire of the Vanities* could just as well be taken as an example of that tradition's demise. There's no reason to denigrate Wolfe's gift for satire and caricature. He is a marvelous journalist (and in his essay correctly celebrates journalism, meaning hard research and reporting, as a component of literature). By dint of many a gruesome subway trek to 161st Street, he has drawn an artful cartoon of the courthouse politics and newspaper life of New York, just as his hero Zola, by descending into the coal mines, caught something of the miners' misery (though if we are to bandy about nineteenth-century comparisons, it might be more appropriate to group Wolfe with a melodramatist like Eugène Sue, whose *Mysteries of Paris*, like *The Bonfire of the Vanities*, began as a series in a periodical). But Wolfe is not especially interested in grand emotions or, for that matter, even in character; he's not naturally a novelist. And among the grand emotions that do not especially engage him are, it must be said, the old-fashioned table-pounding sentiments of social sympathy.

Dickens, Sue, and Zola wrote protest novels against the rich. Today we have protest novels against the poor. *The Bonfire of the Vanities* works up a splendid satiric indignation against the parvenus and the people who spend $350,000 on a fireplace—yet its truest rage hammers at the mendacity and violence of the nameless black and Latin immigrant masses, who never appear as anything but an anonymous muttering mob. And to return to the question of socialism and its doctrines, it does seem that the third component of grandfather's left-wing imagination, his sympathy with the downtrodden, has indeed gone the way of socialism's historical and economic ideas—at least among the leading literary and popular writers. The old-fashioned sympathy hasn't disappeared entirely, of course. But it is no longer very sharply defined. It is seen as an idea from the dusty past. An out-of-date notion. Something that is mostly *remembered,* but not exactly experienced in the present.

◆

I realize that readers are already rushing forward to complain that a debonair journalist with conservative instincts like Tom Wolfe cannot be made to stand for the whole of modern literature; that sympathy for the downtrodden is *not* like the other elements of socialist fundamentalism and has *not* diminished and has, on the contrary, remained entirely accessible to the modern imagination. Perhaps someone will argue that, far from having diminished, sympathy for the downtrodden has grown since the days when grandfather waved his red flag, as shown by the very welfare measures whose incorporation into the modern state has vitiated the old either/or choice between capitalism and socialism. Perhaps someone will mutter that today's poor are not quite up to the higher standards of the poor of yesteryear—that the bottom class of today is morally more wretched, that drugs and crime have given us depths so low as to lie beyond sympathy. Someone may complain that today's bottom class upholds too many crackpot theories and cheers too many demagogic manipulators.

Still, all you have to do is glance at the writers that Grandfather Kramer, if he was a reading man, would have treasured, from Dickens to Jack London, to notice that a difference in generosity between the past and the present is not imaginary—at least in books. Let me cite, just because the books happen to be on my table, an example grandfather wouldn't have known (though his Spanish or Cuban immigrant neighbors might): the novelist Benito Pérez Galdós (1843–1920). Galdós is exactly the kind of writer that Wolfe has in mind when he speaks of the nineteenth-century city realists. As Dickens and Balzac were to London and Paris, Galdós was to Madrid. He wrote about the Spanish royal court, about the revolutionary republicans, about the rising middle class (his special subject), and also about the wretched South Madrid slums that were not, judging from his vivid descriptions, any sweeter or safer than our own South Bronx.

He tells us in the introduction to one of his celebrated studies of South Madrid, *Misericordia* ("Mercy" or "Compassion"), that he "proposed to go to the lowest layers of Madrid society, describing and presenting the humblest types, the greatest poverty, the professional begging, the vice-ridden vagrancy, the poverty that is almost always sad, in some cases picturesque or criminal and meriting correction." His book required, as per Wolfe's injunction, months of research. Was researching the slums easier in 1897 than it is today? The difficulties and dangers of penetrating into Madrid's "evil-smelling" southern districts were such that Galdós was obliged to disguise himself as a doctor from Municipal Hygiene. He didn't soften the ghastliness. He went accompanied by police. He didn't ascribe all problems to the enemy class. He knew that South Madrid was unhealthy not just in the sense of physical disease.

Yet the feeling that he worked up in *Misericordia* and in other novels was an immense sympathy for these wretched persons of the Madrid slums. The beggars gather outside the church and wail with pain, the drunks indulge their vice to the point of suicide, the deluded Quixotesque dreamers sink ever deeper into homelessness, every third person seems half out of his mind, and as the pages turn, Galdós's heart pounds harder and harder for these unfortunate people—if perhaps not for every individual. Sympathy and solidarity were, for a writer like him, as much a theme of literature as any other emotion. Compassion was his guitar. It was rich and colorful, now open to satire, now to frank weeping, now to anger. It was, for him, the biggest of all emotions, the great all-inclusive chord. And when you read such a writer, it is hard not to conclude that emotions and themes like his have indeed withdrawn from the center of modern literature. Among the dominant novelists of our own time, how many would even try to write about the people whom Galdós adopted as his protagonists: a beggar in *Misericordia,* a prostitute in *Fortunata and Jac-*

intal, a stunted victim of industrial pollution in *Marianela?* Of course a variety of works from the present can be named—but not too many of them, and at any rate, they can't claim to speak for our age.

◆

Several reasons can be offered for why such a narrowing of the moral imagination has occurred. For instance, we might cite the kitsch that came out of false leftisms of the past. We might speculate that greater wealth has erected stronger walls around the middle class, such that concerns about poverty and social despair no longer press upon the ordinary writer or reader (though that seems less and less true). But mostly I wonder if the feeling of compassion and solidarity isn't somehow connected, at a deep level, with the other original elements of the socialist idea—with the expectation of a new stage of history based on a new kind of economy. Maybe the writers of the nineteenth century looked to the downtrodden for themes because they felt that the poor were not, as they have come to see today, marginal, but were instead the key to the future. Maybe the writers strummed their sympathetic chords because they had a notion of history and economy that directed them to do so. Maybe they felt that compassion and solidarity were linked to the laws of history and were therefore hardheaded and authentic, not softheaded and false.

The fading of left-wing fundamentalism about history and economics is not to be regretted, given that it comes on the heels of social progress and that, besides, certain of the old hopes lent themselves too easily to disastrous uses. But it may be that, without these sturdy old doctrines to prop them up, sympathy and solidarity begin to sag. We may have reached a place where, due to the general rise of productivity and wealth, we are at last materially capable of eliminating the worst sorts of poverty—only to find that we no longer have the will. Grandfather Kramer is no more; today we have the district attorney. We do not have Zola or even Eugène Sue; we have Tom Wolfe. Socialism's meaning is vaguer; our hearts are smaller.

Children of the Future
1993

◆

MARSHALL BERMAN

Marshall Berman, a member of the *Dissent* editorial board, teaches political theory, urbanism, and cultural history at the City University of New York. He is the author of *All That Is Solid Melts into the Air* and *The Politics of Authenticity.*

> Children of the future Age
> Reading this indignant page,
> Know that in a former time
> Love! sweet Love! was thought a crime. . . .
>
> —WILLIAM BLAKE,
>   "A Little Girl Lost,"
>   1790s

> They fuck you up, your mum and dad,
> They may not mean to, but they do.
> They fill you with the faults they had,
> And add some new ones, just for you. . . .
>
> —PHILIP LARKIN,
>   "This Be the Verse,"
>   1970s

One of the marks of modern times is that masses of ordinary people have come to believe that their children's lives could be a lot better than their own. Over the last two centuries, as the world has opened up, this belief has become one of the driving forces for mass migration. People sell all they have, travel steerage, often declass themselves, anything to get out; when they land, they live in wretched slums, work themselves to death in jobs the natives won't accept, put up with vicious insults and injuries (and every time and place has a racist and xenophobic repertory all its own), subject themselves to enormous amounts of crap, and *alles fur die kindelech,* everything for the kids, as they used to say when I was a kid. They still say it, the Russian bakers and Indian stationers and Korean fruit-and-vegetable people on my block, and the parents of my students at CCNY, in more languages than I can keep track of. Their deepest belief—sometimes, it seems, their only belief—is a belief in progress. "Children of the future age," William Blake's lyrical invocation, evokes this romantic faith. The speaker in Blake's poem is wretched in the present age, but confident that his (her?) children's generation will enjoy a glorious future; the children of the future will be so free and radiant that they will need poetry to feel and understand their parents' inner wounds.

Alas, in the history of culture as much as in the history of families, children tend not to appreciate parental sacrifice; they often come to feel it's they themselves who are the lambs, and their parents' visionary hopes are bonds that chain and crush them. Again and again, since the Age of Revolutions, romantic faith in the future has generated a dialectical antithesis, a counterromance. Sometimes this grim myth has appeared as a counter-American Dream, as in all the great American plays—by Eugene O'Neill, Clifford Odets, Lillian Hellman, Arthur Miller, Tennessee Williams, Sam Shepard—about children who are crushed by their parents and/or their parents' sins. In the Punk Rock of the 1970s, the myth took the form of a counter-Woodstock, spat into the face of the 1960s: "I belong to the blank generation," said Richard Hell and the Voidoids; the Sex Pistols said, "We are the future / there is no future"; one group called themselves Devo, in honor of humanity's Devolution. Christopher Lasch expounded this sort of theory in academic language in his 1970s cultural studies, *The Culture of Narcissism* and *Haven in a Heartless World,* which proclaimed as an incontrovertible fact of modern life "the death of the family." The generally genteel poet Philip Larkin, England's Poet Laureate, when he wrote about the family, sounded just like a punk. His poem, quoted above, reads like an apotheosis of the family counterromance. His rap ends with Swiftian nihilism:

> Man hands on misery to man.
> It deepens like a coastal shelf.
> Get out as early as you can,
> And don't have any kids yourself.

Like the Grinch who stole Christmas, this guy wants to grab hold of everybody's family hopes and smash them against the wall; then he grins at us wickedly while he stomps the shards, even as his own feet are torn up by the broken glass. But still, he upholds an equation proclaimed by the soppiest sentimentalists: "the family" equals the future; to not have kids is to "get out as early as you can" from life.

◆

It's strange to go through this post-sixties material twenty years later. So many people seemed so sure (some sad, some glad) "the family"—as if there were only one—was "dead." What can they have been thinking of? What was happening was that millions of families were reconfiguring themselves. The big thing is that mothers en masse were going to work. Here are some numbers, hot off the presses from the Bureau of Labor Statistics (BLS). If we compare the proportion of working mothers—that is, mothers in the labor force with children under seventeen—we find that in thirty years, from March 1962 to March 1992, it has more than doubled: 30 percent for 1962, 67 percent for 1992. The BLS breaks down this statistic into mothers with children from six to seventeen, and those whose children are under six. Since 1962, the percentage of working mothers with children six to seventeen has risen from 42 percent in 1962 to 76 percent in 1992. The most striking rise has been for mothers with children under six: 20 percent were working in 1962, 58 percent in 1992. So the proportion has tripled, and a family structure that was pretty rare thirty years ago has become typical today.

Can we assess mothers' motivations? There are many layers. Outside of the trust-fund set, there are few families that don't simply need the money. Remember, real wages in the United States have been falling since 1973. But the experiences of going out to work, of being part of an enterprise and a workforce, of having co-workers, of contributing to something outside one's own household, address more than material needs. Millions of women, over the past two decades—not only women who were proud to be called feminists, but also women who scorned or feared the word—have been learning to apply those old Jeffersonian ideals, "life, liberty, and the pursuit of happiness," to their own lives. Many Americans were, and are, disturbed to see the Enlightenment come so close to home. But they shouldn't be surprised. After all, since the 1950s, American society has been going through the most intense agitation, redefining and working through the meaning of civil rights. How much longer could

American women be expected to ignore their own?

What looks so weird, twenty years after, is the assumption that, once modern women cease to be deferent, they are bound to become indifferent; that, given a chance to live for themselves, they will become utterly cruel and uncaring for others—for men and children, for love and nurturing, for any sort of family tie or social bond beyond their momentary whims. So many writers (of both sexes) used to talk this way. Where did they get that perverse equation, FREEDOM = INDIFFERENCE? Was it from John Locke? Or from their own lives? You have to wonder.

In fact, it didn't work that way. What has happened, instead, for the most part, is that men and women discovered how thrilling, as well as grueling, life in a two-income and two-career family could be. Where both people are out in the world, there's more substance of fire, more life to share, more *there* there. Of course, there's not much time for there to be there: a working couple with children pretty much has to make dates to be together, and not many dates will be open. (A comic spinoff: sometimes, say, in interludes when they find themselves with exactly thirty-five minutes alone, and aren't totally worn out, they can enjoy the *frisson* of an illicit affair. Is this what's meant by "Treat your spouse like a lover"?) Two-income families with children have been forced to develop a vast infrastructure of playgroups and sitters and nannies and day-care centers and after-school programs. Americans over the last twenty years have been very imaginative and resourceful in putting these support systems together, with no government help. (In the United States, unlike Western Europe, the only people who get that help are people already on welfare.) But the scaffolding shakes, the props are precarious, the parents lie awake in bed together at night worrying that somebody (or one body too many) will get sick the next morning and the whole structure will crash.

Sometimes it does split, right down the middle. With women as well as men struggling to be who they are, it's no surprise if both sexes feel under intolerable pressure and put intolerable pressure on each other. Today's couples break up far more often than their parents did. The good news is that over the last decade or so the divorce rate has leveled off; the bad news is that it's leveled off at about one out of two. Divorce today, as much as in the Karenins' day, opens floodgates of rage, guilt, and existential panic. But today the unraveling of marriages doesn't mean the destruction of *families*. Here, too, parents have found or created new structures for support. Family law has developed the institution of joint custody: now there don't have to be zero-sum wars between parents, and children can have two solid homes, and ex-spouses who can't agree on much can agree on this and work like hell to keep it intact for the sake of the children. Single parents have developed elaborate networks to share responsibility for each other's children, so they can get at least some slack to take responsibility for themselves. Meanwhile, ex-wives and ex-husbands, thrown on their own, rarely live like swinging singles (as it used to be thought they would); instead, they tend to fall in love again as soon as they can pick themselves off the floor, form new bonds, start new families, have more children (if they're too old, they adopt), and crowd the betting windows to wager on the future again. Today's children of divorce don't skulk alone in corners, as yesterday's did: they are likely to grow up surrounded by stepparents and godparents and stepsiblings who fill their lives and give them all the love they can take. Moreover, the very pervasiveness of divorce has mostly dissipated its stigma, and given the children, for company, plenty of other children like themselves. In the middle class, they will grow up surrounded by networks of psychiatrists, teachers, social workers, counselors, lawyers, mediators, coaches, tutors, nurturing them and helping them survive their parents even as they help their parents hold them together. All these professional helpers and carers work for money, as they must, and yet, in this *la ronde* whose social boundaries are so fluid, any one of them may turn into something very like family, and turn out to stand by their children and stand up for them for life.

◆

These changes can help explain the spectacular backfire of the GOP's "family values" campaign. That campaign highlighted many of the Clinton family's troubles, especially Bill's adultery (but also his brother's drug addiction), and intimated that it was really all Hillary's fault, not just for going to work, but for thinking her work had some value independent of her husband, and generally for having an attitude and not knowing her place. Simultaneously, the Bush family was held up as a sort of Norman Rockwell icon, a family that had stayed together all these years (photo op: Barbara with grandchildren; keep those sleazy sons off camera, please), supposedly because the wife had given up not only her work but her beliefs—most strikingly, her belief in women's right to choice—and had submitted herself unto her husband, just the way St. Paul said she should. It didn't work because so many families, even in those sacred middle-class suburbs, have moved out of Norman Rockwell country and won't look back. When Barbara Bush righteously denied everything—her husband's mistress, her children's crookedness—instead of being admired for her saintliness, she was reproved for living a lie. Hillary Clinton, on the other hand, won admiration for *not* lying, for confirming the rumors, openly expressing her disgust with her husband, but saying she still loved the guy and hoped they could work it through. The Clintons, with two incomes and two careers, an unsubmissive wife, an overachieving husband who comes not only from the wrong side of the tracks but from an abusive, "dysfunctional" family and a past that still haunts him, and a large complex of serious troubles worn openly on their sleeves, turned out to be close to millions of contemporary families' hearts. The most salient of "family values" in 1992 may be honesty in confronting a family's real troubles. (Will the Clintons add a family therapist to the White House staff?)

◆

So what can President Clinton do for real families? The Western European countries that Clinton has shown he knows about suggest some simple basic services that families need: family allowances, day-care centers, public schools that aren't crumbling, after-school and summer programs for children, community health services, including preventative medicine, birth control and abortion, prenatal care, family counseling, psychiatric help before (rather than after) things fall apart. All these services exist differentially around the country today, but they are dependent on private incomes or local budgets, which means they get slashed just when and where they are needed most. The crucial point is that our federal government has to pay for them out of tax money, and has to make them available to all Americans as basic rights. If Clinton's slogan, "Invest in the American people," means anything, it means this: not only to serve and help the children, but to reduce the crushing anxiety level of all the parents who lie awake in the dark and try to make the life forces add up. It can be done, but it is going to cost plenty, and it's time for the Clinton family, which has impressed so many of us with its honesty, to start being honest about this.

I know my picture of family life today leaves out a deep structure of feeling: nostalgic longing for a self-sufficient family of the past, a family that was everything to us, whose love warmed and enveloped us completely. None of us is free from fantasies like this. For people who grew up in the Great Depression, the Joad family formed a prime nostalgic archetype. (And we shouldn't forget the Goldbergs.) Those who grew up with television are likely to find, twenty and thirty years later, the Walton, Ingalls ("Little House on the Prairie"), Nelson, and Cleaver families playing endless reruns in our brains, peremptorily loud, impossible to evict or turn off. Maybe, so that the fantasies don't drown us, our inner networks need supplements. For our nineteenth- and earlier-twentieth-century time slots, we should add a couple of domestic horror shows like *The Case of Dora* and *The Sound and the Fury*. We could enrich our inner 1950s with a program note—maybe from Stephanie Coontz's recent study, *The Way We Never Were* (Basic Books, 1992)—to say how the GI Bill, FHA housing loans, the federal highway system, and the whole vast cold-war defense economy created a new suburban middle class "far more dependent on government handouts than any so-called 'underclass' in recent U.S. history." Many children of those garden suburbs, who grew up on those comedies, have found themselves in tragic deserts now that the cold-war faucets are being turned off.

I've been disparaging nostalgic fantasies. Yet there is a way in which, regardless of the historical reality, everybody's nostalgic fantasies are right. Unconditional love is the condition we all (or almost all) are in when we're born and in our first few months of life. As grownups, we miss this state of total envelopment, and shouldn't we have the right to? We want to be happy, and nothing makes humans happier than feeling loved. But even if we could have this back somehow, it can't last. From the moment we are born, we are beings who are made to grow. Our parents know we are going to grow, and they want to help us grow: that's part of the way, even in the beginning, the way we're loved. And we are reaching out to grow: even before we know anything, reaching out is the way we love. So, if we want to incorporate family values into our lives, our private lives and our collective life, we've got to think of our families as groups of people who are meant to grow.

Actually, Americans know this, even if they don't know they know it. It's why, in 1992, they so decisively rejected "the family" as a symbol of rigidity and regression. Tomorrow's families are going to have a far wider range of forms than yesterday's. They will be, in John Stuart Mill's wonderful phrase, "experiments in living." Plenty of families are experiments in living today: just take a look at the families out shopping with their children any Saturday on Upper Broadway, or check out your favorite mall. Everybody in these families may not be "blood" relations. The parents may not be married. They may be of different races. They may be of the same sex. There will be a lot more stepparents around, and the stepchildren may belong to different generations. The children may spend time shifting homes. They may not understand the relationships among the adults who are taking care of them. (The adults may not understand them either.) But the grownups out there will be giving *alles fur die kindelech,* and the children of the future will be getting a lot of love.

Race

White Man—Listen!
1957

◆

RICHARD WRIGHT

Richard Wright (1908–1960) was one of America's leading novelists and social critics. His first book, *Uncle Tom's Children* (1938), brought him immediate recognition for his depiction of the South. It was followed two years later by his landmark novel, *Native Son*. His other books include *Black Boy*, *The Outsider*, *The Color Curtain*, and *White Man, Listen!*

So great a legion of ideological interests is choking the media of communication of the world today that I deem it advisable to define the terms in which I speak and for whom. In the heated, charged, and violently partisan atmosphere in which we live at this moment, all public utterances are dragged willy-nilly into the service of something or somebody. Even the most rigorously determined attitudes of objectivity and the most passionate avowals of good faith have come to be suspect. And especially is this true of the expressions of those of us who have been doomed to live and act in a tight web of racial and economic facts, facts viewed by many through eyes of political or religious interest, facts examined by millions with anxiety and even hysteria.

Knowing the suspicious, uneasy climate in which our twentieth-century lives are couched, I, as a Western man of color, strive to be as objective as I can when I seek to communicate. But, at once, you have the right to demand of me: What does being objective mean? Is it possible to speak at all today and not have the meaning of one's words construed in six different ways?

For example, he who advocates the use of mass educational techniques today can be, and usually is, accused of harboring secret Soviet sympathies, despite the fact that his advocacy of the means of mass education aims at a quick spreading of literacy so that communism cannot take root, so that vast populations trapped in tribal or religious loyalties cannot be easily duped by self-seeking demagogues. . . . He who urgently counsels the establishment of strong, central governments in the so-called underdeveloped countries, in the hope that those countries can quickly pull themselves out of the mire and become swiftly modernized and industrialized and thereby set upon the road to democracy, free speech, a secular state, universal suffrage, etc., can be and commonly is stigmatized as: "Well, he's no Communist, *but* . . ." He who would question, with all the good faith in the world, whether the philosophical ideas and assumptions of John Stuart Mill and John Locke are valid for all times, for all peoples, and for all countries with their vastly differing traditions and backgrounds, with the motive of psychologically freeing men's minds so that they can seek new conditions and instrumentalities for freedom, can be indicted as an enemy of democracy. . . .

◆

Confronted with a range of negative hostility of this sort, knowing that the society of the Western world is so frantically defensive that it would seek to impose conformity at any price, what is an honest man to do? Should he keep silent and thereby try to win a degree of dubious safety for himself? Should he endorse static defensiveness as the price of achieving his own personal security? The game isn't worth the candle, for, in doing so, he buttresses that which would eventually crush not only him, but that which would negate the very conditions of life out of which freedom can spring. In such a situation one's silence implies that one has surrendered one's intellectual faculties to fear, that one has voluntarily abdicated life itself, and that one has gratuitously paralyzed one's possibilities of action. Since any and all events can be lifted by men of bad faith out of their normal contexts and projected into others and thus consequently condemned, since one's thoughts can be interpreted in terms of such extreme implications as to reduce them to absurdity or subversion, obviously a mere declaration of one's good intentions is not enough. In an all-pervading climate of intellectual evasion or dishonesty, everything becomes dishonest; suspicion subverts events and distorts their meaning; mental reservations alter the character of facts and rob them of validity and utility. . . . In short, if good will is lacking everything is lost and a dialogue between men becomes not only useless, but dangerous, and sometimes even incriminating.

To imagine that straight communication is no longer possible is to declare that the world we seek to defend is no longer worth defending, that the battle for human freedom is already lost. I'm assuming, however naïvely, that such is not quite yet the case. I cannot, of course, assume that universal goodwill will reign, but I have the elementary right, the bounden duty even, to assume that man, when he has the chance to speak and act without fear, still wishes to be man, that is, he harbors the dream of being a free and creative agent. . . .

◆

Then, first of all, let us honestly admit that there is no such thing as objectivity, no such objective fact as objectivity. Objectivity is a fabricated concept, a synthetic intellectual construction devised to enable others to know the general conditions under which one has done something, observed the world or an event in that world.

So, before proceeding to give my opinions concerning tradition and Industrialization, I shall try to state as clearly as possible where I stand, the mental climate about me, the historic period in which I speak, and some of the elements in my environment and my own personality which propel me to communicate. The basic assumption behind all so-called objective attitudes is this: If others care to assume my mental stance and, through empathy, duplicate the atmosphere in which I speak, if they can imaginatively grasp factors in my environment and a sense of the impulses motivating me, they will, if they are of a mind to, be able to see, more or less, what I've seen, will be capable of apprehending the same general aspects and tones of reality that comprise my world, that world that I share daily with all other men. By revealing the assumptions behind my statements, I'm striving to convert you to my outlook, to its essential humaneness, to the generality and reasonableness of my arguments.

Obviously no striving for an objectivity of attitude is ever complete. Tomorrow, or the day after, someone will discover some fact, some element, or a nuance that I've forgotten to take into account, and, accordingly, my attitude will have to be revised, discarded, or extended, as the case may be. Hence, there is no such thing as an absolute objectivity of attitude. The most rigorously determined attitude of objectivity is, at best, relative. We are human; we are the slaves of our assumptions, of time and circumstance; we are the victims of our passions and illusions; and the most that our critics can ask of us is this: Have you taken your passions, your illusions, your time, and your circumstances into account? That is what I am attempting to do. More than that no reasonable man of goodwill could demand.

First of all, my position is a split one. I'm black. I'm a man of the West. These hard facts are bound to condition, to some degree, my outlook. I see and understand the West; but I also see and understand the non- or anti-Western point of view. How is this possible? This double vision of mine stems from my being a product of Western civilization and from my racial identity, long and deeply conditioned, which is organically born of my being a product of that civilization. Being a Negro living in a white Western Christian society, I've never been allowed to blend, in a natural and healthy manner, with the culture and civilization of the West. This contradiction of being both Western and a man of color creates a psychological distance, so to speak, between me and my environment. I'm self-conscious. I admit it. Yet I feel no need to apologize for it. Hence, though Western, I'm inevitably critical of the West. Indeed, a vital element of my Westernness resides in this chronically skeptical, this irredeemably critical outlook. I'm restless. I question not only myself, but my environment. I'm eager, urgent. And to be so seems natural, human, and good to me. Life without these qualities is inconceivable, less than human. In spite of myself, my imagination is constantly leaping ahead and trying to reshape the world I see (basing itself strictly on the materials of the world in which I live each day) toward a form in which all men could share my creative restlessness. . . . Such an outlook breeds criticism. And my critical attitude and detachment are born of my position. Me and my environment are one, but that oneness has in it, at its very core, an abiding schism. Yet I regard my position as natural, as normal, though others, that is, Western whites, anchored in tradition and habit, would have to make a most strenuous effort of imagination to grasp it.

Yet, I'm not non-Western. I'm no enemy of the West. Neither am I an Easterner. When I look out upon those vast stretches of this earth inhabited by brown, black, and yellow men—sections of the earth in which religion dominates, to the exclusion of almost everything else, the emotional and mental landscape—my reactions and attitudes are those of the West. I see both worlds from another and third point of view. (This outlook has nothing to do with any so-called Third Force; I'm speaking largely in historical and psychological terms.)

I'm numbed and appalled when I know that millions of men in Asia and Africa assign more reality to their dead fathers than to the crying claims of their daily lives: poverty, political degradation, illness, ignorance, etc. I shiver when I learn that the infant-mortality rate, say, in James Town (a slum section of Accra, the capital of the

Gold Coast in British West Africa) is 50 percent in the first year of life; and, further, I'm speechless when I learn that this inhuman condition is explained by the statement, "The children did not wish to stay. Their ghost-mothers called them home. . . ." And when I hear that explanation I know that there can be no altering of social conditions in those areas until such religious rationalizations have been swept from men's minds, no matter how devoutly they are believed in or defended. Indeed, the teeming religions gripping the minds and consciousness of Asians and Africans offend me. I can conceive of no identification with such mystical visions of life that freeze millions in static degradation, no matter how emotionally satisfying such degradation seems to those who wallow in it. But, because the swarming populations in those continents are two-time victims—victims of their own religious projections and victims of Western imperialism—my sympathies are unavoidably with, and unashamedly for, them. For this sympathy I offer no apology.

Yet, when I turn to face the environment that cradled and nurtured me, I experience a sense of dismaying shock, for that Western environment is soaked in and stained with the most blatant racism that the contemporary world knows. . . . It is a racism that has almost become another kind of religion, a religion of the materially dispossessed, of the culturally disinherited. Rooted in my own disinheritedness, I know instinctively that this clinging to, and defense of, racism by Western whites are born of their psychological nakedness, of their having, through historical accident, partially thrown off the mystic cauls of Asia and Africa that once too blinded and dazed them. . . . A deeply conscious victim of white racism could even be strangely moved to compassion for that white man who, having lost his mystic vision of a stern Father God, a dazzling Virgin, and a Dying Son Who promises to succor him after death, settles upon racism . . . ! What a poor substitute! What a shabby, vile, and cheap home the white heart finds when it seeks shelter in racism . . . ! One would think that sheer pride would deter Western whites from such emotional debasement!

I stand, therefore, mentally and emotionally looking in both directions, being claimed by a negative identification on one side, and being excluded by a feeling of repulsion on the other.

◆

Since I'm detached, because of racial conditions, from the West, why do I bother to call myself Western at all? What is it that prompts me to make an identification with the West despite the contradiction involved? The fact is that I really have no choice in the matter. Historical forces more powerful than I am have shaped me as a Westerner. I have not consciously elected to be a Westerner; I have been made into a Westerner. Long before I had the freedom to choose, I was molded a Westerner. It began in childhood. And the process continues.

Hence, standing shoulder to shoulder with the Western white man, speaking his tongue, sharing his culture, participating in the common efforts of the Western community, I say frankly to that white man: "I'm Western, just as Western as you are, maybe more; but I don't completely agree with you."

What do I mean, then, when I say that I'm Western? I shall try to define what the terms mean to me. I shan't here, now, try to define what being Western means to all Westerners. I shall confine my definition only to that aspect of the West with which I identify, that aspect that makes me feel, act, and live Western.

The content of my Westernness resides fundamentally, I feel, in my secular outlook upon life. I believe in a separation of Church and State. I believe that the state possesses a value in and for itself. I feel that man—just sheer brute man just as he is—has a meaning and value over and above all sanctions or mandates from mystical powers, either on high or from below. I am convinced that the humble, fragile dignity of man, buttressed by a tough-souled pragmatism, implemented by methods of trial and error, can sufficiently sustain and nourish human life, can endow it with ample and durable meaning. I believe that all ideas have a right to circulate in the marketplace without restriction. I believe that all men should have the right to have their say without fear of the political "powers that be," without having to dread the punitive measures or the threat of invisible forces which some castes of men claim as their special domain—men such as priests and churchmen. (My own position compels me to grant those priests and churchmen the right to have their say, but not at the expense of having my right to be heard annulled.) I believe that art has its own autonomy, a self-sufficiency that extends beyond, and independent of, the spheres of political or priestly power or sanction. I feel that science exists without any *a priori* or metaphysical assumptions. I feel that human personality is an end in and for itself. In short, I believe that man, for good or ill, is his own ruler, his own sovereign, his own keeper. I hold human freedom as a supreme right and good for all men, my conception of freedom being the right of all men to exercise their natural and acquired powers as long as the exercise of those powers does not hinder others from doing the same.

◆

These are my assumptions, my values, my morality, if you insist upon
that word. Yet I hold these values at a time in history when they are
threatened. I stand in the middle of that most fateful of all the world's
centuries: the Twentieth Century. Nuclear energy, the center of the
sun, is in the hands of men. In most of the land-mass of Asia and
Africa the traditional and customary class relations of feudal, capital-
istic societies have been altered, frequently brutally shattered, by
murder and terror. Most of the governments of the earth today rule,
by one pretext or another, by open or concealed pressure upon the
individual, by blacklists, intimidation, fiat, secret police, and machine guns. Among intellectual circles the globe over, the desperate
question has been raised: "What is man?" In the East as in the West,
wealth and the means of production have been taken out of private
hands, families, clans, and placed at the disposal of committees and
state bureaucrats. The consciousness of most men on earth is filled
with a sense of shame, of humiliation, of memories of past servitude
and degradation—and a sense of fear that those periods of servitude
and degradation will return. The future for most men is an apprehen-
sive void which has created the feeling that it has to be impetuously,
impulsively filled, given a new content at all costs. With the freeing of
Asia and most of Africa from Western rule, more active and unbri-
dled religion now foments and agitates the minds and emotions of
men than at any time since 1453! Man's world today lies in the python-
like coils of vast irrational forces which he cannot control.—This is
the mental climate out of which I speak, a climate that tones my being
and pitches consciousness on a certain plane of tension. These are
the conditions under which I speak, conditions that condition me.

   Now, the above assumptions and facts would and do color my view
of history, that record of the rise and fall of traditions and religions.
All of those past historical forces which have, accidentally or intentionally, helped to create the basis of freedom in human life, I extol,
revere, and count as my fervent allies. Those conditions of life and of
history which thwart, threaten, and degrade the values and assumptions I've listed, I reject and consider harmful, something to be
doggedly resisted. . . .

From a Harlem School
1968

◆

DEBORAH MEIER

Deborah Meier is a member of the *Dissent* editorial board and a 1987 MacArthur Fellow. She is co-director of the Central Park East Secondary School, a New York public high school, and member of the Coalition of Essential Schools, a nationwide network of schools involved in educational reform. She wrote this piece at the start of her teaching career, as a kindergarten teacher at PS 144 in Central Harlem.

For some time now I have been teaching in a Harlem elementary school and trying to understand the attitudes shown by the parents toward the school. Last September, the teacher's strike forced me to speculate on how the hostilities of a minority and the passivity of the majority fit together.

After Labor Day, the season was on for community protest meetings. One night I found myself among a hundred Negro and Puerto Rican women on Manhattan's West Side. I was torn between sympathetic admiration at their determination to do "something" and irritation at the perversity of that "something." Vengefulness and suspicious fury had dulled their ability to distinguish targets. Anything said against schools was guaranteed to produce enthusiastic anger. Speaker after speaker expanded on how the teachers destroyed children, and the audience cheered, stomped, and shouted "You tell 'em!"

At one point, a white mother rose and suggested that she also was bitter about the school system, but she could not, as many speakers had suggested, scab on the teachers. The teachers' demands were of a kind parents had always favored and besides, she said, in the long run weren't teachers needed to rebuild a good system and wouldn't their cooperation be important in any community decentralization? Would we really be any better off if the union were destroyed? At which point one woman shouted out: "No teachers allowed here! We don't want no teachers!"

I slumped down in my seat, since I had been explicitly told that no teachers were allowed, and had come only because I was, after all, the mother of three neighborhood public-school pupils. For the moment it was, fortunately, this other mother who had been mistaken for the spy in their midst. And despite her assurance that she was not a teacher, the audience continued to bait her. A woman shouted furiously, shaking her fist: "Has a teacher ever told you your home was unfit?" The white mother paused, looked forlorn, shook her head sadly, and said, "No . . . you're right, there is no way to communicate." The chairman concluded the white mother's defeat by saying it was pointless to have her remarks translated into Spanish, as was customary.

I left that packed meeting with fear and sadness. How would I work with children whose parents' angers are so intense? And the anger, directed at both the system and the teachers, seemed for the moment logical. Here we are, a nation that has the know-how and wealth to send rockets to Saturn and spend billions in Vietnam. How can we face parents and tell them we cannot teach their children to read properly? In a world becoming hopeless for those with only minimal literacy, this failure is no mere "pity."

In the past the poor "knew their place," and few of them took seriously the idea that they could share in affluence. Now opportunity has been dangled before their eyes, only to prove unavailable in fact—and the resulting frustration is perfectly normal and understandable. Yet the sad truth is that together with this response there are confusions which make things worse still.

The urban Negro poor suffer from a heightened sense of grievance based on four widely held myths. These myths make their problems appear both more grotesque and simpler than the reality.

- First of all, they believe that the lower classes of the past—the immigrants of the early twentieth century who came from rural and deprived European communities—were, unlike Negroes today, given an adequate education which enabled them to "make it" in the mainstream of American society. When Negroes ask for the same, they are told about "cultural deprivation" and "bad speech patterns." But didn't the immigrants suffer from these too? Yes; and precisely these former immigrants are constantly reminding Negroes that they succeeded, after all, despite all these handicaps. "What's wrong with you?" they chide. The Negro community answers, defensively, "But you had a good education, and they won't let us give our children one."

In fact, however, America did not give the lower-class Italian, Pole, or Irishman a good education. Nor did he obtain one. He "made it" not because of his good schooling, but because the expansion of the labor market, the development of new skilled trades, and the organization of unions coincided with the period of mass immigration. Since for him there were no color barriers, the expanding economy helped the immigrant escape from the lower class. Most immigrants or their youngsters got only a sixth- to ninth-grade schooling; the high-school graduate was still in the minority and the college student a novelty. Most were content with basic literacy skills—skills Negroes also obtain today but which we correctly label as totally inadequate. The poor, in fact, are asking the school to do something it has never had to do before, and neither they nor the rest of society realize it.

The myth of education as the great social leveller has been with us so long that it has obscured the historical reality. Only today is the school a crucial factor in obtaining any kind of decent employment. Thus, the intense demands made on the schools by Negroes is paralleled by the fiercest pressures from the middle class on the educational establishment, as social and economic status is more and more tied in with academic success.

♦ A second related myth, often heard in Harlem, is that things used to be better: Harlem schools really used to teach and children really learned in them, Southern segregated schools are superior to Northern ghetto schools, teachers in the South and teachers in the old Harlem were less biased than they are now, etc. In this nostalgia Negroes are forgetting that it was not assumed then that children would remain in school until the twelfth grade, and that simply learning to read and write was then considered sufficient schooling. They are also mistaking the orderliness that used to exist in segregated and thoroughly authoritarian all-Negro schools for a true learning experience. The statistics belie these claims, and we know that the quiet, passive, orderly Negro children were in fact learning almost nothing. But in such environments teachers also appeared less mean and less hostile. And because they were rarely confronted with the anger or rebelliousness of the black student, they were probably less aware of their own biases. Because prejudice was built into the system openly, the teacher's own prejudice could be more disguised.

- ◆ A third myth believed by urban Negroes and Puerto Ricans is that only those of color are deprived of an adequate education. Like my own children, raised in urban interracial neighborhoods where the poor were always black, they basically disbelieve the claim that there are many more poor whites than poor Negroes in America, and that these poor whites are equally powerless and handicapped in school. (It is probably true, however, that poor blacks are more sensitive to educational failure and more motivated to change it.)
- ◆ The fourth myth involves a belief in the omnipotence of American know-how and the complicity of all whites in the "power structure." It is assumed that all whites have access to fairly unlimited power and could, if they chose, do almost anything with it. And teaching seems a simple skill compared to some others white America has conquered. The failure of teachers, most of whom are white, is thus explicable only as a conscious decision not to let black children learn: the "ins" run schools so that they and their kind alone will learn; despised minorities in the past succeeded only when they took over the system and saw to it that teachers didn't get away with not teaching or replaced the "in" teachers with others of their own ethnic background; only when blacks "take over" can the current conspiracy be foiled.

How is this conspiracy now carried out? The logical, simple, "scientific" explanation is easy to see. What, after all, is learning anyway? It's absorbing information and remembering it. If one is made to listen, if one is told true facts, if one is forced to repeat such facts and frequently tested on them, then learning must occur. If learning is not occurring, it follows that the teachers must either not make children listen, or not be telling them the truth, or refusing to make them repeat the correct answers, or failing to test them often enough. Or, if all these techniques fail, the teacher is causing the children to be disruptive so that they can be kicked out altogether.

◆

Mother after mother got up that hot September night on the West Side of Manhattan and repeated bits and pieces of these myths. And the more I heard, the less I felt able to refute. In a world in which the hypocrisy of men in authority seems increasingly clear, it is certainly fitting that those with the most to be angry at should revert to the simplest beliefs about society, history, and the nature of education—beliefs easily understood and resting not on magical thinking but on simple assumptions about cause-and-effect.

I realized that in one form or another I had been hearing these theories for almost a year—ever since I moved to New York City—at one hysterical meeting after another. They were expressed in more traditional "Marxist" terminology by the Progressive Labor Party in a pamphlet widely distributed in the ghetto: *We Must Rule the Schools.* It says, simply, "The rich ruling class wants SERVICE . . . unthinking workers who will be forced to work in low-pay jobs. They want soldiers. They don't want to give our boys and girls good schooling." While the PLP may, for Marxistic reasons, partially exempt workers and union teachers from this conspiracy and place the blame on some abstract "capitalists," the parents transpose this explanation into more concrete personal experience with teachers.

It was this approach that made the parents shout with approval when one white leader of EQUAL said: "Once we go into the schools during the strike we will take over the classes; it will be us who will be in charge when that teacher decides to come back. And let them try to get us out! We'll stay and we'll see that they teach!" When I asked her afterward whether she expected any good teacher could be effective in such a parent-run classroom, subjected to such humiliating working conditions, she answered, "Why not? Is there something wrong with working for these parents? Aren't they good enough for the teachers? If the parents were middle-class, would the teachers be so horrified? The parents won't be doing the teaching, after all; we know we need experts for that. The parent's job is just telling the teacher when and what to teach—the how is up to her." Mothers in Westchester and Queens and mothers in private schools, she claimed, already are doing just this.

What the parents in the slums fail to realize is that parents in good suburban schools (of course there are bad ones run according to this EQUAL mother's fantasy) know how to organize schools so that professionals, in fact, have very great freedom. Because the professionals respect the general range of social values that are part of their students' world and succeed in producing students who succeed in that world, there is not the same distrust of professionalism and professional power.

The dispute over decentralization reflects the same mythology. "We

must use our children as a whip to crack over the heads of professionals," said a sober statement passed without protest by a well-attended
meeting of the West Side Committee for Decentralization. The rest of
the statement denounced all the fancy explanations for learning failure and placed responsibility where "it belonged": on teachers.
Speaker after speaker got up to expand upon the statement's denunciation of the UFT on the issue of "disruptive children." They declared
with certainty that there were no disruptive children, "just disruptive
teachers." No psychologists, guidance workers, or social workers are
needed in our schools, said EQUAL chairman Rosalie Stutz (who had
some otherwise perceptive things to say about the schools). Just teach
them to read and stop psychologizing them, she declared. Psychological problems do not handicap learning, they are merely the result of
bad teaching. Children who know how to read and write properly
(which she also tends to see as the only proper function of the school)
will not cause trouble. (And, of course, it is undeniable that the failure of ghetto schools to teach and the anger, chaos, and bias present
in such schools does harm children psychologically.)

Manhattan's West Side, Bedford-Stuyvesant, East Harlem, Central
Harlem—all were rife in September with new *ad hoc* organizations,
formed to represent parents and the community and organized
around antiteacher and prodecentralization slogans. The names of
the leaders were often familiar and the same ones popped up many
times over. A United Federation of Parents was organized by Rev-
erend Milton Galamison for the express purpose of keeping an eye
on teachers and textbooks. Most were paper groups, lasting only for a
meeting or two, producing new steering committees, resolutions,
and press releases. But in shouting out that something is rotten in
our school system, they spoke, I felt sure, for something deeply felt in
Harlem, Spanish Harlem, and even in anxious, increasingly suspicious middle-class communities.

The night before the strike began all of this seemed crystal clear
and inescapably sensible to me. I dreaded going to Central Harlem,
where I taught and where I would be easily identifiable as a teacher
(white women in Harlem are generally either teachers or social workers). While I wholeheartedly supported the UFT and felt proud of the
teachers for going out on nonwage demands, their position seemed
impossible to communicate to the people who most needed just what
the UFT was demanding.

◆

Yet, when I came to Lenox Avenue to join my picket line, I found a normal atmosphere, the same casual friendliness or indifference of past years, neither more intense nor more angry, although more confused.

And the relationships I developed with the parents of my students had never begun more favorably. When I called upon parents for help in arranging an emergency program, I got my share of evasively pleasant and polite answers—"anything you say, teacher." As I talked on the phone I heard, in one case, some abusive remarks in the background about where teachers belonged, while the mother politely assured me she was all for the teachers and the Union. But during the next three weeks, as our program got under way, many parents worked with me; they spent time and money helping the class, in a way I had never before experienced.

My students come mostly from families on welfare, yet several parents offered financial assistance during the strike. While on the picket line, while riding in Harlem subways, while walking down Lenox Avenue to school, I saw no angry looks, heard no angry words. I spent three weeks walking the streets with children—bringing them to and from their homes, playing with them in various parks, and visiting area stores—and there were no incidents. Many who remembered me from the year before greeted me warmly. The cluster of unemployed men on the corner of Lenox Avenue engaged in their usual passing comments: "How're the kids behaving today?" "If they get out of line, just tell me." "How about teaching me to read?" It was no different this year, although it was clear I was a teacher on strike. And my experience was not unique or based on a special personal reputation. It was the experience of most of the teachers at my school and most of those I knew who worked in Harlem. There were of course a number of well-publicized exceptions, in places such as IS 201.

Despite all the claims about how the parents were going to man the schools and begin their "takeover" during the strike, few black volunteers showed up. (Antiunion efforts in conservative white neighborhoods also had difficulty producing volunteer scabs on any regular basis.) Most of the volunteers who did show up were not black militants but appeared to be the usual middle-class Harlem ladies who thought all strikes a disgrace, or retired teachers who believed striking was "unprofessional." Most of the parents shied away from all trouble, routinely condemning all parties concerned. The majority, for example, did not take advantage of the Emergency or Freedom Schools set up by the union teachers, but neither did they send their children to the regular schools unless desperate for baby-sitting.

While antiwhite feeling in Harlem is surely on the increase and probably no Negro is immune from it, still it was the parents at Harlem's PS 175, and not the Board of Education, the UFT, or the white principal, who decided that Ralph Poynter and his able promoter Queen Mother Moore (one of the newly fashionable spokesmen for black power—a witty, perceptive, oratorically skilled evangelist) did not represent them. It was they who roundly repudiated Poynter's attempt to take over the school on behalf of black parent power and black male power. They voted him out of his self-appointed principalship (which the TV cameras helped promote) and reappointed the white principal.

Despite the furor at IS 201, the parents at 201 and its four feeder schools were not often heard from or seen. They were not the ones who shoved and kicked other parents or threatened teachers. They remained in the background, uneasy, frightened, sometimes protesting, and perhaps sometimes vicariously pleased at the actions of the black nationalists. Even months later, however, when the much-publicized elections for the governing board of IS 201 were held, less than a third of the twelve hundred parents from the five schools who had registered to vote actually did so.

While the West Side Committee for Decentralization—an amalgam of black and Puerto Rican nationalists, just plain angry parents, and more moderate school "reformers"—held meetings of hundreds in September, today its meetings are poorly attended. A few months ago the attendance was primarily Negro and Puerto Rican; today it is mostly the white middle-class parents who still show up and vie among themselves for the support of the few nonwhites present (who in confusion often drift away altogether).

The mothers who were so angry in September are no doubt still unhappy. But for them the concerns of daily life must take priority, and bitterness that leads to no immediate change in the scenery of life cannot long be sustained at fever pitch.

The average parent in Harlem remains inactive in regard to school issues, and if he becomes active, it is still in the more traditional Parent Associations which, despite poor participation, probably involve more parents than all the black-power groups combined. The average PA meeting is a quiet and ineffective affair indeed, with desperate PA presidents trying to produce life, stir discussion, get new parents to volunteer for office, hold cake sales and arrange for class pictures, organize polite luncheons for the teachers, get along with principals, and occasionally to agitate on some issue.

Principals in Harlem now are more tense and teachers more wary. They feel that parents are more likely than in the past to raise a fuss if a child claims to have been hit or pushed, if children are not getting enough homework, if a fight breaks out in the school yard, if the teacher is not sending home the proper change from the milk money, if a child is transferred to another class or placed in a special program without properly notifying the parents, or, of course, if children are suspended from school.

◆

While the majority of parents in Harlem repudiated their more militant leaders by not volunteering as scabs and by maintaining a semi-friendly or neutral posture toward the teachers, it would be a mistake to assume that the hostile response was symptomatic only of a mad minority or that it is a put-up job of "outside agitators."

There were moments those first few weeks of school when I did wonder whether I had been completely fooled and deceived by those hysterical parents at hysterical meetings. The parents I knew personally seemed so reasonable and communicative. But I soon concluded that the hysteria was not unrepresentative of parent attitudes even at my seemingly calm school.

For some of my friendliest parents responded with approval, nodding their head and adding their own points, to stories repeated to them about those angry speeches of the EQUAL and CORE leaders. They sometimes smiled in open pleasure at the antiteacher denunciations, even as they added their own qualifiers. They were almost totally confused about the ruckus going on at IS 201, but they were clearly open to believing the worst about the school system. The angry leaders speak, I believe, to something deep within all Harlem parents—those whose anger runs over into a kind of desperate paranoia, and those whose "sense of proportion" prevents them from rude behavior, who still want to "get along," whether from apathy or hope.

The feelings of the extremists are, I believe, shared by the vast majority. The vast majority is merely unwilling or unable to deal with life on these extreme and frightening terms.

Part of this I knew from years of teaching in ghetto schools in New York and Chicago. Like most teachers I remember how shocked I was at first when parents would tell me that I had their permission to beat their child for the slightest infraction. Still others, too intimidated themselves to enter the school, would nevertheless "support" the teachers by harshly punishing their children if the teacher sent home a disapproving note. Few parents ever seemed to listen to their own child's version of school life. They turned a deaf ear, it seemed to me, to the legitimate anxieties, fears, and defeats that their children daily underwent in our school system. What they seemed to tell their children was:

> Don't come to me for support. Don't complain to me about injustice. Don't expect me to appeal your case to any higher authorities. I don't like or trust them myself. But if I responded to my likes and dislikes, I'd have to tear this world apart. All that would accomplish would be to endanger you and myself without the slightest chance of changing things for the better. The white folks have the power; the teachers represent them. Learn what you can from them, pick up any tricks they can teach you. Stay in line and, at all costs, avoid trouble. If trouble comes, you are always wrong. That's what life is all about. If the school teaches you only that, it's worth it, and you might as well learn it young, when the penalties for making a mistake are less severe.

This may have been an apt approach to coping with survival in the South, even though its psychological and intellectual toll was incalculable. But times have changed. The penalties are less murderous. Yesterday's children are today's parents. And they grew up not in the South but in the North, where such an attitude can be disastrous.

There appear to be three general responses to the ghetto-school problem. There are those who remain passive, motivated by the old fear of trouble. Underneath they may identify with the anger, but many are probably unable to express it even to themselves and have buried their rage beneath an apathetic view of life. A second group can no longer bear to see another generation destroyed. But they have been embittered, if not altogether shattered, by the present collapse of the nonviolent integrationist movement. If that beautiful new world we used to sing about cannot be created, at least they are determined that those who have made them and their children suffer will henceforth suffer too. No longer will only black people be humiliated in our schools—let teachers experience a little humiliation too. Still many others, sometimes confused with the passive, at other times with the "extremists," are parents who cling to hope and cannot, at least as yet, accept mere vengeance. While they do not dissociate themselves from the black-power extremists, they are still "victims" of a hope that something less than complete destruction might suffice. Their desire for a less racially bitter world for their youngsters makes them willing to work with their children's teachers in order to produce a better school system.

The attempt neatly to define who is who and which group is bigger or smaller is probably impossible and even useless. What the UFT does, what white Americans do, and what the city and federal government decide the next few years will be decisive in pushing black parents one way or another.

The New Black Intellectuals
1969

◆

MARTIN KILSON

Martin Kilson, a member of the *Dissent* editorial board, is professor of government at Harvard and a leading authority on American and African politics. His books include *Political Awakening of Africa, Key Issues in the Afro-American Experience,* and, with Clement Cottingham, *African Autocracy: Political Development in Third World States.*

The Negro Intelligentsia in the United States has recently faced several critical points in its evolution. These crises have been both sociological—including a new social composition, shifting intellectual activities, a changing relationship to whites—and indirectly political, as the Negro lower classes express their violent estrangement through urban riots and demand black separatism or nationalist political leadership.

These two dimensions are intimately related; for it is the addition of persons from the lower classes that has changed the social composition of the Negro intelligentsia and led to the pressure for nationalism or separatism. As this composition changes, there are new claimants to Negro leadership, who transform traditional emphases within the black intellectual community. Formerly, activities were carried out through the NAACP, the Negro Medical Association, or other professional groups; at Negro colleges; and in closely knit groups of middle- to upper-class literati (e.g., the Harlem Renaissance movement of the 1920s and 30s). Now, intellectual activity is found more and more on the street corner, among popular groups with charismatic leaders, or in community organizations—often funded by the Office of Economic Opportunity. This shift is not complete; but it already indicates a major change in the character of the black intelligentsia.

A black intelligentsia first appeared in the United States during the late nineteenth century. From then until almost the present day, the middle and upper class of the Negro community formed the main social base of this group. An illustration is the data we have on forty Negro writers who were members of the Harlem Renaissance movement: 55 percent came from professional homes and 45 percent from solid middle-class, white-collar families. Persons of similar background dominated law, medicine, college teaching, and other professions. In as much as the social structure of the Negro intelligentsia conditioned its intellectual style and ideology, a pragmatic intellectual style and political outlook prevailed. Because of the racism in American life, Negro professionals practiced largely within an all-Negro context: lawyers and doctors, for example, had their own law and medical associations, which serviced their members in dealing with white society. As a rule, these associations were viewed as stop-gap or transitory agencies, for Negro doctors and lawyers hoped ultimately to integrate, both as professionals and members of the middle class, into white institutions.

Only a few significant tendencies toward deviant or antiestablishment behavior could be found among the Negro intelligentsia during the years between the world wars, and these were displayed almost exclusively by writers, artists, and a few college teachers. The lawyers, doctors, dentists, engineers, clergymen, and other professionals remained generally unaffected by these trends. Dependent upon and accepting the roles provided by the white establishment, they were less free to participate in oppositional movements. Writers and artists, on the other hand, were quite independent of the establishment for their livelihood. A few had independent means—often provided by fathers who were lawyers, doctors, engineers—others earned enough from published works and artistic performances. Some had lucrative patrons: wealthy whites, or white radical movements, for example, the Communist Party. As a result, they could experiment with new, and self-determined, intellectual trends. From the 1920s through the 1940s the most important of such trends was the movement toward a race-conscious literature and art—the objectives of the Harlem Renaissance movement, also known as the New Negro Movement. Through the folkways of blacks, the New Negro Movement sought to redefine the meaning of Negro life in particular and human existence in general. Intellectually, it owed much to Paul Lawrence Dunbar, whose novels and poetry drew heavily upon Negro folk material, in speech, lore, humor, and wit.

Politically, the New Negro Movement was diffuse, with few goals, though a few writers participated in both the Communist and Socialist movements. Rather curiously, the New Negro Movement remained independent of another racialist movement, formed by Marcus Garvey during World War I, which *was* political. There were several reasons for this: The Garvey movement, officially called the Universal Negro Improvement Association, depended heavily on a charismatic leadership that was not disposed to let intellectuals play an independent or critical role. Garvey, who designated himself Provisional President of Africa, possessed a strong ego and nursed intellectual ambitions of his own. Though he had little formal training, Garvey wrote numerous pamphlets and articles on historical, cultural, and political issues relating to Negroes. To leaders of the New Negro Movement, Garvey seemed like something of an upstart, gifted but half literate, who had chanced upon an important cause. Alain Locke, the finest theoretical thinker in the New Negro Movement, remarked in 1926 that "Garveyism may be a transient, if spectacular, phenomenon, but the possible role of the American Negro in the future development of Africa is one of the most constructive and universally helpful missions that any modern people can lay claim to."

Conflicts in social outlook and style also kept the New Negro Movement at a distance from Garveyism. The Garvey movement was led by small businessmen. It was pretty much a petty-bourgeois phenomenon, and far less interested in the intellectual claims of black nationalism than in using black awareness in order to achieve concrete economic gains.

On the other hand, the intellectuals in the New Negro Movement, though mainly from middle-class families, were antibourgeois in outlook: some sympathized with the anticapitalist sentiments then widespread among American intellectuals, and others looked down upon economics and politics as too mundane. The latter group of black intellectuals saw it as their mission to help their fellow blacks alter their self-image. As James Weldon Johnson put it in his poem "To America":

> How would you have us, as we are?
> Or sinking 'neath the load we bear,
> Our eyes fixed forward on a star,
> Or gazing empty at despair?

When members of the New Negro Movement did occasionally assume a political posture they did so through white radical politics rather than Garveyism or its offshoots.

By the end of World War II the first two major militant racialist movements among Negroes had no effective links. It is this failure of the New Negro Movement to connect with the more popular and political nationalism of the Garvey movement that sharply distinguishes the prewar Negro intellectuals from their present equivalents. Today a sizable segment of the Negro intelligentsia is at the center of, or at least responding to, a popular black-nationalist movement that often releases xenophobic attitudes toward white society.

◆

In the past decade there has been a powerful thrust toward a fusion of the two currents of black ethnocentrism inherited from the pre–World War II era. The basis of this tendency has been a generic change, which was both sociological and ideological, in the Negro intelligentsia. The ranks of the Negro intelligentsia have been extended, almost willy-nilly, to include a new set of persons, men and women who hitherto would hardly have been called "intellectuals." They may be described, for want of a better term, as "paraintellectuals": self-made intellectuals, lacking for the most part formal education in literature, the expressive arts, and the liberal and technical or scientific professions.

These "paraintellectuals," now a major force in the Negro intelligentsia, are largely upper-lower-class, though sometimes lower-middle-class in background. They possess at best secondary schooling, and more commonly are drop-outs from high school. But they are usually persons of high talent, and they display a high degree of motivation within the context of Negro lower-class culture. In general, they are adept at verbal and other skills, which enables them to become what may be called "cultural celebrities" within the Negro lower class.

Their occupational careers before their debut as "paraintellectuals" are quite varied and carry high prestige within the Negro lower class. These occupations include "hustling" roles: pimp, numbers writer, narcotics pusher, etc. Other occupations of Negro "paraintellectuals" are rather more conventional: petty shopkeeper, poolroom operator, storefront preacher.

The entry of these paraintellectuals into the ranks of the black intelligentsia is mainly the direct result of the urban riots of 1964 and, later, an expression of Negro outrage against racist restrictions in American society. Though a handful of paraintellectuals had surfaced before these events (e.g., Malcolm X, Louis X, and others who were transformed into paraintellectuals by way of the Black Muslim movement), they were exceptions. Only after the first flush of urban riots in 1964 did a large stratum of persons distinguishable as paraintellectuals emerge. Every American city with a sizable Negro population (say 10 percent or more) has experienced the rise of such a stratum. In Boston, Guido St. Laurent emerged as founder and leader of NEGRO (New England Grass Roots Organization); in San Francisco there was Eldridge Cleaver, a leader of the Black Panther Party. These two newcomers to the black intelligentsia had occupational careers like others of their group, and as a result of these careers had spent time in prison.

The revolutionary implications of the entry into the Negro intelligentsia of men like Malcolm X, Louis X, and Eldridge Cleaver are clear enough. Until recently, if movement of lower-class blacks into the intelligentsia occurred at all, high-school education was the minimum and college education the usual requirement. Thus the rise of what I have termed black paraintellectuals represents a hitherto unknown stratum not only within the black but also within the white intelligentsia.

◆

Tension and conflict are unavoidable in this kind of structural change. Unlike the established elements in the Negro intelligentsia, the paraintellectuals share a cultural experience similar to that of the black lower classes. They share too, as Claude Brown's *Manchild In the Promised Land* shows, the lower classes' brutalizing experience with the coercive arm of white-controlled cities, especially the police power. These common experiences enabled the paraintellectuals to be spokesmen for the Negro masses as they emerged into a militant politicalization through riots. The paraintellectuals came onto the scene as legitimate and *natural* leaders. Moreover, they advance the politicalization of the black urban masses, after a fashion, by formulating cathartic descriptions of black-white relations, past and present, and policies for altering these relations that the Negro lower class finds meaningful. Few of the established elements among the black intelligentsia have, until very recently, had such success.

As a result, the paraintellectuals pose a major crisis for the established Negro intelligentsia. Several resolutions of the crisis are available to the established intelligentsia: (1) It could leave the emergent militant politics in the hands of the paraintellectuals, concentrating instead on broadening and consolidating traditional roles made available through the moderate politics of the civil-rights movement. (2) It could compete with the paraintellectuals for leadership of the new nationalist militancy, adopting or fabricating a lower-class-oriented black militancy of its own. (3) It could join forces with the paraintellectuals, more or less on the latter's terms.

These strategies, with one or another variation, have recently characterized the responses of the established Negro intelligentsia. In general, the upper strata of the black intelligentsia (lawyers, doctors, dentists, college teachers, large-scale entrepreneurs) tend to avoid competing with the paraintellectuals in manipulating nationalist or antiwhite militancy and violent rhetoric. Instead, they persist in a commitment to nonracialist approaches to political and social change for Negroes.

Yet the upper strata of the Negro intelligentsia also increasingly display interest in the nationalist militancy of the paraintellectuals, insofar as they hope such militancy will impress upon the white power structure the need to open greater opportunities to blacks. Indeed, some members of the established Negro intelligentsia (notably businessmen, city civil servants, and others whose careers may be readily advanced through politics) have gone so far as to adopt or simulate a nationalist militancy of their own. They hope thereby to bring their own needs and interests more forcefully to the attention of the white power structure.

Furthermore, when the white power structure concedes new roles and benefits to the politically active segments of the established Negro intelligentsia as a result of antiwhite militancy, these segments perceive an additional use for militancy: it enables them to appear legitimate in the eyes of the urban black lower class.

Such militant-linked legitimacy is necessary in view of the paraintellectuals' new role as the *natural* leaders of the black city-dwellers. The paraintellectuals virtually control the terms according to which legitimacy in the urban black community is defined, and it is very difficult for other black leadership groups to ignore these criteria. It can therefore be expected that the politically active segments of the established Negro intelligentsia will continue for some time to utilize a variant of antiwhite militancy as one of their political weapons.

Indeed, some groups among the established Negro intelligentsia have operationalized a militant antiwhite posture, one as genuine as that of the paraintellectuals. This militancy is displayed most often by schoolteachers, writers, and artists, and it results partly from the intellectual persuasion of paraintellectuals like Malcolm X and Eldridge Cleaver. Some black writers and artists also have utilitarian ends in mind when they convert to militancy: new opportunities are more readily conceded by the white power structure in artistic and literary fields, particularly among liberal whites, when confronted by Negro militancy.

Another important characteristic of that portion of the Negro intelligentsia that inclines toward the nationalist rhetoric of the paraintellectuals and is a sociological tie with the black lower classes. During the past decade we have seen a sizable increase of college-trained black teachers, writers, and artists who enter the Negro intelligentsia, yet their roots in the black lower-class community remain strong. It was largely among such persons that men like Malcolm X first found their audience, for it was among them that a sense of outrage could be articulated with some freedom and coherence. They were drawn to the readiness of Malcolm X to say things that they might feel too but hesitate to express. And as urban riots became a regular feature of the political expression of the black lower classes, these teachers, writers, and artists were the first within the Negro intelligentsia to welcome this mode of attack on the white power structure.

Indeed, antiwhite violence in general is now celebrated by growing numbers. It is seen as serving a dual function: validating Negro manhood and forcing concessions from white institutions. In several cities, especially New York, some teachers, writers, and artists have joined forces with the paraintellectuals in disseminating a veritable cult of violence. Negro teachers, moreover, will have an increasingly important role in this development: for, as ghetto school districts come under Negro control through administrative decentralization, a cult of violence might well be enshrined in the curriculum of many black ghetto schools.

◆

Right now we are too close to the processes of change and crisis in the Negro intelligentsia to know precisely what future trends will be. Patterns of militancy that appear immutable might well turn out to be merely ephemeral or tactical postures. Some paraintellectuals, the catalytic agents of black militance and violent rhetoric, have already modified their militancy in exchange for concessions from the white power structure. As they are co-opted into the power structure by assuming influential and well-paying roles in the plethora of community organizations funded by the Office of Economic Opportunity or on governing boards of the Model Cities program, the propensity of some paraintellectuals toward militancy and violent rhetoric seems to diminish. This is especially true in cities where the paraintellectuals feel secure about co-optation into the power structure. Whether this sense of security prevails depends upon the intensity and form of competition both among paraintellectuals, and between them and the established Negro intelligentsia.

Most questionable here is the assumption of many black-nationalist students that the validation of Negro manhood and culture through black-controlled Afro-American studies programs on white campuses is more "relevant" than the acquisition of professional skills. What, then, will be the long-run outcome of this development? At best the nationalist linkage of Negro self-identification and militance on white campuses will produce a generation of college-trained blacks who will be highly motivated to return to the urban black community to advance its fortune. At worst, this development will produce, for many college-educated blacks, a vicious psychological dependence upon antiwhite violent rhetoric. Moreover, their perception of the black community's basic needs (which are, mainly, more skills and resources in order to participate effectively in our society) will be pathetically distorted. And such faulty perception will in turn help perpetuate black-nationalist political posturing and sporadic unrest as substitutes for serious politics.

The worst, however, need not occur. The new Negro intelligentsia will no doubt be militant in racial outlook and political style; but its use of militancy will probably be tempered by practical considerations. Like it or not, the militants' goal of black social and economic advancement—even along black-separatist lines—can be realized only through such structures as political parties, pressure groups, trade unions, professional associations, and the like. As the new militants in the Negro intelligentsia adapt their aims to institutionalized structures and processes, the therapeutic and normless features of black militancy will be filtered out or neutralized; they will, in a word, be reduced to mere trappings of the political process, though symbolically important ones.

This development, however, will depend upon the emergence within the new Negro intelligentsia of political leaders skilled at redirecting into viable political channels the enormous energy now wasted by black nationalists in political posturing or role-playing. Fortunately, such politicians are already surfacing. The paraintellectuals, particularly those organized in the Black Panther Party, represent one type of Negro leader potentially capable of facilitating the political institutionalization of black nationalism. Based in West Coast cities like Oakland and San Francisco and rapidly spreading to Midwestern and Eastern cities, the Black Panther Party (BPP) is mostly a secular variant of the Black Muslim movement. Like the Black Muslims, the BPP seeks the transformation or rebirth of the Negro personality. But it shuns the religious forms of the Black Muslims, seeking legitimacy instead through assertive or violent political action. Violence, rhetorical or actual, had a special role in the early phase of the BPP because the idea of black renascence was rooted in the paraintellectuals' need to link Negro self-identification with violence. Thus the BPP's early political acts invariably entailed confrontation with such features of the white power structure in urban ghettos as the police and the courts.

Currently, however, the BPP is entering a second phase of political development, including organization among Negro workers, community development activity, campus organization, and some electoral activity. But it is doubtful that the limited educational and technical skills possessed by the paraintellectual leaders of the BPP will allow it to evolve very far in this new direction without outside aid from more skilled groups. This is already recognized by some BPP leaders who have sought the assistance of middle-class white radicals and their organizations, such as the Progressive Labor Party and the Peace and Freedom Party. But inasmuch as the BPP is sensitive to the need to remain legitimate in the eyes of the growing segment of lower-class blacks who are hostile to whites, it must obtain a large part of the skills required by its new political development from Negroes themselves.

At this point enter the established Negro intelligentsia as the source of the second type of black politician able to facilitate the political institutionalization of black nationalism. A new crop of professionally educated black politicians is now emerging in urban ghettos—and the growth of this group seems certain as more Negroes enter and complete college. Lawyers currently predominate in the new group of Negro professional politicians; Hatcher in Gary, Stokes in Cleveland, Thomas Atkins in Boston, Conyers in Detroit, and Tom Bradley in Los Angeles are among the best. These men are fashioning a black-militant style of their own, within the established framework of urban politics: and as they perfect the assimilation of a black ethnicity to the basic patterns of American politics, they may prove legitimate recipients of alliance with such paraintellectual elements as the Black Panther Party.

Such an alliance could well be mutually beneficial: the paraintellectuals will derive from it the professional skills and relationships they badly need; the professional politicians will acquire greater legitimacy in the eyes of the black lower class, as well as valuable political workers. It is an alliance that will not, of course, proceed without conflict, either between the parties to it or between them and the white power structure. (Hatcher's experience in Gary illustrates both forms of conflict.) But it is a feasible alliance, with political possibilities, not the least of which is lending political order to the Negro intelligentsia's endeavor to offer new leadership to the crisis-ridden black ghetto.

Blackness Without Blood
1989

◆

HENRY LOUIS GATES, JR.

Henry Louis Gates, Jr., is W. E. B. Du Bois Professor of the Humanities
and chairman of the Afro-American Studies Department of Harvard University. He is both a MacArthur Fellow and the winner of a 1989 American Book Award. His books include *Figures in Black, The Signifying
Monkey, Loose Canons: Notes on the Culture Wars,* and *Colored People: A Memoir.*

The question of color takes up much space in these pages, but the
question of color, especially in this country, operates to hide the graver
questions of the self.

—JAMES BALDWIN, 1961

... blood, darky, Tar Baby, Kaffir, shine ... moor, blackamoor, Jim
Crow, spook ... quadroon, meriney, red bone, high yellow ... Mammy,
porch monkey, home, homeboy, George ... spearchucker, schwarze,
Leroy, Smokey ... mouli, buck, Ethiopian, brother, sistah ...

—TREY ELLIS, 1989

I had forgotten the incident completely, until I read Trey Ellis's essay,
"Remember My Name," in a recent issue of the *Village Voice* (June 13,
1989). But there, in the middle of an italicized list of the by-names of
"the race" ("the race" or "our people" being the terms my parents
used in polite or reverential discourse, "jigaboo" or "nigger" more
commonly used in anger, jest, or pure disgust) it was: "George." Now
the events of that very brief exchange return to mind so vividly that I
wonder why I had forgotten it.

My father and I were walking home at dusk from his second job. He "moonlighted" as a janitor in the evenings for the telephone company. Every day but Saturday, he would come home at three-thirty from his regular job at the paper mill, wash up, eat supper, then at four-thirty head downtown to his second job. He used to make jokes frequently about a union official who moonlighted. I never got the joke, but he and his friends thought it was hilarious. All I knew was that my family always ate well, that my brother and I had new clothes to wear, and that all of the white people in Piedmont, West Virginia, treated my parents with an odd mixture of resentment and respect that even we understood at the time had something directly to do with a small but certain measure of financial security.

He had left a little early that evening, because I was with him and I had to be in bed early. I could not have been more than five or six, and we had stopped off at the Cut-Rate Drug Store (where no black person in town but my father could sit down to eat, and eat off real plates with real silverware) so that I could buy some caramel ice cream, two scoops in a wafer cone, please, which I was busy licking when Mr. Wilson walked by.

Mr. Wilson was a very quiet white man, whose stony, brooding, silent manner seemed designed to scare off any overtures of friendship, even from white people. He was Irish, as was one-third of our village (another third being Italian), the more affluent among whom sent their children to "Catholic School" across the bridge in Maryland. He had white straight hair, like my Uncle Joe, whom he uncannily resembled, and he carried a black worn metal lunch pail, the kind that Riley carried on the television show. My father always spoke to him, and for reasons that we never did understand, he always spoke to my father.

"Hello, Mr. Wilson," I heard my father say.

"Hello, George."

I stopped licking my ice-cream cone, and asked my Dad in a loud voice why Mr. Wilson had called him "George."

"Doesn't he know your name, Daddy? Why don't you tell him your name? Your name isn't George."

For a moment I tried to think of who Mr. Wilson was mixing Pop up with. But we didn't have any Georges among the colored people in Piedmont; nor were there colored Georges living in the neighboring towns and working at the mill.

"Tell him your name, Daddy."

"He knows my name, boy," my father said after a long pause. "He calls all colored people George."

A long silence ensued. It was "one of those things," as my Mom would put it. Even then, that early, I knew when I was in the presence of "one of those things," one of those things that provided a glimpse, through a rent curtain, at another world that we could not affect but that affected us. There would be a painful moment of silence, and you would wait for it to give way to a discussion of a black superstar such as Sugar Ray or Jackie Robinson.

"Nobody hits better in a clutch than Jackie Robinson."

"That's right. Nobody."

I never again looked Mr. Wilson in the eye.

◆

But I loved the names that we gave ourselves when no white people were around. And I have to confess that I have never really cared too much about what we called ourselves publicly, except when my generation was fighting the elders for the legitimacy of the word "black" as our common, public name. "I'd rather they called me 'nigger,' " my Uncle Raymond would say again and again. "I can't *stand* the way they say the word 'black.' And, by the way," he would conclude, his dark-brown eyes flashing as he looked with utter disgust at my tentative Afro, "when are you going to get that nappy shit *cut?*"

There was enough in our public name to make a whole generation of Negroes rail against our efforts to legitimize, to naturalize, the word "black." Once we were black, I thought, we would be free, inside at least, and maybe from inside we would project a freedom outside of ourselves. "Free your mind," the slogan went, "and your behind will follow." Still, I value those all-too-rare, precious moments when someone "slips," in the warmth and comfort of intimacy, and says the dreaded words: "Was he colored?"

I knew that there was power in our name, enough power that the prospect frightened my maternal uncles. To open the "Personal Statement" for my Yale admission application in 1968, I had settled upon the following: "My grandfather was colored, my father is Negro, and I am black." (If that doesn't grab them, I thought, then nothing will.) I wonder if my daughters, nine years hence, will adapt the line, identifying themselves as "I am an African American." Perhaps they'll be Africans by then, or even feisty rapper-dappers. Perhaps, by that time, the most radical act of naming will be a return to "colored."

I began to learn about the meanings of blackness—or at least how to give voice to what I had experienced—when I went off to Yale. The class of 1973 was the first at Yale to include a "large" contingent of Afro-Americans, the name we quickly and comfortably seized upon at

New Haven. Like many of us in those years, I gravitated to courses in Afro-American studies, at least one per semester, despite the fact that I was premed, like almost all the other black kids at Yale—that is, until the ranks were devastated by organic chemistry. (The law was the most common substitute.) The college campus, then, was a refuge from explicit racism, freeing us to read and write about our "racial" selves, to organize for recruitment of minority students and faculty, and to demand the constitutional rights of the Black Panther Party for self-defense—an action that led, at New Haven at least, to a full-fledged strike in April of 1970, two weeks before Nixon and Kissinger invaded Cambodia. The campus was our sanctuary, where we could be as black as the ace of spades and nobody seemed to mind.

Today the white college campus is a rather different place. Black studies, where it has survived—and it has survived only at those campuses where someone believed enough in its academic integrity to insist upon a sound academic foundation—is entering its third decade. More black faculty members are tenured than ever before, despite the fact that only eight hundred or so black students took the doctorate in 1986, and fully half of these were in education. Yet, for all the gains that have been made, racial tensions on college campuses appear to be on the rise, with a monitoring group finding incidents, reported at over 175 colleges since the 1986–87 academic year (and this is just counting the ones that made the papers). The dream of the university as a haven of racial equity, as an ultimate realm beyond the veil, has not been realized. Racism on our college campuses has become a palpable, ugly thing.

Even I—despite a highly visible presence as a faculty member at Cornell—have found it necessary to cross the street, hum a tune, or smile, when confronting a lone white woman in a campus building or on the Commons late at night. (Once a white coed even felt it necessary to spring from an elevator that I was about to enter, in the very building where my department was housed.) Nor can I help but feel some humiliation as I try to put a white person at ease in a dark place on campus at night, coming from nowhere, confronting that certain look of panic in their eyes, trying to think grand thoughts like Du Bois but—for the life of me looking to them like Willie Horton. Grinning, singing, scratching my head, I have felt like Steppin Fetchit with a Ph.D. So much for Yale; so much for Cambridge.

◆

The meanings of blackness are vastly more complex, I suspect, than they ever have been before in our American past. But how to explain?

I have often imagined encountering the ghost of the great Du Bois, riding on the shoulders of the Spirit of Blackness.

"Young man," he'd say, "what has happened in my absence? Have things changed?"

"Well, sir," I'd respond, "your alma mater, Fair Harvard, has a black-studies department, a Du Bois Research Center, and even a Du Bois Professor of History. Your old friend Thurgood Marshall sits like a minotaur as an associate justice on the Supreme Court. Martin Luther King's birthday is a *federal* holiday, and a black man you did not know won several Democratic presidential primaries last year. Black women novelists adorn the *New York Times* best-seller lists, and the number-one television show in the country is a situation comedy concerning the lives and times of a refined Afro-American obstetrician and his lovely wife, who is a senior partner in a Wall Street law firm. Sammy Davis, Jr.'s second autobiography has been widely—"

"Young man, I have come a long way. Do not trifle with the Weary Traveler."

"I would not think of it, sir. I revere you, sir, why, I even—"

"How many of them had to die? How many of our own? Did Nkrumah and Azikwe send troops? Did a nuclear holocaust bring them to their senses? When Shirley Graham and I set sail for Ghana, I pronounced all hope for our patient people doomed."

"No, sir," I would respond. "The gates of segregation fell rather quickly after 1965. A new middle class defined itself, a talented tenth, the cultured few, who, somehow, slipped through the cracks."

"Then the preservation of the material base proved to be more important than the primal xenophobia that we had posited?"

"That's about it, Doctor. But regular Negroes still catch hell. In fact, the ranks of the black underclass have never been larger."

I imagine the great man would heave a sigh, as the Spirit of Blackness galloped away.

From 1831, if not before, to 1965, an ideology of desegregation, of "civil rights," prevailed among our thinkers. Abolitionists, Reconstructors, neoabolitionists, all shared one common belief: that if we could only use the legislature and the judiciary to create and interpret the laws of desegregation and access, all else would follow. As it turns out, it was vastly easier to dismantle the petty forms of apartheid in this country (housing, marriage, hotels, and restaurants) than anyone could have possibly believed it would be, *without* affecting the larger patterns of inequality. In fact, the economic structure has not changed one jot, in any fundamental sense, except that black adult and teenage unemployment is much higher now than it has been in my lifetime. Considering the out-of-wedlock birthrate, the high school drop-out rate, and the unemployment figures, the "two nations" predicted by the Kerner Commission in 1968 may be upon us. And the conscious manipulation of our public image, by writers, filmmakers, and artists, which many of us *still* seem to think will bring freedom, has had very little impact in palliating our structural social problems. What's the most popular television program in South Africa? The "Cosby Show." Why not?

Ideology, paradoxically, was impoverished when we needed it most, during the civil-rights movement of the early 1960s. Unable to theorize what Cornel West calls "the racial problematic," unwilling (with very few exceptions) to theorize class, and scarcely able even to contemplate the theorizing of the curious compound effect of class-cum-race, we have—since the day after the signing of the Civil Rights Act of 1964—utterly lacked any instrumentality of ideological analysis, beyond the attempts of the Black Power and Black Aesthetic movements, to *invert* the signification of "blackness" itself. Recognizing that what had passed for "the human," or "the universal," was in fact white essentialism, we substituted one sort of essentialism (that of "blackness") for another. That, we learned quickly enough, was just not enough. But it led the way to a gestural politics captivated by fetishes and feel-bad rhetoric. The ultimate sign of our sheer powerlessness is all of the attention that we have given to declaring the birth of the African American, and pronouncing the Black Self dead. Don't we have anything better to do?

Now, I myself happen to like African American, especially because I am, as a scholar, an Africanist as well as an African-Americanist. Certainly the cultural continuities among African, Caribbean, and Black American cultures cannot be denied. (The irony is that we often thought of ourselves as "African" until late into the nineteenth century. The death of the African was declared by the Park school of sociology in the first quarter of this century, which thought that the hyphenated ethnicity of the Negro American would prove to be ultimately liberating.) But so tame and unthreatening is a politics centered on onomastics that even *The New York Times,* in a major editorial, declared its support of this movement.

> If Mr. Jackson is right and blacks now prefer to be called African-Americans, it is a sign not just of their maturity but of the nation's success. . . . Blacks may now feel comfortable enough in their standing as citizens to adopt the family surname: American. And their first name,

African, conveys a pride in cultural heritage that all Americans cherish. The late James Baldwin once lamented, "Nobody knows my name." Now everyone does [December 22, 1988].

To which one young black writer, Trey Ellis, responded recently: "When somebody tries to tell me what to call myself in all uses just because they come to some decision at a cocktail party to which I wasn't even invited, my mama raised me to tell them to kiss my black ass" (*Village Voice*, June 13, 1989). As he says, sometimes "African American" just won't do.

Ellis's amused rejoinder speaks of a very different set of concerns, and made me think of James Baldwin's prediction of the coming of a new generation that would give voice to blackness:

> While the tale of how we suffer, and how we are delighted, and how we may triumph is never new, it always must be heard. There isn't any other to tell, it's the only light we've got in all this darkness. . . . And this tale, according to that face, that body, those strong hands on those strings, has another aspect in every country, and a new depth in every generation [*The Price of the Ticket*].

In this spirit, Ellis has declared the birth of a "New Black Aesthetic" movement, comprising artists and writers who are middle-class, self-confident, and secure with black culture, and not looking over their shoulders at white people, wondering whether or not the Mr. Wilsons of their world will call them George. Ellis sees creative artists such as Spike Lee, Wynton Marsalis, Anthony Davis, August Wilson, Warrington Hudlin, Joan Armatrading, and Lisa and Kelly Jones as representatives of a new generation who, commencing with the publication in 1978 of Toni Morrison's *Song of Solomon* (for Ellis a founding gesture), "no longer need to deny or suppress any part of our complicated and sometimes contradictory cultural baggage to please either white people or black. The culturally mulatto *Cosby* girls are equally as black as a black teenage welfare mother" ("The New Black Aesthetic," *Before Columbus Review*, May 14, 1989). And Ellis is right: something quite new is afoot in African-American letters.

In a recent *New York Times* review of Maxine Hong Kingston's new novel, Le Anne Schreiber remarks: "Wittman Ah Singh can't be Chinese even if he wants to be. . . . He is American, as American as Jack Kerouac or James Baldwin or Allen Ginsberg. . . ." I remember a time, not so very long ago, when almost no one would have thought of

James Baldwin as typifying the "American." I think that even James Baldwin would have been surprised. Certainly since 1950, the meanings of blackness, as manifested in the literary tradition, have come full circle.

Consider the holy male trinity of the black tradition: Wright, Ellison, and Baldwin. For Richard Wright, "the color curtain"—as he titled a book on the Bandung Conference in 1955, when "the Third World" was born—was something to be rent asunder by something he vaguely called the "Enlightenment." (It never occurred to Wright, apparently, that the sublime gains in intellection in the Enlightenment took place simultaneously with the slave trade in African human beings, which generated an unprecedented degree of wealth and an unprecedentedly large leisure-and-intellectual class.) Wright was hardly sentimental about Black Africa and the Third World—he actually told the first Conference of Negro-African Writers and Artists in Paris, in 1956, that colonialism had been "liberating, since it smashed old traditions and destroyed old gods, freeing Africans from the 'rot' of their past," their "irrational past" (James Baldwin, *Nobody Knows My Name*). Despite the audacity of this claim, however, Wright saw himself as chosen "in some way to inject into the American consciousness" a cognizance of "other people's mores or national habits" ("I Choose Exile," unpublished essay). Wright claimed that he was "split": "I'm black. I'm a man of the West. . . . I see and understand the non- or anti-Western point of view. . . ." But, Wright confesses, "when I look out upon the vast stretches of this earth inhabited by brown, black and yellow men . . . my reactions and attitudes are those of the West" *(White Man, Listen!)*. Wright never had clearer insight into himself, although his unrelentingly critical view of Third World cultures will certainly not make him required reading among those of us bent upon decentering the canon.

James Baldwin, who parodied Wright's 1956 speech in *Nobody Knows My Name*, concluded that "this was, perhaps, a tactless way of phrasing a debatable idea. . . ." Blackness, for Baldwin, was a sign, a sign that signified through the salvation of the "gospel impulse," as Craig Werner characterizes it, seen in his refusal "to create demons, to simplify the other in a way that would inevitably force him to simplify himself. . . . The gospel impulse—its refusal to accept oppositional thought; its complex sense of presence; its belief in salvation—sounds in Baldwin's voice no matter what his particular vocabulary at a particular moment" (Craig Werner, "James Baldwin: Politics and the Gospel Impulse," *New Politics*, Winter 1989). Blackness, if it would be anything, stood as the saving grace of both white *and* black America.

Ralph Ellison, ever the trickster, felt it incumbent upon him to show that blackness was a metaphor for the human condition, and yet to do so through a faithful adherence to its particularity. Nowhere is this idea rendered more brilliantly than in his sermon "The Blackness of Blackness," the tradition's classic critique of blackness as an essence:

"Brothers and sisters, my text this morning is the 'Blackness of Blackness.' "
And a congregation of voices answered: "That blackness is most black, brother, most black . . ."
"In the beginning . . ."
"At the very start," they cried.
". . . there was blackness . . ."
"Preach it . . ."
". . . and the sun . . ."
"The sun, Lawd . . ."
". . . was bloody red . . ."
"Red . . ."
"Now black is . . ." the preacher shouted.
"Bloody . . ."
"I said black is . . ."
"Preach it, brother . . ."
". . . an' black ain't . . ."
"Red, Lawd, red: He said it's red!"
"Amen, brother . . ."
"Black will git you . . ."
"Yes, it will . . ."
". . . an' black won't . . ."
"Naw, it won't!"
"It do . . ."
"It do, Lawd . . ."
". . . an' it don't."
"Hallelujah . . ."
"It'll put you, glory, glory, Oh my Lawd, in the WHALE'S BELLY."
"Preach it, dear brother . . ."
". . . an' make you tempt . . ."
"Good God a-mighty!"
"Old aunt Nelly!"
"Black will make you . . ."
"Black . . ."

". . . or black will un-make you."
"Ain't it the truth, Lawd?"

ELLISON, *Invisible Man*

Ellison parodies the idea that blackness can underwrite a metaphysics or even a negative theology; that it can exist outside and independent of its representation.

And it is out of this discursive melee that so much contemporary African-American literature has developed.

◆

The range of representation of the meanings of blackness among the post–*Song of Solomon* (1978) era of black writing can be characterized—for the sake of convenience—by the works of C. Eric Lincoln (*The Avenue, Clayton City*), Trey Ellis's manifesto "The New Black Aesthetic," and Toni Morrison's *Beloved*, in many ways the Ur-text of the African-American experience.

Each of these writers epitomizes the points of a post–Black Aesthetic triangle, made up of the realistic representation of black vernacular culture: the attempt to preserve it for a younger generation (Lincoln), the critique through parody of the essentialism of the Black Aesthetic (Ellis), and the transcendence of the ultimate horror of the black past—slavery—through myth and the supernatural (Morrison).

The first chapter of Eric Lincoln's first novel, *The Avenue, Clayton City* (1988), contains an extended re-creation of the African-American ritual of signifying, which is also known as "talking that talk," "the dozens," "nasty talk," and so on. To render the dozens in such wonderful detail, of course, is a crucial manner of preserving it in the written cultural memory of African Americans. This important impulse to preserve (by recording) the vernacular links Lincoln's work directly to that of Zora Neale Hurston. Following the depiction of the ritual exchange, the narrator of the novel analyzes its import in the following way:

Guts shook his head sadly as he could hear the unmistakable repartee of the dirty dozens above the clapping and the loud laughter which always somehow seemed to be louder and somehow more pitiful whenever they were talkin' that talk. Two quick-tongued contestants were already hacking away at each other's family tree, prodded on to ever more colorful and drastic allegations by the third-party agitators whose job it was to keep the verbal skirmish at high heat.

"Hey, man, your daddy's so funny he'd make a three-dollar bill look real!"

"Yeah! And your mama's so ugly that when she saw her reflection in the millpond, she thought it was a turtle an' jumped in an' tried to catch it!"

"That ain't nothin'. If your A'nt Letty was in a beauty contest with a buffalo and a bulldog, she'd be second runner-up."

"Around the bend came the L&N, an' it was loaded down with your mammy's men!"

"Well, your mammy's in the po'house; your daddy's in the jail. An' your sister's on the corner tryin' to work up a sale!"

"I'm gon' tell you 'bout *your* sister. She wears so many flour sack drawers she flapjacks twice a day!"

"Yeah! An' you-all eat so many black-eyed peas 'til if your mama had a baby, she'd have to shell it!"

"I hear that when your daddy opens his lunch box, all he finds in it is two air sandwiches an' a long drink of water!"

"The first time your daddy went to church they buried him!"

"Yeah. Now when God made Adam, He made him quick, but when God made your daddy, it made Him Sick!"

"You better watch out. You know I don't play no dozens!"

"If you don't play, just lay dead an' pat your foot while me and your mama play!"

As Guts neared the circle of revelers, he could see a tall, skinny youth of light complexion moving around in a tight circle, cutting some kind of step to the handclap rhythm of nine or ten other boys gathered under the light. It was Finis Lee Jackson, Mamie Jackson's boy who dropped out of the Academy school to work for Mr. Bimbo loading rags and scrap iron down by the railroad. Guts couldn't hear what Finis Lee was saying, but he guessed it must have been nasty or the crowd wouldn't be whooping and hollering like they were. And he knew that as soon as Finis got through, somebody else would step into the ring and the show would go on. But he never did have a chance to find out what nastiness Finis was up to because somebody spotted him leaving the Flame and put the word out.

"Ol' Creeper comin'! Cool it."

The clapping stopped. There was a long moment of silence, and then Finis Lee, determined not to forfeit his time in the ring, took on a pious look like a Methodist preacher and intoned:

> Amazin' grace, how sweet the sound
> It done saved a wreck like me. . . .

"A-man! A-man!" came a chorus of responses liberally interposed with sniggles and suppressed whoops.

"Evening, Mr. Gallimore," one of the boys said as Guts shuffled on toward the circle.

"Don't be tryin' to 'good evening' me," Guts said, looking at nobody in particular. "An' ain't no use to try to get so holy all of a sudden an' mess up no church song jest because you see me comin'. I know what you been up to. I heard you talkin' that ol' nasty talk. It's jest a sin an' a shame before Jesus in His heaven. That's what it is!"

"That's right, Mr. Gallimore. You sho' right. I been tryin' to tell these ol' nasty-talkin' boys to shape up an' get on the ball!" It was Nero Banks, one of the younger boys who had only recently begun to hang out under the light.

Without bothering to even search him out in the crowd, Guts warned, "Boy, don't you play with me. I know who you is, an' I'm old enough to be your daddy twice if I wanna be, an' I don't take no sass. If you ain't got no respect for grown folks, try to have a little bit for yourself. That's the reason colored folks like you don't never git nowhere. You spend your time tryin' to impress a no-good passel of nasty-talkin' niggers an' you end up bein' jest like them—nasty an' good-for-nothin'-but-trouble!"

The circle gave way, and Guts Gallimore shuffled on up The Avenue to his wife, Rosie, and his hot tub to soak his feet and pray for a call to preach. But other calls echoed after him through the hot and steamy darkness.

"That's right, Mr. Gallimore! You're right 'til you're left, an' when you're left, right don't make no difference."

"Good night, Guts. Don't let your meat loaf, your gravy might curdle!"

"So long, Mr. Gallimore, 'cause so short can't cut no mustard."

Trey Ellis, whose first novel, *Platitudes*, is a satire on contemporary black cultural politics, is an heir of Ishmael Reed, the tradition's great satirist. Ellis describes the relation of what he calls "The New Black Aesthetic" (NBA) to the black nationalism of the sixties, engaged as it is in the necessary task of critique and revision:

Yet ironically, a telltale sign of the work of the NBA is our parodying of the black nationalist movement: Eddie Murphy, 26, and his old *Saturday Night Live* character, prison poet Tyrone Green, with his hilariously awful angry black poem. "Cill [sic] My Landlord," ("See his dog Do he bite?"); fellow Black Packer Keenan Wayans's upcoming blaxploitation parody *I'm Gonna Git You Sucka!;* playwright George Wolfe, and his parodies of both "A Raisin in the Sun" and "For Colored Girls . . ." in his hit play "The Colored Museum" ("Enter Walter-Lee-Beau-Willie-Jones. . . . His brow is heavy from 300 years of oppression"); filmmaker Reginald Hudlin, 25, and his sacrilegious *Reggie's World of Soul* with its fake commercial for a back scratcher, spatula and toilet bowl brush all with black clenched fists for their handle ends; and Lisa Jones's character Clean Mama King who is available for both sit-ins and film walk-ons. There is now such a strong and vast body of great black work that the corny or mediocre doesn't need to be coddled. NBA artists aren't afraid to publicly flout the official, positivist black party line.

This generation, Ellis continues, cares less about what white people think than any other in the history of Africans in this country. "The New Black Aesthetic says you just have to *be* natural, you don't necessarily have to *wear* one."

Ellis dates the beginning of this cultural movement with the publication of *Song of Solomon* in 1978. Morrison's blend of magical realism and African-American mythology proved compelling: this brilliantly rendered book was an overnight bestseller. Her greatest artistic achievement, however, and most controversial, is her most recent novel, *Beloved,* which won the 1988 Pulitzer Prize for Fiction.

In *Beloved,* Morrison has found a language that gives voice to the unspeakable horror and terror of the black past, our enslavement in the New World. Indeed, the novel is an allegorical representation of this very unspeakability. It is one of the few treatments of slavery that escapes the pitfalls of kitsch. Toni Morrison's genius is that she has found a language by which to thematize this very unspeakability of slavery.

Everybody knew what she was called, but nobody knew her name. Disremembered and unaccounted for, she cannot be lost because no one is looking for her, and even if they were, how can they call her if they don't know her name? Although she has claim, she is not claimed. In the place where long grass opens, the girl who waited to be loved and cry shame erupts into her separate parts, to make it easy for the chewing laughter to swallow her all away.

It is not a story to pass on.

They forgot her like a bad dream. After they made up their tales, shaped and decorated them, those that saw her that day on the porch quickly and deliberately forgot her. It took longer for those who had spoken to her, lived with her, fallen in love with her, to forget, until they realized they couldn't remember or repeat a single thing she said, and began to believe that, other than what they themselves were thinking, she hadn't said anything at all. So, in the end, they forgot her too. Remembering seemed unwise. They never knew where or why she crouched, or whose was the underwater face she needed like that.

Where the memory of the smile under her chin might have been and
was not, a latch latched and lichen attached its apple-green bloom to
the metal. What made her think her fingernails could open locks the
rain rained on?

It was not a story to pass on.

Only by stepping outside of the limitations of realism and entering a
realm of myth could Morrison, a century after its abolition, give a
voice to the silence of enslavement.

For these writers, in their various ways, the challenge of the black
creative intelligence is no longer to *posit* blackness, as it was in the
Black Arts movement of the sixties, but to render it. Their goal seems
to be to create a fiction *beyond* the colorline, one that takes the blackness of the culture for granted, as a springboard to write about those
human emotions that we share with everyone else, and that we have
always shared with each other, when no white people are around.
They seem intent, paradoxically, in escaping the very banality of
blackness that we encountered in so much Black Arts poetry, by *assuming* it as a legitimate ground for the creation of art.

To declare that race is a trope, however, is not to deny its palpable
force in the life of every African American who tries to function every
day in a still very racist America. In the face of Anthony Appiah's and
my own critique of what we might think of as "black essentialism,"
Houston Baker demands that we remember what we might character-
ize as the "taxi fallacy."

Houston, Anthony, and I emerge from the splendid isolation of the
Schomburg Library, and stand together on the corner of 135th Street
and Malcolm X Boulevard attempting to hail a taxi to return to the
Yale Club. With the taxis shooting by us as if we did not exist, Anthony and I cry out in perplexity: "But sir, it's only a trope."

If only that's *all* it was.

My father, who recently enjoyed his seventy-sixth birthday, and I attended a basketball game at Duke this past winter. It wasn't just any
game; it was "the" game with North Carolina, the ultimate rivalry in
American basketball competition. At a crucial juncture of the game,
one of the overly avid Duke fans bellowing in our section of the auditorium called J. R. Reid, the Carolina center, "rubber lips."

"Did you hear what he said?" I asked my father, who wears *two* hearing aids.

"I heard it. Ignore it, boy."

"I can't, Pop," I replied. Then, loud-talking all the way, I informed the crowd, while ostensibly talking only to my father, that we'd come too far to put up with shit like this, that Martin Luther King didn't die in vain, and we won't tolerate this kind of racism again, etc., etc., etc. Then I stood up and told the guy not to say those words ever again.

You could have cut the silence in our section of that auditorium with a knife. After a long silence, my dad leaned over and whispered to me, "Nigger, is you *crazy?* We am in de Souf." We both burst into laughter.

Even in the South, though, the intrusion of race into our lives usually takes more benign forms. One day my wife and father came to lunch at the National Humanities Center in Research Triangle Park, North Carolina, where I'm currently a fellow. The following day, the only black member of the staff cornered me and said that the kitchen staff had a bet, and that I was the only person who could resolve it. Shoot, I said. "OK," he said. "The bet is that your daddy is Mediterranean—Greek or Eyetalian, and your wife is High Yellow." "No," I said, "it's the other way around; my dad is black; my wife is white."

"Oh, yeah," he said, after a long pause, looking at me through the eyes of the race when one of us is being "sadiddy," or telling some kind of racial lie. "You know, *brother*," he said to me in a low but pointed whisper, "we black people got ways to *tell* these things, you know." Then he looked at me to see if I was ready to confess the truth. Indeterminacy had come home to greet me.

◆

What, finally, is the meaning of blackness for my generation of African-American scholars? I think that many of us are trying to work, rather self-consciously, within the tradition. It has taken white administrators far too long to realize that the recruitment of black faculty members is vastly easier at those institutions with the strongest black studies departments, or at least with the strongest representation of other black faculty. Why? I think the reason for this is that many of us wish to be a part of a community, of something "larger" than ourselves, escaping the splendid isolation of our studies. What can be lonelier than research, except perhaps the terror of the blank page (or computer screen)? Few of us—and I mean *very* few—wish to be the "only one" in town. I want my own children to grow up in the home of intellectuals, but with black middle-class values as common to them as the air they breathe. This I cannot achieve alone. I seek out, eagerly, the company of other African-American academics who have paid their dues, who understand the costs, and the pleasures, of achievement, who care about "the race," and who are determined to leave a legacy of self-defense against racism in all of its pernicious forms.

Part of this effort to achieve a sense of community is understanding that our generation of scholars is just an extension of other generations, of "many thousands gone." We are no smarter than they; we are just a bit more fortunate, in some ways, the accident of birth enabling us to teach at "white" research institutions, when two generations before we would have been teaching at black schools, overworked and underfunded. Most of us define ourselves as extensions of the tradition of scholarship and academic excellence epitomized by figures such as J. Saunders Redding, John Hope Franklin, and St. Clair Drake, merely to list a few names. But how are we *different* from them?

A few months ago I heard Cornel West deliver a memorial lecture in honor of James Snead, a brilliant literary critic who died of cancer recently at the age of thirty-five. Snead graduated valedictorian of his class at Exeter, then summa cum laude at Yale. Fluent in German, he wrote his Scholar of the House "essay" on the uses of repetition in Thomas Mann and William Faulkner. (Actually, this "essay" amounted to some six hundred papers, and the appendices were written in German.) He was also a jazz pianist and composer and worked as an investment banker in West Germany, after he took the Ph.D. in English literature at Cambridge University. Snead was a remarkable man.

West, near the end of his memorial lecture, told his audience that he had been discussing Snead's life and times with St. Clair Drake, as Drake lay in bed in a hospital recovering from a mild stroke that he had experienced on a flight from San Francisco to Princeton, where Drake was to lecture. When West met the plane at the airport, he rushed Drake to the hospital, and sat with him through much of the weekend.

West told Drake how Snead was, yes, a solid race man, how he loved the tradition, and wrote about it, but that his real goal was to redefine *American studies* from the vantage point of African-American concepts and principles. For Snead, taking the black mountaintop was not enough; he wanted the entire mountain range. "There is much about Dr. Snead that I can understand," Drake told West. "But then again," he concluded, "there is something about his enterprise that is quite unlike ours." Our next move within the academy, our next gestures, is to redefine the whole, simultaneously institutionalizing African-American studies. The idea that African-American culture was exclusively a thing apart, separate from the whole, having no influence on the shape and shaping of American culture, is a racialist fiction. There can be no doubt that the successful attempts to "decenter" the canon stem in part from the impact that black-studies programs have had upon traditional notions of the "teachable," upon what, properly, constitutes the universe of knowledge that the well-educated should know. For us, and for the students that we train, the complex meaning of blackness is a vision of America, a refracted image in the American looking-glass.

Snead's project, and Ellis's—the project of a new generation of writers and scholars—is about transcending the I-got-mine parochialism of a desperate era. It looks beyond that overworked masterplot of victims and victimizers so carefully scripted in the cultural dominant, beyond the paranoid dream of cultural autarky, and beyond the seductive ensolacements of nationalism. Their story—and it is a new story—is about elective affinities, unburdened by an ideology of descent; it speaks of blackness without blood. And this *is* a story to pass on.

Nihilism in Black America
1991

◆

CORNEL WEST

Cornel West is a member of the *Dissent* editorial board and director of Afro-American Studies at Princeton University. His books include *Prophetic Fragments, Race Matters,* and *Keeping Faith: Philosophy and Race in America.*

Recent discussions about the plight of African Americans—especially those at the bottom of the social ladder—tend to divide into two camps. On the one hand, there are those who highlight the *structural* constraints on the life chances of black people. This viewpoint involves a subtle historical and sociological analysis of slavery, Jim Crowism, job and residential discrimination, skewed unemployment rates, inadequate health care, and poor education. On the other hand, there are those who stress the *behavioral* impediments on black upward mobility. This focuses on the waning of the Protestant ethic—hard work, deferred gratification, frugality, and responsibility—in much of black America.

Those in the first camp—the liberal structuralists—call for full employment, health, education, and child-care programs, and broad affirmative action practices. In short, a new, more sober version of the best of the New Deal and the Great Society: more government money, better bureaucrats, and an active citizenry. Those in the second camp—the conservative behaviorists—promote self-help programs, black business expansion, and nonpreferential job practices. They support vigorous "free market" strategies that depend on fundamental changes in how black people act and live. To put it bluntly, their projects rest largely upon a cultural revival of the Protestant ethic in black America.

Unfortunately, these two camps have nearly suffocated the crucial debate that should be taking place about the prospects for black America. This debate must go far beyond the liberal and conservative positions in three fundamental ways. First, we must acknowledge that structures and behavior are inseparable, that institutions and values go hand in hand. How people act and live is shaped—though in no way dictated or determined—by the larger circumstances in which they find themselves. These circumstances can be changed, their limits attenuated, by positive actions to elevate living conditions.

Second, we should reject the idea that structures are primarily economic and political creatures—an idea that sees culture as an ephemeral set of behavioral attitudes and values. Culture is quite as structural as the economy or politics; it is rooted in institutions like families, schools, churches, synagogues, mosques, and communication industries (television, radio, video, music). Similarly, the economy and politics are not only influenced by values but also promote particular cultural ideals of the good life and good society.

◆

Third, and most important, we must delve into the depths where neither liberals nor conservatives dare to tread, namely, into the murky waters of despair and dread that now flood the streets of black America. To talk about the depressing statistics of unemployment, infant mortality, incarceration, teenage pregnancy, and violent crime is one thing. But to face up to the monumental eclipse of hope, the unprecedented collapse of meaning, the incredible disregard for human (especially black) life and property in much of black America is something else.

The liberal/conservative discussion conceals the most basic issue now facing black America: *the nihilistic threat to its very existence.* This threat is not simply a matter of relative economic deprivation and political powerlessness—though economic well-being and political clout are requisites for meaningful black progress. It is primarily a question of speaking to the profound sense of psychological depression, personal worthlessness, and social despair so widespread in black America.

The liberal structuralists fail to grapple with this threat for two reasons. First, their focus on structural constraints relates almost exclusively to the economy and politics. They show no understanding of the structural character of culture. Why? Because they tend to view people in egoistic and rationalist terms according to which they are motivated primarily by self-interest and self-preservation. Needless to say, this is partly true about most of us. Yet people, especially degraded and oppressed people, are also hungry for identity, meaning, and self-worth.

The second reason liberal structuralists overlook the nihilistic threat is a sheer failure of nerve. They hesitate to talk honestly about culture, the realm of meanings and values, because to do so may seem to lend itself too readily to conservative conclusions in the narrow way Americans discuss race. If there is a hidden taboo among liberals it is to resist talking about values *too much*, because it takes the focus away from structures, especially the positive role of government. But this failure leaves the existential and psychological realities of black people in the lurch. In this way, liberal structuralists neglect the battered identities rampant in black America.

As for the conservative behaviorists, they not only misconstrue the nihilistic threat but inadvertently contribute to it. This is a serious charge, and it rests upon three claims. First, conservative behaviorists talk about values and attitudes as if political and economic structures hardly exist. They rarely, if ever, examine the innumerable cases in which black people do act on the Protestant ethic and still remain at the bottom of the social ladder. Instead, they highlight the few instances in which blacks ascend to the top, as if such success is available to all blacks, regardless of circumstances. Such a vulgar rendition of Horatio Alger in blackface may serve as a source of inspiration to some—a kind of model for those already on the right track. But it cannot serve as a substitute for serious historical and social analysis of the predicaments and prospects for all black people, especially the grossly disadvantaged ones.

Second, conservative behaviorists discuss black culture as if acknowledging one's obvious victimization by white-supremacist practices (compounded by sexism and class condition) is taboo. They tell black people to see themselves as agents, not victims. And on the surface, this is comforting advice, a nice cliché for downtrodden people. But inspirational slogans cannot substitute for substantive historical and social analysis. While black people have never been simply victims, wallowing in self-pity and begging for white giveaways, they have been—and are—*victimized*. Therefore, to call on black people to be agents makes sense only if we also examine the dynamics of this victimization against which their agency will, in part, be exercised. What is particularly naïve and peculiarly vicious about the conservative behavioral outlook is that it tends to deny the lingering effect of black

history—a history inseparable from though not reducible to victimization. In this way, crucial and indispensable themes of self-help and
personal responsibility are wrenched out of historical context and
contemporary circumstances—as if it is all a matter of personal will.

This ahistorical perspective contributes to the nihilistic threat
within black America in that it can be used to justify right-wing cutbacks for poor people, struggling for decent housing, child care,
health care, and education. And, as I pointed out earlier, while liberals are deficient in important ways, they are right on target in their
critique of conservative government cutbacks for services to the poor.
These ghastly cutbacks are one cause of the nihilist threat to black
America.

◆

The proper starting point for the crucial debate about the prospects
for black America is the nihilism that increasingly pervades black
communities. *Nihilism is to be understood here not as a philosophic doctrine
that there are no rational grounds for legitimate standards or authority; it is,
far more, the lived experience of coping with a life of horrifying meaninglessness, hopelessness, and (most important) lovelessness.* This usually results
in a numbing detachment from others and a self-destructive disposition toward the world. Life without meaning, hope, and love breeds a
cold-hearted, mean-spirited outlook that destroys both the individual
and others.

Nihilism is not new in black America. The first African encounter
with the New World was an encounter with a distinctive form of the
Absurd. The initial black struggle against degradation and devaluation in the enslaved circumstances of the New World was, in part, a
struggle against nihilism. In fact, the major enemy of black survival in
America has been and is neither oppression nor exploitation but
rather the nihilistic threat—that is, loss of hope and absence of
meaning. For, as long as hope remains and meaning is preserved, the
possibility of overcoming oppression stays alive. The self-fulfilling
prophecy of the nihilistic threat is that without hope there can be no
future, that without meaning there can be no struggle.

The genius of our black foremothers and forefathers was to create
powerful buffers to ward off the nihilistic threat, to equip black folk
with cultural armor to beat back the demons of hopelessness, meaningless, and lovelessness. These buffers consisted of cultural structures of meaning and feeling that created and sustained
communities; this armor constituted ways of life and struggle that

embodied values of service and sacrifice, love and care, discipline and excellence. In other words, traditions for black surviving and thriving under usually adverse New World conditions were major barriers against the nihilistic threat. These traditions consist primarily of black religious and civic institutions that sustained familial and communal networks of support. If cultures are, in part, what human beings create out of antecedent fragments of other cultures, in order to convince themselves not to commit suicide, then black foremothers and forefathers are to be applauded. In fact, until the early seventies black Americans had the lowest suicide rate in the United States. But now young black people lead the nation in suicides.

What has changed? What went wrong? The bitter irony of integration? The cumulative effects of a genocidal conspiracy? The virtual collapse of rising expectations after the optimistic sixties? None of us fully understands why the nihilistic threat is more powerful now than ever before. I believe that the commodification of black life and the crisis of black leadership are two basic reasons. The recent shattering of black civil society—black families, neighborhoods, schools, churches, mosques—leaves more and more black people vulnerable to the nihilistic threat. This shattering spawns a deracinated and denuded people with little sense of self or existential moorings.

Black people have always been in America's wilderness in search of a promised land. Yet many black folk now reside in a jungle with a cutthroat morality devoid of any faith in deliverance or hope for freedom. Contrary to the superficial claims of conservative behaviorists, these jungles are not primarily the result of pathological behavior. Rather, this behavior is the tragic response of a people bereft of resources in confronting the workings of U.S. capitalist society. This does not mean that individual black people are not responsible for their actions—black murderers and rapists should go to jail. But it does mean that the nihilistic threat contributes to criminal behavior—a threat that feeds on poverty *and* shattered cultural institutions. The nihilistic threat is now more powerful than even before because the armor to ward against it is weaker.

◆

But why this shattering of black civil society, this weakening of black cultural institutions in asphalt jungles? *Corporate market institutions* have contributed greatly to this situation. By corporate market institutions I mean that complex set of interlocking enterprises that have a disproportionate amount of capital, power, and influence on how our society is run and on how our culture is shaped. Needless to say, the primary motivation of these institutions is to make profits, and their basic strategy is to convince the public to consume. These institutions have helped create a seductive way of life, a culture of consumption that capitalizes on every opportunity to make money. Market calculations and cost-benefit analyses hold sway in almost every sphere of U.S. society.

The common denominator of these calculations and analyses is usually the provision, expansion, and intensification of *pleasure*. Pleasure is a multivalent term; it means different things to many people. In our way of life it involves comfort, convenience, and sexual stimulation. This mentality pays little heed to the past, and views the future as no more than a repetition of a hedonistic-driven present. This market morality stigmatizes others as objects for personal pleasure or bodily stimulation. On this view, traditional morality is not undermined by radical feminists, cultural radicalists in the sixties, or libertarians, as alleged by conservative behaviorists. Rather, corporate market institutions have greatly contributed to undermining traditional morality in order to stay in business and make a profit. This is especially evident in the culture industries—television, radio, video, music—in which gestures of foreplay and orgiastic pleasure flood the marketplace.

Like all Americans, African Americans are influenced greatly by the images of comfort, convenience, machismo, femininity, violence, and sexual stimulation that bombard consumers. These seductive images contribute to the predominance of the market-inspired way of life over all others and thereby edge out nonmarket values—love, care, service to others—handed down by preceding generations. The predominance of this way of life among those living in poverty-ridden conditions, with a limited capacity to ward off self-contempt and self-hatred, results in the possible triumph of the nihilistic threat in black America.

◆

A major contemporary strategy for holding the nihilistic threat at bay is to attack directly the sense of worthlessness and self-loathing in black America. This *Angst* resembles a kind of collective clinical depression in significant pockets of black America. The eclipse of hope and collapse of meaning in much of black America is linked to the structural dynamics of corporate market institutions that affect all Americans. Under these circumstances black existential *Angst* derives from the lived experience of ontological wounds and emotional scars inflicted by white-supremacist beliefs and images permeating U.S. society and culture. These wounds and scars attack black intelligence, black ability, black beauty, and black character daily in subtle and not-so-subtle ways.

The accumulated effect of these wounds and scars produces a deep-seated anger, a boiling sense of rage, and a passionate pessimism regarding America's will to justice. Under conditions of slavery and Jim Crow segregation, this anger, rage, and pessimism remained relatively muted because of a well-justified fear of brutal white retaliation. The major breakthroughs of the sixties—more psychically than politically—swept this fear away. Sadly, the combination of the market way of life, poverty-ridden conditions, black existential *Angst*, and the lessening of fear toward white authorities has directed most of the anger, rage, and despair toward fellow black citizens, especially black women. Only recently has this nihilistic threat—and its ugly inhuman outlook and actions—surfaced in the larger American society. And it surely reveals one of the many instances of cultural decay in a declining empire.

◆

What is to be done about this nihilistic threat? Is there really any hope, given our shattered civil society, market-driven corporate enterprises, and white supremacism? If one begins with the threat of concrete nihilism, then one must talk about some kind of *politics of conversion*. New models of collective black leadership must promote a version of this politics. Like alcoholism and drug addiction, nihilism is a disease of the soul. It can never be completely cured and there is always the possibility of relapse. But there is always a chance for conversion—a chance for people to believe that there is hope for the future and a meaning to struggle. This chance rests neither on an agreement about what justice consists of nor an analysis of how racism, sexism, or class subordination operates. Such arguments and analyses are indispensable. But a politics of conversion requires more. Nihilism is not overcome by arguments or analyses; it is tamed by love and care. Any disease of the soul must be conquered by a turning of one's soul. This turning is done by one's own affirmation of one's worth—an affirmation fueled by the concern of others. This is why a love ethic must be at the center of a politics of conversion.

This love ethic has nothing to do with sentimental feelings or tribal connections. Rather, it is a last attempt at generating a sense of agency among a downtrodden people. The best exemplar of this love ethic is depicted on a number of levels in Toni Morrison's *Beloved*. Self-love and love of others are both modes toward increasing self-valuation and encouraging political resistance in one's community. These modes of valuation and resistance are rooted in a subversive memory—the best of one's past without romantic nostalgia—and guided by a universal love ethic. For my purposes here, *Beloved* can be construed as bringing together the loving yet critical affirmation of black humanity found in the best of black nationalist movements, the perennial hope against hope for transracial coalition in progressive movements, and the painful struggle for self-affirming sanity in a history in which the nihilistic threat *seems* insurmountable.

The politics of conversion proceeds principally on the local level—in those institutions in civil society still vital enough to promote self-worth and self-affirmation. It surfaces on the state and national levels only when grass-roots democratic organizations put forward a collective leadership that has earned the love and respect of and, most important, that has proved itself *accountable* to these organizations.

Like liberal structuralists, the advocates of a politics of conversion never lose sight of the structural conditions that shape the sufferings and the lives of people. Yet, unlike liberal structuralism, the politics of conversion meets the nihilistic threat head-on. Like conservative behaviorism, the politics of conversion openly confronts the self-destructive and inhuman actions of black people. Unlike conservative behaviorists, the politics of conversion situates (not exonerates) these actions within inhumane circumstances. The politics of conversion shuns the limelight—a limelight that solicits status seekers and ingratiates egomaniacs. Instead, it stays on the ground among the toiling everyday people, ushering forth humble freedom fighters—both followers and leaders—who have the audacity to take the nihilistic threat by the neck and turn back its deadly assaults.

◆

The nihilistic threat to black America is inseparable from a crisis in black leadership. This crisis is threefold.

First, at the national level, the courageous yet problematic example of Jesse Jackson looms large. On the one hand, his presidential campaigns based on a progressive multiracial coalition were *the* major left-liberal response to Reagan's conservative policies. For the first time since the last days of Martin Luther King, Jr.—with the grand exception of Harold Washington—the nearly *de facto* segregation in

U.S. progressive politics was confronted and surmounted. On the other hand, Jackson's televisual style resists grass-roots organizing and, most important, democratic accountability. His brilliance, energy, and charisma sustain his public visibility—but at the expense of programmatic follow-through. We are approaching the moment in which this style exhausts its progressive potential.

Other national nonelectoral black leaders—like Benjamin Hooks of the NAACP and John Jacobs of the National Urban League—rightly highlight the traditional problems of racial discrimination, racial violence, and slow racial progress. Yet their preoccupation with race—the mandate from their organizations—downplays the crucial class, environmental, and patriarchal determinants of black life chances. Black politicians—especially new victors like Mayor David Dinkins of New York City and Governor Douglas Wilder of Virginia—are part of a larger, lethargic electoral system riddled with decreasing revenues, loss of public confidence, self-perpetuating mediocrity, and pervasive corruption. Like most American elected officials, few black politicians can sidestep these seductive traps. So black leadership at the national level tends to lack a moral vision that can organize (not just periodically energize), subtle analyses that enlighten (not simply intermittently awaken), and exemplary practices that uplift (not merely convey status that awes) black people.

Second, this relative failure creates vacuums to be filled with even narrower visions, one-note racial analyses, and sensationalist practices. Louis Farrakhan, Al Sharpton, and others vigorously attempt to be protest leaders in this myopic mode—a mode often, though not always, reeking of immoral xenophobia. This kind of black leadership is not only symptomatic of black alienation and desperation in a country more and more indifferent or hostile to the quality of life among black working and poor people; it also reinforces the fragmentation of U.S. progressive efforts that could reverse this deplorable plight. In this way, black nationalist leaders often inadvertently contribute to the very impasse they are trying to overcome: inadequate social attention and action to change the plight of America's "invisible people," especially disadvantaged black people.

Third, this crisis of black leadership contributes to political cynicism among black people; it encourages the idea that we cannot really make a difference in changing our society. This cynicism—already promoted by the larger political culture—dampens the fire of engaged *local* activists who have made a difference, yet who also have little interest in being in the national limelight. Rather, they engage in protracted grass-roots organizing in principled coalitions that bring power and pressure to bear on specific issues.

Without such activists there can be no progressive politics. Yet state, regional, and national networks are also required for an effective progressive politics. That is why local-based collective (and especially multigendered) models of black leadership are needed. These models must shun the idea of one black national leader; they also should put a premium on critical dialogue and democratic accountability in black organizations.

Work must get done. Decisions must be made. But charismatic presence is no legitimate substitute for collective responsibility. Only a charisma of humility and accountability is worthy of a leadership grounded in a genuine democratic struggle for greater freedom and equality. This indeed may be the best—and last—hope to hold back the nihilistic threat to black America.

Feminism

Perspectives on the Women's Movement
1975

♦

CYNTHIA FUCHS EPSTEIN

Cynthia Fuchs Epstein is Distinguished Professor of Sociology at the Graduate Center of the City University of New York. Her books include *Deceptive Distinctions, Women in Law,* and *Woman's Place.*

The current woman's movement is unique in the American experience. This movement, multidimensional in character, is striking toward change in the structure of our major institutions, in the quality and content of our culture, and at the level of interpersonal dynamics. Not even a decade old, it has permeated the fabric of modern life.

Women, forever intimate and integrated with men, have been subservient to them, to a greater or lesser extent, in all societies. The women's movement is without precedent because of the special ambivalences that mark the relationship of women to men—the components of attraction and withdrawal; love and hate; need and distaste—which have not been characteristic of other subordinate groups. Furthermore, through the current movement women have sought to do more than demand greater access to the resources of society; they have wanted redefinition of who they are and what they are worth both in private relationships and in public ones.

It is difficult to analyze the extent of these changes within American society. One can look at the data—statistics that indicate rates of change in terms of numbers of women who now work in fields they never worked in before; numbers of women entering business and professional schools. Such changes are extensive if one measures what has happened since the beginning of the woman's movement in the mid-sixties. But statistics do not indicate the cause of change, or whether it is rooted or ephemeral.

Because more has happened to alter the position of women in the past ten years than for a score of decades before, I think it is safe to assume that the woman's movement was the driving force. Neither past changes in the economy nor the two world wars, which utilized womanpower as never before, caused real alterations in women's roles. Although "the pill" surely made a large difference, contraception was widely used prior to its invention, and fertility, which increased or decreased according to the impact of other experiences, showed in general a downward trend.

Although millions of women had left home to take jobs during World War II, traditional ideology convinced them to yield these jobs to male veterans after the war. And while there is some debate as to whether women left factory jobs voluntarily or were laid off because of low seniority, veterans' job priorities, and the closing of war-producing factories, women did not assert their "right" to jobs previously defined as men's work. They were also persuaded that their first commitment was to the home, whether or not they worked. Myth conquered reality, and few recognized that a growing proportion of the labor force—close to one-third and increasing every year—were women. "Should or could women work?" was the eternal debate, while in fact women were working.

Most social commentators agree that Betty Friedan's book *The Feminine Mystique* provided the ideological underpinning for a woman's movement.

In writing *The Feminine Mystique,* Friedan became a Tom Paine for women. It was an analytic book, and it had popular appeal. In it Friedan sketched the problems women faced in a society that judged itself by the degree of equality it offered its citizens while excluding women from that judgment. The problems of black people were obvious to all—even to those who chose not to do anything about them. But whether women had a problem, or how important it was, seemed unclear to women themselves.

Friedan's book described a malaise, "the problem that had no name." She gave form to women's distress, and provided sound social structural reasons for it. She indicated how women's powerlessness drove them to lives of vicarious fulfillment, and how as consumers but not producers they were playing a frustrating role, but one necessary for the continuation of the economic system.

Friedan translated ideas into action when she organized the National Organization for Women (NOW) in 1966, and ever since she has been at the forefront of the enterprise, from the organization of the Women's Political Caucus to the first women's bank, and currently the Economic Think Tank on Women.

Friedan does not follow any "great man" model of leadership. Lacking both conventional charisma of person and the charisma of family or office, but with a compelling intensity, she became a person with a message to be reckoned with, at a time when conditions in the economy and the ideological structure of the society were ripe for change.

We have no model of leadership for women; there is only the model of the ideal woman whose qualities of dedication to demure service and soft nurturance are inconsistent with the demands of a leader's office. Men might fight for liberty, but women were to defend only the sanctity of the home and morality; liberty, with its connotations of self-realization, was not deemed her province.

While Susan B. Anthony, Elizabeth Cady Stanton, and others who organized the first woman's-rights conference, in Seneca Falls, New York, in 1848, were regarded as revolutionaries and insurrectionists, Friedan has drawn fire from both the Left and the Right—accused of both middle-class reformism and disruption of the family. Part of the attack is directed at the alleged impropriety of her personal style and appearance.

How curious that not only is the leader of the woman's movement judged by how well she fits the acceptable modes for a proper lady, but so too is the *movement itself!* Polls indicate a growing sentiment in support of more equality for women, but they show that women not associated with women's groups do not care to be thought of as "women's lib" types. In fact, a current poll by the Roper organization shows that 57 percent of the women questioned favored efforts to strengthen their status, an increase over the figures reported in 1971 and 1972 by Louis Harris, in which 40 percent and 48 percent expressed support. But in 1972, 49 percent were still unsympathetic with efforts of women's liberation groups.

Perhaps it is characteristic of subjugated groups to become convinced that they have little right to question the views of their "betters." It has certainly been true of women, who, in public debate and in philosophical and psychoanalytic tracts, have accepted such definitions and the rationales supporting them. The antiegalitarian views—the Old and New Testaments; the writings of Nietzsche, Freud, and even of political theorists such as Jefferson—have gained popular support through time, while competing views—those of John Stuart Mill, Charlotte Gilmans Perkins, and later Karen Horney—did not.

I suggest that this is not because the competing ideas were less philosophically or scientifically sound, but because the gatekeeping, both formal and informal, of the males in power created support for the explanations they preferred. Furthermore, the longer these views were supported and adopted by a majority of people, the more "normal" they appeared to be.

The change of the feminist movement at the turn of the century from a radical ideology demanding change throughout society to one of relative moderation was probably caused by the powerlessness of women. Earlier, just getting the vote had been dismissed by Elizabeth Cady Stanton as "not even half a loaf; . . . only a crust, a crumb."

Getting the vote did not even put women into the *political* mainstream. Aside from pressure in the 1920s, which led to protective work legislation, women did not create focused political interest or do much lobbying. Under pressure from the Catholic bishops, Congress had by 1929 cut appropriations for the Women's Bureau and the Children's Bureau. The vote became like money in the bank that its owners were afraid to spend even as it lost value through inflation. At most, women's suffrage may have put a brake on the further enactment of regressive legislation.

If women were not exercising political power, they were moving into the labor market in increasing numbers and played active nontraditional worker roles during the two world wars. A general movement toward mass primary and secondary education, and then toward higher education for many students, meant that women were no longer confined to the home. The home may have been where their heart was, or was expected to be, but their feet were often off and running.

Yet each bit of advancement was met with severe opposition. Educating women or opening opportunities to work have not necessarily been indicators of public sentiment supporting women's rights to equality. What made the women's movement in the U.S. unique was that changes in behavior and attitudes were demanded, not only in the society but in personal life as well.

In that way American women were more avant-garde than their sisters in the Eastern European countries. We know that Soviet women physicians (75 percent of all doctors) must also perform household duties unassisted by husbands and without the mechanical aids available to American housewives. The Soviet grandmother is the chief child-care institution in that country, as she is still in Italy, France, Germany, and, to some extent, in the United States. Child care and housework still seem to be assigned to women universally, and this checks their ability to assume commanding positions in other areas of life, even where they constitute dominant numbers. In all countries, and in the "socialist" ones too, despite the ideological claims of writers from Engels to Mao, entrenched habits of mind linked with the vested interests of men in power have kept women assigned to roles men don't respect or wish to perform. In no country has women's equality yet been accomplished, or has there been complete reevaluation of modes of thought that define women's capacities and roles.

◆

To return to the American situation: in initiating a new woman's movement in 1966, Betty Friedan took a step that was to raise the consciousness of millions of American women and result in the formation of thousands of groups, both formal and informal. Moving swiftly, organizations such as NOW and WEAL (Women's Equity Action League) sought to implement the Civil Rights Act of 1964. This act, intended to stop discrimination against minorities, was amended to include sex in a last-minute effort by Representative Howard W. Smith (D. Va.) who thought the added word might send the entire act to defeat. Not only did the act pass, it provided the major foundation for movement activity. The combination of law and the organization of women was powerful. There were other allies. The Equal Economic Opportunities Commission (EEOC), which before had handled only cases of discrimination against minority people, established guidelines for compliance with Civil Rights Act provisions relating to women. It was the EEOC and a number of feminist lawyers who took on the American Telephone and Telegraph Company, the largest employer of women in the world, and won a landmark agreement forcing AT&T to provide goals and timetables for the hiring and promotion of women and minorities. AT&T was also forced to pay $15 million in back pay to persons who had been denied promotion because of discrimination and $23 million in immediate annual pay increases to women and minority males who were deemed underpaid in their job classifications.

The EEOC action against AT&T demonstrated not only that women had power if they cared to use it, but that there was support for their position in and out of government. Contrary to critics who labeled the women's movement an enterprise of privileged white middle-class women, the AT&T case proved that women working for women were working for women at all levels of the socioeconomic pyramid. It showed that women were oppressed as a class and that legislation giving middle-class women an opportunity to be hired as lawyers also gave lower-income women the opportunity to be promoted as supervisors in factories and businesses.

Middle-class women had louder voices than lower-income ones; perhaps because their aspirations were spurred by rising opportunities, they were more discontented. Many of the women most involved in "causes" were drawn from those who had been active in the civil-rights movement or had been student activists. In the late 1960s these women started realizing the extent to which they themselves were victims of discrimination. Assigned to the kitchen to cook for striking students in Columbia University; hooted off the platform at the SDS national convention for introducing women's liberation resolutions; mocked by Stokely Carmichael in his classic remark that the only position for women in the movement was "prone"—young women, finding themselves somehow excluded from all social-reform programs, sought focus for their rights.

Splinter groups broke away from NOW in the late 1960s over issues of radical politics and on the role of lesbians in the movement. As Friedan was asking for women to be "in equal partnership with men," some women's groups were campaigning for separatism. A few groups argued that women should join together in their own communities, away from man, the enemy. Lesbianism, in this context was seen politically as a way of life for women who could express their sexuality apart from men. In fact, sexuality and sexual activity became targets of attack. Beliefs concerning women's sexuality had long been used to legitimate their second-class status. Biology, it turned out, was more politics than science. New freedoms in sexual morality, which gave women permission to discard the ideal of chastity, had their repressive side. Young men expected them to be more available sexually outside of marriage and the women felt a compulsion to comply. There were no longer unequal costs to women for having sexual relationships, and some were beginning to initiate them, but sexual equality, women soon found out, was not necessarily linked to equality in other spheres.

Although sexual mores had been changing toward greater liberality since the Victorian period, the talk about sex still seemed radical to many Americans. It was one thing to be for equal pay for equal work. It was another thing to be in on the discussion about the "big O." Women's liberationists campaigned for the clitoral orgasm as Freud, in his way, had campaigned for the vaginal orgasm. Women were insisting on their right to orgasm in reaction to older claims that women weren't as capable of sexual fulfillment as men. Here, as in other spheres, new freedoms created backlash. It was claimed that men not only disliked all this talk about sexual rights for women, but were "turning off" and becoming impotent in response to these sexually emancipated women. All changes in the direction of emancipation effected by the women's movement could expect to be sabotaged in newer and more subtle ways.

Before the modern woman's movement existed, Philip Wylie was complaining that "Momism" was killing the manhood of American men, and indeed there was a spate of scientific studies that proved mothers were responsible for traits ranging from juvenile delinquency and homosexuality to aggressive achievement motivation. Now American women were reminded of their responsibility for maintaining the intensity of sexual drives in men. So vulnerable were men, it was claimed, their very sexuality was dependent on women's submissive behavior. Science also provided a number of studies to back up that notion and showed case after case where female animals had to present themselves submissively to males in order for sex to work.

Intellectual and political arguments over sexual capacity, sexual etiquette, and sexual "rights" were fought in the laboratory, movement meetings, the media, and in the bedroom. But it was clear that, whatever truths were discovered, their interpretation could be used to serve any side of an issue. Science, like alcohol, can apparently make people sexier by loosening their inhibitions, or frigid by depressing them. Science had still not provided the answer to who was fit to make decisions in society.

◆

The women's movement has been working steadily and expanding into academic and professional organizations of all types. Formally excluded from male societies, women sometimes had formed separate professional associations (which had low prestige and little power) or served peripherally in service roles in the "integrated" organizations. In the past six or seven years, however, these major associations have had to cope with emergent women's caucuses, which pressed for representation in decision-making committees and offices. (A recent count showed women's units within 67 professional organizations as diverse as the Society for Cell Biologists and the American Management Association.) These organized professional women were instrumental in increasing the representation of women in professional and graduate schools.

As women became more vocal in these male domains, they also insisted that sexism was embodied in the work of the professions and that it had to be identified and routed out. Thus women in medicine urged more respect for women as patients and the more serious study of diseases associated with their sex. There was pressure for demystification of the male medical establishment by feminists and young male physicians who had become alert to the problems of minority groups in getting good medical care. Many women had felt physicians often treated them as hypochondriacal half-wits whose gynecological pains seemed less worthy of medical concern than pains associated with more androgenous zones of the body. Young feminists formed self-help clinics and recruited sympathetic women doctors, although there were few to choose from. Quotas on women in medical schools, like those in law and business schools, had been kept at a fairly constant 3–10 percent from the first opening of the doors to women until the late 1960s. Feminists also analyzed medical texts in current use and exposed stereotyped characterizations of women's psychological makeup which had no basis in reality, in the same way they monitored the media and schoolchildren's texts for stereotyping of women in classic housewife roles.

In law, a number of vigorous women students' associations were formed. Slowly, the barriers to admission of women eased. That change did not come about by feminist effort alone. The movement was gaining strength in a context of concern with civil rights and it was also the time of debate over the Vietnam War. Women found it easier to get into law schools, not because the doors were opened in immediate accord with their demands, but because there were fewer male applicants (draft exemptions were not granted for law school). Furthermore, young women were beginning to feel that by going to law school they could "be something"—a lawyer—an experience few could have had after earning a degree in history or literature.

Young women lawyers (as well as interested male researchers) learned that in a number of states women offenders were likely to receive stiffer sentences than men for the same crimes, because women's criminality was perceived as more threatening to the moral structure of society than men's. The attitudes of judges and other lawyers toward women clients and attorneys became the target of feminist attack.

Still there was evidence that in some professions the study of women or problems relating to women was not considered as serious as study of other problems. Family matters, or any areas related too closely to women, have always been at a disadvantage in the prestige structure of the professions; to be a marriage-and-divorce lawyer always meant to be less of a lawyer, as to be a family sociologist meant to be of lower rank than a sociologist of organizations.

Certainly, word was spreading throughout the U.S. Although much media news about women's endeavors to improve their situation was tinged with derision and humor, and often only the dramatic and radical activities gained attention (picketing and those oft-cited but infrequent bra-burning demonstrations), women throughout America were reporting that they were reassessing their roles as housewives and mothers. They were becoming sensitive to the discrimination they were facing in getting jobs, getting credit, the dependency problems they had in marriage, and the disorienting anomie that divorce created in their lives. Consciousness-raising groups started in suburban neighborhoods with middle-aged women following the models set by young, college-aged women in urban centers. In fact, college-aged women, infused with a sense of the waste they saw as the tragedy of their mothers' lives, seemed to be turning more toward planning careers that could be held (still in conjunction with marriage) throughout life.

Women not counted among the many thousands in feminist organizations were nevertheless following feminist principles even as they rejected the "taint" of identification with the movement. A 1974 poll reported that almost half (46 percent) the women polled in a national sample preferred a marriage "where husband and wife share responsibilities more—both work, both share homemaking and child-care responsibilities."

Still, large questions remain. The great fear of feminists is that the movement's apparent great strides will turn out to be token changes or the result of fads. There are also fears of the repercussions that may result from entrance of very large numbers of women into professions where they were virtually absent before. Now that many law schools have classes that are nearly half female, the question remains whether substantial numbers will be able to get jobs. Law firms often were pleased to hire a few exceptionally able women attorneys; and the few women engineers who graduated in the early 1970s can pick and choose among companies looking for minority recruits. But feminists are aware that affirmative-action programs in these organizations are the motivating factor in their hiring, and not a sudden appreciation of women's talents.

Increasingly tight economic conditions create another source of trouble. Employers may feel freer to retreat to older hiring practices, especially when their token group has been completed. In 1970, 65 percent of American women polled by Gallup believed they got as good a break in life as men, and the 1974 Roper poll reported that three out of four women interviewed said that being a woman has not prevented them from doing the things they wanted to do in life. There is always the chance that, having won more equality in a few areas, as women did at the time they won the vote, they may lower their guard and their militancy.

◆

It is too early to be certain of the lasting consequences of the women's movement. We can sketch some areas of major change, and others where change is significant but countered by other conditions.

- Item: While women have increased their percentages in law (from 3 percent to 4.9 percent between 1960 and 1970) and medicine (from 7 percent to 9 percent), this has not substantially affected the generally unchanging sex-division of labor. There continue to be tendencies toward creating boundaries between "men's work" and "women's work."

- Item: While more women are now getting jobs in the male-dominated professions, they are still being directed into types of work considered "suitable" for women, and avoiding, or being kept out of, male preserves. In the legal profession, for example, women could only find work in the trusts and estates divisions of large firms, or had specialties in divorce, child custody, and real-estate work in smaller firms. Today women lawyers are "choosing" specialties that seem largely the same or their equivalent. For example, newly created women's firms are dealing with "women's matters" (such as sex discrimination and rape as well as divorce) and thus come to be professional ghettos.

  The "ghetto" phenomenon is manifested in other ways. Many new women professors in law schools are asked to teach "women and the law" courses and find they are often lecturing mainly to women.

- Item: More women have entered graduate schools of business administration and are then getting management trainee positions in government and business. But it is clear that many of them are made assistants to senior executives, or administrative assistants in charge of personnel or affirmative-action programs. Although these are "management" positions (and thus count on the charts monitored by government agencies) and pay executive-level salaries, these jobs are not on the track to high administrative offices. Women, like blacks, are given separate work, apparently equal to male executive jobs but unequal in career potential.

♦ Item: Many more women seem to be running for political office. Those who are elected are highly visible and some (Bella Abzug and Shirley Chisholm) have spectacular images. An important qualitative change over the past is that a growing number of women in political life seem to have made their mark without attachment to a male politician. It was not so in the past. Becoming a widow of a congressman or senator was a common route for women in American legislative life. Yet Ella Grasso, just elected governor in Connecticut, or Congresswomen Bella Abzug, Shirley Chisholm, and Elizabeth Holtzman of New York, and Yvonne Braithewaite of California all seem to be their "own women."

♦ Item: The woman's movement gained strength during a time of high employment and a vigorous economy. There is great fear that a depression would destroy the now uneasy balance between the feminists and the gatekeepers of the opportunity structure. Young men, now seen as more egalitarian than their elders, may become more conservative as they face the competition of increasing numbers of women for a limited supply of jobs. At the level of middle management, men express fears that they are increasingly deprived of chances for upward mobility because blacks and women are favored for promotions. The statistics do not substantiate these fears, but it is certainly possible they may be realized as more women become trained.

♦ Item: Women are going to work at all levels of the economic pyramid, and married women, even with preschool children, have become more firmly attached to the labor force. The number of working mothers whose youngest child is in the age group from three to five rose by 13.2 percent since 1960; it is now 38.3 percent of employed women. Those with children under three went up to 29.4 percent.

An increasing number of female heads of households, both black and white, have no choice but to work. And as inflation puts a greater strain on family incomes, it creates a need for both spouses to work. Currently 56 percent of husband-wife families are multiple-worker families, an increase over the 47 percent of 1963.

◆

All of these factors create new conditions for the playing out of the ambiguous commitment Americans have to women's equality. Clearly, backlash is mobilizing in many forms. Employers are protesting the economic costs of special training for women. (The whole notion of the need for special training may be a bugaboo. It seems clear that women need jobs more than training, especially because most work is learned on the job.) Many groups are protesting what they regard as preferential treatment for designated minorities. The reaction of some Jewish groups against quotas (e.g., the DeFunis case) speaks to the sensitivity caused by competition between minority groups for a limited number of places.

There is also the insidious backlash many women are experiencing in their personal relations with men. Although most men today find it necessary to indicate a commitment to the ideals of equality, the translation of it into their personal lives is difficult and often cumbersome. Marriages seem ever more fragile under the new assaults of the incongruent needs for autonomy and privacy, for rest and support on the part of both partners.

Any set of freedoms creates problems of disharmonies between the rights and needs of the individuals involved. Not only the men, the women too tire of the battle and may retreat into traditional models of marriage to reestablish equilibrium in their lives. But even this is often no solution, because neither partner is really convinced of the ideological worthiness of the compromise.

All movements need momentum, and an ever-militant corps who will unceasingly maintain pressure. Many women are consolidating the gains they have achieved in the struggle for equality by uncovering myths, by advancing in their work, without letting a sense of defeat stop their efforts. But there is often little time for movement activity if they have a job and are also doing the dishes and being the mothers in a society still unresponsive to the needs of women for household assistance and child care.

Furthermore, there is some indication that attention directed toward improving the status of women is now being diverted into other realms. Energy and the economy have the headlines. With a sense that enough has been done, government and the private sector may lean back and lessen their efforts.

There is indication that the issue of women's equality is still a joke at high levels. Witness President Gerald Ford's first address to a joint session of Congress on August 12, and his egregious assertion that he would be "the President of black, brown, red and white Americans, of old and young, of women's liberationists and male chauvinists and all the rest of us in between. . . ." But consider the uproar he would have generated had he asserted he fell somewhere "between" the racists and egalitarians. The next day, his wife, when questioned on her views of women's liberation, apparently felt it a thorny issue, and only committed herself as far as "equal pay and equal opportunity" were concerned.

The achievements of the women's movement are not a joke, nor are those women who are committed to winning full equality. The swiftness with which they have advanced probably acts in their favor. Many remember the quality of life and work before (was it only ten years ago?), and none will forget the hard work that went into changing them. None will easily let the new freedoms slip away. Today there is enough organizational structure in local communities and nationally, in business and the professions, to keep movement projects going and recruit new adherents. A major recession would hurt everyone and probably minority groups most, but this society's general acceptance of the idea of equality will make it difficult substantially to undo the work of these past ten years.

A Gender Diary

1989

◆

ANN SNITOW

Ann Snitow was one of the founding members of New York Radical Feminists in 1969. Most recently she founded the Network of East-West Women in response to the post-1989 changes in Eastern and Central Europe. She teaches at the New School for Social Research and with Rachel DuPlessis is editing *The Feminist Memoir Project*. A longer, footnoted version of "A Gender Diary" appears in *Conflicts in Feminism*, edited by Marianne Hirsch and Evelyn Fox Keller.

In the early days of this wave of the women's movement, I sat in a weekly consciousness-raising group with my friend A. We compared notes recently: What did you think was happening? How did you think our own lives were going to change? A. said she had felt, "Now I can be a woman; it's no longer so humiliating. I can stop fantasizing that secretly I am a man, as I used to, before I had children. Now I can value what was once my shame." Her answer amazed me. When I sat in the same meetings during those years, my thoughts were roughly the reverse: "Now I don't have to be a woman anymore. I need never become a mother. Being a woman has always been humiliating, but I used to assume there was no exit. Now the very idea 'woman' is up for grabs. 'Woman' is my slave name; feminism will give me freedom to seek some other identity altogether."

On its face this clash of theoretical and practical positions may seem absurd, but it is my goal to explore such contradictions, to show why they are not absurd at all. Feminism is inevitably a mixed form, requiring in its very nature such inconsistencies. In what follows I try to show, first, that a common divide keeps forming in both feminist thought and action between the need to build the identity "woman" and give it solid political meaning and the need to tear down the very category "woman" and dismantle its all-too-solid history. Feminists often split along the lines of some version of this argument, and that splitting is my subject. Second, I argue that, though a settled compromise between these positions is currently impossible, and though a constant choosing of sides is tactically unavoidable, feminists—and indeed most women—live in a complex relationship to this central feminist divide. From moment to moment we perform subtle psychological and social negotiations about just how gendered we choose to be.

This tension—between needing to act as women and needing an identity not overdetermined by our gender—is as old as Western feminism. It is at the core of what feminism is. The divide runs, twisting and turning, right through movement history. The problem of identity it poses was barely conceivable before the eighteenth century, when almost everyone saw women as a separate species. Since then absolute definitions of gender difference have eroded, and the idea of "woman" has become a question rather than a given.

In the current wave of the movement, the divide is more urgent and central a part of feminism than ever before. On the one hand, many women moved by feminism are engaged by its promise of solidarity, the poetry of a retrieved worth. It feels glorious to "reclaim an identity they taught [us] to despise." (The line is Michelle Cliff's.) Movement passion rescues women-only groups from contempt; female intimacy acquires new meanings and becomes more threatening to the male exclusiveness so long considered "the world."

On the other hand, other feminists, often equally stirred by solidarity, rebel against having to be "women" at all. They argue that, whenever we uncritically accept the monolith "woman," we run the risk of merely relocating ourselves inside the old closed ring of an unchanging feminine nature. But is there any such reliable nature? These feminists question the eternal sisterhood. It may be a pleasure to be "we," and it may be strategically imperative to struggle as "we," but who, they ask, are "we"?*

---

*The "we" problem has no more simple solution than does the divide itself, but, in spite of its false promise of unity, the "we" remains strategically important. In this piece "we" includes anyone who calls herself a feminist, anyone who is actively engaged with the struggles described here.

Names for a Recurring Feminist Divide

In every case, the specialness of women has this double face, though often, in the heat of new confrontations, feminists suffer a harmful amnesia; we forget about this paradox we live with. Feminist theorists keep renaming this tension, as if new names could advance feminist political work. But at this point new names are likely to tempt us to forget that we have named this split before. In the service of trying to help us recognize what we are fated—for some time—to repeat, here is a reminder of past categories.

MINIMIZERS AND MAXIMIZERS

The divide so central as to be feminism's defining characteristic goes by many names. Catharine Stimpson cleverly called it the feminist debate between the "minimizers" and the "maximizers." Briefly, the minimizers are feminists who want to undermine the category "woman," to minimize the meaning of sex difference. (As we shall see, this stance can have surprisingly different political faces.) The maximizers want to keep the category (or feel they can't do otherwise), but they want to change its meaning, to reclaim and elaborate the social being "woman," and to empower her.

RADICAL FEMINISTS AND CULTURAL FEMINISTS

In *Daring to Be Bad: A History of the Radical Feminist Movement in America, 1967–1975,* Alice Echols sees this divide on a time line of the current women's movement, with "radical feminism" more typical of the initial feminist impulse in this wave succeeded by "cultural feminism." Echols's definition of the initial bursts of "radical feminism" shows that it also included "cultural feminism" in embryo. She argues that both strains were present from the first—contradictory elements that soon proclaimed themselves as tensions in sisterhood. Nonetheless, the earlier groups usually defined the commonality of "women" as the shared fact of their oppression by "men." Women were to work separately from men not as a structural ideal but because such separation was necessary to escape a domination that only a specifically feminist (rather than mixed left) politics could change.

On the other side stands Echols's category "cultural feminism." In her depiction of the divide, the cultural-feminist celebration of being

female was a retreat from "radical feminism": "[I]t was easier to reha-
bilitate femininity than to abolish gender." She offers as a prime example of the growth of cultural feminism the popularity of Jane
Alpert's "new feminist theory," published in *Ms.* magazine in 1973 as
"Mother Right":

> [F]eminists have asserted that the essential difference between women
> and men does not lie in biology but rather in the roles that patriarchal
> societies (men) have required each sex to play. . . . However, a flaw in
> this feminist argument has persisted: *it contradicts our felt experience of
> the biological difference between the sexes as one of immense significance.* . . .
> The unique consciousness or sensibility of women, the particular at-
> tributes that set feminist art apart, and a compelling line of research
> now being pursued by feminist anthropologists all point to the idea
> that *female biology is the basis of women's powers.* Biology is hence the
> source and not the enemy of feminist revolution.

Echols concludes that, by 1973, "Alpert's contention that women were
united by their common biology was enormously tempting, given the
factionalism within the movement." Ironically, then, the pressure of
differences that quickly surfaced in the women's movement between
lesbians and straight women, between white and black, between
classes, was a key source of the new pressure toward unity. The female
body offered a permanence and an immediately rich identity that
radical feminism, with its call to a long, often negative struggle of resistance, could not.

As her tone reveals, in Echols's account, "radical feminism" is a relatively positive term and "cultural feminism" an almost entirely negative one. As I'll explain later, I have a number of reasons for sharing
this judgment. Finally, though, it won't help us to understand recurring feminist oppositions if we simply sort them into progressive versus reactionary alignments. The divide is nothing so simple as a split
between truly radical activists and benighted conservative ones, or
between real agents for change and liberal reformers, or between
practical fighters and sophisticated theorists. The sides in this debate
don't line up neatly in these ways. Maximizers and minimizers have
political histories that converge and diverge. A pretense of neutrality
won't get us anywhere either. I'm describing a struggle here, and
every account of it contains its overt or covert tropism toward one
side or the other.

ESSENTIALISTS AND SOCIAL CONSTRUCTIONISTS

One has only to move from an account of movement politics to one of feminist theory in order to reverse Echols's scenario of decline. In academic feminist discussion, the divide between the "essentialists" and the "social constructionists" has been a rout for the essentialists. Briefly, essentialists (like Alpert, above) see gender as rooted in biological sex differences. Hardly anyone of any camp will now admit to being an essentialist, since the term has become associated with a naïve claim to an eternal female nature. All the same, essentialism, like its counterpart, cultural feminism, is abundantly present in current movement work. When Barbara Deming writes that "the capacity to bear and nurture children gives women a special consciousness, spiritual advantage rather than a disadvantage," she is assigning an enduring meaning to anatomical sex differences. When Andrea Dworkin describes how through sex a woman's "insides are worn away over time, and she, possessed, becomes weak, depleted, usurped in all her physical and mental energies . . . by the one who occupies her," she is asserting that in sex women are immolated as a matter of course, in the nature of things.

"Social construction"—the idea that the meaning of the body is changeable—is far harder to embrace with confidence. As Ellen Willis once put it, culture may shape the body, but we feel that the body has ways of pushing back. To assert that the body has no enduring, natural language often seems like a rejection of common sense. Where can a woman stand—embodied or disembodied—in the flow of this argument?

Writing not about gender in general but about that more focused issue of bodies and essences, sexuality, Carole Vance muses over the strengths and vicissitudes of "social construction" theory. She observes that the social constructionists who try to discuss sexuality differ about just what is constructed. Few would go so far as to say that the body plays no part at all as a material condition on which we build desire and sexual mores. But even for those social constructionists who try to escape entirely from any *a priori* ideas about the body, essentialism makes a sly comeback through unexamined assumptions. For example, how can social constructionists confidently say they are studying "sexuality"? If there is no essential, transhistorical biology of arousal, then there is no unitary subject, "sexuality," to discuss: "If sexuality is constructed differently at each time and place, can we use the term in a comparatively meaningful way? . . . [H]ave constructionists undermined their own categories? Is there an 'it' to study?"

In the essentialist–versus–social-constructionist version of the divide, one can see that one term in the argument is far more stable than the other. Essentialism such as Jane Alpert's in "Mother Right" assumes a relatively stable social identity in "male" and "female," while, as Carole Vance argues, social construction is at its best a source of destabilizing questions. By definition, social-construction theory cannot offer a securely bounded area for the study of gender; instead it initiates an inspiring collapse of gender verities.

CULTURAL FEMINISTS AND POSTSTRUCTURALISTS

The contrast between more and less stable categories suggests yet another recent vocabulary for the feminist divide. In "Cultural Feminism versus Post-Structuralism: The Identity Crisis in Feminist Theory," Linda Alcoff puts Echols's definition of "cultural feminism" up against what she sees as a more recent counterdevelopment: feminist poststructural theory. By speaking only of "the last ten years," Alcoff lops off the phase of "radical feminism" that preceded "cultural feminism" in movement history, leaving the revisionist image of extreme essentialism (such as Mary Daly's in *Gyn/Ecology*) as the basic matrix of feminist thought from which a radical "nominalism" has more recently and heroically departed, calling all categories into doubt. It is no accident that, with attention to detail, Alice Echols can trace a political decline from "radical feminism" to "cultural feminism" between 1967 and 1975, whereas Linda Alcoff can persuasively trace a gain in theoretical understanding from "cultural feminism" to "post-structuralism" between 1978 and 1988. Put them together and both narratives change: instead of collapse or progress, we see one typical oscillation in the historical life of the divide.

These two accounts are also at odds because they survey very different political locations: Echols is writing about radical feminist activism, Alcoff about developments in academic feminist theory. Though political activism has developed a different version of the central debate from that of the more recent academic feminism, both confront the multiple problems posed by the divide. Nor will a model that goes like this work: *thesis* (essentialism, cultural feminism), *antithesis* (poststructuralism, deconstruction, Lacanian psychoanalysis), *synthesis* (some stable amalgam of women's solidarity that includes radical doubts about the formation, cohesion, and potential power of the group).

Instead, the divide keeps forming *inside* each of these categories. It is fundamental at any level one cares to meet it: material, psychological, linguistic. For example, U.S. feminist theorists don't agree about whether poststructuralism tends more often toward its own version of essentialism (strengthening the arguments of maximizers by recognizing an enduring position of female Other) or whether poststructuralism is instead the best tool minimalists have (weakening any universalized, permanent concept such as Woman). Certainly poststructuralists disagree among themselves, and this debate around and inside poststructuralism should be no surprise. In feminist discourse a tension keeps forming between finding a useful lever in female identity and seeing that identity as hopelessly compromised.

I'm not regressing here to the good old days of an undifferentiated, undertheorized sisterhood, trying to blur distinctions others have usefully struggled to establish, but I do want to explore a configuration—the divide—that repeats in very different circumstances. For example, in an earlier oscillation, both radical feminism and liberal feminism offered their own versions of doubt about cultural feminism and essentialism. Liberal feminists refused the idea that biology should structure women's public and sometimes even their private roles. Radical feminists saw the creation and maintenance of gender difference as the means by which patriarchs controlled women. Though neither group had the powerful theoretical tools later developed by the poststructuralists, both intimated basic elements in poststructuralist work: that the category "woman" was a construction, a discourse over which there had been an ongoing struggle; and that the self, the "subject," was as much the issue as were social institutions. To be sure, these early activists often foolishly ignored Freud; they invoked an unproblematic "self" that could be rescued from the dark male tower of oppression; and they hourly expected the radical deconstruction of gender, as if the deconstruction of what had been constructed was relatively easy. Nonetheless, radical, philosophical doubts about the cohesion of "woman" have roots that go all the way down in the history of both liberal and radical feminism.

Recently I asked feminist critic Marianne DeKoven for a piece she and Linda Bamber wrote about the divide for the Modern Language Association in 1982. "Feminists have refined our thinking a great deal since then," she said. Yes, no doubt; but there is not much from the recent past that we can confidently discard. In fact, the Bamber-DeKoven depiction of the divide remains useful because we are

nowhere near a synthesis that would make these positions relics of a
completed phase. One side of the divide, Bamber says in her half of
the paper, "has been loosely identified with American feminism, the
other with French feminism."

> But in fact these labels are inadequate, as both responses can be found
> in the work of both French and American feminists. Instead of debat-
> ing French vs. American feminism, then, I want to define the two poles
> of our responses non-judgmentally and simply list their characteristics
> under Column A and Column B.
>
>   Column A feminism is political, empirical, historical. A Column A
> feminist rebels against the marginalization of women and demands ac-
> cess to "positions that require knowledge and confer power." A Col-
> umn A feminist insists on woman as subject, on equal pay for equal
> work, on the necessity for women to be better represented in political
> life, the media, history books, etc. Column A feminism assumes, as
> Marks and de Courtivron put it, "that women have (always) been pre-
> sent but invisible and if they look they will find themselves."
>
>   The Column B feminist, on the other hand, is not particularly inter-
> ested in the woman as subject. Instead of claiming power, knowledge
> and high culture for women, Column B feminism attacks these privi-
> leged quantities as "phallogocentric." . . . The feminine in Column B is
> part of the challenge to God, money, the phallus, origins and ends,
> philosophical privilege, the transcendent author, representation, the
> Descartian cogito, transparent language, and so on. The feminine is
> valorized as fragment, absence, scandal. . . . Whereas the Column A
> feminist means to occupy the center on equal terms with men, the Col-
> umn B feminist, sometimes aided by Derrida, Lacan, Althusser, Levi-
> Strauss and Foucault, subverts the center and endorses her own
> marginality.

No doubt Bamber and DeKoven would restate these terms now in the
light of seven more years of good, collective feminist work, but I am
trying to write against the grain of that usually excellent impulse
here, trying to suggest a more distant perspective in which seven
years become a dot.

Alcoff is only the latest in a long line of frustrated feminists who
want to push beyond the divide, to be done with it. She writes typically: "We cannot simply embrace the paradox. In order to avoid the
serious disadvantages of cultural feminism and post-structuralism,
feminism needs to transcend the dilemma by developing a third
course. . . ." But "embracing the paradox" is just what feminism cannot choose but do. There is no transcendence, no third course. The

urgent contradiction women constantly experience between the pressure to be a woman and the pressure not to be one will change only through a historical process; it cannot be dissolved through thought alone.

This is not to undervalue theory in the name of some more solid material reality but to emphasize that the dualism of the divide requires constant work; it resists us. It's not that we can't interrupt current patterns, not that trying to imagine our way beyond them isn't valuable, but that such work is continual. What is more, activists trying to make fundamental changes, trying to push forward the feminist discourse and alter its material context, don't agree about what sort of synthesis they want. Nor can activists turn to theorists in any direct way for a resolution of these differences. Activism and scholarship have called forth different readings of the divide, but neither of these locations remains innocent of the primary contradiction. There is no marriage of theoretical mind and activist brawn to give us New Feminist Woman. And the recognition that binary thinking is a problem doesn't offer us any immediate solution.

In other words, neither cultural feminism nor poststructuralism suggests a clear course when the time comes to discuss political strategy. Though we have learned much, we are still faced with the continuing strategic difficulty of *what to do*. As Michèle Barrett puts it: "It does not need remarking that the postmodernist point of view is explicitly hostile to any political project beyond the ephemeral." The virtue of the ephemeral action is its way of evading ossification of image or meaning. Ephemerally, we can recognize a possibility we cannot live out, imagine a journey we cannot yet take. We begin: the category "woman" is a fiction; then, poststructuralism suggests ways in which human beings live by fictions; then, in its turn, activism requires of feminists that we elaborate the fiction "woman" as if she were not a provisional invention at all but a person we know well, one in need of obvious rights and powers. Activism and theory weave together here, working on what remains the same basic cloth, the stuff of feminism.

Some theorists, like Alcoff, reach for a synthesis, a third way, beyond the divide, while others, like Bamber and DeKoven, choose instead the metaphor of an inescapable, irreducible "doubleness"—a word that crops up everywhere in feminist discussion. To me, the metaphor of doubleness is the more useful: it is a reminder of the unresolved tension on which feminism continues to be built. As Alice Walker puts it in her formal definition of a "womanist" (her word for black feminism): "Appreciates and prefers women's culture, women's emotional flexibility . . . committed to survival and wholeness of entire people, male and female. Not a separatist, except periodically, for health."

This is not to deny change but to give a different estimate of its rate. Mass feminist consciousness has made a great difference; we have created not only new expectations but also new institutions. Yet, inevitably, the optimism of activism has given way to the academic second thoughts that tell us why our work is so hard. For even straightforward, liberal changes—like equal pay or day care—are proving far more elusive than feminists dreamed in 1970. We are moving more slowly than Western women of the late twentieth century can easily accept—or are even likely to imagine.

MOTHERISTS AND FEMINISTS

If the long view has a virtue beyond the questionable one of inducing calm, it can help feminists include women to whom a rapid political or theoretical movement forward has usually seemed beside the point—poor women, peasant women, and women who for any number of reasons identify themselves not as feminists but as militant mothers, fighting together for survival. In a study group convened by Temma Kaplan since 1985, Grass Roots Movements of Women, feminists who do research about such movements in different parts of the world, past and present, have been meeting to discuss the relationship among revolutionary action, women, and feminist political consciousness. As Meredith Tax described this activism:

> There is a crux in women's history/women's studies, a knot and a blurry place where various things converge. This place has no name and there is no established methodology for studying it. The things that converge there are variously called: community organizations, working-class women's organizations, consumer movements, popular mass organizations, housewives' organizations, mothers' movements, strike support movements, bread strikes, revolutions at the base, women's peace movements. Some feminist or proto-feminist groups and united front organizations of women may be part of this crux. Or they may be different. There is very little theory, either feminist or Marxist, regarding this crux.

The group has been asking: Under what class circumstances do women decide to band together as women, break out of domestic space, and publicly protest? What part have these actions actually played in gaining fundamental political changes? How do women themselves define what they have done and why? Does it make any sense to name feminist thinking as part of this female solidarity? Is there reason to think some kind of feminist consciousness is likely to emerge from this kind of political experience? Is the general marginality of these groups a strength or a weakness?

Almost all the women we have been studying present themselves to the world as mothers (hence, "motherists") acting for the survival of their children. Their groups almost always arise when men are forced to be absent (because they are migrant workers or soldiers) or in times of crisis, when the role of nurturance assigned to women has been rendered impossible. Faced with the imperatives of their traditional work (to feed the children, to keep the family together) and with the loss of bread, or mobility, or whatever they need to do that work, women can turn into a militant force, breaking the shop windows of the baker or the butcher, burning the pass cards, assembling to confront the police state, sitting-in where normally they would never go—on the steps of the governor's house, at the gates of the cruise-missile base.

As feminists, it interested us to speculate about whether the women in these groups felt any kind of criticism of the social role of mother itself, or of the structural ghettoization of women, or of the sexism that greets women's political efforts. As Marysa Navarro said of the women she studies, the Mothers of the Plaza de Mayo, who march to make the Argentine government give them news of their kidnapped, murdered children: "They can only consider ends that are mothers' ends." The surfacing of political issues beyond the family weakened the Mothers of the Plaza de Mayo. Some wished to claim that party politics don't matter and that their murdered children were innocent of any interest in political struggle. Others felt political activism had been their children's right, one they now wished to share. These argued that their bereavement was not only a moral witnessing of crime and a demand for justice but also a specific intervention with immediate and threatening political implications to the state.

This kind of difference has split the mothers of the Plaza de Mayo along the feminist divide. To what extent is motherhood a powerful identity, a word to conjure with? To what extent is it a patriarchal construction that inevitably places mothers outside the realm of the social, the changing, the active? What power can women who weep, yell, mourn in the street have? Surely a mother's grief and rage removed from the home, suddenly exposed to publicity, are powerful, shocking. Yet, as Navarro also points out, the unity of this image was misleading; its force was eventually undermined by differences a group structured around the monolith "mother" was unable to confront.

But, finally, to give the argument one more turn, many Plaza de Mayo women experienced a political transformation through their mothers' network. No group can resolve all political tensions through some ideal formation. The mothers of the disappeared, with their cross-party unity, have been able to convene big demonstrations, drawing new people into the political process. Women can move when a political vacuum develops; by being women who have accepted their lot, they can face the soldiers who have taken their children with a sense of righteous indignation that even a usually murderous police find it hard to dispute. On whatever terms, they have changed the political climate, invented new ways to resist state terrorism.

Using examples like these, the Grass Roots study group gave rise to a particularly poignant exploration of the feminist divide. In each member's work we saw a different version of how women have managed the mixed blessing of their female specialness. Actions like bread riots are desperate and ephemeral, but also effective. With these street eruptions, women put a government on notice; they signal that the poor can be pushed no further. It is finally women who know when the line has been crossed to starvation. But what then? Prices go down; the women go home—until the next time.

Women's movements for survival are like fire storms, changing and dissolving, resistant to political definition. We asked: Would a feminist critique of the traditional role of women keep these groups going longer? Or might feminist insights themselves contribute to the splits that quickly break down the unity shared during crisis? Or, in yet another shift of our assumed values, why shouldn't such groups end when the crisis ends, perhaps leaving behind them politicized people, active networks, even community organizations capable of future action when called for? If the left were to expand its definition of political culture beyond the state and the workplace more often, wouldn't the political consciousness of women consumers, mothers, and community activists begin to look enduring in its own way, an important potential source of political energy? Perhaps, our group theorized, we are wrong to wish the women to have formed ongoing political groups growing out of bread riots or meat strikes. Maybe we would see more if we redefined political life to include usually invisible female networks.

The more we talked, the more we saw the ramifications of the fact that the traditional movements were collectivist, the feminist ones more individualistic. Women's local activism draws on a long history of women's culture in which mutual support is essential to life, not (as it often is with contemporary urban feminists) a rare or fragile achievement. The community of peasant women (or working women, or colonized women, or concerned mothers) was a given for the motherists; crisis made the idea of a separate, private identity beyond the daily struggle for survival unimportant. Here was another face of the divide: Collectivist movements are powerful but they usually don't raise questions about women's work. Feminism has raised the questions, and claimed an individual destiny for each woman, but remains ambivalent toward older traditions of female solidarity. Surely our group was ambivalent. We worried that mothers' social networks can rarely redefine the *terms* of their needs. And, rich as traditional forms of female association may be, we kept coming on instances in which the power of societies organized for internal support along gender lines was undermined by the sexism of those very organizations.

For example, historian Mrinalini Sinha's research describes how the Bengali middle class of nineteenth-century India used its tradition of marrying and bedding child brides as a way of defining itself against a racist, colonial government. The English hypocritically criticized Bengali men as effeminate because they could not wait. Bengali men answered that it was their women who couldn't wait: the way to control unbounded female sexuality—in which, of course, the English disbelieved—was to marry women at first menstruation.

In Sinha's account one rarely hears the voices of Bengali women themselves, but the question of which sexism would control them— the English marriages of restraint or the Bengali marriages of children—raged around these women. Neither side in the quarrel had women's autonomy or power at heart. Both wanted to wage the colonial fight using women as the symbolic representatives of their rivalry. Because Bengali men wanted control of their women just as much as the English wanted control of Bengali men, the anticolonial struggle had less to offer women than men. In general, our group found that sexism inside an oppressed or impoverished community—such as rigidity about gender roles, or about male authority over women, or about female chastity—has cost revolutionary movements a great deal. Too often, gender politics goes unrecognized as an element in class defeat.

Our group disagreed about the women's solidarity we were studying: was it a part of the long effort to change women's position and to criticize hierarchy in general, or did motherist goals pull in an essentially different direction from feminist ones? And, no matter where each one of us found herself on the spectrum of the group's responses to motherist movements, no resolution emerged of the paradox between mothers' goals and the goals of female individuals no longer defined primarily by reproduction and its attendant tasks. We saw this tension in some of the groups we studied, and we kept discovering it in ourselves. (Indeed, some of us were part of groups that used motherist rhetoric, as Ynestra King and I were of women's peace networks, or Amy Swerdlow had been of Women Strike for Peace.)

Drawing hard lines between the traditional women's movements and modern Western feminist consciousness never worked, not because the distinction doesn't exist but because it is woven inside our movement itself. A motherist is in some definitions a feminist, in others not. And these differing feminisms are yoked together by the range of difficulties to be found in women's current situation. Our scholarly distance from the "motherists" kept collapsing. The children's toy-exchange network that Julie Wells described as one of the political groupings that build black women's solidarity in South Africa couldn't help striking us urban women in the United States as a good idea. We, too, are in charge of the children and need each other to get by. We, too, are likely to act politically along the lines of association our female tasks have shaped. We sometimes long for the community the women we were studying took more for granted, although we couldn't help remarking on the ways those sustaining communities—say of union workers, or peasants, or ghettoized racial groups—used women's energy, loyalty, and passion as by right, while usually denying them a say in the group's public life, its historical consciousness.

Culture offers a variety of rewards to women for always giving attention to others first. Love is a special female responsibility. Some feminists see this female giving as fulfilling and morally powerful. Others see it more negatively, as a mark of oppression, and argue that women are given the job of "life," but that any job relegated to the powerless is one undervalued by the society as a whole. Yet in our group there was one area of agreement: traditional women's concerns—for life, for the children, for peace—should be everyone's. Beyond that agreement the question that recreates the feminist divide remained: how can the caring that belongs to "mother" travel out to become the responsibility of everyone? Women's backs hold up the world, and we ached for the way women's passionate caring is usually taken for granted, even by women themselves. Some Western feminists, aching like this, want above all to recognize and honor these mothers who, as Adrienne Rich writes, "age after age, perversely, with no extraordinary power, reconstitute the world." Others, also aching, start on what can seem an impossible search for ways to break the ancient, tireless mother's promise to be the mule of the world.

EQUALITY AND DIFFERENCE

By now anyone who has spent time wrangling with feminist issues has recognized the divide and is no doubt waiting for me to produce the name for it that is probably the oldest, certainly the most all-encompassing: "equality" versus "difference." Most feminist thought grapples unavoidably with some aspect of the equality-difference problem at both the level of theory and of strategy. In theory, this version of the divide might be stated: Do women want to be equal to men (with the meaning of "equal" hotly contested), or do women see biology as establishing a difference that will always require a strong recognition and that might ultimately define quite separate possibilities inside "the human"?

Some difference feminists would argue that women have a special morality, or aesthetic, or capacity for community that it is feminism's responsibility to maximize. Others would put the theoretical case for difference more neutrally and would argue that woman, no matter what she is like, is unassimilable. Because she is biologically and therefore psychologically separable from man, she is enduring proof that there is no universally representative human being, no human wholeness. In contrast, the equality feminists would argue that it is possible for the biological difference to wither away as a basis for social organization, either by moving men and women toward some shared center (androgyny) or toward some experience of human variety in which biology is but one small variable.

Difference theory tends to emphasize the body (and more recently the unconscious, where the body's psychic meaning develops); equality theory tends to deemphasize the body and to place faith in each individual's capacity to develop a self not ultimately circumscribed by a collective law of gender. For difference theorists the body can be either the site of pain and oppression or the site of orgasmic ecstasy and maternal joy. For equality theorists neither extreme is as compelling as the overriding idea that the difference between male and

female bodies is a problem in need of solution. In this view, therefore, sexual hierarchy and sexual oppression are bound to continue
unless the body is transcended or displaced as the center of female
identity.

At the level of practical strategy, the equality-difference divide is
just as ubiquitous as it is in theory. Willingly or not, activist lawyers
find themselves pitted against each other because they disagree
about whether "equal treatment" before the law is better or worse for
women than "special treatment," for example, in cases about pregnancy benefits or child custody. (Should pregnancy be defined as
unique, requiring special legal provisions, or will pregnant women
get more actual economic support if pregnancy, when incapacitating,
is grouped with other temporary conditions that keep people from
work? Should women who give birth and are almost always the ones
who care for children therefore get an automatic preference in custody battles, or will women gain more ultimately if men are defined
by law as equally responsible for children, hence equally eligible to be
awarded custody?) Sometimes activists find themselves pressured by
events to pit the mainstreaming of information about women in the
school curriculum against the need for separate programs for
women's studies. Or they find themselves having to choose between
working to get traditionally male jobs (for example, in construction)
and working to get fair pay in the women-only jobs they are already
doing.

One rushes to respond that these strategic alternatives should not
be mutually exclusive, but often, in the heat of local struggles, they
temporarily become so. No matter what their theoretical position on
the divide, activists find themselves having to make painfully unsatisfactory short-term decisions about the rival claims of equality and difference.*

Regrettably, these definitions, these examples flatten out the oscil-
lations of the equality-difference debate; they obscure the class struggles that have shaped the development of the argument; they offer
neat parallels where there should be asymmetries. Viewed historically, the oscillation between a feminism of equality and one of difference is a bitter disagreement about which path is more progressive,
more able to change women's basic condition of subordination.

*If I had to come up with an example of a feminist strategy that faces the power of
the divide squarely, yet at the same time undermines the oppression the divide represents, I'd choose recent feminist comparable-worth legislation.

In this history each side has taken more than one turn at calling
the other reactionary and each has had its genuine vanguard moments. "Difference" gained some working women protection at a
time when any social legislation to regulate work was rare, and
"equality" lay behind middle-class women's demand for the vote, a
drive Ellen DuBois has called "the most radical program for women's
emancipation possible in the nineteenth century." At the same time,
bourgeois women's demands that men should have to be as sexually
pure as women finessed the divide between difference and equality
and gave rise to interesting cross-class alliances of women seeking
ways to make men conform to women's standard, rather than the
usual way round—a notion of equality with a difference. As DuBois
points out, it is difficult to decide which of these varied political con-
structions gave nineteenth-century women the most real leverage to
make change:

> My hypothesis is that the significance of the woman suffrage move-
> ment rested precisely on the fact that it bypassed women's oppression
> within the family, or private sphere, and demanded instead her admis-
> sion to citizenship, and through it admission to the public arena.

In other words, at a time when criticism of women's separate family
role was still unthinkable, imagining a place outside the family where
such a role would make no difference was—for a time—a most radical act.

Equality and difference are broad ideas and have included a range
of definitions and political expressions. Equality, for example, can
mean anything from the mildest liberal reform (this is piece-of-the-
pie feminism, in which women are merely to be included in the world
as it is) to the most radical reduction of gender to insignificance. Difference can mean anything from Mary Daly's belief in the natural superiority of women to psychoanalytic theories of how women are
inevitably cast as "the Other" because they lack penises.

Just now equality—fresh from recent defeats at the polls and in the
courts—is under attack by British and U.S. theorists who are developing a powerful critique of the eighteenth- and nineteenth-century
roots of feminism in liberalism. In what is a growing body of work,
feminists are exploring the serious limitations of a tradition based on
an ideal of equality for separate, independent individuals acting in a
free, public sphere—either the market or the state. This liberalism,
which runs as an essential thread through Anglo-American feminism,

has caused much disappointment. Feminists have become increasingly aware of its basic flaws, of the ways it splits off public and private, leaves sexual differences entirely out of its narrative of the world, and pretends to a neutrality that is nullified by the realities of gender, class, and race. A feminism that honors individual rights has grown leery of the liberal tradition that always puts those rights before community and before any caring for general needs. Liberalism promises an equal right to compete, but as bell hooks puts it: "Since men are not equals in white supremacist, capitalist, patriarchal class structure, which men do women want to be equal to?"

These arguments against the origins and tendencies of equality feminism are cogent and useful. They have uncovered unexamined assumptions and the essential weakness in a demand for a passive neutrality of opportunity. But there are cracks in the critique of equality feminism that lead me back to my general assertion that neither side of the divide can easily be transcended. The biggest complaint against a feminist demand of "equality" is that this construction means women must become conceptual men, or rather that to have equal rights they will have to repress their biological difference, to subordinate themselves in still new ways under an unchanged male hegemony. In this argument the norm is assumed to be male, and women's entry into public space is assumed to be a loss of the aspects of experience they formerly embodied—privacy, feeling, nurturance, dailiness. Surely, though, this argument entails a monolithic and eternal view both of public space and of the category "male." How successfully does public space maintain its male gender markers, how totally exclude the private side of life? (The city street is male, yet it can at times be not only physically but also conceptually invaded, say, by a sense of neighborhood or by a demonstration of mass solidarity.) Does male space sometimes dramatically reveal the fact of women's absence? How well does the taboo on public women hold up under the multiple pressures of modernity? Even if public and private are conceptually absolutes, to what extent do individual men and women experience moments in both positions?

Or, if one rejects these hopeful efforts to find loopholes in the iron laws of gender difference, the fear that women will become men still deserves double scrutiny. Is the collapse of gender difference into maleness really the problem women face? Or are we perhaps quite close to men already at the moment when we fear absorption into the other?

None of this is meant as a refutation of the important current work that brings skepticism to the construction of our demands. When health activist Wendy Chavkin notes that making pregnancy disappear by calling it a "disability" is one more way of letting business and government evade sharing responsibility for reproduction, she is right to worry about the invisibility of women's bodies and of their work of reproduction of which their bodies are one small part. When philosopher Alison Jaggar gives examples of how male norms have buried the often separate needs of women, she is sounding a valuable warning. When critic Myra Jehlen describes how hard it is for the concept of a person to include the particular when that particular is female, she is identifying the depth of our difficulty, men's phobic resistance to the inclusion of women into any neutral or public equation.

Nonetheless, I want to reanimate the problem of the divide, to show the potential vigor on both sides. On the one hand, an abstract promise of equality is not enough for people living in capitalism, where everyone is free both to vote and to starve. On the other, as Zillah Eisenstein has pointed out in *The Radical Future of Liberal Feminism,* the demand for equality has a radical meaning in a capitalist society that claims to offer it but structurally often denies it. Feminism asks for many things the patriarchal state cannot give without radical change. Juliet Mitchell's rethinking of the value of equality feminism reaches a related conclusion: when basic rights are under attack, liberalism feels necessary again. At best, liberalism sometimes tips in action and becomes more radical than its root conceptions promise. Certainly, no matter which strategy we choose—based on a model of equality or of difference—we are constantly forced to compromise.

It's not that we haven't gotten beyond classical liberalism in theory but that in practice we cannot live beyond it. In their very structure, contemporary court cases about sex and gender dramatize the fact of the divide, and media questions demand the short, one-sided answer. Each "case," each "story" in which we act is different and we are only at moments able to shape that difference, make it into the kind of "difference" we want.

The Divide Is Not a Universal

After having said so much about how deep the divide goes in feminism, how completely it defines what feminism is, I run the risk of seeming to say that the divide has some timeless essence. In fact, I want to argue the opposite, to place Western feminism inside its two-hundred-year history as a specific possibility for thought and action that arose as one of the possibilities of modernity.

When Mary Wollstonecraft wrote one of the founding books of feminism in 1792, *A Vindication of the Rights of Woman,* she said what was new then and remains fresh, shocking, and doubtful to many now: that sex hierarchy—like ranks in the church and the army or like the then newly contested ascendancy of kings—was social, not natural. Though women before her had named injustices and taken sides in several episodes of an ancient *querelle des femmes,* Wollstonecraft's generation experienced the divide in ways related to how feminists experience it now. At one and the same time she could see gender as a solid wall barring her way into liberty, citizenship, and a male dignity she envied, and could see how porous the wall was, how many ways she herself could imagine stepping through into an identity less absolute and more chaotic.

Modern feminists often criticize her unhappy compromise with bourgeois revolution and liberal political goals, but if Wollstonecraft was often an equality feminist in the narrowest sense, eager to speak of absolute rights, of an idealized male individualism, and to ignore the body, this narrowness was in part a measure of her desperation. The body, she felt, could be counted on to assert its ever-present and dreary pull; the Enlightenment promised her a mind that might escape. She acknowledged difference as an absolute—men are stronger; then, with cunning, wheedling a bit, Wollstonecraft made men the modest proposal that, if women are inferior, men have nothing to fear; they can generously afford to give women their little chance at the light. This is a sly, agnostic treatment of the issue of equality versus difference. Experimental and groping spirit, Wollstonecraft *didn't know* how much biological difference might come to mean; but that she suffered humiliation and loss through being a woman she did know, and all she asked was to be let out of the prison house of gender identity for long enough to judge what men had and what part of that she might want.

When Wollstonecraft wrote, difference was the prevailing wind, equality the incipient revolutionary storm. She feared that, if women could not participate in the new civil and political rights of democracy, they would "remain immured in their families groping in the dark." To be sure, this rejection of the private sphere made no sense to many feminists who came after her, and left modern feminists the task of recognizing the importance of the private and women's different life there, yet it is a rejection that was absolutely necessary as one of feminism's first moves. We in turn have rejected Wollstonecraft's call for chastity, for the end of the passionate emotions "which disturb the order of society"; we have rejected her confidence in objective reason and her desire to live as a disembodied self (and a very understandable desire, too, for one whose best friend died in childbirth and who was to die of childbed fever herself), but we have not gotten beyond needing to make the basic demands she made—for civil rights, education, autonomy.

Finally, what is extraordinary in *A Vindication* is its chaos. Multivalent, driven, ambivalent, the text races over most of feminism's main roads. It constantly goes back on itself in tone, thrilling with self-hatred, rage, disappointment, and hope—the very sort of emotions it explains are the mark of women's inferiority, triviality, and lascivious abandon. Though its appeals to God and virtue are a dead letter to feminists now, the anger and passion with which Wollstonecraft made those appeals—and out of which she imagined the depth of women's otherness, our forced incapacity, the injustice of our situation—feel thoroughly modern. Her structural disorganization derives in part from a circular motion through now familiar stages of protest, reasoning, fury, despair, contempt, desire. She makes demands for women, then doubles back to say that womanhood should be beside the point. Her book is one of those that mark the start of an avalanche of mass self-consciousness about gender injustice. So, in the midst of the hopeful excitement, the divide is there, at the beginning of our history.

◆

If the divide is central to feminist history, feminists need to recognize it with more suppleness, but this enlarged perspective doesn't let one out of having to choose a position in the divide. On the contrary, by arguing that there is no imminent resolution, I hope to throw each reader back on the necessity of finding where her own work falls and of assessing how powerful that political decision is as a tool for undermining the dense, deeply embedded oppression of women.

Though it is understandable that we dream of peace among feminists, that we resist in sisterhood the factionalism that has so often disappointed us in brotherhood, still we must carry on the argument among ourselves. Better, we must actively embrace it. The tension in the divide, far from being our enemy, is a dynamic force that links very different women. Feminism encompasses central dilemmas in modern experience, mysteries of identity that get full expression in its debates. The electricity of its internal disagreements is part of feminism's continuing power to shock and involve large numbers of people in a public conversation far beyond the movement itself. The dynamic feminist divide is about difference; it dramatizes women's differences from each other—and the necessity of our sometimes making common cause.

Gender Diary: Some Stories, Some Dialogues

If, as I've said, the divide offers no third way, no high ground of neutrality, I certainly have not been able to present this overview so far without a constant humming theme beneath, my own eagerness to break the category "woman" down, to find a definition of difference that pushes so far beyond a settled identity that "being a woman" breaks apart.

Though sometimes I have found the theoretical equality arguments I have described blinkered and reactive, when it comes to strategy, I almost always choose that side, fearing the romance of femaleness even more than the flatness and pretense of undifferentiated, gender-free public space.

I suspect that each one's emphasis—equality or difference—arises alongside and not after the reasons. We criticize Wollstonecraft's worship of rationality, but how willing are we modern ones to look at the unconscious, the idiosyncratic, the temperamental histories of our own politics? It is in these histories—private, intellectual, and social—that we can find why some women feel safer with the equality model as the rock of their practice (with difference as a necessary condition imposed on it), while other women feel more true to themselves, more fully expressed, by difference as their rock (with equality a sort of bottom-line call for basic reforms that cannot ultimately satisfy).

Why do I decide (again and again) that being a woman is a liability, while others I know decide (again and again) that a separate female culture is more exciting, more in their interests, more promising as a strategic stance for now than my idea of slipping the noose of gender, living for precious moments of the imagination outside it? An obvious first answer is that class, race, and sexual preference determine my choices, and surely these play their central part. Yet, in my experience of splits in the women's movement, I keep joining with women who share my feminist preferences but who have arrived at these conclusions from very different starting points.

This is not to understate the importance of class, race, and sexual preference but merely to observe that these important variables don't segment feminism along the divide; they don't provide direct keys to each one's sense of self-interest or desire, nor do they yield clear directions for the most useful strategic moves. For example, lesbian and straight women are likely to bring very different understandings and needs to discussions of whether or not women's communities work, whether or not the concept is constricting. Yet, in my own experience, trust of women's communities does not fall out along the lines of sexual preference. Instead, up close, the variables proliferate. What was the texture of childhood for each one of us? What face did the world beyond home present?

In the fifties, when an earlier, roiled life of gender and politics had subsided and the gender messages seemed monolithic again, I lived with my parents in the suburbs. My mother's class and generation had lived through repeated, basic changes of direction about women, family, and work, and my own engaged and curious mother passed her ambivalent reception of the world's mixed messages on to me in the food. With hindsight, I can see that of course gender, family, and class weren't the settled issues they seemed then. But the times put a convincing cover over continuing change. In "Second Thoughts on the Second Wave," Deborah Rosenfelt and Judith Stacey describe this precise historical moment and the particular feminist politics born from it:

> [T]he ultradomestic nineteen fifties [was] an aberrant decade in the history of U.S. family and gender relations and one that has set the unfortunate terms for waves of personal and political action to family issues ever since. Viewed in this perspective, the attack on the breadwinner/homemaker nuclear family by the women's liberation movement may have been an overreaction to an aberrant and highly fragile cultural form, a family system that, for other reasons, was already passing from the scene. Our devastating critiques of the vulnerability and cultural devaluation of dependent wives and mothers helped millions of women to leave or avoid these domestic traps, and this is to our everlasting credit. But, with hindsight, it seems to us that these critiques had some negative consequences as well. . . . [F]eminism's overreaction to the fifties was an antinatalist, antimaternalist moment. . . .

I am the child of this moment, and some of the atmosphere of rage generated by that hysterically domestic ideology of the fifties can now feel callow, young, or ignorant. Yet I have many more kind words to say for the reaction of which I was a part in the early seventies than

Rosenfelt and Stacey seem to: I don't think the feminism of this phase would have spoken so powerfully to so many without this churlish outbreak of indignation. Nothing we have learned since about the fragility of the nuclear family alters the fundamental problems it continues to pose for women. It is not really gone, though it is changing. And though feminism seeks to preside over the changes, other forces are at work, half the time threatening us with loneliness, half the time promising us rich emotional lives if we will but stay home—a double-punch combination. In this climate, feminist resistance to pronatalism—of either the fifties or the nineties—continues to make sense.

It's hard to remember now what the initial feminist moves in this wave felt like, the heady but alarming atmosphere of female revolt. As one anxious friend wondered back then, "Can I be in this and stay married?" The answer was often "no," the upheaval terrifying. Some of us early ones were too afraid of the lives of our mothers to recognize ourselves in them. But I remember that this emotional throwing off of the mother's life felt like the only way to begin. Black women whose ties to their mothers were more often a mutual struggle for survival rarely shared this particular emotion. As Audre Lorde once said, "We [black children] were not meant to survive," so parents and children saw a lifeline in each other that was harder for the prosperous or the white to discern. The usually white and middle-class women who were typical members of early women's consciousness-raising groups often saw their mothers as desperate or depressed in the midst of their relative privilege. Many had been educated like men and had then been expected to become . . . men's wives. We used to agree in those meetings that motherhood was the divide: before it, you could pretend you were just like everyone else; afterward, you were a species apart—invisible and despised.

But if motherhood was despised, it was also festooned—then as now—with roses. Either way, in 1970, motherhood seemed an inevitable part of my future, and the qualities some feminists now praise as uniquely women's were taken for granted as female necessities: Everyone wanted the nice one, the sweet one, the good one, the nurturant one, the pretty one. No one wanted the women who didn't want to be women. It's hard to recover how frightening it was to step out of these ideas, to resist continuing on as expected; it's hard to get back how very naked it made us feel. Some of the vociferousness of our rhetoric, which now seems unshaded or raw, came partly from the anxiety we felt when we made this proclamation, that we didn't want to be women. A great wave of misogyny rose to greet us. So we said it even more. Hindsight has brought in its necessary wisdom, its temporizing reaction. We have gotten beyond the complaint of the daughters, have come to respect the realities, the worries, and the work of the mothers. But to me "difference" will always represent a necessary modification of the initial impulse, a reminder of complexity, a brake on precipitate hopes. It can never feel like the primary insight felt, the first breaking with the gender bargain. The immediate reward was immense, the thrill of separating from authority.

◆

Conversation with E. She recalls what the new women's movement meant to her: You don't have to struggle to be attractive to men anymore. You can stop working so hard on that side of things. I was impressed by this liberation so much beyond my own. I felt the opposite. Oppressed and depressed before the movement, I found sexual power unthinkable, the privilege of a very few women. Now angry and awake, I felt for the first time what the active eroticism of men might be like. What men thought of me no longer blocked out the parallel question of what I thought of them, which made sexual encounters far more interesting than they had once been. Like E., I worried about men's approval less, but (without much tangible reason) my hopes for the whole business of men and women rose. For a brief time in the early seventies, I had an emotional intimation of what some men must feel: free to rub up against the world, take space, make judgments. With all its hazards, this confidence also offered its delight—but only for a moment of course. The necessary reaction followed at once: Women aren't men in public space. There is no safety. Besides, I had romanticized male experience; men are not as free as I imagined. Still, I remember that wild if deluded time—not wanting to be a man but wanting the freedom of the street. The feminist rallying cry "Take Back the Night" has always struck me as a fine piece of movement poetry. We don't have the night, but we want it, we want it.

◆

Another memory of the early seventies: An academic woman sympathetic to the movement but not active asked what motivated me to spend all this time organizing, marching, meeting. (Subtext: Why wasn't I finishing my book? Why did I keep flinging myself around?)

I tried to explain the excitement I felt at the idea that I didn't have to be a woman. She was shocked, confused. This was the motor of my activism? She asked, "How can someone who doesn't like being a woman be a feminist?" To which I could only answer, "Why would any-one who likes being a woman need to be a feminist?"

Quite properly, my colleague feared woman-hating. She assumed that feminism must be working to restore respect and dignity to women. Feminism would revalue what had been debased, women's contribution to human history. I, on the other hand, had to confess: I could never have made myself lick all those stamps for a better idea of what womanhood means. Was this, as my colleague thought, just a new kind of misogyny? I wouldn't dare say self-hatred played no part in what I wanted from feminism from the first. But even back then, for me, woman-hating—or loving—felt beside the point. It was the idea of breaking the law of the category itself that made me delirious.

◆

The first time I heard "women" mentioned as a potentially political contemporary category I was already in graduate school. It was the mid-sixties and a bright young woman of the New Left was saying how important it was to enlist the separate support of women workers in our organizing against the Vietnam War. I remember arguing with her, flushed with a secret humiliation. What good was she doing these workers, I asked her, by addressing them and categorizing them separately? Who was she to speak so condescendingly of "them"? Didn't she know that the inferior category she had named would creep up in the night and grab her, too?

I'm ashamed now to admit that gender solidarity—which I lived inside happily, richly, every day in those years—first obtruded itself on my conscious mind as a threat and a betrayal. So entirely was I trapped in negative feelings about what women are and can do that I had repressed any knowledge of femaleness as a defining characteristic of my being.

I can see now that women very different from me came to feminist conclusions much like my own. But this is later knowledge. My feminism came from the suburbs, where I knew no white, middle-class woman with children who had a job or any major activities beyond the family. Yet, though a girl, I was promised education, offered the pretense of gender neutrality. This island of illusions was a small world, but if I seek the source for why cultural feminism has so little power to draw me, it is to this world I return in thought. During the day, it was safe, carefully limited, and female. The idea that this was all made me frantic.

◆

S. reads the gender diary with consternation. In Puerto Rico, where she grew up, this fear of the mother's life would be an obscenity. She can't recognize the desire I write of—to escape scot free from the role I was born to. Latina feminists she knows feel rage, but what is this shame, she wants to know. In her childhood both sexes believed being a woman was magic.

S. means it about the magic, hard as it is for me to take this in. She means sexual power, primal allure, even social dignity. S. became a feminist later, by a different route, and now she is as agnostic about the meaning of gender as I am. But when she was young, she had no qualms about being a woman.

After listening to S., I add another piece to my story of the suburbs. Jews who weren't spending much of our time being Jewish, we lived where ethnicity was easy to miss. (Of course it was there; but I didn't know it.) In the suburbs, Motherhood was white bread, with no powerful ethnic graininess. For better and worse, I was brought up on this stripped, denatured product. Magical women seemed laughably remote. No doubt this flatness in local myth made girls believe less in their own special self, but at the same time it gave them less faith in the beckoning ideal of mother. My gifted mother taught me not the richness of home but the necessity of feminism. Feminism was her conscious as well as unconscious gift.

It is not enough for the diary to tell how one woman, myself, came to choose—again and again—a feminism on the minimalizers' side of the divide. Somehow the diary must also tell how this decision can never feel solid or final. No one gets to stay firmly on her side; no one gets to rest in a reliably clear position. Mothers who believe their daughters should roam as free as men find themselves giving those daughters taxi fare, telling them not to talk to strangers, filling them with the lore of danger. Activists who want women to be very naughty (as the women in a little zap group we call No More Nice Girls want women to be) nonetheless warn them there's a price to pay for daring to defy men in public space. Even when a woman chooses which shoes she'll wear today—is it to be the running shoes, the flats, the spikes?— she's deciding where to place herself for the moment on the current possible spectrum of images of "woman." Whatever one's habitual position on the divide, in daily life one travels back and forth, or, to change metaphors, one scrambles for whatever toehold one can.

◆

Living with the divide: In a room full of feminists, everyone is saying that a so-called surrogate mother, one who bears a child for others, should have the right to change her mind for a time (several weeks? months?) after the baby is born. This looks like agreement. Women who have been on opposite sides of the divide in many struggles converge here, outraged at the insulting way one Mary Beth Whitehead has been treated by fertility clinics, law courts, and press. She is not a "surrogate," we say, but a "mother" indeed.

The debate seems richer than it's been lately. Nobody knows how to sort out the contradictions of the new reproductive technologies yet, so for a fertile moment there's a freedom, an expressiveness in all that's said. Charged words like "birth" and "mothering" and "the kids" are spilling all around, but no one yet dares to draw the ideological line defining which possibilities belong inside feminism, which are antithetical to it. Some sing a song of pregnancy and birth while others offer contrapuntal motifs of child-free lesbian youth, of infertility, all in different keys of doubt about how much feminists may want to make motherhood special, different from parenting, different from caring—a unique and absolute relation to a child.

But just as we're settling in for an evening that promises to be fraught, surprising, suggestive, my warning system, sensitive after eighteen years of feminist activism, gives a familiar twitch and tug. Over by the door, one woman has decided: Surrogacy is baby-selling and ought to be outlawed. All mothering will be debased if motherhood can be bought. Over by the couch, another woman is anxiously responding: Why should motherhood be the sacred place we keep clean from money, while men sell the work of their bodies every day? Do we want women to be the special representatives of the moral and spiritual things that can't be bought, with the inevitable result that women's work is once again done without pay?

Here it is, then. The metaconversation that has hovered over my political life since 1970, when I joined one of the first women's consciousness-raising groups. On the one hand, sacred motherhood. On the other, a wish—variously expressed—for this special identity to wither away.

Only a little later in the brief, eventful history of this ad hoc Mary Beth Whitehead support group, a cleverly worded petition was circulated. It quoted the grounds the court used to disqualify Whitehead from motherhood—from the way she dyed her hair to the way she played pattycake—and ended: "By these standards, we are all unfit mothers." I wanted to sign the petition, but someone told me, "Only mothers are signing." I was amazed. Did one have to be literally a mother in order to speak authentically in support of Whitehead? Whether I'm a mother or not, the always obvious fact that I am from the mother half of humanity conditions my life.

But after this initial flash of outrage at exclusion, I had second thoughts: Maybe I should be glad not to sign. Why should I have to be assumed to be a mother if I am not? Instead of accepting that all women are mothers in essence if not in fact, don't I prefer a world in which some are mothers—and can speak as mothers—while others are decidedly not?

To make a complicated situation more so: while I was struggling with the rights and wrongs of my being allowed to sign, several other women refused to sign. Why? Because the petition quoted White-head's remark that she knew what was best for her child because she was the mother. The nonsigners saw this claim as once again imputing some magic biological essence to motherhood. They didn't want to be caught signing a document that implied that Mother always knows best. They supported Whitehead's right to dye her hair but not her claim to maternal infallibility.

I saw the purity of this position, recognized these nonsigners as my closest political sisters, the ones who run fast because the old world of mother-right is just behind them. But in this case I didn't feel quite as they felt. I was too angry at the double standard, the unfair response to Whitehead's attempts to extricate herself from disaster. I thought that given the circumstances of here, of now, Mary Beth Whitehead was as good an authority about her still-nursing baby as we could find any-where in the situation. It didn't bother me at all to sign a petition that in-cluded her claim to a uniquely privileged place. The press and the court seemed to hate her for that very specialness; yet they all relegated her to it, execrating her for her unacceptable ambivalence. Under such con-ditions she was embracing with an understandable vengeance the very role the world named as hers. Who could blame her?

Eventually, I signed the petition, which was also signed by a number of celebrities and was much reported in the press. It is well to remem-ber how quickly such public moments flatten out internal feminist de-bates. After much feminist work, the newspapers—formerly silent about feminism's stake in surrogacy questions—began speaking of "the femi-nist position." But nothing they ever wrote about us or our petition came close to the dilemma as we had debated it during the few intense weeks we met. Prosurrogacy and antisurrogacy positions coexist inside feminism. They each require expression, because neither alone can re-

spond fully to the class, race, and gender issues raised when a poor woman carries a child for a rich man for money.

Over time I've stopped being depressed by the lack of feminist accord. I see feminists as stuck with the very indeterminacy I say I long for. This is it, then, the life partway in, partway out. One can be recalled to "woman" anytime—by things as terrible as rape, as trivial as a rude shout on the street—but one can never stay inside "woman," because it keeps moving. We constantly find ourselves beyond its familiar cover.

Gender markers are being hotly reasserted these days—U.S. defense is called "standing tough" while the Pope's letter on women calls motherhood woman's true vocation. Yet this very heat is a sign of gender's instabilities. We can clutch aspects of the identity we like, but they often slip away. Modern women experience moments of free fall. How is it for you, there, out in space near me? Different, I know. Yet we share—some with more pleasure, some with more pain—this uncertainty.

About Women and Rights
1991

♦

JEAN L. COHEN

Jean L. Cohen, a member of the *Dissent* editorial board, is associate professor of political science at Columbia University. She is the author of *Class and Civil Society: The Limits of Marxian Critical Theory* and, with Andrew Arato, *Civil Society and Political Theory*.

That rights are controversial for women is neither a new nor an obvious idea. Although some of us would be quick to attribute only to men the view that women do not need equal rights, this would be misleading. How many of us realize that the main activists against women's rights in the past century have been women? In fact, the women's rights movement is the only one I know that has occasioned countermovements by its intended beneficiaries—by women and at times even by feminists.

The struggle for the right to abortion and the counter "right-to-life" movement (peopled mainly by women) is just the most recent example. It was primarily women who organized and ran the antisuffrage movement at the turn of the century. Many women oppose the use and legalized availability of contraceptives. The vast majority of women's organizations in the first third of this century fought against passage of an Equal Rights Amendment, insisting that women in the workplace needed protection more than equality. Recently, women (need I mention Phyllis Schlafly?) mobilized against the ERA, on the grounds that it would undermine women's status and prestige in our society. I know of no similar movements by blacks, workers, or ethnic groups in the United States against their own enfranchisement or against the acquisition of equal rights in the polity, the workplace, or civil society. Nor has the issue been resolved. On the contrary, it has become one of the most hotly debated topics within feminist legal and political theory.

What is behind this controversy? In spring 1989 *Dissent* carried an article by Ann Snitow, "A Gender Diary." Snitow identified a divide that in one form or another permeates all feminist theory: on one side those who want to undermine the category "woman" so as to minimize the legal impact of sex difference and gender; on the other, those who want to keep the category while changing its meaning and value in order to challenge existing gender hierarchies and to empower women. The first group embraces an androgynous ideal focusing on what women and men have in common; the second insists on the positive aspects of women's "difference."

Snitow convincingly argued that there is no theoretical high ground of neutrality and no obvious strategy that can offer a clear way out of this divide. I agree. The reason for this is the new sense of indeterminacy regarding gender identity. We have come to recognize that the meanings of sex, gender, and the body are not given but are socially constructed. As a result, we have to learn to live with the following complexity: women (like men) lead gendered lives and yet are not and refuse to be overdetermined by gender or gender stereotypes. All that is solid has indeed melted into air. Small wonder that the battle concerning gender is now drawn over who gets to interpret its meaning and who controls the practical implications of such interpretations.

◆

The contemporary debate over which kinds of rights women should demand reflects the continued force of the divide pinpointed by Snitow. This debate takes place within feminist legal theory under the general rubric of "equality" versus "difference"—the specific legal problem it poses is whether women ought to seek equal rights or "special" treatment from the law. Should women fight for truly gender-neutral laws and rights, or should they insist upon rights and benefits that reflect the gender-specific experiences of their lives? Those who champion the first position are called equality advocates; those embracing the second are labeled positive-action theorists. The problem is that each approach involves double binds and seemingly intractable dilemmas.

Let me cite as an example the controversy that recently emerged within the feminist community over the legal treatment of pregnancy-related disabilities at work. Invoking the 1978 congressional amendment to the Civil Rights Act of 1964, equal-rights feminists argue that women affected by pregnancy, childbirth, and related medical conditions should be treated the same as all other persons in their ability or inability to work, that is, by gender-neutral laws. However, if a company does not grant disability benefits to anyone, the logic of this position is that pregnant women then have no claim to benefits.

Positive-action theorists, on the other hand, insist that, since only women can bear children and the vast majority of women do become pregnant, formally equal-rights or gender-neutral laws would deny women needed benefits and unfairly disadvantage women workers. On this view, women can be treated equally in the workplace only by being treated differently. Thus, special rights for women as a class seem to be indispensable in this case and probably in some others, if we are to have equality of opportunity. The problem is how to discern when truly gender-neutral laws can achieve this goal on their own and when the acknowledgment of difference and special treatment (without stigma) is necessary.

Although the debate over rights in general is often couched in strategic terms, there are important underlying theoretical and normative issues that point far beyond the doctrinal matters raised in law journals. Debates over whether equal or special treatment will help women most raise questions about the meaning of equality and its relation to sameness or difference. Debates over whether one should argue for abortion by invoking the right to privacy or the equality provision of the Fourteenth Amendment force one to rethink the meaning of privacy, autonomy, personhood, and identity with reference to the moral postulate of equality. If all individuals are moral equals entitled to equal autonomy and respect as subjects capable of pursuing their own life plans, then abortion rights raise fundamental issues of equality despite the fact that they apply only to women. And arguments over the need for and against gender-specific divorce laws and the overall meaning of sex discrimination raise questions as to whether the law can ever be both gender-neutral and just. In short, the debates within the feminist legal community should force serious rethinking not only about sex, gender, and the Constitution, but also the meaning of rights in general and of equality, privacy, autonomy, and neutrality, in particular.

◆

Some have argued, however, that underlying the controversy over which kinds of rights women should seek is a more fundamental issue: namely, whether the language of rights in either form is appropriate to empowering women at all. As I've said, women's resistance to rights is as old as the women's rights movement. The reasoning by women who define themselves primarily as wives and mothers is simple: equal rights seem a threat to the doctrine of separate spheres and to the traditional concept of the family, by bringing women into a direct relation with the state, independent of their mates or brood. If the bearers of rights are seen as individuals, the heart of the feminist struggle for equal rights lies in the recognition of a woman's selfhood—of her existence as a unique person, different from other women, and with particular interests that might conflict with those of her husband, or even her children, at work, in politics, and in the home. Individual rights for women define women as individuals, outside a family frame of reference. They thus appear as a serious threat to those women who define themselves *within* that frame of reference, as wives and mothers. This is why supporters of the traditional family and of separate spheres mobilize against equal rights for women. This is also a source of the ideology that insists on a natural, biologically based (and morally superior) female identity rooted in the maternal role that requires recognition and protection of women as a group. We should not underestimate the continued strength of this view. In many parts of the country, traditional forms of life survive and so do efforts at strengthening them, often initiated by women understandably disenchanted with what the labor market or the world of politics has to offer them.

◆

To be sure, almost none of the equal-rights feminists prior to the 1960s sought to challenge women's traditional roles in the family. They saw no conflict between these roles and equal rights or the full inclusion of women in all spheres of life on formally equal terms with men. Since the 1960s, however, the second wave of equal-rights feminists did and still does seek to undermine the doctrine of separate spheres. At first, however, these feminists also ignored the difficulties involved in trying to include women in the public spheres of work and politics on the same terms as men. However, this happy consciousness soon became undermined, in part because of women's successes in gaining formal equality and in part because of the issues raised by the younger "third wave" in the late 1960s and 1970s.

As the examples of divorce-law reform and sex-discrimination jurisprudence show (see Okin's and Cornell's essays), formal equality and gender-neutral laws do not on their own undermine male privilege and power or seriously threaten substantive gender inequality in the labor market or the family. Still, the challenge to the public/private dichotomy and the doctrine of separate spheres initiated by radical feminists with their slogan that "the personal is political" revealed that women could not gain inclusion in economic or political life on equal terms unless there were fundamental changes in gender relations outside these spheres.

By the 1970s both "radical" and "equal-rights" feminists raised issues that opened the private sphere to public scrutiny. New breakthroughs in biotechnology have contributed to this development. But as the unresolved controversies over abortion rights (Olsen), the treatment of rape and domestic battery victims, pornography, child care, surrogacy contracts, and so on show, attempts to apply the principles of justice to the "private" sphere (Brill, Okin) have encountered intense resistance. This resistance, more than anything else, has led many feminists to conclude that apparently gender-neutral laws and rights regarding paid work and politics are often based on a male standard, backed up by hierarchical relations within the private sphere. Two new catchphrases capture the difficulties that women face under these circumstances: the "double burden of the working mother" and the "feminization of poverty."

◆

There are several ways to respond to this conflict. One might conclude that only the extension of women's rights from the political and economic into the private sphere could make rights operate in a genuinely egalitarian manner for women. The model of rights cannot stop at the threshold of the family any more than at the doors of the workplace. The second approach, in opposition to the first one, involves new types of arguments against rights and has led to a "third wave" of feminist theory. The arguments of the third wave are no longer based on traditionalist or biological conceptions of either women's difference or woman's place. Rather, they challenge what are taken to be the conceptual presuppositions of liberal-rights theory. Drawing variously on Marxist, communitarian, and postmodern theory, contemporary feminist claims that rights are inimical to women reject the conception of the self and the model of society that is allegedly attached to the idea of rights. Let me briefly explain.

The old Marxist critique of rights drew upon two arguments: first, that formal equality (equal rights) in a society based on substantive economic inequalities is an ideology that conceals and reinforces class hierarchies; second, that the rights-bearing person enshrined by the various declarations of the Rights of Man is modeled on the bourgeois proprietor. In short, the idea of basic rights rests on the ideology of possessive individualism: it presupposes a competitive, atomistic, ego- istic conception of the individual that has been generalized from mar- ket relations. As such it shores up the class hierarchies typical of capitalist society. For feminists resorting to the Marxist critique it was not a big step to add that the person presupposed by the idea of rights is not only a bourgeois but also a male. I would argue that these ap- proaches confuse history with conceptual structure, for, while it is true that property and gender have been invoked to restrict rights, it does not follow that rights are conceptually bourgeois or male.

The communitarian critique of rights-oriented liberalism is a varia- tion on these themes. The central issue for communitarians is of course not class, but community. From this perspective, the liberal ideals of moral autonomy and individual self-development that un- derlie claims for basic rights presuppose an abstract and ultimately incoherent concept of the self as the subject of rights. As the commu- nitarians see it, the bearers of equal rights are individuals whose rela- tions are purely instrumental or self-regarding. But what the communitarians fail to consider, in my judgment, is that rights have never been defended as the sole source of morality, and that they come into play in conflict situations when community is already rent asunder. Like the Marxists, communitarians argue that the type of so- ciety presupposed by the theory of individual rights is a competitive market society. Thus, a society in which individual rights are para- mount cannot be a solidaristic community but is alienated, anomic, privatized, and without moral substance. Still, it is easy to notice that the communitarian critics continue to dream of a society without di- vision, without conflict, and without the risk of the tyranny of majori- tarian consensus.

◆

The feminist version of the communitarian critique of rights draws not upon women's biology but on their experience as nurturers. Ac- cording to this view, rights thinking, especially if applied to the pri- vate sphere, devalues and threatens intimacy, care, relational responsibility, love, friendship, marriage, and the family. Thus, the ideal of individual rights is neither an appropriate ethical category for healthy personal relations (whoever said it was?) nor an accept- able ideal for the good life. But is the good life in a modern society

conceivable without rights? Indeed, some feminists allege that thinking in terms of rights is part of a male style of identity that threatens
what is most valuable in women's experience. They argue that, instead of struggling for equal rights in the public sphere or applying
the principles of justice to the private sphere, women should defend
the experience of nurturance and care in the private sphere and seek
to generalize concrete duties of loyalty and membership from the private to the public.

One wonders if this supposedly advanced version of feminist ideology has not in the end converged with its erstwhile opponent, tradi-
tionalism. In any case, its advocates leave few instruments in the
hands of women encountering traditional forms of oppression in the
family. Thus, one could easily grant that when the principles of justice are applied to the private sphere they tend to undermine the
family—that is, the patriarchal family and the power of the paterfa-
milias. But in modern civil societies, which are supposed to be regulated by egalitarian values, it is inegalitarian gender relations that are
the real threat to family life.

Finally, the postmodern argument against basic rights involves a
challenge to the very conceptions of subjectivity, universality, and human nature that the idea of rights seems to entail. Postmoderns insist
that there is no abstract subject or human essence that can be invoked to justify basic rights; rather, the subject is merely another position in language. The concept of universality is a myth that
illegitimately privileges the values of unity, totality, homogeneity, and
closure over multiplicity, fragmentation, and diversity. And the metaphysical assumption that there is a real, unitary human nature open
to discovery and representation by philosophy, which in turn can
ground fundamental rights, is here dismissed as a misguided effort to
find ultimate foundations. The possibility that there can be postmeta-
physical justifications for universal rights seems to escape the advocates of this position.

Recently, many feminists have taken up postmodern arguments
from the standpoint of gender relations. Accordingly, the discourse
of the sovereign self-identical subject is seen as the discourse of the
male subject of reason. The universalistic ideal that has informed
philosophies of history since the Enlightenment is taken to be based
on the suppression of women's difference, history, and temporality,
while the ahistorical and unitary conception of human nature enshrined in the idea of rights obliterates the hierarchical reality of
gender relations. In short, postmodern feminist theory challenges

the idea of basic moral or human rights as a dangerous Western, male myth that levels difference while constituting otherness (woman) as inferior. Since, on this view, there can be no justice without taking *difference* into account, rights and justice turn out to be antithetical. That the rights model can incorporate difference on the basis of a wider, more pluralistic, procedural notion of universality is hardly considered by advocates of this approach.

   That is, I believe, a shortsighted view. The challenge that feminist theory poses to those of us who recognize the connection between rights and freedom is the following: for women (and one hopes for men) to continue to take the idea of rights seriously, the core values underlying the idea must be reworked so that women can come to be considered both as individuals, persons, citizens, and as historically situated and embodied women who merit equal concern, respect, recognition, and solidarity.

Labor Under Siege

Diary from the Grape Strike
1973

♦

NICOLAUS MILLS

Nicolaus Mills, a member of the *Dissent* editorial board, is professor of American Studies at Sarah Lawrence College. His books include *Debating Affirmative Action, Like a Holy Crusade: Mississippi 1964—The Turning of the Civil Rights Movement in America,* and *The Crowd in American Literature.* "Diary from the Grape Strike" was written while he was working for the United Farm Workers.

When we are really honest with ourselves, we must admit that our lives are all that really belong to us.

To try to change conditions without power is like trying to move a car without gasoline.

—CESAR CHAVEZ

Los Angeles, 1967

I pronounce it like FDR's middle name, and the man at the Greyhound ticket window stares at me. "The bus don't stop at no place like that!"

"You sure?" He nods, and then I spell it out, "D-E-L-A-N-O!"

"De-*lay*-no. That's different. Sure, we got a six-thirty bus goin' there."

I buy a one-way ticket and start looking for a place to sit. It is close to midnight, but the bus station is still crowded. There is no room on the wooden benches for stretching out, so I prop my feet on my duffel bag and hunch down in a corner. I am half asleep when two cops come by and ask to see my ticket. They barely look at it once I take it out. They are checking to make sure no one is using the bus station as a flop house, and they go up and down the rows of benches like armed railroad conductors, prodding those who are sleeping with their billy clubs. Only rarely do they touch anyone with their hands. It's as if they were worried about infection. The police who ask for my identification when the bus stops at Bakersfield are the same way. I am asked to show my driver's license, but the minute it is out of my wallet, they nod and move on to the man across the aisle from me. We are the only two on the Greyhound they bother with, and they address us both in Spanish.

The Pink House

The bus trip to Delano is made up of sprints down freeways, then sudden turnoffs for small towns, and more freeway driving. The foothills along the way are one gray-brown mound after another. Their monotony is broken only by an occasional orange or lemon grove, and I sleep most of the time. I am tired when we reach Delano, but all I want to do is walk. A man outside the bus station gives me directions for the Farm Worker offices, and I start out for them. His directions, I soon realize, are almost unnecessary. Delano is as racially divided as any Southern city, and after a few blocks it becomes clear which part of town is for Anglos and which part for everyone else. I head west, past a cluster of stores and cafés and across the overpass that lets Route 99 cut through the center of town. I am surprised by the heat. It is not just that the sun is hot but that everything around me is. It feels as if there were radiators hidden in the trees and telephone poles. I am twenty minutes outside of town when a car pulls up. I wave it on. My instincts, this first morning in Delano, are to refuse a ride from anyone white. The driver ignores my wave and asks, "You going to the Union offices?" I laugh and get in. He is, it turns out, Jim Drake, Cesar's administrative assistant. He drives me to the Union's main office, a stucco bungalow with pink paint coming off on all four sides. The dirt road in front of the Pink House is lined with beat-up cars, and a half dozen people are sitting under a nearby tree. I am introduced to the people under the tree, most of whom have also just come to Delano, and then taken to Filipino Hall for breakfast. It is three days before I am assigned to work with the organizers who are laying the groundwork for a strike against the Giumarra Company, the principal grape grower in the area. I have been fearful of getting an office or a research assignment, and now the worst seems over. There is a shortage of sleeping spaces in the houses the union rents and so, with two others, I move into the back room of *El Malcriado,* the Farm Worker newspaper.

Card Checks

The organizers' meetings begin at eleven o'clock in the morning. They start this late because most organizing is done in the evening, after the workers come home from the fields, and Bakersfield, where the majority of Giumarra workers live, is an hour from Delano. Ten-thirty is usually the earliest an organizer can get back home. The only exception is Friday night, when organizing is cut short so that everyone can be at the Union's general meeting. Friday is also special because it is the day on which the Union's $5-a-week salary is paid. After the general meeting, most of the organizers end up drinking beer at People's Café, where prices are cheap and nearly all the customers are farm workers.

The organizers' meetings are run by Fred Ross, a tall, gaunt man, somewhere in his middle fifties. It is Ross who, while he was working for Saul Alinsky's Community Services Organization, started Cesar organizing, and the two have been close ever since. Ross introduces me and another new organizer to the group, but that is it as far as our newness goes. We are assigned to work with older organizers, but there is no theorizing, no special explanation for our benefit. It is assumed we will learn what needs to be done by having to do it ourselves.

The first organizers' meeting I attend begins with Ross asking for newly signed union cards. He is like a schoolteacher who has consciously decided to put his students in competition with each other. For those who have brought in only a few cards, there is very close questioning, sometimes sarcasm. For those who have brought in a good many cards, there is praise and usually a much greater willingness to hear out their stories. Most of the teams of organizers have brought in between five and eight cards; the exception is a pair who have brought in nineteen. The cards represent commitments by the workers at Giumarra to have the United Farm Workers as their union, and they put the Union in a position to call for a card-check election and know that it has the support to win. Still, this is not the main value of the cards. For it is clear that the Giumarras, who insist that their workers don't want a union, will never voluntarily agree to an election. What the cards do is prepare the way for a strike at Giumarra. They give the workers a chance to express their feelings and the Union a chance to make plans: to know the names and addresses of workers, to begin calculating who is or isn't likely to leave the fields when that time comes.

After the card check Ross asks, "Any more new crews?"

"Two more back in the mountains," one of the organizers answers.

There is a groan, and then a decision on who should make the first contact. This will happen at least three more times in the next weeks. Crews we never knew existed will be reported working in some remote part of the Giumarra vineyards. It is this kind of isolation that has made it difficult for the men to know their own strength or numbers, and when I drive to Bakersfield the next night to meet with a family that has not yet signed with the union, I am immediately confronted with this situation. We meet with a father and his two sons, and most of our time is spent answering questions they put to us about the union. It isn't that they don't hate the Giumarras but that they don't know how many other workers are willing to sign union cards and that they fear being blacklisted. They are also new enough to be afraid of their crew leader, and so, even when no one from the company is around, they keep to themselves during the day.

House Meetings

By the end of June, I have gotten used to the pattern of organizing. Meetings at eleven, late-afternoon dinner at Filipino Hall, into Bakersfield by five-thirty. There are still only about twenty of us doing full-time organizing, but it is going much faster now. We are no longer finding new crews, and more and more help is being given us by the workers themselves. They are bringing in as many cards as we are. We feel sure we already have the signatures of at least 80 percent of the workers eligible to vote in a union election. We are weak only among the Anglo workers. They are suspicious of a union in which the leadership is Mexican American and Filipino, aware that at the very least they can no longer expect to monopolize the higher-paying jobs, such as trucker and irrigator. Many of these men are from families that came to California during the Depression years, and they leave me with a vision of John Steinbeck's Joads accepting everything they once fought against.

With one other organizer, I share responsibility for five different crews. In three of them, we meet with the crew leader himself. In the other two, we concentrate on a group of men who rent the same house. We are in contact with each crew at least several times a week, sometimes to get new names, other times just to talk about how the grapes are ripening. From our point of view the ideal time for a strike is when the seedless Thompsons, the Giumarras' biggest cash crop, are ready for picking.

Early in July, Fred Ross makes a decision to hold a house meeting for the crew leaders we absolutely trust. It is a crucial step. So far, the workers have committed themselves only to wanting union representation. They have said nothing about a strike, and our problem is to see how many are willing to leave the fields when it comes to a showdown with the Giumarras. The meeting takes place early in the evening at a farm house just outside Bakersfield. Some of the men arrive in their own cars, others in the trucks they use to take their workers into the fields. We have to introduce at least half the crew leaders to each other, although many of them have been working at Giumarra for more than a dozen years. There is much joking about the need for introductions. They set the tone for the meeting: the men don't feel anonymous.

When Cesar speaks, it is not to rouse the men but to ask questions. "Do you want a strike? Will your crews stay out? Who else is to be trusted?" These are questions all of us have been asking, but now it is possible to compare replies and have the men judge one another's accuracy. Most of the crew leaders have never seen Cesar before, and he moves among them slowly, listening, asking questions, nodding in sympathy. Although there is nothing striking in anything he does or says, he sets off reactions we have not gotten in the last month. At the end of the evening Fred Ross asks the crew leaders if they are willing to help us arrange house meetings with their men. They say they are, and the stage is set for the most crucial part of the organizing.

El Mosquito

We try to hold the house meetings early enough in the evening so that we can remain outside and not have to turn on lights and be bothered with bugs. Occasionally we bring beer or soft drinks but usually not very much. We worry that, if the meetings seem like a party, people will think the union is trying to trick them. The questions we get asked are nearly always the same. No one believes the company will allow a union without a fight. What they want to know is how they can endure a strike. "Will the Union help with money? What if the Giumarras find out about the strike ahead of time? What about strike-breakers?" We make no promises. We talk about the union giving support, but only to those who come to work for it full-time. And we insist the strike must be nonviolent. It is slow going, and often we have a second or third meeting with workers from the same crew. At this time we also begin to publish *El Mosquito Zumbador* ("the buzzing mosquito"). It is a one-page paper, written in Spanish and English. We take it to the crew leaders at night, or deliver it ourselves in the morning by riding the trucks carrying workers to the fields. Sometimes *El Mosquito* does nothing more than list the Union's demands and compare them with the wages the Giumarras are paying. Other times it explains new benefits, such as health and accident insurance. But always it lives up to its name, and whenever there is a rumor or an incident, it appears in *El Mosquito*. At first *El Mosquito* circulates like an underground newspaper, with workers afraid to read it on the job. Then it breaks into the open. We distribute it one morning in front of the Giumarra packing sheds at Edison. Some of the office employees refuse copies, but virtually everyone else takes a paper. One of the Giumarra brothers drives by in a yellow Cadillac and tears up the *El Mosquito* he is offered. It is hard to think of anything more helpful he could do.

Fiesta

By the end of the month we have gone as far as we can with house meetings. It is necessary to see if the workers feel confident enough to turn out in mass for a Union gathering at which they know there will almost certainly be company spies. We decide on a fiesta. It will have free food and mariachi bands, and anyone can use these as an excuse for coming, although it is obvious that the fiesta will be for something more. We are worried that not enough workers will come, but we plan for two thousand anyway and spend the ten days before the fiesta urging our crews to come. Other problems in managing the fiesta become comic, especially the matter of what to serve. Cesar wants brains as the main dish and says he knows just the man to cook them. Everyone else groans, and for days the organizers' meetings open with someone asking if Cesar has given in on the brains. Finally, it turns out that the man who is supposed to cook them can't be gotten, and we settle on lamb instead.

Our fears about attendance prove wrong. We have more than two thousand, as farm workers who have nothing to do with Giumarra also come. We run out of lamb after several hours of serving, and by the time the speeches begin, we are serving only rice and beans and salad. It is hot inside the arena in Bakersfield where we are meeting, and the crowd is restless at the start, wanting the Union to prove itself, not really believing that they hold the key to a showdown with Giumarra. Only five people have been scheduled to speak, but it is still too many, and when Cesar's turn comes, the crowd is uneasy. He begins in a low voice, not moving his arms, barely moving his feet. He talks the whole time in Spanish, not doing what he usually does, stopping every few sentences and translating into English. I have a hard time following him, but the man next to me translates whenever I ask him a word, and I keep up that way.

It is the Union, much more than the Giumarras, which Cesar wants to talk about.

> I want to tell a story about a man with a whip [he says]. This man was an expert with a whip. He could flick the ashes off a man's cigarette while he smoked it . . . even pull a handkerchief out of a pocket with the whip. He could also kill a man with this whip, and because of his temper and his reputation, everyone was afraid of him. His workers always did what he told them, no matter how much they hated it, and his wife and his children were very quiet when he was around the house. . . . After a while, it got so that nobody would stand up to this man, and to keep in practice he began using his whip on anything that bothered him. A stray dog, a cat, even flies. He was so good, he could take the whip and kill a fly while it was still in midair.
>
> All this went on for many years and then, one day, as the man was sitting on his porch, a bee came buzzing around him. It flew in his hair and around his ears and didn't pay any attention when he tried to brush it away. One of the man's workers was passing by at the time, and when he noticed what was happening, he was very surprised. "Why don't you use your whip on the bee?" he asked. "It's no bigger than any of the other things you've gone after." But the man with the whip just smiled. "You don't understand," he said. "I can kill the bee all right. That would be easy for someone like me. But bees are different from anything I've whipped before. If you go after one, they all come after you. So, if I took my whip to this bee, there would be the whole hive to fight. I'd get stung for sure . . . !"

Cesar stops at this point. There is no sound, no movement, just waiting. Then he begins again.

That is what the union means. The union is like the bees, and the man with the whip is like the grower. He cannot do anything to one of us without having all of us come after him.

It could not have been more than a few seconds between when Cesar stopped speaking and when people began shouting. But it seemed to take forever, and I remember feeling that silence as important as everything that came after it.

Strike Vote

We call for a strike vote the first week in August, on the night after the men get their paychecks. We want to make sure no one has a reason for going to work the next day. The strike vote is unanimous, and the tension is so great after it that speeches are unnecessary. The meeting ends with the singing of *Nosotros Venceremos,* and for a brief moment I feel as if I were in Mississippi again, leaving a civil-rights meeting. In less than half an hour we are back in the office the union has rented in Bakersfield, planning for the next morning. So far, everything is going better than expected, but we still worry about workers we have not seen at the fiesta or the strike meeting. What will they do? How much influence will they have on their friends? Is it just fear that keeps them away?

The next morning all of us are up by three. Four of the five crews I share responsibility for have said they will join the strike. We drive to the fifth crew leader's house before he is up, and when he leaves, we follow his truck. At every house he stops, we get out of our car and ask the men who are up to stay away from work. More than half do, and by the time the truck gets to its last stop—an ice store—it is carrying only a dozen men. We get out and begin talking with the men, but this time less about the union than who they are loyal to: those who have joined the strike or the Giumarras. Just as I think we have failed, the man sitting nearest me climbs down from the truck, then two more follow, then everyone climbs down. We promise them rides back home, and they start heading for our station wagon. Suddenly, we realize we will never fit everyone into it, and it is not until their crew leader (who has been opposing us) says that he will drive every-one home that our problem is solved. We follow his truck to make sure everyone gets back home all right, and then we go out to the fields.

The sun is up, and it is still cool, the ideal time in the day for picking grapes. But the Giumarra fields are empty. The only people at the gates I go to are pickets and police. Later we learn that, except for the few Anglo workers, only two crews have broken the strike. Despite the number of men involved, our strategy has been kept a secret and the Giumarras are caught by surprise. It is not until the following week that they realize most of their workers are not coming back, and they start breaking the strike by bringing in crews from Texas and Arizona or border cities like Calexico.

The crews are bused in late at night so they can avoid our picket lines, but they cannot be kept under cover for more than a day or two. Most of the new workers were not told a strike was going on, and getting them to leave the fields is difficult. Roving picket lines, equipped with bull horns, speak to the workers whenever they get close to the road, and sometimes whole crews will throw down their boxes of grapes and leave the job. But most of the new workers are a long way from home and feel trapped. They have no money or transportation, and they don't know where else to look for a job. As the week goes on, new workers are brought in at a much faster rate than we can turn them away. The Giumarras also begin radio advertisements saying the strike is over, and before we can get the advertisements stopped, they have done us enormous harm.

Boycott

We ask the Department of Labor and Department of Immigration to check on what the Giumarras are doing (the men in a number of the new crews do not have legal work permits, and it is a violation of the law for the Giumarras not to inform anyone they hire that a strike is going on). But the government officials we speak to are of no help. Unprotected by the National Labor Relations Act, we are as handicapped as any union was before the New Deal. Even with a strike, we have no legal right to a representation election. We can only have one if the company agrees to it. Another week goes by, and it becomes clear that, if the strike is going to be successful and nonviolent, we must move to a national boycott of Giumarra grapes (we later include all California-Arizona grapes when other growers start letting the Giumarras use their labels). Organizers are sent out to key cities, and we begin cutting down on our work in California. Still, we maintain a picket line in front of the Giumarra packing sheds, and when word comes that some Teamster locals are prepared to honor the line, we run it around the clock. Along with a crew of five workers, I have a midnight-to-eight shift. Our one compensation is that it is cool at night. Not cool enough to wear a jacket but cool enough so that we don't sweat.

Most of our time is spent trying to keep awake. We get threats from some of the white packing-shed workers and from some of the high-school boys who have been hired to break the strike, but while I am there, nothing happens. I will be in Cambridge, doing research of my own and working part-time for the Boston boycott, when I will learn that the men I have been picketing with were beaten up so badly they had to be hospitalized. Two of the men were in their sixties. It is enough to make me stop imagining in more detail.

Winning: 1970

I am in the office of the Ladies' Garment Workers' Union in New York when word comes that the Giumarras are about to sign a contract and that the other Delano growers are ready to follow their lead. There has been talk of victory for weeks, and now, when it is official, the news seems flat. I look around me at the office the Garment Workers let the New York Grape Boycott Committee share. We have a picture of Cesar and some *Huelga* posters on the wall, but basically the typewriters and the telephones and the fluorescent lights belong here most of all. How different from the Pink House or Filipino Hall, where one never stops running into children. I cannot believe we would take the news about the Giumarras so calmly there. But then I wonder. Somewhere along the way, our organizing has come to take on a life of its own. The satisfaction it provides lies in the effort itself. When it is over and we win, there is a feeling of relief, above all, of purpose, but the intensity is gone. Perhaps we are punch-drunk in a way? I can imagine an outsider seeing us in that light. And then I stop thinking about it. A lettuce strike has begun in Salinas, and I have calls to make.

Human Capital and Economic Policy

1983

◆

ROBERT B. REICH

Robert B. Reich is the U.S. Secretary of Labor. He has taught at Harvard's John F. Kennedy School of Government and has been a commentator for National Public Radio and public television. He is the author of *The Work of Nations, The Next American Frontier, The Resurgent Liberal,* and *Tales of a New America.*

Dead-End Labor

Persistent unemployment and pervasive mismatches between skills and job opportunities are symptoms of a basic problem: America's labor force is not participating in the growing segments of the world economy. One out of every six jobs in the American economy now depends on the automobile industry. One out of every five unskilled manufacturing jobs in America is in the textile industry. All told, one out of every three American workers now depends for a livelihood, directly or indirectly, on American industries that are losing rapidly in international competition.

True, the economy performed extraordinarily well during the last decade in terms of creating twenty-one million new jobs for the surge of young people and married women who entered the labor force. But a large percentage of these jobs were dead ends. Seventy percent of them (outside government) were in services and retailing; almost all these jobs are sheltered from international trade. Thirty percent of the new jobs (employing more than seven million people) were in eating and drinking places (mostly as waiters, waitresses, cooks, and kitchen helpers), health services (hospital orderlies and attendants), and business services (typists, clerks, messengers, deliverymen, security guards, low-paid salesclerks, cashiers, janitors). Since 1973 the increase in employment in eating and drinking places alone has been greater than the total employment in America's auto and steel industries combined. Employment in finance, insurance, and real estate has increased substantially, but most of the new jobs in these industries also have been in low-level clerical and sales positions. Some new jobs also have been created in the shoe, textile, and tanning industries, but many of these have gone to illegal immigrants (an estimated six million of them are now working in the United States), who work for subminimum wages in order to compete with workers doing much the same tasks in Southeast Asia.

Even America's high-technology industries are filling almost as many dead-end jobs as skill-intensive ones. Production workers now constitute 45 percent of the American electronics-industry work force. They do such things as assemble integrated circuits, stuff circuits into printed boards, and transfer silicon wafers from ovens to acid baths and electroplating tanks—unskilled and tedious work. And because these production workers compete directly with workers in Taiwan, South Korea, and China, their pay is low, and declining in real terms. Between 1972 and 1978 their average salary increased by only 7 percent. By 1979 they were earning $4.52 an hour, or about $9,000 a year. (In contrast, between 1972 and 1978 the average salary of electronics engineers increased 33 percent; by 1979 they were earning an average of $48,000 yearly.)

Most of these new jobs in the American economy—in menial occupations sheltered from international trade or in low-paying assembly operations in direct competition with foreign workers—have no future. Wages do not increase with experience. Few or no benefits attach to these jobs. There is almost no job security. The majority of Americans in jobs like these are unprotected against an incapacitating accident, a heart attack, an illness, or a sudden layoff.

It is true that, even if America were to adapt itself to flexible-system production, there still would be some routine jobs to be filled by relatively unskilled workers. Not everyone is capable of maintaining precision machinery, developing software, or participating on a problem-solving team. But it seems a safe guess that, among the millions of Americans now locked into dead-end jobs, there are vast numbers whose latent talents and untapped capacities for learning could be put to far more productive uses.

◆

America has no mechanisms to shift its work force out of unemployment and dead-end jobs into the kinds of flexible-system industries
where Americans can gain and maintain competitive advantage while
preserving or increasing their real incomes.

Unemployment insurance is the main public program for Americans out of work. But it is designed to tide people over during temporary periods of unemployment, not to help the large numbers of
workers who are unemployable because they have no marketable
skill. Coverage is limited, providing only a fraction of the worker's
previous earnings (usually one-half) for only twenty-six weeks. It is
not available at all to people who have not yet entered the work force.
And there are wide variations among the states in eligibility and benefits. Six states and the District of Columbia provide benefits that extend slightly beyond twenty-six weeks. Another thirteen weeks are
available under a federally mandated scheme applying to states
where unemployment has been particularly severe. Most states also
place a ceiling on the amount of weekly benefits that can be obtained; where the ceiling is low, as in New York, Texas, and California,
workers who before had held relatively high-paying jobs may have to
get by on only a small fraction of their previous salaries. Given these
restrictions and inconsistencies, it is not surprising that only one-half
of America's unemployed receive unemployment insurance at any
given time.

Public welfare, in the form of Aid to Families with Dependent Children, is of little help. In half the states the program is available only
to single-parent families; in the other twenty-five states it also applies
to two-parent families in which the principal wage earner is unemployed. But in order to qualify, the family's assets (including house
and car) must not exceed $1,000. At most, the program reaches only
the hard core of America's poor.

The United States does have job-training programs, but they are
generally restricted to the unskilled. There are no programs to re-
train people with obsolete skills or those who wish to improve their
skills. America's publicly financed job-training programs do not prepare even the unskilled for real careers. They are oriented primarily
toward "public-service" jobs rather than toward new jobs in the private sector. In 1980, $6 billion of $11 billion in job-training money
was spent on public-service employment. Many states and localities
have used these job-training programs to hire people they would

have hired anyway. And even these public-service jobs have been temporary. In 1980, 40 percent of the job trainees were unemployed after
leaving the program. In any event, the Reagan administration is cutting back these programs severely: Department of Labor outlays for
job-training programs declined to $4.5 billion in 1982 from $7.8 billion in 1981, despite the addition of almost two million men and
women to the unemployment rolls.

The private sector does provide some training. In 1981 American
firms spent more than $30 billion on courses for their employees, af-
fecting about 6 percent of the labor force. (This is roughly half the
cost of higher education in America.) The Bell System, for example,
spent $1.7 billion conducting twelve thousand courses for up to thirty
thousand employees daily at thirteen hundred training sites around
the country. Xerox opened a $75-million training-and-management
center, training twelve thousand employees a year.

The vast majority of these programs, however, provide training in
narrow jobs or in processes unique to the company rather than in
broadly applicable skills. There is an obvious reason for this. Broader
training would render employees much more marketable, and therefore require that the firm pay them a higher wage in order to retain
them. Few firms are so generous (or foolish) as to want to bid up the
wages of their workforce in this way. In any event, companies are now
spending about the same amount on training per employee that they
spent in 1969—even though the need for such training is much
greater now that America's competitive position is in jeopardy.

Special government assistance has been available to workers and
communities injured by foreign trade—to provide relocation, retraining, and extended unemployment insurance to workers whose
jobs have been eliminated because of imports, and to aid communities facing economic decline. But, like unemployment compensation
and job training, these "trade-adjustment" programs have been dis-
connected from the process of industrial change in America. As a result, they, too, have failed to help ease the transition of the labor
force to sophisticated-system production. Administered by the Department of Labor and far removed from such forums as the Trea-
sury, Commerce, and the office of the U.S. trade representative,
where tariffs, quotas, and bailouts for industry are formulated,
worker-adjustment programs have been encumbered by administrative problems of determining whether imports are to blame for job
loss and of deciding where workers should relocate and for what jobs
they should seek retraining. In practice, these programs have provided workers with little more than extended unemployment com-

pensation. Since 1975, 1.2 million American workers have received cash payments under these programs, totaling $4 billion. Yet only thirty-six thousand workers have obtained any training, and only four thousand have received job-search allowances. In 1981 cash benefits totaled $1.5 billion, but the training budget was only $17 million. A survey of laid-off workers who had exhausted their unemployment benefits revealed that only 20 percent had received counseling, only 8 percent had received job referrals, and only 7 percent job training. (The Reagan administration has also targeted trade-adjustment assistance for substantial reductions.)

The only job-training programs with direct ties to the nation's economic development have been conducted by the Defense Department. Since World War II the military has trained generations of Americans. A survey undertaken in 1964 showed that 18 percent of all nuclear-power workers and 45 percent of all licensed nuclear operators learned their skills in the U.S. Navy. Many of the nation's skilled machinists, electricians, machine operators, and computer programmers also received their training while in military service. Defense-related education programs spawned new skills: the GI Bill following the war enabled 7.5 million veterans to attend college or technical school. The National Defense Education Act of 1958, inspired by Sputnik, provided low-interest education loans, teacher training, and funds for doctoral research. All these programs, in turn, helped ensure a well-trained workforce, which contributed to America's economic development well into the 1960s.

But defense-related job-training and education programs can no longer be relied upon to shift America's labor force into higher-valued production. These programs have been reduced in recent years, as more defense resources have been channeled to advanced weapons systems and other sorts of military hardware. Because new weapons technology is so specialized, the training that is provided has tended to be less broadly applicable to civilian occupations than before.

Most community and regional development programs have been similarly irrelevant to real economic progress. Firms seeking to diversify or to develop new products in an effort to regain competitiveness seldom, if ever, base their location decisions on the financial lures offered by needy communities—such as tax abatements, low-interest financing, or transportation facilities, most of which are made possible by federal grants. For one thing, the real value of these offerings constitutes, at most, a very small fraction of the costs of starting and operating a new enterprise, particularly when compared to factors such as prevailing wage rates, the availability of workers with particular skills, access to raw materials and suppliers, and local energy costs. Perhaps more significantly, so many jurisdictions now offer these inducements that they largely offset one another. As communities bid to attract businesses, one city's gain is another's loss, and little or no additional investment occurs. Federal programs finance much of this competition. For example, program eligibility standards have been drawn so loosely for grants from the Commerce Department's Economic Development Administration that 80 percent of American communities are now eligible; more than half the nation's locales have been deemed eligible for urban-development action-grant programs administered by the Department of Housing and Urban Development; and as a practical matter, every community in America can offer low-interest loans financed by federally subsidized industrial-development bonds.

The problems of worker and community adjustment are exacerbated by other public policies. The tax code, for example, effectively subsidizes capital mobility, but not the use of unemployed labor or underused public infrastructures. Firms in declining industries can typically take a tax loss on the plant and equipment that they leave behind, treat the cost of moving their headquarters as a deductible business expense, and take advantage of accelerated depreciation and tax credits for their investments in new plant and equipment elsewhere. But they reap no advantage from keeping their former employees or from utilizing the infrastructures of their former communities. Thus the tax code biases firms' incentives against staying put.

Similarly, American antitrust laws recognize that restrictions on mergers should be relaxed for failing firms, which otherwise might be deprived of the capital they need to regain competitive strength. But businesses that have been granted such antitrust immunity have not been required to accept even limited responsibility for their workers or communities. On the contrary, the resulting mergers have often meant closing or relocating the failing firm's facilities, with no provisions for labor or community adjustment.

The net result of all these programs has been the continued atrophy of the American labor force. Workers' skills are not upgraded to fit them for flexible-system production. . . .

◆

Other social policies (or their absence) have conspired to render much of America's labor force physically immobile. The fragmented administration of welfare and unemployment insurance, imposing different requirements and offering different benefits in every state, itself has discouraged mobility. Many unemployed Americans are reluctant to look for work in another part of the country for fear that they will lose the minimal assistance they have.

Federal housing policies have locked the labor force into stricken communities and regions. Generous credit assistance to homeowners (available through the Farmers Home Administration, the Federal National Mortgage Assistance Administration, and the Veterans Administration), coupled with tax breaks (in the form of mortgage-interest deductions and the ability to "roll over" proceeds from the sale of one's old house to purchase a new house without paying any tax on the transaction), have transformed the nation's housing stock into many middle-class Americans' primary form of savings. With so much at stake in one's home, the financial and psychological costs of moving are extremely high. This is particularly true if local housing prices are depressed as a result of a plant closing or any other manifestation of local economic decline, while housing prices in growing areas of the country are driven up by the increasing demand.

Those who cannot afford to own their homes are often even more trapped. The nation's stock of low-cost rental housing units is decreasing rapidly. In Washington, D.C., alone, 13,600 housing units have been converted to condominiums in the last five years. Only 2 percent of Washington's rental units are available for occupancy at any given time. More than ten thousand area residents are now on the waiting list for public housing. For America's poor, it takes a long time to obtain adequate accommodation. Once a rental unit is obtained, the occupants are understandably reluctant to leave. Rent-control laws in many jurisdictions further discourage the unemployed or underemployed from looking for jobs elsewhere, since the laws deter private builders from erecting other low-cost housing while allowing rents on existing units to shoot up if the current tenant forays out in search of work in another city.

Other social policies also are rendering the nation's labor force less adaptable. America's fragmented and expensive system of health care causes many Americans to fear that a debilitating illness will use up their savings and impoverish their families. Planned cutbacks in Medicare will only heighten this fear. Medical insecurity discourages people from searching for new jobs in locations far removed from family and friends who might sustain them in time of hardship.

Mass transit and day care represent other failed opportunities for

helping American labor shift into new production. If adequately
funded, both sorts of programs would allow workers to search for
work within a large radius of their homes. But mass transit and day
care are becoming some of the first victims of America's economic
decline. Subway systems in Boston, New York, Philadelphia, and
Chicago are near collapse, plagued by aging equipment, vandalism,
and frequent breakdowns and derailments. Bus systems in other major cities are experiencing periodic shutdowns because of insufficient
funding. And the demand for day-care facilities is far outrunning
their availability.

   In all these ways America is inadvertently accelerating its economic
decline. By failing to appreciate and act on the link between these social programs and future productivity, America is condemning itself
to a long and painful economic transition. Insecurity born of the fear
of sudden, arbitrary, and unanticipated loss—whether of job, home,
or health—does not inspire people to new productive feats. To the
contrary, insecurities like these discourage risk-taking and constrain
adaptability. People who feel insecure want to keep what they have,
even at the cost of some hardship and discomfort; the unknown
could be far worse. In the face of such insecurity, people will seek better lives for themselves and their families only when their situation is
truly desperate—as generations of immigrants will attest. . . .

The Era of Human Capital

Above all, a false choice—the free market versus central planning,
business culture versus civic culture—has prevented us from understanding the central importance of human capital to America's future.

   Unlike high-volume production, where most of a firm's value is
represented by physical assets, the principal stores of value in sophisticated-system enterprises are human assets. Specialized machines
and unskilled workers cannot adapt easily to new situations. Flexible
machines and teams of skilled workers can. Only people can recognize and solve novel problems; machines can merely repeat solutions
already programmed within them. The future prosperity of America
and every other industrialized country will depend on their citizens'
ability to recognize and solve new problems, for the simple reason
that processes that make the solution to older problems routine are
going to be the special province of developing nations. Industries of
the future will not depend on physical "hardware," which can be du-

plicated anywhere, but on the human "software," which can retain a technological edge.

Financial-capital formation is becoming a less important determinant of a nation's well-being than human-capital formation. Financial capital is highly mobile. It crosses international borders with the speed of an electronic impulse. International savings are flowing around the globe to wherever they can be put to use. The eagerness of Western bankers to recycle petrodollars to Poland and other high-risk countries is evidence enough. But a nation's store of human capital is relatively immobile internationally, apart from a few high-flying scientists and engineers. The skills, knowledge, and capacity for teamwork within a nation's labor force will determine that nation's collective standard of living.

The preeminence of human capital in sophisticated-system production gives new urgency to the old problem that markets alone fail to generate enough investment in human skills. Incentives to invest in human capital differ fundamentally from incentives to invest in physical capital because human-capital investment and the productivity that flows from it are necessarily social. A firm contemplating worker training knows that some employees, once trained, will leave the company. It invests less in human capital than it would if it could somehow ensure that the workers would stay on and apply their new productivity to benefit the firm. Meanwhile, the next company neglects developing its own workforce, confident that luring qualified workers away from the other firm will be cheaper than setting up its own training program. Because companies cannot force their workers to remain in their jobs and pay off the investment in increased productivity, no firm spends as much on human capital as it should (and would, if it could only reap the full benefits).

Even individual workers are apt to underinvest in their own training. When a person decides how much and what kind of training to get, he is usually ill-informed about the value of a certain skill, since that value is determined in the context of a job. He is uncertain about how well the investment will pay off for him, and the uncertainty makes him reluctant to spend much of his time or money on learning new skills. And even if he could be certain of the future value of investing in his own human capital (in terms of increased earnings), he may not be able to afford a year or two of training in new skills. Though loans are available for investments in physical capital, many workers are forced to finance their human-capital investments themselves. They cannot offer lenders an interest in their more productive future selves as collateral against a training loan. The lesson is that unaided market forces lead workers, like firms, to underinvest in human capital.

◆

This pattern of "market failures" is complicated by the fact that in flexible-system enterprises the real value of a worker's skill depends not solely on his own training but also on how his abilities complement and enhance the skills of his co-workers. When productivity gains flow over time from an integrated working unit, it makes no sense to depend wholly on individuals' cost-and-return calculations to set the level of human-capital investment.

In short, we are entering a new era of productivity in which the costs, the process, and the return from investments in human capital all are inescapably social. In the era of human capital and flexible-system production, failing to recognize this and to respond with the right mechanisms to supplement the market means stifling the sources of future economic growth.

But the fact is that America now is doing little to build new human capital, and the nation is wasting its present stock. We have organized production in a way that squanders our talents. Some of America's most gifted citizens are engaged in manipulating abstract symbols, with no result other than the rearrangement of industrial assets and the replacement of names on organization charts. Other citizens are unemployed or working in dead-end jobs that are sheltered from international competition. America displays great ingenuity in revitalizing its old physical assets: a Procter & Gamble factory that once made the ill-fated Pringle's potato chips now produces Pampers; many of bankrupt Braniff's jets now fly the "friendly skies." But America is sadly neglectful of its human assets. All too often, when a company fails, its plant and equipment are quickly redeployed, but its workers are—in effect—scrapped.

Unless America moves quickly into a new era in which upgrading and using our human capital become a central concern, however, our future wealth will come primarily from extracting coal, timber, and grain from our lands, from assembling advanced components that have been designed and fabricated elsewhere, and from distributing the resulting products to our own citizens. We will become a nation of extractors, assemblers, and retailers—relatively poor by the standards of the rest of the world.

Already America's gross national product per person (a crude measure of economic well-being, to be sure) is lower than it is in several other industrialized countries. Our average life expectancy is lower than in fourteen other industrialized countries, and our unemployment rate higher. We have higher rates of infant mortality. We enjoy less job security. These are illustrations of long-term trends that had already begun fifteen years ago. They will worsen, unless we act deliberately and strategically to speed the movement of capital and labor into higher-valued production.

◆

But ideologies resist change, particularly when change seems to threaten people's economic security. The process of long-term decline, once under way, has a self-perpetuating quality. It rigidifies old ideologies and engenders a widespread conservatism. It also breeds divisiveness as each group discovers it can preserve its own standard of living only by appropriating a portion of another group's declining wealth.

The dilemma is that the groups seeking to seize assets from each other are often the very ones that must collaborate if real growth is to occur. The clearest example is in labor-management relations. Here the portion of the pie shared by workers has been declining as inflation has outstripped wage hikes. Trying to recoup, unions demand catch-up raises, only to find that other unions do the same, generating another round of inflation. And as corporate managers harden their positions in the face of declining profits, they are apt to resort to hostile counterstrategies: hiring consultants to "bust" their unions; moving factories to other states or countries. The result is likely to be a breakdown in cooperation between unions and management, possibly sparking crippling rounds of strikes, which will ensure there will be even less product to spread around. Only when an entire industry faces collapse—as is now the case with automobiles, steel, and rubber—do labor and management begin to recognize their common interests, and by then it is usually too late for affirmative change. There is only time enough to make wage concessions and to form political coalitions seeking protection against imports, both of which merely perpetuate the underlying problems or pass them on to consumers and other industries.

American society is now rife with other "beggar-thy-neighbor" tactics, many of which are rational from the standpoint of the individual actor but tragically irrational for society as a whole:

- ◆ the asset rearranging undertaken through conglomerate merger, manipulation of balance sheets, and schemes of tax avoidance;

- exorbitant salaries and bonuses provided to executives in America's largest companies;
- the rising incidence of employee theft and insider dealings;
- the political demands for tariffs, quotas, and bailouts to protect companies against foreign competitors;
- and the refusal by many middle-income taxpayers to foot any longer the bill for social services.

The vicious circle has closed: As the economy continues to decline, Americans grow more cynical about collective endeavor. Their consequential retreat into egoism merely accelerates the decline, since collaboration is the only way to reverse direction.

Altering the ideological lenses through which many Americans have come to view government, business, and the economy will be difficult. It ultimately will depend on the quality of U.S. politics (a subject to which we will return). But in the short term, several changes can be made at least to slow the decline and reduce the fear and insecurity that fuel it.

◆

America could take several immediate steps to help shift into higher-valued production. These steps could overcome bottlenecks and constraints that now retard economic change and also serve to ameliorate the burdens that make change disproportionately painful to certain groups. They could be accomplished by merely altering the mix of tax incentives and subsidies flowing to American business, which now encourage paper entrepreneurialism and historic preservation and discourage investments in human capital. For example, in place of public-service job-training programs that merely perpetuate dead-end labor, we could provide unemployed workers with vouchers that they could cash in at companies for on-the-job training. Firms that accepted the vouchers would have half their training costs paid by the government, for up to three years. The program could be financed by a payroll tax paid by employees and employers. Any worker unemployed longer than three months would be eligible. The virtue of such a program is that it would match training to specific industrial needs and, by ensuring that companies themselves finance part of the training, help target program funds to firms that are serious about employing the newly trained workers. The program also would create incentives for companies to locate in high-unemployment, low-skilled regions, the work forces of which would collectively represent a substantial subsidy.

One variation on this theme would feature retraining vouchers. These would be available to any worker who had been employed for more than two years at his present job and wished to upgrade his skills. The vouchers could be cashed in at universities or accredited training facilities, which would be reimbursed by the government.

Programs like these would quickly pay for themselves. In West Germany, which has similar programs, the cost per participant is approximately $14,000 per year, once savings from reduced unemployment costs are netted out. This sum is likely to be far smaller than the new productivity benefits that are generated. Also, empirical evidence suggests that companies do respond to wage subsidies by increasing employment as well as by reducing their rate of price increases.

In addition to such direct subsidies, tax incentives could be used to encourage companies to invest in upgrading their workforces and communities. The tax code now provides incentives leading in just the opposite direction: companies that wish to desert their workers and communities in pursuit of greener pastures now can deduct their costs of moving as a business expense, write off the plant and machinery left behind, and obtain tax credits and accelerated depreciation against new plant and machinery purchased at the new location. On the other hand, education and training costs expected to be incurred for the purpose of preparing employees for new jobs in which they are not currently engaged cannot be deducted from current income. This policy preference generates large social costs as workers and communities are left stranded within vast pockets of unemployment.

To reverse this policy preference, the tax code might permit companies to claim tax benefits for retraining their older workers for new jobs. Just as a tax depreciation now can be taken against machines that are gradually becoming obsolete, the tax code might also permit employers to set aside an annual tax-deductible reserve fund for human-capital development, based on the number of workers on the payroll. The accumulated funds would be used for retraining and upgrading the work force within a certain number of years of their being set aside, or else the deduction would be lost. The tax code also might reward companies for remaining in their communities by giving them deductions proportional to their length of stay. In effect, this would be a kind of reverse depreciation—recognizing that the social benefits of remaining within a community (and the social costs of leaving it) often increase with the duration of a company's stay.

Tax reform might also eliminate the inconsistencies that invite paper entrepreneurialism. As of now, the tax code rewards corporations and individuals for rearranging assets and speculating on their future

value. The code confuses economically sterile transactions and productive investments in new wealth. It does this by, among other
things, making interest payments on loans for any investment tax-deductible. One avenue of reform would be to allow interest deductions
to be taken only for the purchase of new assets or the modernization
of old ones. Under this rule, mergers and acquisitions would not
qualify for tax deductions. Nor would commodity futures, paintings
by old masters, or real estate. Lest millions of middle-class homeowners suddenly be impoverished by this measure, however, mortgage-interest payments on one's principal residence would still be deductible
even for older houses, but the deduction would be limited to, say,
$5,000 per year.

There are many other ways in which incentives could be restructured to encourage human-capital investment. For example, companies now have little to lose by laying off their employees during
downturns. By foisting their payroll expenses onto the states' unemployment-insurance funds, they reduce their fixed costs. Then, when
the economy improves, the companies hire back their employees.
This merely encourages employers to consider their employees as
fungible commodities and discourages them (and their employees)
from making long-term investments in training. It also promotes
needless unemployment.

An alternative scheme would be to make companies' payroll contributions to the unemployment-insurance system depend directly on
the extent to which their former employees have been forced to use
the system in the past. If a company's practice was to lay off many of
its employees every time there was a downturn in the business cycle—
shifting the carrying costs for its labor "stock" onto the community—
its unemployment-insurance premium would be substantially higher
than that of an identical company that had kept its workers employed. Like any other insured entity, the former company would be
deemed a relatively bad risk and would pay accordingly. If unemployment-insurance rates were directly pegged to a company's employment history in this way, companies would have more of an incentive
to maintain their work forces intact and to invest in their long-term
development.

Other changes could be made in programs that use business subsidies to attract investment to various regions of the country. America's
economy has come to be based on distinct economic regions, each
with its own climate, raw materials, demographics, and special needs.
Major business investments ripple throughout a region, fostering

skills, spinning off new innovations (consider "Silicon Valley" around Stanford University, and Route 128 around Harvard and MIT), and spawning networks of suppliers that are dependent on the region's major industries. Similarly, a region's special problems—traffic congestion, inadequate sewage treatment, disposal of toxic wastes, water shortages—are largely a function of the regional pattern of industry. Within these regional economies, public and private investments are inextricably linked. But as capital markets have become national and even international, bank lenders and institutional investors have become almost oblivious to these linkages. Private-capital markets now focus narrowly on an individual company's bottom line. Across America, money that used to remain within regions is now pouring out. Money-market funds have grown to more than $200 billion, from only $11 billion at the end of 1978; most of this growth has been at the expense of financial institutions, mainly in small towns. The public response to this problem has been a welter of local tax-abatement schemes, industrial-development bonds, urban-development action-grants, and Community Development Administration loans—all spread so widely and so thinly across the land that their net effects cancel one another out, burdening taxpayers and granting companies pure windfalls that fail to influence location decisions.

Instead of this patchwork, and with no greater expenditure, the federal government might establish regional banks to provide low-interest long-term loans to industries that agree to restructure themselves to become more competitive. The banks would also supply cities and towns in the region with low-interest financing for maintaining and developing infrastructure such as roads and sewage-treatment plants. Bank directors would be appointed by state governors. The banks would finance themselves by issuing government-guaranteed bonds and shares of stock.

Some of these bonds and stocks could be made available to union pension funds. Pension funds are rapidly becoming a primary source of industry financing in America. Public-employee pension-fund assets now exceed $200 billion; private-employee funds, $450 billion. AT&T's pension fund alone is up to $31 billion. Indeed, such funds are now America's largest single source of investment, underpinning stock values as individual investors abandon the equity market. While private investors have dumped more than $20 billion worth of stocks since 1978, pension funds have increased their equity holdings by a greater amount. This year pension funds are expected to absorb $11 billion of new corporate debt and most of the new equity issues.

But a substantial part of this investment has been unrelated to America's human and economic development. Pension funds now hold $12 billion in foreign securities and another $13 billion in real estate. By 1990, if present trends continue, 22 percent of pension-fund assets will be invested in these ways. The potential social benefits flowing from investment in a regional economy have not been considered in these investment decisions. The investment of a given proportion of pension-fund assets in regional-development banks would help spur the economy and thereby benefit American workers over the long term.

Regional development also could be promoted through regional-based training programs. Participating companies within a geographic region might pool their training activities, with each company paying one-half of 1 percent of its payroll costs into a common training fund. The government would provide matching funds. The resulting training centers would contract with the participating companies to provide employees with appropriate training and re-training. The companies would help in the design of these programs.

Many companies are too small to provide their employees with adequate training and retraining. But through combining their efforts and receiving additional public funding, training programs could reach a scale that would make them worthwhile. With participating companies directly involved, the programs could have a multiplier effect throughout the area, increasing the quality of the regional work force and attracting more sophisticated jobs to the area.

◆

Whatever form these programs might take, the government programs flowing to businesses cannot be redirected to economic adjustment unless government has the institutional capacity to view all its programs in light of the nation's long-term economic health. The government now has no way to monitor the aggregate impact of these programs on particular industries. Defense procurement has a powerful effect on the economic development of the nation, spawning entirely new industries, setting the direction for their future development, enriching or impoverishing regions whose economies depend on defense contracts, employing one-third of the nation's scientists and engineers, contributing more than one-third of its total research-and-development budget, and training a large number of its skilled machinists. Other policies—tariffs, quotas, marketing orders, price supports, bailouts, federal loans and loan guarantees, subsidized insurance, and special tax breaks—also affect the pattern of industrial development. Government programs that promote certain industries or businesses amount to 13.9 percent of the nation's gross national product.

But these programs have been unrelated to the goal of long-term economic growth. The government now gives $445 million in tax breaks to the timber industry and $2 billion in subsidies to the dairy industry, but offers no special encouragement to the semiconductor industry. It spends five times as much on research and development for commercial fisheries as it does for steel; $6 billion in loans and loan guarantees go to the shipbuilding industry, compared with $940 million to the automobile industry. Without the institutional capacity to focus these programs on the competitive performance of our economy as a whole, government policy will inevitably serve the politically strongest or most active industries and businesses.

One small step toward a more strategic and more publicly accountable approach to national economic policy, therefore, would be to establish a public board to monitor these programs, perhaps located in the White House's Office of Management and Budget. As part of its responsibility, the board would each year recommend to Congress and to the president what changes should be made in programs that may be retarding national economic development.

Taken together, changes like these would constitute a modest start toward a dynamic economy. Of course, before we were to launch on any one of them, we would want to know a great deal more about its likely effects on business strategies and possible substantive or administrative difficulties. But even if they all were to be successfully implemented, they would not be a panacea. For America to enter fully into the era of human capital will require more dramatic changes in the way we organize ourselves.

The Breakdown of Labor's Social Contract

1992

◆

DAVID BRODY

David Brody is professor of history emeritus at the University of California at Davis and one of America's leading labor historians. His books include *Steelworkers in America, Labor in Crisis,* and *Workers in Industrial America.*

In 1950, John L. Lewis, head of the United Mine Workers of America (UMWA), and leading operators representing the entire soft-coal industry negotiated the first National Bituminous Wage Agreement. It was a triumphant moment for Lewis, culminating an entire career of dogged effort at constructing a collective-bargaining system that would stabilize the cutthroat soft-coal industry. With the formation, after the 1950 agreement, of the Bituminous Coal Operators Association (BCOA), Lewis had the industrial partner he ardently desired. For the next decade, the BCOA-UMWA agreement worked as Lewis had intended. Although production declined by 20 percent, coal prices remained stable. Wages rose from $14.75 a day in 1950 to $24.25 in 1958, and royalty payments of 40 cents per ton financed a generous welfare-and-retirement fund. The high-wage structure stimulated the mechanization Lewis had long championed. Output per miner jumped from 6.77 to 12.83 tons during the decade, so that, despite steeply rising wages, labor costs actually fell by 8 percent. Economists estimated that the union impact on wages—the 30 percent of earnings beyond what the labor market for miners would have commanded—exceeded that of any other basic industry.

The BCOA-UMWA agreement was emblematic, if in exaggerated

form, of the industry-wide bargaining systems that took wages out of competition, linked rising earnings to productivity gains, and integrated collective bargaining into the regulated national markets of postwar American capitalism. "An astonishing degree of unanimity in our judgment of industrial relations" now existed, remarked the Cornell scholar George Brooks at a 1961 symposium. "Almost all the articulate members of the community now accept the same objectives in industrial relations, variously called maturity, industrial stability, responsibility, or statesmanship." This consensus, in turn, signified an enduring social contract between labor, capital, and the state that at long last put behind the country a century of endemic industrial strife. Brooks's conclusion was very like Francis Fukuyama's famous response to the end of the cold war in our own time: the triumph of the postwar settlement meant the end of labor history. To see what actually happened, let us return to the coal industry.

No sooner had Lewis retired in 1960 than the economic underpinnings of his grand strategy started to unravel. After half a century of secular decline, the demand for coal began to rise, but almost exclusively from the electric utilities, which were consuming 80 percent of output by 1980. The structure of the industry was transformed by the entry of conglomerates: by 1976, only three of the forty largest coal producers remained under independent management. And, in the strip-mining fields of the west that produced a quarter of the nation's coal by 1980, there was a new and potent nonunion sector to contend with. As an economic regulator—a mechanism for stabilizing a highly competitive, overdeveloped industry—the BCOA-UMWA agreement had effectively been superseded. On top of this came a crisis over productivity, induced by the clash between union work rules rooted in the premechanization era and the rationalizing demands of an increasingly capital-intensive industry. Amid widespread workplace strife, output per worker in the underground mines plunged during the 1970s.

The best union leadership in the world would have been pressed to manage these problems. Under Lewis's incompetent successors, beginning with the corrupt Tony Boyle, the UMWA never had a chance. The BCOA-UMWA structure still exists, but, with only twenty signatories to the 1988 contract, scarcely matters for the industry. Once almost fully organized, the UMWA represents fewer than 15 percent of the nation's miners, and, despite Richard Trumka's robust leadership and the courage of the Pittston strikers, today faces a bleak future.

In its decline, as in its moment of collective-bargaining triumph, the Mine Workers Union is emblematic—again, to an exaggerated degree—of what has happened to the labor movement in recent years. As in coal mining, transforming changes have everywhere swept across the economic landscape. In some industries, as in communications, the airlines, and trucking, labor's problems stemmed from government deregulation; in others, as in autos, steel, clothing, and shoes, from foreign competition; and elsewhere, from construction to retailing, from a host of other destabilizing market and technological changes. Whatever the particularities, the recent economic revolution has been remarkably consistent in its impact on the labor movement: in the private sector, collective-bargaining systems are everywhere under siege, and antiunionism is resurgent. The social contract of the postwar era is, for practical purposes, dead.

Individual unions have responded with varying degrees of flexibility and resourcefulness. The performance of the Mine Workers by no means represents the norm. But even the most inventive of unions— for example, the Steelworkers in the face of its industry's extraordinary collapse in the early 1980s—could not prevent the deep erosion of their membership bases. The Steelworkers emerged with its union-management relations largely intact, but with a membership cut in half: in basic steel, production jobs shrank from half a million in 1975 to 120,000 in 1990.

The depth of labor's crisis is best captured in the numbers. In 1970, membership in the private sector stood at an all-time high of seventeen million. That translated into a union density of 29.1 percent, down only by six points from the peak of 35.7 percent in 1953. By the mid-1980s, union density in the private sector had fallen to roughly 17 percent, and membership was down by five million from the 1970 high mark. Today, union representation in the private sector stands at 12 percent. But for union successes in the public sector, a phenomenon that began in the 1960s, the labor movement would be down perilously close to pre–New Deal levels.

◆

In accounting for this calamitous decline, my premise is that the operative forces are economic. In the American case that is an unarguable truth. But there is no automatic or universal translation of market competition and structural change into trade-union decline. What is happening in the United States is after all part of a global phenomenon, affecting, if not necessarily to the same degree or in precisely the same ways, the labor markets of all the advanced industrial economies. Indeed, if one credits the influential argument of the *Régulation* school of French political economy, a new stage of late capitalism has set in worldwide, displacing the regulated national economies of the postwar era with a global economic order characterized by capital mobility and competitive labor markets.

Yet no other labor movement has been so hard hit as the American by these global developments—at least, as reflected in the numbers. Of fifteen industrialized countries, only in three others did the percentage of organized workers actually fall between 1970 and 1985–86, and nowhere with anything like the magnitude of the American decline. In 1970, the United States was at the bottom end of the scale, but it shared the 30–39 percent decile with six other countries. At 17 percent in 1985–86, it stood in a class by itself, eleven points behind the next-most-laggard movement.

Consider, moreover, the diverging fates of Canadian and U.S. unionism in these years. No two movements could have been more alike in institutional makeup and historical experience. The early and persistent tendency of Canadian local unions to affiliate with the emerging national trade unions south of the border—not the contrary impulses of Canadian nationalism—was the determining fact in the evolution of Canadian unionism. The decisive moment came in 1902, when the Trades and Labour Congress (TLC—the Canadian counterpart to the American Federation of Labor) expelled the Knights of Labor bodies and adopted the AFL principle of opposition to dual unionism, thereby granting the Canadian branches of the U.S. internationals a virtual monopoly over trade-union representation in the TLC. It became, in effect, the Canadian wing of the American movement. And thereafter, with certain deviations, the two movements came close to having a unitary institutional history, with the Canadians generally marching a half step to the rear. There was the same split over industrial unionism in the 1930s, a Canadian version of the Wagner Act in 1944, anticommunist purges in 1949–50, and, in the wake of AFL-CIO reunification in 1955, the Canadian Labour Congress the next year. At that time, 70 percent of all organized workers in Canada belonged to AFL-CIO unions. The 1950s marked the apex of the historic tendency toward an integrated North American labor movement.

That tendency no longer governs. From the 1960s onward, the Canadian unions entered a period of sustained growth, more than doubling their membership in twenty years and, by the early 1980s, boasting a unionized sector approaching 40 percent—this in stark contrast to the devastating spiral below 20 percent in the United States. The historic linkages between the two movements are disintegrating. Increasingly, the Canadian branches have been inclined to go their own way, either by asserting more autonomy or, like the Canadian Auto Workers in 1984, by declaring their independence. A dwindling share of the Canadian movement—35 percent or less by the late 1980s—retains ties to the AFL-CIO, and the sense that the Canadian movement has a separate destiny is palpable. The Canadian Auto Workers split off from the UAW citing the responsibility that they had "to play a lead role" in fulfilling "a Canadian labour movement programme."

How are we to account for this remarkable divergence of institutional fortunes? For auto, an economic explanation might suffice. The Canadian industry boomed after the 1982 recession. With output and employment on the rise—the Canadian share of North American production expanded by 25 percent during the decade— Canadian auto-workers were spared the plant closings and draconian cost-cutting demands confronting their U.S. brothers and sisters. The vaunted Canadian militancy against concessions was well grounded in a markedly more favorable bargaining environment. But for Canada as a whole that was decidedly not the case. Since 1973, manufacturing productivity has increased even more slowly than in the United States, the unemployment rate has run almost consistently higher during the 1980s (it currently stands at 10 percent), and, as in the United States, the downward pressure on wages has been (in the words of the Canadian scholar Daniel Drache) "far-reaching and broad-based." It cannot be said that the economic environment for collective bargaining is more favorable in Canada than in the United States.

What has become more favorable is, in the broadest sense, political. In the United States, the legal framework for collective bargaining has deeply eroded since the days of the Wagner Act. Employers today feel free to thwart unionization and, perhaps even more important in the current economic climate, to break out of established contractual relations—hence the current eagerness of the AFL-CIO for legislation prohibiting the permanent replacement of strikers. It signifies the political weakness of organized labor that this modest strengthening of union protections stands so little chance of passage.

In Canada, on the other hand, the collective-bargaining process is closely regulated by conciliation requirements, strike votes, and prohibitions against stoppages during the life of contracts (with mandatory arbitration of grievances required). In flush times, these state restraints might seem burdensome (in practice, of course, they become incorporated into the bargaining strategy of the parties), but under adverse conditions, they preserve the collective bargaining process itself. The rights of workers to organize and bargain collectively are much more effectively protected under Canadian law because of swift certification procedures and the mandatory signing of first agreements. And in a variety of ways—in the agency-shop requirements in the major provinces (as compared with the right-to-work laws in many states) and in limitations on the freedom of employers to move from unionized sites—Canadian law signals the legitimacy of collective bargaining. This is reflected in the bargaining rights granted public employees, who are organized at twice the U.S. rate and are identified with the militant wing of the Canadian movement. In Canada corporate employers—even those with nasty records south of the border—do not sing the praises of a union-free environment, and, of course, there is no Canadian counterpart to the action by the Reagan administration breaking the strike of air-traffic controllers in 1981. There has emerged what the Canadian scholar Christopher Huxley and his associates have called a distinctively Canadian "labor regime."

By way of explanation, the sociologist Seymour Lipset and others point to collectivist values inhering in the Canadian political culture that accord legitimacy to the labor movement and shelter it from the market-driven antiunionism rampant in the United States. There is much to be said for this as a basic explanation, but the fact is that, although Canadian statist tendencies go far back (for example, to MacKenzie King's Industrial Disputes Investigative Act of 1907), the legal and political climate was no more favorable to trade unionism, nor was the unionized sector larger, in Canada than in the United States up to quite recent times. The catalytic element sparking Canada's modern "labor regime" is to be found in the country's changing party system and in a new path taken by Canadian labor. In the 1960s, a political divergence occurred no less remarkable than the divergence in the institutional fortunes of the two movements.

◆

The AFL-CIO remained steadfastly nonpartisan, although, as compared with the old AFL, with far more potent force and in firm alliance with the Democratic Party. In Canada, on the other hand, the two-party system itself came under attack, initially by the Cooperative Commonwealth Federation in the western provinces and then more decisively with the formation of the New Democratic Party (NDP) in 1961. Canadian labor threw off the nonpartisanship fostered by the AFL-CIO linkage and entered into a robust social-democratic third-party politics. As the NDP made headway—its progress capped by the capture of Ontario in the 1990 elections—Canadian unionism not only gained political muscle but increasingly became a progressive force in the nation's political life. It assumed the mantle of what the Canadian scholar Pradeep Kumar calls "social unionism." In the meanwhile, the AFL-CIO fell on hard political times, becoming more marginal to electoral politics after the collapse of the Johnson administration in 1968 and reduced increasingly to fighting for its own sectional interests rather than for the larger social-justice objectives that since the New Deal had animated labor's legislative agenda. This is "the most striking difference," remark Huxley and his associates in the essay referred to earlier—"the increasing importance of more adversarial and political unionism in Canada, marked above all by the interdependence and mutual aid between key unions and the New Democratic party, and analogous developments in Quebec."

Are we to conclude that U.S. labor took a historic misstep, and should have followed the Canadian example? By no means. The more apt historical question runs the other way: why was Canadian labor so long in finding the empowering political role it currently enjoys? The comparative history in which I have indulged does pose an inescapable question on the American side: what was there about the nation's politics that denied such an empowering role to U.S. labor? But, inviting as that question is, it is not one that can be pursued in this essay. If we can agree that, at least after the triumph of the New Deal, the fundamental conditions of American politics did preclude the Canadian option, that will suffice for my purposes. For what I want to argue is that American labor's recent decline should not be seen as a contingent event, one that, with better leaders or better policies, might have turned out differently, but rather that, given the changes in the U.S. economy, its decline was historically determined. In short: no other labor movement stands so exposed to the forces of its economic environment.

The Canadian comparison suggests the insulating powers of a more favorable political culture. But it does not explain how, in the absence of such a culture, the American movement made headway in the past. So, in thinking about prospects for its future recovery, we have to turn to the best historical instance we have of how trade unionism has triumphed in the American environment—the 1930s.

◆

In 1929, organized labor was an arrested movement. In the areas of its historical strength—construction, mining, and transportation—it represented in the range of 25 to 30 percent of eligible workers. The modern movement represents roughly the same proportion of workers in the sectors of its historical strength (that is, as of 1950). At both moments, the crisis confronting the labor movement came not primarily from these mature sectors, which, even totally organized, could by themselves not have sustained a robust national movement, but from the dynamic new sectors of economic growth seemingly beyond the reach of trade unionism. In 1929, of course, the dynamic core was the technologically advanced mass-production industries. Today it is the white-collar consumer and business services.

It would be hard to say whether the changing complexion of the modern movement, which is already more than half white-collar, gives it any relative advantage over the 1929 movement, where the craft/industrial mix had shifted much less—only a quarter of the organized came from the manufacturing sector—but also with class barriers not so distinct between the organized and unorganized. No one would argue, however, that the obstacles facing organized labor seemed any less daunting in 1929 than they do today. There are, too, quite striking parallels in how the labor movement responded to adversity. In politics, for example, there were comparably desperate initiatives: the abortive entry into the Democratic nominating process in 1984 has a counterpart in the farmer-labor insurgency within the party primaries that petered out in LaFollette's Progressive ticket of 1924. And there was an eerily familiar retreat in the 1920s from adversarial unionism, evident not only in the sharp decline in strike activity but, more significantly, in the AFL's conversion to cooperative labor-management relations. In the context of the mass-production systems at the cutting edge sixty years ago, the efforts of organized labor to jump on board bear a striking similarity to the anxious receptivity of today's trade unions toward a more flexible and mutualistic system of labor relations. The Baltimore and Ohio Railroad had very much the same cachet for the 1920s that GM's NUMMI plant has today.

The breakthrough of the 1930s, of course, came from an entirely different direction. With the onset of the Great Depression, the balance of forces in the United States shifted dramatically. The elemental events were, first, the rise of the New Deal and, second, the rebellion of the industrial workers. From these events there issued the particular conditions making possible the unionization of the mass-production sector.

First, the state began to protect the rights of workers to organize and engage in collective bargaining, initially under Section 7a of the National Industrial Recovery Act (1933) and then decisively with the passage of the Wagner Act (1935). Employers were deprived of the enormous power advantage they had long enjoyed in the struggle over collective bargaining.

At the same time, the New Deal moved to mitigate the market pressures that had driven their antiunionism. Section 7a was part of the industrial-recovery legislation that, through codes of fair competition, enabled industries to cartelize their depression-ridden markets. The exchange was entirely deliberate—representational rights for workers as a price for market controls for industry. This key linkage survived the early demise of the National Industrial Recovery Act. The Wagner Act contained an explicit economic rationale: collective bargaining would give rise to the mass purchasing power necessary for sustained economic growth. This, in turn, prefigured the Keynesian economic policy that underwrote the New Deal collective-bargaining system. With macroeconomic policy (as specified by the Employment Act of 1946) responsible for long-term demand, and price competition firmly controlled by the restored oligipolistic structures or, as in the transport and communications sectors, by direct state regulation, the market-driven basis for American antiunionism had seemingly run its course after World War II.

Much the same could be said for the labor-process sources of antiunionism. The crisis over job control touched off by Taylorism had passed by the 1930s. In the mass-production sector, the question was no longer whether managers had the authority, but only how they exercised it. There were, moreover, compelling reasons, almost systemic in nature, for the formalization of work rules. Where tasks were subdivided and precisely defined, for example, job classification necessarily followed and, from that, the principle of pay equity. Time-and-motion study meant objective—that is, testable—standards for the pace of work. Internal labor markets implied uniform rules governing layoff, recall, and even promotion. Corporate commitment to this formalized system was imperfect, however, and broke down entirely in the early years of the Great Depression.

Rank-and-file fury over job insecurity and intolerable speed-up forced management's hand during the NRA period. Between 1933 and 1936—*before* collective bargaining began—all the elements of the modern workplace regime were more or less in place: specified, uniform rights for workers (beginning with seniority and pay equity); a formal procedure for adjudicating grievances arising from those rights; and a structure of shop-floor representation to implement the grievance procedure. Corporate employers would have much preferred to operate this regime under nonunion conditions. Indeed, it had taken shape in the course of their efforts to implant the employee-representation plans (that is, company unions) that employers hoped would satisfy the requirements of New Deal labor policy. But when that strategy failed, they were prepared to have the workplace regime incorporated into contractual relations with independent unions under the terms of the Wagner Act.

Thus there emerged the key elements—the legal framework, the market regulation, an agreed-upon workplace regime—buttressing the modern collective-bargaining system. It is, of course, the breakdown of these sustaining elements that accounts for labor's recent decline. By the same token, something like them in new forms will have to take shape to bring into being the next expansionist period.

◆

But what does the history I have described say about the labor movement as the agent of its own revival? It was a bystander in the cataclysmic economic collapse that set things in motion, and a very minor player in the emergence of the New Deal and upsurge of rank-and-file militancy. Nor was it ever in a position to make or break the key developments in law, economic policy, or workplace relations on which labor's future depended. The AFL never had the power to shape the environment within which it operated. But what it did have was an acute and true sense of what, as a job-conscious labor movement, it wanted from that environment. That may sound like an odd claim, given the notorious failure of the AFL to surmount the jurisdictional impasse over industrial unionism that split the movement in 1935. But, at a more fundamental level, the labor movement—both the AFL and CIO wings—was unerring and, at the critical junctures, astonishingly successful in advancing its trade-union interests.

This is best observed in the battle over New Deal collective-bargaining policy. What was at issue, once Section 7a was adopted, was really a competition between rival conceptions of labor organization. Corporate employers argued that labor's rights could be fulfilled through employee-representation plans (ERPs), that is, by a system of works councils. In resisting that claim, the AFL faced a hard, uphill struggle. For one thing, corporate industry seized the initiative, put the ERPs into place unilaterally in 1933; and thereafter largely defined the terms of the debate. The AFL never had the power during the NRA period to impose collective bargaining on unwilling employers. Nor was much help forthcoming from the New Deal. The ERP scheme, as it evolved from its transparently cynical beginnings, became attractive to many in the administration, including Roosevelt himself, as an alternative to collective bargaining.

What the AFL had on its side, in the long, dispiriting battle over Section 7a, was an absolutely clear and unwavering conception of what it wanted: a system of state regulation that conformed to its conception of collective bargaining through trade-union representation. And through the Wagner Act, against all odds, the labor movement prevailed. Everything in the law's provisions was keyed to promoting collective bargaining: majority rule in the selection of bargaining agents; exclusive representation by the certified bargaining agents; the obligation of good-faith bargaining imposed on employers; labor's right to strike specifically guaranteed. Yet, despite its far reach, the law was specifically circumscribed, setting collective bargaining in motion but leaving the process itself within the realm of contractual freedom. A voluntaristic labor movement would not have had it otherwise. Never mind that in later years a darker side to the law would be revealed and the wisdom of departing from Gompers's antistatist principles called into question. At the time, the Wagner Act represented a remarkable triumph for American trade unionism.

The rise of industrial unionism enables us to identify the enduring historical determinants of the fate of organized labor in the American environment. The essential developments at the time in politics, market structure, and workplace relations have to be taken as autonomous events. Yes, the labor movement played a role; it joined the New Deal, advocated market regulation, participated in the workplace struggles of 1933–36; in any proper history, all this would have to be fully explicated.

But these transforming events were not of labor's making. Nor can we expect that they will be when—if—another historic moment like the 1930s arrives. What we can hope is that the labor movement will know how to seize that moment, and that depends, as it did in the 1930s, on a sure sense of its job-conscious character.

◆

Back in the darkest days of the 1982 recession, the business analyst Peter Drucker wrote a column for the *Wall Street Journal* of September 22, 1982, entitled "Are Unions Becoming Irrelevant?" There was something very particular—and prescient—about how Drucker put that question. It suggested some fundamental disjuncture: the industrial order had gone off in one direction, the labor movement in another, and, in so doing, was in danger of becoming "irrelevant." Drucker's question has had a remarkable resonance: it defines the dominant strain of current thinking about the problems of American labor. And, from that perspective, there seems to have developed a broad consensus about the locus of that fatal disjuncture. It is at the workplace.

In *The Transformation of American Industrial Relations,* Thomas Kochan and his fellow authors write:

> Over the course of the past half century union and nonunion systems traded positions as the innovative force in industrial relations. . . . An alternative human resources management system . . . gradually overtook collective bargaining and emerged as the pacesetter by emphasizing high employee involvement and commitment and flexibility in the utilization of individual employees.

Involvement, commitment, flexibility—these are the watchwords of the new industrial relations, and they are required, Ben Fischer tells us, "by very new forces in the patterns of ownership, management and market behavior, along with radical new technology. . . . The type of work being performed by workers is changing. The manner in which performance is sought contrasts drastically with yesterday's strategies." The conclusion drawn by a distinguished panel of business and labor leaders for the Economic Policy Council (1990) is that

> a "them and us" system of workplace relations [is] simply inadequate in today's social and economic environment. Finding the common interests of employees and employers, of unions and managers, and developing a process for overcoming the division between workers and managers, is the critical challenge that labor and capital must address in the decade ahead.

The foregoing quotations, which could be duplicated many times over, fairly convey a broad consensus of what might be called "progressive" thinking (including inside the labor movement) about the obsolescence of the contractual system of workplace relations that took shape under industrial unionism.

The attack on that system has powerful programmatic implications. The way Peter Drucker initially defined the question—are unions becoming irrelevant?—embodied the most important part of the answer: namely, it identified the unions as the problem. And if the gap between institution and environment was wide enough, then it would follow—as indeed Drucker says—that "the labor union will have to transform itself drastically." Those who have focused on the workplace (as Drucker himself did not) draw the same conclusion. To adapt to the new industrial relations, says Ben Fischer, "will dictate a redefinition of what is a union." So labor's crisis has brought the movement to a juncture where this question is seriously contemplated: should institutional change be undertaken of the scope needed to promote a shift from adversarial to cooperative workplace relations?

◆

Let us assume, for the sake of argument, that the mass-production regime to which that adversarial system was responsive is in fact coming to an end. Why should we believe that the succeeding regime will not in its turn set in motion a process that, like the one we have just surveyed, will end with a new adversarial system, a postmodern version, so to speak, of what Sumner Slichter half a century ago called industrial jurisprudence? The answer, at its most basic, would have to be that past experience no longer applies. Indeed, that is precisely what Ben Fischer does say about "the new face of much of industrial relations": it "is not a replay of history."

If that is true, then of course not much can be learned from labor's past. But we need to specify quite precisely the historical discontinuity that must occur: namely, that the new industrial relations not give rise to a crisis over industrial justice.

Proponents do indeed make that assumption. New modes of flexible production and knowledge-based operation, they argue, require an abandonment of the Taylorist reliance on hierarchical control and a rationalized division of labor. The emerging post-Taylorist system of industrial relations is characterized by what Charles Heckscher calls "managerialism," whose aim it is "that every employee be a manager, involved in decisions and contributing intelligently to the goals of the corporation." To achieve these results, corporations have enlisted a sophisticated human-resources science that Kochan, Katz, and McKersie assure us has mastered the mysteries of employee motivation. Under its guidance, a wide range of programs have taken shape—all-salaried compensation, profit-sharing, work-sharing, flexible work schedules, payment for knowledge, autonomous work teams, ingenious systems of communication and grievance handling. "At its best," concludes Heckscher, "the managerialist order offers genuine improvements in the situation of employees as well as in the effectiveness of the organization."

If the managerialist order at its "best" becomes the norm, what are the prospects for the labor movement? The critical question really is not how successful the existing unions can be at transforming their relations with organized employers. Without penetrating the new dynamic sectors, as it did in mass production fifty years ago, the labor movement can look forward only to stagnation and decline. In these sectors, no amount of union enthusiasm for cooperative relations and employee involvement is likely to persuade employers that collective bargaining is preferable to a union-free environment. And if Heckscher's managerialist order lives up to its promise, what incentive would their employees have for joining a union?

But there are contrary facts to consider. Surveys show a startling rise in the levels of dissatisfaction in all categories of white-collar employees in recent years. Consider what the Opinion Research Corporation (ORC) found in surveys among managers at about two hundred companies over a thirty-year period from the 1950s to the early 1980s: Those who rated their companies favorably in terms of fair application of policies and rules dropped from almost 80 percent to less than 40 percent, those who felt secure in their jobs declined from nearly 100 percent to 65 percent, those who thought their company was a better place to work than when they had started stood at a little higher than 25 percent. Among clerical workers, ORC figures indicated an approval rating of company fairness down from 70 percent in the 1950s to 20 percent in 1979. This is happening partly because of a new spirit of entitlement to state-mandated due process and antidiscriminatory rights, and even more because of the injury that cost-cutting programs and corporate restructuring in its various guises has inflicted on the privileged status of white-collar and semi-professional employees. The current recession, moreover, suggests that their troubles may not be short-term. In a striking reversal of historic trends, it is the service sector that is lagging in an economic recovery. Heckscher sees signs of an emergent movement, still inchoate and divided among many interest groups, but acting "on a single premise: that corporations, while they may have property rights, have no right to abuse their employees."

"This is quite different from the premise that fueled industrial unionism," Heckscher adds. His error here is absolutely fundamental, masking as it does a vital continuity between past and present. Recall the moment at which industrial unionism crystallized during the 1930s. There had been a prior period of struggle driven, as now, by a deepening sense of industrial injustice among factory workers. That its roots may have been somewhat different from those animating the incipient movement that Heckscher describes seems to me not especially germane, so long as we are not prepared to deny that injustice can be as potent a conception for industrial workers as for middle managers and semiprofessionals, and as potent if it arises from the factory regime as from a sense of legal entitlement (although, with the adoption of Section 7a, there developed in the minds of industrial workers as well a strong sense of legal entitlement.) During the battles over employee representation of the NRA period, the terms of a just workplace system took shape and gained the broad assent of all parties (including, in large measure, management). Empowered by the Wagner Act, the industrial unions then seized that system, gave it contractual form, and, in short, made themselves the institutional embodiment of the job interests of the mass-production workers.

◆

In this achievement resides the essential historical continuity on which I am insisting: that what made trade unionism compelling to American workers in the past—and is likely to do so in the future—was its job-conscious capacity to link itself to their aspirations for industrial justice. The labor movement cannot itself define those aspirations, nor very much influence the processes that give rise to them. This was true for the industrial workers of the 1930s and true likewise of the incipient movement for employee rights to which Heckscher calls our attention. Should that movement reach crisis proportions, however, the stage would be set, so to speak, for the next CIO.

American industrial relations have arrived at an odd juncture. How can we be moving at once toward a cooperative labor-management system and also toward a deepening crisis over employee rights? The explanation would seem to be that basic structural forces are in contradiction: postindustrial technology demands involvement and commitment from employees, but the competitive market and corporate restructuring now deny to all but the most sheltered firms the means for assuring the job security and predictable treatment on which employee commitment depends. How that contradiction is resolved remains to be seen, but on its resolution probably rides the future of the American labor movement. Insofar as the outcome favors managerialism, to that extent labor's prospects are surely foreclosed. It was because the contrary happened in the 1930s—because welfare capitalism failed under the stress of the Great Depression—that the occasion was provided for the rise of the industrial unions.

Embattled as it is, the labor movement hears on all sides today calls for an end to "adversarialism." Insofar as this means responsiveness to the logic of a post-Taylorist system of production, the advice is sound, and altogether consistent with historical experience. It bears repeating that, after all, the "adversarial" work-rules system now so roundly condemned was adopted not in opposition to, but directly in conformity with, the logic of the mass-production regime. But retreating from "them and us" as a basic orientation is a different matter.

The labor movement will not prevail by trying to persuade non-union employers. It is their employees who have to be persuaded, and, if and when that time comes, what will persuade them will be the only kind of appeal that has worked with American workers since the days of Samuel Gompers: namely, the identification of the union with their demand for industrial justice. The source of that appeal is the abiding job-consciousness of American trade unionism. In this sense, labor's past is deeply and irrevocably implicated in whatever future it has.

VII

The Cold War
and After

Requiem for Utopia
1969

◆

Erazim V. Kohák

Erazim V. Kohák is professor of philosophy at Boston University and a member of the *Dissent* editorial board. A native of Czechoslovakia, he lived in exile in the United States from 1948 to 1990. His books include *Embers and the Stars: A Philosophical Inquiry into the Moral Sense of Nature, Ideas and Experience: Edmund Husserl's Project of Phenomenology in Ideas*, and *Jan Patocka: Philosophy and Selected Writings*. Since his return to Czechoslovakia he has taught philosophy alternately at Boston University and at the Faculty of Philosophy at Charles University in Prague, Czechoslovakia (currently the "Czech Republic").

Two days before the Soviet army entered Czechoslovakia, I received a letter from a student friend in Prague. The writer is an intelligent young man who received his entire formal education under the Communist regime. He had participated vigorously in the Czechoslovak reform in the spring of 1968, and had spent his vacation the following summer visiting first Nanterre, then Berlin. He speaks German and French fluently, reads English, and has made extensive contacts with his Western colleagues. His reflections on socialism East and West are worth quoting:

Western socialism, especially in its radical form, took me completely by surprise. It seemed so completely unreal, something from a different planet or a different era. You have completely dissociated theory and practice. The men I met are all properly repelled by the realities of authoritarian rule, but they keep on preaching the same weary Utopian ideologies that can lead to nothing else. They live in a romantic dream-world in which their dear radical rhetoric is perfectly consistent with their apparently sincere faith in freedom and justice. But do they really

think they could apply their radical Utopia in a real world and still respect their libertarian commitments? Do they really think their utopia
could be benign if their revolutions were not comic-opera coups on in-
dulgent campuses but real ventures in the exercise of power?

I met a few hard-headed colleagues, but most of the men who clam-
ored for attention were three-semester intellectuals, pampered children of your permissive, affluent society, throwing tantrums because
Father gave them only education, security, and freedom, but not
utopia. They bitterly resent society because it does not treat them as
the fulcrum of the universe: though from what they told me about
themselves it seemed that their families did treat them that way. I can't
take them seriously. They seem to have no idea of the cost or the value
of the privileges they receive abundantly and *gratis.* They dismiss
them as "bourgeois"—in Czechoslovakia we are struggling for just a
fraction of what they dismiss. I suppose their histrionics do have some
individual cathartic value, like the old dueling fraternities, but socially they seem infinitely irrelevant. Can you imagine one of them in
Czechoslovakia?

What surprises me most is not that they take themselves seriously—
students always do, and we are no exception—but that their elders take
them seriously. In the West it seems possible to grow quite old without
having to grow up—you have so much slack, so much room, so much
padding between yourselves and reality. You can afford a great deal: we
can't. For instance, can you imagine reading Sartre's *Les Communistes et
la Paix* here in 1952? That was just at the time of the Slansky trials. Or
reading Marcuse on repressive tolerance, in Prague at the time of the
Writers' Union Congress? It was not until I started visiting the West
that I began to understand that a Sartre or a Marcuse can simply afford
a great deal of illusion. You all live in a different era—you still believe
in Utopia. You simply haven't faced up to the fact that you can't build a
Utopia without terror, and that, before long, terror is all that's left. You
have little stomach for terror—after twenty years, we have even less.
But you like your radical illusions too well.

We've had our fill of Utopia. No more. Now we are building piece-
meal, building a democratic society that will be as imperfect as the
people who live in it. It will be socialist because it is an industrial and
a democratic society—it just doesn't work the other way around. It
won't be a Utopia, but it will be a human kind of society, fit for people
to live in.

I read this letter while listening to the Soviet Ambassador explain that
the armed might of his country had descended upon the Czechoslovak Socialist Republic in order to protect socialism.

II

Not that I think my friend right in everything—there is much he does not know and understand. Still, his grasp of the dynamics of socialism is uncomfortably accurate.

The strength of socialism has always been its steady effort to build the prerequisites of democracy and social justice in an industrial society. But the appeal of socialism has been something different, something much less tangible—the promise of the millennium. Social Democratic parties in the nineteenth century were transforming society through a persistent, unspectacular effort to build a place in the social structure for the underprivileged, and to assure them the means and ability to assume that place. But what drew workers and still moves intellectuals to the party had little to do with concrete social progress. It was the ageless vision of a millennium, a fairy-tale kingdom in which men would still live together, but all the frictions of social existence—and, by implication, all the frustrations of individual life—would disappear. For the tedious, frustrating work of social progress the party needed a vision and the myth of apocalyptic revolution or, later, of the *Massenstreik,* the apocalyptic General Strike which would usher in the millennium, filled that need.

The millennial rhetoric was always grossly inconsistent with the evolutionary, progressive practice of socialism. On the one hand, the party worked to give the workers the wherewithal of social progress, to help them gain self-respect, economic and social security, education, legal protection, and to transform social structures in depth, "radically," making them responsive to the needs of all men. On the other hand, its orators dismissed all such effort as irrelevant and proclaimed the coming of a Hegelian cataclysm from which a perfect society would arise as if by magic, in which depraved workers would suddenly become capable of establishing and administering a perfectly humane society, and in which new, just institutions would spontaneously spring up precisely from the depth of deprivation.

The pattern here is that of the familiar romantic myth in which the very handicaps of the underprivileged become an asset. Touched by the magic wand, the princess loves the peasant lad precisely because he is crude (unaffected) and boorish (spontaneous). In revolutionary mythology, the magic wand was Hegelian dialectic. While in practice imperfect progress was won in patient, tedious, determined work, in millennial rhetoric the law of negation was to produce

utopia in an exhilarating cataclysm, with the necessity of a law of nature. In his "Critique of Hegel's *Philosophy of Right*" in the *Deutsch-
Französische Jahrbücher*, Marx announced that, precisely because the
German working class was completely depraved, precisely because its
condition was beneath critique, it would establish a genuinely humane society.

There is nothing particularly socialistic about this apocalyptic
utopianism. Quite the contrary. Socialism is first of all realistic, tack-
ling the concrete problems of making human existence possible in
an industrial age. Marx himself damned utopianism in his controversy with Schapper-Willich, citing the undeveloped condition of the
German workers as reason for fifty years of preparation required for
political power (Mehring, *Die Geschichte der deutschen Sozialdemokratie*,
vol. I, p. 430).

But, as Marx himself noted, men can stand only limited doses of reality. They need their illusions, and as long as actual power with its
limitations and responsibilities was not a real consideration, the revolutionary mythology could seem harmless enough.

◆

With the upheaval of World War I and the collapse of the Russian empire, the situation changed radically. Russia in 1917 was a society virtually devoid of overt structure, radically open to experiment. At the
same time, it was hopelessly backward. The problems it faced were
not those of an industrial society, and Western socialist programs
were wildly inapplicable to it. Its urgent need was presocialist, practical—the need to build a modern society. Socialists might have been
able to contribute to the process, but the only way some of them
knew to profit from it was to emphasize the Hegelian ideological su-
perstructure of socialism, the revolutionary fairy tale of the peasant
lad becoming a shining prince at the touch of a magic cataclysm.

The men who carried out the communist revolution finally did just
that. They were not practical men. In temper, they were intellectual
aristocrats interested in changing the ideological façade but having
little patience for the unspectacular, ambiguous work of concrete,
deep-reaching ("radical") change. A truly basic change requires
work, the detailed, tedious, patient, persistent work of rebuilding basic attitudes and relations. A revolution is necessarily a poor instrument for such basic change. No matter how spectacular and
exhilarating it may be, it leaves basic attitudes, habits, and relations
among men unchanged; the social structures that emerge from it,

though their ideology reflects the revolution, still articulate the old social orientation. Not surprisingly, Russian society, its paternalism, its stratification, its police apparatus, its provincialism, its primitivism—even the foreign policy of its government, in both goals and technique—remained relatively constant in spite of the revolutionary change of façade. T. G. Masaryk's sociological study *The Spirit of Russia,* published in 1913, may have appeared momentarily out of date in 1920, but it is quite accurate in 1968. Ideological labeling has changed—for Orthodox Church read Communist Party, for Czar read First Secretary, for Okhranka read MVD; but basic attitudes and relations, those which socialists recognize as the real fabric of society, have remained unchanged.

Unfortunately socialists, long accustomed to their revolutionary mythology, are easily dazzled by ideological trappings. Hammer and sickle on the flag of a sovereign state, the whispered names in an official hagiography, red stars on soldiers' caps, all the trappings of power and success easily outshone both the sordid realities of Russian life and the tangible social progress of unspectacular Western socialism. With the Russian Revolution, the Hegelian ideological myth became respectable. Worse, it became "socialism."

To be sure, even the dazzling façade of Russian *Parteistaatssozialismus* could not quite conceal the persistent Czarist mentality. It was Lenin who characterized tsarist Russia as "a state which is a cross between Asiatic despotism and European absolutism . . . not an organ of any class of Russian society but a military-administrative machinery whose task is to resist the pressure of a higher Western civilization" (*Iskra,* March 5, 1904). That description fitted the new Communist regime all too well. But men who desperately wanted to believe could always find excuses as to why the magic failed to work. Russia was backward, it was encircled by hostile states, etc., etc., and of course all of that was true. For fifty years the energies of socialists have been drawn away from the urgent tasks of social progress to a cataclysmic Utopian fantasy. In Czechoslovakia in 1920, the socialists lost their considerable parliamentary majority and the chance to build a social democracy because the ideological, Communist-led wing of the party chose to withdraw from Parliament and wait for an apocalyptic revolution. Ever since, the pattern they set has been repeated throughout the West, down to the young ideologues of today whose conception of becoming involved is to abstain from elections.

III

The significance of the Czechoslovak experience is that with us the millennium did come, under conditions as ideal as an imperfect world can offer. Czechoslovakia was an advanced industrial country, far more so than the England or Germany of Marx's time. Culturally it was part of the West, with a mature democratic tradition; yet it was surrounded by friendly "socialist" countries. Its industries had been socialized several years earlier, and there was no hard-core political opposition. The Communist Party had won, in 1946, some 38 percent of the vote in a reasonably free election, yet had subsequently seized power in an armed coup, and so was unhindered by any constitutional guarantees of personal or social freedom. The Hegelian myth that had lured socialists for half a century was finally being acted out exactly as three generations of visionaries had imagined. The men who guided the experiment were true believers. From the beginning, they applied the theory of a radical break in all aspects of personal and social life. Tight internal and external censorship sealed off the country from the outside world and from its own past. History was rewritten and rebuilt. Organizations and men, whether Communist or noncommunist, who had any pretensions to autonomy disappeared. Not that the Czechoslovak communists were any more crude or repressive than their rhetorical colleagues in the West—they weren't. But they were engaged in rule, not rhetoric—and in practice. A theoretical revolutionary can speak of "protecting the freedom of the people to develop along a socialist path unhampered by reactionary propaganda"—the ruling revolutionary has to censor the press and liquidate offending writers, and that is what the Czech Communists did. The human, social, and economic cost was tremendous, but the break was complete—everything and everyone even vaguely associated with the past was wiped out. The new Czechoslovakia was a completely "liberated" country, free of anything that might have repressed its development.

According to Utopian rhetoric from Lenin on, new institutions, social relations, and new men, free, unalienated, should have sprung from socialist praxis. Life had been liberated from all impediments, it should have blossomed, free and abundant. But nothing of the sort happened. The new institutions expressed nothing but the new masters' conception of Utopia. Creatures of theory, they remained theoretical alien, lifeless, apathetic. The people proved apathetic rather than zealous, preferring their lost freedom, even their folly, to perfection. They were willing to be socialists, and they were willing to be enthusiastic, but they were not willing to be enthusiastic about socialism. At the height of the Stalin period, a Czech friend told me, "At home they expect us to have sex orgies with socialism." The story, in a nutshell, of Czechoslovakia's Utopian experiment is that Czechs and Slovaks continued to prefer women.

It was at this point that the hidden logic of all social messianism came to the fore. The rhetorical Utopians convinced themselves that they had found the recipe for perfection. When their fellow men failed to share their enthusiasm, they embarked on a crusade to eliminate whatever was blinding them to their superior insight—Jews, capitalists, sinners. But when their crusade succeeded and men still failed to conform to their true faith, they found themselves forced to resort to coercion. Like all utopians, they were convinced they were coercing men for their own good, and that in time the coercion would become unnecessary. But as Masaryk pointed out about Marx in *The Foundations of Marxism* in 1898, the Utopians are shoddy psychologists. Coercion produces not enthusiasm and agreement, but alienation and apathy, which in turn can be dislodged only by greater coercion, leading to still greater apathy. The escalating spiral of apathy and terror is the real *mors immortalis* of social messianism. The Czechoslovak experiment proved that the temptation to prod progress with a bayonet, so attractive to powerless radical rhetoricians, leads not to progress but to apathy and terror, regardless of the ideology in whose name it is exercised.

IV

What is it like, living in Utopia? Perhaps the most eloquent testimony is the recent Czech film *The Fifth Horseman Is Fear*. Western reviewers interpreted it as just another wartime melodrama with bad Germans pitted against good Czechs and/or suffering Jews. That story is there, and the film does include some rather obvious period pieces. The resistance worker, his acts, even his clothes and his apartment clearly belong to the war years. So does the surrealistic brothel scene, with its gas-chamber showers and Wehrmacht uniforms. But Czech audiences could not fail to recognize another dimension—Prague landmarks erected long after the war, late-model cars in the streets, contemporary clothes, all-Czech posters pasted over wartime bilingual ones.

This second dimension stands out most clearly in the official notices which appear in prominent close-ups throughout the film. Their format (though not their color—German notices were dark-red) is that of the wartime bilingual notices, a German eagle in the center, with parallel German and Czech columns below. In the film, the parallel columns are retained, but both sides are set in Czech. The point of the film is clear: for the man who must live in utopia, there is no difference between right and left Hegelians. The forties and the fifties, Hitler years and Stalin years, merge. The only difference is that this time both the oppressors and the victims are Czech.

The Fifth Horseman is only one of the countless testimonies, produced both in the last months of gunpoint "socialism" and in the seven months of freedom, that the basic common fact of life in any utopia is alienation. The word has become so fashionable that to restore it as a tool of social analysis we need to give it a more precise meaning. By "alienation" we shall mean a dissociation of an individual's public identity from his private one. Under ideal conditions, the two would be integrally related. Public life would serve to act out private identity; private identity would in turn be enriched, reinforced, and challenged by the demands of praxis. When this relation breaks down, for whatever reason, we can speak of alienation—public life becomes formal, empty, lifeless, while private identity becomes involuted, explosive, and distorted.

That much is commonplace. The reason why alienation can today serve as a revolutionary slogan, and not simply as a tool in the perennial attempt to rescue Karl Marx from irrelevance, is that it can be used as a bridge between private problems and public issues, mobilizing the energy of individual failure and frustration for the purposes of social action. But it is an ambiguous tool, because it blurs two phenomena which, though never altogether dissociated, are still basically distinct and require different strategies: pathological alienation and social alienation.

Pathological alienation is the dissociation of public acts and private identity brought about by a defect in the latter. The subject is unable to relate his private identity to any sustained public role, regardless of social conditions, because his definition of personal identity is in principle solipsistic, incompatible with the strains and stresses of social existence. This is a phenomenon characteristic, for instance, of both the extreme "Left" and the extreme "Right," and one reason why the far "Left" rejects all concrete social progress as capitulation to "the system." If the cause of alienation is a pathological inability of the subject to function in any social system, only the fairy-tale land of revolutionary apocalypse will do—and even that only as long as it does not become reality—witness the regular disenchantment of the far "Left" with its successive Robin Hood heroes whenever they actually succeed in bringing their experiment into practice. Pathological alienation is only symptomatically relevant to social theory.

The alienation which the Utopian experiment produced in Czechoslovakia is an entirely different phenomenon. It is social alienation, brought about by the structure of society rather than by that of private identity. It is more closely analogous to the alienation of American blacks, to whom the structure of society denies opportunity for participation, than to the alienation of disaffected students. The Czech protesters were generally adults; workers, students, writers, men from every social stratum, ready and able to sustain the responsibility of being adults in a society. It was the utopian ideology of the regime which made successful integration of (any) private identity with social existence effectively impossible.

Social alienation is as characteristic of Utopian societies as pathological alienation is of affluent, permissive ones. Utopian regimes invariably pay lip service to freedom and participation, but the logic of Utopia forces them to deny their subjects the materials from which a satisfactory private identity is built—privacy, personal security, and especially freedom. Freedom inevitably includes the possibility of error, and utopia in principle demands perfection. The Czechoslovak regime was Utopian, committed to remolding men in its image, and so, quite independently of the content of its ideology, it was also committed to paternalistic authoritarianism and its practical enforcement. Quite logically, the basic reality of life in Utopia was apathy—and terror.

V

Czechoslovak reform under Alexander Dubcek signified essentially a rejection of the utopia that sacrifices men to the demands of a prescription. First of all democratic, it was determined to safeguard personal freedom and personal security, because twenty years of gunpoint "socialism" had taught the Czechs and Slovaks, Communists included, that the logic of terror is self-defeating. In Czechoslovakia there could be no question of whether personal freedom and security can be violated for the sake of a social ideal. Czechs and Slovaks have learned that, once freedom and security are violated, any ideology becomes simply a rationale for self-perpetuating terror. The reform was democratic—and it was also fundamentally and emphatically socialist. Czechoslovakia is an advanced industrial country, in which democracy necessarily means economic democracy as well. In all its aspects, the heady Czechoslovak spring of 1968 was an experiment moving toward postmillennial socialism or, in traditional terms, toward social democracy.

Not that Dubcek and his colleagues were in any sense social democrats when they came to power. They weren't; they were Communists who still shared the aristocratic assumption of all Utopians that a monopoly of power must remain in the hands of the enlightened elect, the Party. But they were determined to be humane authoritarians, respecting the rights of their subjects. In their seven months in power they discovered that the idea of a humane authoritarianism, the standard illusion of well-intentioned rhetorical revolutionists, is an illusion, a *contradictio in adiecto*. A humane authoritarianism would respect the rights and freedom of its subjects, and so inevitably create the possibility of dissent and opposition. Faced with opposition, the humane authoritarian faces the choice of ceasing to be authoritarian—or ceasing to be humane. Repression, whatever its overt aim, can be humane only in rhetoric—in practice it necessarily means breaking men. Czechs and Slovaks, including Dubcek, were too familiar with the logic of terror to opt for the latter alternative. After seven months, the program which started out as a program of humane communism became a program of social democracy.

To be sure, Czechoslovakia did not and could not become a social democracy overnight. The reformers worked in detail, steadily, on a hundred concrete programs, from rehabilitation of political prisoners to economic reform and social restructuring. They built consciously on Czechoslovakia's tradition of freedom and social progress. But the change was too radical to be spectacular. By August only the first steps had been taken. Still, the direction of change was clear, and received the full support of the whole nation. The experiment in democratic socialism was succeeding beyond the fondest hopes of its leaders and supporters.

VI

The end came on August 21, when the Hegelian left repeated the pattern set by the Hegelian right thirty years earlier. The workers of the Skoda Works, who painted swastikas on Russian tanks, made it clear that they failed to appreciate the difference.

But why did the Russians move in? The occupation of Czechoslovakia cost them much and won them little. The usual explanations
about the threat posed by Czech liberalism sidestep the crucial question—why should liberalism be a threat? It was no threat to Russian
national interest. Czechoslovak security on the crossroads of super-
powers is necessarily tied to a Soviet alliance, and the Czechs proved
themselves fully aware, in both word and deed, of this fact. Nor was
Czech liberalism a threat to socialism. Czechoslovakia is an industrial
country in which socialism is a necessary consequence of democracy,
and, again, the Czechs and Slovaks were obviously aware of this. Neither the Soviet alliance nor socialism was ever an issue in the
Czechoslovak reform—both were taken entirely for granted by the
whole spectrum of national opinion.

Liberalism was a threat precisely because it *supported* socialism and
the Soviet alliance, and so brought into question the very legitimacy
of the Utopian claim to power. This is no abstract consideration. Not
only the Soviet regime, but any government in the world can exercise
power effectively only as long as the governed recognize, tacitly at
least, its right to rule—as long as they recognize it as a legitimate government. They might, and usually do, consider it a very bad government indeed. They might criticize it at every turn and resolve to
replace its personnel or policies at the earliest opportunity. They
might look forward to its fall and feel unhappy and alienated under
its rule. Yet, as long as they consider it a legitimate bad government,
society will continue to function. The recognition of the legitimacy of
power in the making and enforcing of social decisions is the constituting factor in society, and failure to acquire legitimacy in the eyes
of the governed reduces even the most benign attempt at government to arbitrary tyranny.

Since the last echoes of "divine right" or "right of conquest" died
out in the nineteenth century, legitimation in Europe has invariably
meant legitimation by public interest. The democratic model interpreted acts in the public interest as acts receiving popular support:
the legitimacy of a democratic government derives at least theoreti-
cally from the ability of the governed to confirm or reject their rulers.
The model has achieved such prestige that even totalitarian regimes
have felt the need to stage plebiscites and elections to give themselves
an aura of legitimacy. Soviet elections in the past have invariably
been elaborate, ostentatious affairs. They have also been invariably
uncontested—a Utopian revolutionary regime, finally, cannot equate
public interest with public support. The governed, being unregener-

ate, cannot be expected to realize that the particular Utopia, whether nationalist or socialist, is in their true interest. They are too accustomed to their old self and the old order.

Soviet Communism, both at home and abroad, has always claimed the legitimacy of superior insight. The basic proposition of Soviet political philosophy, so basic that it is taken for granted in most rhetoric, is that the Soviet regime—or any regime—is legitimate because it is "socialist," orthodox, and so in the true interest of the people, whether they realize it or not. Anyone who dissents must be either a knave or a fool. It was this logic which led to the startling conclusion that a Tukhachevsky or a Beria, a Slansky or a Clementis, since they obviously were not fools, must have been imperialist agents. This is the logic which led to the condemnation of Dubcek as a traitor, and which makes the Russians insist that the Czechs produce acceptable scapegoats to explain their recent dissent. The grotesque insistence on Byzantine adulation of all things Russian, paralleled by men as disparate as Hitler, Franco, Trujillo, and Mao, is not simply a psychological quirk—it is a necessary corollary of the claim that utopian revolutionism legitimizes its own acts.

The Czechoslovak reform did not threaten the Soviet Union or socialism, but by supporting them challenged the basic premise of their rule. Soviet rule is predicated on the premise that it is legitimate because it is "socialist"—whereas Czechoslovak democracy admitted that socialism itself requires legitimation by popular consent.

VII

As a Czech, I find little consolation in the fact that tanks can exercise power but cannot make it legitimate or restore the shattered Hegelian illusions of utopian revolutionism. Czechs and Slovaks might be able to mitigate the impact of Russian rule through passive resistance, but the Russians are in effective control of the country, and able to impose absolute limits on its development. There will in all likelihood be periods of relative relaxation. This is to be expected—coercion produces apathy, and has to be relaxed periodically to allow for some life and spontaneity. But such relaxation creates the possibility of dissent, and, the harsher the earlier coercion, the more radical the dissent will be. Unless the Soviet leadership is prepared to abdicate its authoritarian position, it must follow each period of relaxation with another freeze, as the purges of the thirties, postwar Stalinism, or the present hardening of internal and external policy. But the cycles are not progressive or cumulative—today's neo-Stalinism is no more benign than Lenin's War Communism half a century ago, and it would be naïve to pin one's hopes on a gradual mellowing of communism. The internal dynamics of utopianism make such mellowing most unlikely.

The ideals of human freedom and social justice remain valid. Democracy—democracy for blacks as well as whites, in economics as well as politics, at home as well as in remote reaches of Latin America or Eastern Europe—remains valid. Socialism, the ideal of social justice and social responsibility in industrial society, remains valid. Human and civil rights, the right of every man to personal identity and social participation, all remain valid. But the utopian myths of self-proclaimed rhetorical radicals do not advance these ideals. The detour on which too many socialists embarked in 1917 is over, finished, discredited, revealed as an exhilarating, aristocratic, and ultimately reactionary social sport, not the radical social progress it claimed to be. The task that remains is the work of social progress—not the aristocratic sport of revolution, but the solid work of radical, deep-rooted transformation of society. Men may still demand their daily dose of illusion, the exhilaration of revolution or "confrontation" rather than the down-to-earth facts and figures of a Freedom Budget; but those who cater to this demand can no longer do so in the name of social progress—or in the name of socialism.

Utopia is dead. Czechoslovakia has been a graveyard of illusions. As a Czech social democrat, I can only hope that it will also prove the cradle of a new social progress.

Solzhenitsyn's Gulag Archipelago

1976

◆

ROY MEDVEDEV

Roy Medvedev is a Russian historian, whose problems with the communist bureaucracy achieved worldwide notoriety in 1970, when his twin brother, Zhores, an eminent biologist and author, was held against his will in a psychiatric clinic. Medvedev launched a successful publicity campaign to free his brother, and then the two wrote a book about the affair, *A Question of Madness*. His major writings published in English include *Let History Judge: The Origins and Consequences of Stalinism* and *The Soviet Union Since Stalin*.

The second volume of Solzhenitsyn's *Gulag Archipelago* has now appeared. Where the first volume consisted in a detailed investigation of everything that preceded the arrival of millions of Soviet people in Stalin's concentration camps—the system of arrests, the various forms of confinement, interrogation with torture, judicial and extra-judicial persecution, prisoner transports and transit prisons—the second volume gets down to the study of the primary and fundamental part of the Gulag empire, the corrective or, as Solzhenitsyn rightly calls them, the "destructive" labor camps. Here nothing escapes the author's attention: the origin and history of the camps, the economics of forced labor, the administrative structure, the categories of prisoners and everyday life of the inmates, the position of women and juveniles, the relations between ordinary zeks and the trusties,* between criminals and politicals, the camp guards, the convoy guards,

*Zek: in camp slang, abbreviation of the Russian word for "prisoner," *zaklyuchenny*.

the "information" service and the recruiting of stool pigeons, the system of punishments and "incentives," the functioning of the hospitals and medical stations, the way prisoners died and were killed, and the unceremonious way they were buried—all these things find their place in Solzhenitsyn's book. The author describes the various types of hard labor and the starvation diet imposed on the zeks; he studies not only the world of the camps but also the world immediately surrounding them, the world of "campside"; and he surveys the peculiarities of psychology and behavior found among the prisoners and their jail keepers (or "camp keepers," in Solzhenitsyn's terminology).

Like the first volume, which came out in December 1973, this volume deserves the highest estimation, especially because it is a conscientious investigation, artistically presented and based on authentic fact. True, the second volume did not have the moral shock effect of the first, did not stun and shake the reader so. Perhaps because it was the second volume; or perhaps, for me, this impression has to do with the fact that I have read dozens and dozens of memoirs by former camp inmates (most of them, of course, never published) and have recorded hundreds of accounts and pieces of testimony about camp life. It is also significant that, though the basic facts are reliable (and there are noticeably fewer petty factual inaccuracies in the second volume of *Gulag Archipelago* than in the first), many of the author's judgments and opinions are too one-sided and categorical and his general observations are by no means always well grounded. This is particularly true of the way he obviously lays his colors on too thickly in depicting the world of "the free" in his chapter "Our Muzzled Freedom."

But, of course, none of the shortcomings of the second volume overshadow the artistic and social significance of this book, which has no equal in all our literature on the camps.

Several years ago I heard of a certain occurrence—from a former "son of Gulag" who had gone to visit Vorkuta as a free citizen (many such veterans of the camps feel the urge to visit the places where their years had been spent working behind barbed wire; Solzhenitsyn too writes about this). It was an occurrence common in those parts. A foundation pit for a new school in Vorkuta had been started. No sooner had the thin topmost layer of soil been removed than the teeth of the excavating machines revealed a huge deposit of human bones. This was not of course the site of a primitive human settlement, and no archaeologists came there. It was one of those giant mass graves that grew near the northern camps—great pits, already dug in the autumn, into which thousands of corpses were thrown during the winter—prisoners who died or were shot—to be covered over later on, with the arrival of the brief northern summer. Construction of the school was temporarily halted, not for the purpose, naturally, of setting up a monument to the unknown convicts; the freshly bared bones of these zeks were carted off by night and buried somewhere outside the city limits, and this new cemetery was not marked in any noticeable way. At the original site of the mass grave, school construction was resumed and completed.

Alas, we can have little hope that memorials will be erected even where the largest concentration camps stood, or that the camp barracks, compounds, towers, and mines will be restored in museum form, or that some sort of markings will be placed at the countless camp cemeteries, where there are probably more Soviet people buried than fell in the war against Nazi Germany. There is little hope that an eternal flame will burn here or that the names of those who died and were killed will be chiseled in marble. It is quite possible that books will remain the only monuments to these people. One such book, *The Gulag Archipelago,* will easily outlive those who wish to suppress it and will stand as an unforgettable tribute for those to whom its author dedicated it, all those who perished in the camps, "all those who did not live to tell it."

Camp Myths

In our country, where there is no freedom of the press or freedom of information, where most information circulates by certain secret channels, a multitude of rumors inevitably arise and dozens of different myths have public currency and are accepted by many as unquestionable truths. Under the conditions existing in the camps, such legends, rumors, and myths—often far removed from reality—were all the more likely to find fertile ground. Natalya Reshetovskaya has recently contended that Solzhenitsyn's book is essentially based on this camp folklore.* That is certainly not so. Of course Solzhenitsyn,

*Natalya Reshetovskaya (born 1920): Solzhenitsyn's first wife; they married in 1940, were separated by the war, then by his imprisonment in 1945; she divorced him in 1950 while he was in the camps. After his release and rehabilitation (1956–57) they remarried, in the late 1950s, before be won fame with *Ivan Denisovich.* In the late 1960s they separated again, and he established a relationship with his present wife, Natalya Svetlova. The authorities, to harass him further, long supported Reshetovskaya in her refusal to agree to a divorce. They were finally divorced by the time he was expelled from the U.S.S.R.

through no fault of his own, had no chance to check documentary evidence in order to verify much of the information he obtained from fellow inmates and from subsequent corespondents and informants. However, both his own camp experience and his intuition as an investigator and an artist enable him in most cases to distinguish sharply enough between truth and invention in the accounts he has recorded. If some legends do crop up in the pages of *Gulag Archipelago*, rare as they may be, this happens for the most part when the topic is the distant past or the lives and "affairs" of those high up in the "organs," for example, Minister of State Security Abakumov.

I think that among such myths we must include Solzhenitsyn's story of the fourteen-year-old boy who on June 20, 1929, during Gorky's visit to the Solovetsky Special Purpose Camp, asked to speak with Gorky in private and then spent an hour and a half telling the famous writer about all the illegalities committed in that camp. According to Solzhenitsyn's account, Gorky, after talking with the boy, left the room in tears. But not only did he do nothing for the prisoners at Solovki; he even praised the Solovetsky Cheka agents many times thereafter—while the truth-loving lad was shot the same night by those Chekists.*

Now, Solzhenitsyn himself writes that the first juveniles came to Solovki only in mid-March 1929. How could the newly arrived inhabitants of the children's colony, isolated from the adult prisoners, find out everything that had gone on at Solovki for years before? But if this particular anecdote related by Solzhenitsyn seems dubious, no such doubts arise over his own story of the many illegal and arbitrary actions committed at Solovki, a narrative that can be confirmed by other accounts and other witnesses.

Where the Camps Came From

Solzhenitsyn dates the existence of concentration camps for political opponents in our country from 1918. This is not slander, as some of his detractors contend. Solzhenitsyn quotes Lenin's telegram to Yevgeniya Bosh, president of the Penza Province Executive Committee, advising, "lock up all the doubtful ones in a concentration camp out-

---

*Solovki, Solovetsky; Cheka, Chekist: Solovki is slang for the Solovetsky camp, on the Solovetsky Islands; see the description of the camp in *Gulag Archipelago,* vol. II, ch. 2.

side the city" (Lenin, *Polynoye Sobraniye Sochineniy* [Collected Works], 5th Russian ed., vol. 50, pp. 143–44). Other official documents may be cited to the same effect. Thus, a special resolution of the Council of People's Commissars of the Russian Soviet Federated Socialist Republic (RSFSR) of September 5, 1918, says in part, "It is necessary to secure the Soviet Republic against its class enemies by isolating them in concentration camps" (*Yezhenedelnik ChK* [Weekly Bulletin of the Cheka], no. 1 [September 22, 1918], p. 11). In February 1919 Grigory Sokolnikov, a member of the Central Committee of the Russian Communist Party (Bolsheviks) and of the Military Revolutionary Council of the Southern Front, objecting to Central Committee directives on "de-Cossackization," the mass shooting of Cossacks who gave aid to Krasnov or served in the White Army, proposed that instead of being shot they be employed in socially useful labor in the coal-mining districts, for building railroads and digging shale and peat. For this purpose Sokolnikov requested by telegram that "work begin immediately on the construction of facilities for concentration camps" (Central Party Archives, collection 17, shelf 4, file 53, sheet 54). The concentration camps of civil-war times were quite primitive structures, and the regimen enforced in them bore very little resemblance to that of the camps of the 1930s. Sometimes the people in them were put to work. In other cases, in districts near the battlefronts, an area outside a city would simply be fenced off, the "socially dangerous elements" would be detained there but would not work, and their relatives and friends would bring them food and hand it to them through the fences. Toward the end of 1920 most of those confined in concentration camps were peasants arrested for "speculation," as can be seen from documents of the Cheka. With the end of the civil war many of these camps were dismantled and their inmates sent home. At the beginning of NEP,* the camps for political prisoners were apparently abolished nearly everywhere, with the exception of the Solovetsky Special Purpose Camp and several "political isolators"†—of which Solzhenitsyn writes.

Space does not allow us to explore here the question of which ele-

---

*NEP: The New Economic Policy, introduced in 1921, under which peasants were allowed to trade on the market and were taxed a certain amount of grain or other produce instead of having it requisitioned by the state. Grain requisitioning had been the policy under "war communism" during the 1918–20 civil war. The NEP ended with the beginning of forced collectivization and industrialization in 1929–30.

†"Political isolators": separate Soviet prisons for holding political oppositionists of the noncommunist left or dissident communists.

ments in the early history of these political camps were dictated by the stern necessities of those years and which constituted plainly excessive and unnecessary cruelty. But it would be wrong to place the camps of the civil-war period and those of Stalin's time on the same plane and ignore the fact that in 1918–20 the Soviet Republic was fighting a war on several fronts against foreign-backed White governments and that the numerous concentration camps set up on territory held by the White armies and foreign interventionist forces were usually far more savage than those in the RSFSR. In Stalin's time, on the other hand, the terror of the camps was directed against people who were unarmed and defenseless, and were not hostile toward the sole existing, and firmly established, power in the land. For Solzhenitsyn this distinction seems not to exist.

The 1937 Wave

Solzhenitsyn does not hide his distaste for the government, party, and economic leaders, top commanders of the Red Army, leading cadres of the Young Communist League and the trade unions, and especially the high-ranking personnel of the NKVD and the prosecutor general's office, who themselves became the object of brutal repression in 1937 and '38. Even in the first volume of *Gulag Archipelago* Solzhenitsyn wrote:

> If you study in detail the whole history of the arrests and trials of 1936 to 1938, the principal revulsion you feel is not against Stalin and his accomplices, but against the humiliatingly repulsive defendants—nausea at their spiritual baseness after their former pride and implacability.

All these people, during the civil war or during collectivization and industrialization, so Solzhenitsyn asserts, were pitiless toward their political opponents and therefore deserved no pity when their own "system" turned against them.

In the second volume, we find the same attitude on the author's part toward the "1937 wave." With obvious satisfaction Solzhenitsyn cites the names of dozens of major Communist Party figures shot on Stalin's orders in 1937–38. These people deserved their fate, he suggests; they got what they had made ready for, or given to, others.

> And though [he writes], when the young Tukhachevsky returned victoriously from suppressing the devoted Tambov peasants, there was no

Mariya Spiridonova waiting at the station to put a bullet through his head, it was done sixteen years later by the Georgian priest who never graduated.

But we can in no way share these sentiments and opinions of Solzhenitsyn's.

First, one cannot ignore the fact that the leaders who perished in the 1930s were not all the same kind of people, either in their personal characters or in the degree of responsibility they had for the crimes of the preceding years. There were people who had already degenerated greatly, who had been so caught up in Stalin's system that they carried out the most savage and inhuman orders without thinking of the country or the people, but only of themselves and their power. These people not only carried out orders but "demonstrated initiative" on their own, helping Stalin and the NKVD organs to "expose" and annihilate "enemies of the people." But there were quite a few who acted in error, who were simultaneously victims and instruments of another cult—the cult of party discipline. Among them were many honest, self-sacrificing, and courageous people who, too late, came to understand a great deal. There were quite a few who thought about what was happening in the country and were tormented by it, but who believed in the party and the party's propaganda. It would seem, from today's vantage point, that we could speak of the historical and political guilt of the entire active party membership for the events of the 1920s and 1930s. But we cannot simply lump all these people together indiscriminately as criminals who got what they deserved. The fate of the majority of the revolutionary Bolsheviks remains one of the most awesome tragedies in the history of our country, and we cannot in any way condone Solzhenitsyn in his mocking suggestion that in the obituaries published in our country the words "perished tragically during the period of the cult" should be replaced by the words "perished comically." The best Russian writers never indulged in mockery of the dead. Let us recall Pushkin, who wrote these lines:

> Riego did transgress against Spain's king.
> There I agree. But for that he was hanged.
> Is it seemly, tell me now, for us
> To hotly curse the hangman's fallen victim?

Earlier, in reading the first volume of *Gulag Archipelago,* I was unpleasantly surprised by Solzhenitsyn's words that he had somehow been "consoled"—when describing the trials at which People's Commissar of Justice Krylenko appeared as the accuser—"consoled" by the thought of the degradation to which Krylenko was reduced in Butyrka Prison before he was shot, the same Krylenko who had condemned others to similar degradation. It seems to me that the author's attitude here is quite far removed from the simple standard of human decency, not to mention the Christian virtues of "understanding mildness" and "uncategorical judgments," which Solzhenitsyn proclaims at the end of the second volume.

Solzhenitsyn's position seems wrong to us not only because the government and party leaders destroyed were most often replaced by people who, it is common knowledge, were even worse. Thus, in Yezhov's and Beria's times one could with reason regret the passing of such Chekists as Latsis and Peters. The brutality of Latsis and Peters, sometimes justified and sometimes not, was at any rate never self-seeking, sadistic, or aimed at currying favor. Those men apparently could not have gone down the road of crime as far as Yezhov, Beria, Zakovsky, and their kind.

It must be said, simply, that no one deserved the dreadful fate that befell the leaders arrested in 1937–38. It is impossible to take satisfaction in the thought of their degradation and torment, even knowing that many of them deserved death.

One of Shalamov's *Kolyma Stories* tells the fate of a deputy head of the Leningrad NKVD, Nikonov, an accomplice of Yezhov and Zakovsky, who during "interrogation" had his testicles crushed. Solzhenitsyn himself, in the first volume, wrote about this method of torture as the worst kind, one that cannot be endured. In reading Shalamov's story, I did not feel any gratification. It is quite likely that this Nikonov fully deserved to be tried and shot for his crimes. But even he did not deserve such cruel torture and abuse. It is a profoundly mistaken notion of morality to think that Stalin's reprisals against the main cadres of the Communist Party and Soviet government represented, even in an extremely distorted form, the triumph of some sort of historical justice. No, the death of these people was the prologue to a reign of injustice still more terrible, affecting not only the party but our entire people.

Solzhenitsyn is prepared, oddly enough, to regard the entire Soviet people, Russians and non-Russians alike, as having deserved the unhappy fate they suffered in the 1920s, 1930s, and 1940s. Even in the first volume, having in mind not just the party but the most ordinary people of our land, he exclaimed: "We spent ourselves in one unrestrained outburst in 1917, and then we hurried to submit. We submitted with pleasure! . . . We purely and simply *deserved* everything that happened afterward." (Solzhenitsyn's emphasis.) Many similar pronouncements can be found in the second volume as well. The error and injustice of this view seems too obvious for me to spend any time refuting it.

The Communist Captives of Gulag

Apparently the majority of those shot in 1937–38 were communists. In addition, however, hundreds of thousands of rank-and-file members and middle-level cadres of the party and youth organizations were arrested and sent to the camps along with other prisoners. Solzhenitsyn devotes one of the chapters of his second volume to their fate and discusses the communists at some length in other chapters of this volume. Touching very briefly on those for whom "Communist convictions were inward and not constantly on the tips of their tongues," who did not make a great show of their "party attitude" and did not separate themselves from the other prisoners, Solzhenitsyn directs his attention mainly to those "orthodox Communists" and "loyalists" (the chapter on the communists is entitled "The Loyalists") who sought to justify Stalin and his terror while they were in the camps, who would sing the (party-song) lines "I know no other country / Where a person breathes so freely" while en route in prisoner transports, and who considered virtually every other zek to have been justly condemned and only themselves to be suffering by accident. Solzhenitsyn finds a number of occasions for making fun of such "loyalists" and "orthodox Communists." Sometimes his irony is fully deserved. It is true that among the communists arrested in 1937–38 there were quite a few who continued to believe not only in Stalin but even in Yezhov, and who held themselves aloof from, or were even hostile toward, the other prisoners. But insight came rather quickly, although for understandable reasons it was not always complete, and after several months of "interrogation" the number of the "loyalists" and "orthodox" among arrested party members fell off rapidly. And there were very few of them in the camps. For the majority of communists, however, condemnation of Stalin and the NKVD organs did not mean the repudiation of socialist and communist convictions.

Solzhenitsyn plainly sins against the truth when, in describing the fate of the communists in the camps, he declares that they never objected to "the dominance of the thieves in the kitchens and among the trusties" and that "all the orthodox Communists . . . soon [got] themselves well fixed up." The author of *Gulag Archipelago* even raises the following hypothesis: "Yes, and were there not perhaps some written or at least oral directives: to make things easier for the Communists?"

No, Aleksandr Isayevich, no such directives ever existed, and you knew it well when, in your novel *One Day in the Life of Ivan Denisovich,* you told of the fate of the communist Buinovsky, thrown into the cold punishment block for no reason. From the fate enjoyed in the camps by Boris Dyakov and Galina Serebryakova, you cannot draw conclusions about the position and conduct of the bulk of the communists who found themselves in Stalin's camps. In many respects their circumstances were even worse than those of prisoners in other categories, and quite a few of them died in the camps—in fact, it is likely they died in greater numbers than other prisoners. On this point there are of course no reliable statistics. However, we know from the materials of party conferences, held after the Twenty-second Soviet Communist Party Congress, that of the party members arrested in Moscow in 1936–39 only about 6 percent returned there in 1955–57. The remaining 94 percent were rehabilitated *posthumously*. And throughout the U.S.S.R., out of a million party members arrested in the latter half of the 1930s, not more than sixty to eighty thousand returned after fifteen to eighteen years' imprisonment. The suffering they endured left a deep mark on these people, and very few were left among them who in any way resembled those Solzhenitsyn now writes of with such sarcasm.

Socialism, Revolution, or Religion?

In part four of this book, on "The Soul and Barbed Wire," Solzhenitsyn specifically discusses his spiritual rebirth in the camps, his return to the belief in God instilled in him as an adolescent but abandoned by him as a young man in favor of Marxism. Although with reservations, the author, surprisingly enough, even expresses gratitude for the experience of the camps, for it was precisely the suffering he underwent in them that helped him return to the fold of Christianity. *"Bless you, prison!"* the author writes in emphatic type at the close of his chapter "The Ascent."

In this part of his book Solzhenitsyn expresses some profound though very bitter thoughts. But much of what is written here strikes

a false note (at least to my ears). All these extremely impassioned out-
cries against Marxism, "the infallible and intolerant doctrine," which
demands only results, only matter and not *spirit*, all these arguments
about how only faith in God saved and elevated the human spirit in
the camps, while faith in the future triumph of social justice, in a better way of organizing society, failed to prevent spiritual corruption
and virtually led one straight into the ranks of stool pigeons—all this
has an unproved and arbitrary sound. A regrettable state of embitter-
ment leads the author to that very "intolerance and infallibility" of
judgment of which he accuses Marxism.

Solzhenitsyn does not even consider it possible for nonreligious
people to distinguish between good and bad.

Equating socialism with Stalinism, he naturally cannot understand
that there are people for whom the tragedy they or their countrymen
experienced can only become a further incentive to struggle for social justice and for a better life for humanity on this earth, for the
elimination of all forms of oppression of one person by another, including pseudosocialist forms of such oppression. Solzhenitsyn does
not understand that socialist convictions can be the basis for a genuinely humanist set of values and a profoundly humane morality. And
if up to now the problems of ethics and morals have not yet found satisfactory treatment in Marxist-Leninist theory, this by no means implies that scientific socialism is incapable by its very nature of
establishing moral values.

Summing up the thinking he did in camp, Solzhenitsyn writes:

> Since then I have come to understand the truth of all the religions of
> the world: They struggle with the evil inside a human being (inside
> every human being). It is impossible to expel evil from the world in its
> entirety, but it is possible to constrict it within each person.
>
> And since that time I have come to understand the falsehood of all
> the revolutions in history: They destroy only *those carriers* of evil con-
> temporary with them (and also fail, out of haste, to discriminate the
> carriers of good as well). And they then take to themselves as their her-
> itage the actual evil itself, magnified still more.

This juxtaposition seems to me neither accurate nor just. For it is necessary to fight against evil not only within each person, but also
against the carriers of evil contemporary with us, and against unjust
social institutions. This struggle goes on in various forms. Well and
good if it takes the form of peaceful competition between ideologies

and is realized through reforms and gradual changes for the better. But there still will be times when revolutionary forms of struggle must be resorted to, and although these may be accompanied by many sacrifices and disappointments, they by no means necessarily lead to the magnification of evil in the world. It is not socialist doctrine alone that can be distorted and turned against individuals and against all of humanity; so can the tenets of any religion. History offers more than a few examples of this, including the history of the Russian Orthodox Church, which has its own peculiar traditions of obscurantism. It is well known that in the sixteenth century the Russian Church was still burning heretics alive. Incidentally, one may find in Stalin's behavior and criminal actions not only the pragmatic attitude held by many revolutionaries toward violence and the use of extreme measures but also the dogmatism, casuistry, intolerance, and other qualities that are undoubtedly, to some extent, the result of his five years in an Orthodox school and three in an Orthodox seminary.

Terrible are the crimes Solzhenitsyn so vividly depicts in his book, and we are all as one with him in the condemnation of those crimes. But I continue to believe that only the victory of a genuinely socialist society, of genuinely socialist human and moral relations, can provide humanity with a firm guarantee that such crimes will never be repeated.

Translated by George Saunders

Dissent as a Personal Experience
1984

♦

ANDREI SINYAVSKY

Andrei Sinyavsky made his debut in *Dissent* in 1960 with an unsigned article, "On Socialist Realism." In 1973, after serving a prison term for his dissident writings (published under the pseudonym Abram Tertz), Sinyavsky and his family were allowed to emigrate to France, where he lives today. His books include *The Trial Begins, The Makepeace Experiment,* and *A Voice from the Chorus.*

My experience of dissent is extremely individual, even though, like any personal experience, it reflects in some way broader, more general, and more ramified developments, and not only the events of my own life. I have never belonged to any dissident movement or dissident community, and my heterodoxy has manifested itself not in public activity but exclusively in my writing; moreover, in a kind of writing that initially was esoteric, stylistically obscure for the general public, and not meant to evoke any openly political resonance.

The first period of my dissent as a writer takes up approximately ten years, from 1955 to my arrest. In those days I sent manuscripts abroad through secret channels and, hiding my real name, I published in the West under the pseudonym Abram Tertz. I was wanted as a criminal: this I knew, and I understood that I would be caught sooner or later, for, as the saying goes, "Crime does not pay."

As a result the process of writing itself assumed the nature of a rather thrilling detective story, although I do not write detective fiction and dislike it, and personally I do not care for the adventuresome. I just did not see any other way for my literary work to be published than this slippery path, which was condemned by the state, and was similar to a dangerous game of chance in which it was necessary to stake everything, one's existence, one's human interests, and one's personal attachments on a single card. There was simply no other way. It was necessary to choose, in one's own mind, between one's existence as a human being and one's existence as a writer. The more so since the destiny of writers in the Soviet Union shows that literature is a risky and at times fatal path, and under Soviet conditions the writer who combines literature with his well-being often stops being a real writer.

From the very beginning of my literary career there was, whether I liked it or not, a kind of split personality, which still has not been obliterated. This is a split between the authorial persona Abram Tertz and my human self (as well as my scholarly likeness), Andrei Sinyavsky. As a man I prefer a quiet, peaceful, and secluded life, and I am quite an ordinary person. Accordingly, people are usually nice and well meaning to me as a human individual. The same may be said about my research and teaching activities, which even today run parallel to my work as a writer. To be sure there have also been various inconveniences in this regard—in connection, for example, with my study of the poetry of Pasternak—but, after all, those are trifles.

On the whole my career as a scholar and a literary critic has developed successfully enough. And very likely I would still be a perfectly happy member of the Soviet Academy of Science and a prosperous literary critic of the liberal direction, if it were not for my dark literary double by the name of Abram Tertz. This person is, in contrast to Andrei Sinyavsky, inclined to go on forbidden paths and to take risky steps of different kinds, which has brought a great amount of trouble upon him and, accordingly, upon me. I think, however, that this "split personality" is not a question of my moral psychology, but rather a problem of the artistic style employed by Abram Tertz—an ironic, outré style, with elements of the fantastic and the grotesque.

To write as is customary or as is ordered is simply of no interest to me. Supposing I were asked to describe ordinary life in an ordinary realistic manner, I would refrain from writing at all. Inasmuch as politics and the social structure are not my discipline, it can be said jokingly that my disagreements with the Soviet government were basically aesthetic. As a result, Abram Tertz is a dissident primarily by virtue of his stylistic qualities. But he is an impudent, incorrigible dissident, who provokes indignation and aversion in a conservative and conformist society.

◆

Here it is fitting to deviate a bit and point out that any real literature in modern times is most often a transgression of the rules *"du bon ton."* By its nature literature is heterodoxy (in the broader sense of the word) with regard to the prevailing view of things. Any writer is a heterodox element within a society of people who think in an orthodox manner or, in any event, think alike. Any writer is an outcast, a degenerate, a not fully legitimate person in the world, because he thinks and writes in opposition to the opinion of the majority—at least if he writes in defiance of the existing style and the already determined, accepted course in literature.

In principle the writer should probably be killed—if for no other reason than because, when all people live like real people, he writes. Writing itself is heterodoxy in relation to life. In Russia one of the jailers admitted to me in a moment of intimacy, "I would put all writers, without exception and independent of their greatness—Shakespeare, Tolstoy, Dostoevsky—into one big madhouse, because writers only disturb the normal development of life." I think that this man is somehow right in his own way. He is right in that the writer, by the mere fact of his existence, introduces a kind of anxiety into the social system.

This is particularly the case in a standardized society, which lives and thinks according to state orders. In such a society the writer is a criminal, a more dangerous criminal than a thief or a murderer. In prison I was told with regard to my work, "It would have been better had you killed somebody!" Yet I had not written anything terrible in these works, and had not called for the overthrow of the Soviet government. It was sufficient that you think differently in some way, that you compose words in your own way and thereby enter into contradiction with the general official style, and with the official jargon, which determines everything. For such authors, as for dissidents in general, there exists a special juridical term in the Soviet Union: "especially dangerous state criminals." I personally fell into this category, and I hope to remain to the end of my days, in the eyes of Soviet society, an "especially dangerous state criminal."

However, I was not always such a bad fellow. My childhood and adolescence, in the 1930s, were spent in a wholesome Soviet atmosphere, in a normal Soviet family. My father was admittedly no Bolshevik. He had been a left Social Revolutionary, and, after renouncing the aristocratic milieu by 1909 he had already joined the revolution. He took an extremely loyal position toward the Bolshevik government, no matter how they persecuted him for his former revolutionary activities.

Accordingly, I was raised in the best traditions of the Russian Revolution, or, more precisely, in the traditions of revolutionary idealism, which, by the way, I do not by any means regret. I do not regret it because in my childhood I adopted from my father the notion that one should not live in accordance with narrow, egotistic, "bourgeois" interests, and that it is necessary to see some higher meaning in life. Subsequently, art became this "higher meaning" for me. When I was fifteen, on the eve of the war, I was an enthusiastic Communist-Marxist, for whom there was nothing finer than the world revolution and the future universal brotherhood.

Let me remark in passing that, to the extent that we are talking about dissent as a concrete historical phenomenon, this is a very typical biography for Soviet dissidents in general. Most of the time, dissidents were formerly very high-minded Soviet individuals, people with strong convictions, with principles, and with revolutionary ideals. On the whole, dissidents are the product of the Soviet society of the post-Stalin era, and not some alien elements in this society or remnants of some old, shattered opposition.

In all periods of Soviet history there have been enemies of the Soviet government—people who have not been satisfied with it or who have suffered from it; people who have criticized it, but who nevertheless cannot be called dissidents. Nor can we call, for instance, Pasternak, Mandelstam, and Akhmatova dissidents, although they were heretics in Soviet literature. Through their heterodoxy they anticipated dissent; they supported and still support this later development. But one cannot call them dissidents for the simple reason that their roots go back to bygone, prerevolutionary traditions of Russian culture.

Dissidents, on the other hand, are a totally new phenomenon, which grew directly from the soil of Soviet reality. They are the people who were raised in Soviet society, who are children of the Soviet system, and who came into conflict with the ideology and the psychology of their fathers. And this, it seems to me, partly explains the interest of the contemporary West in the problems of Soviet dissent, because the dissidents represent a view of Soviet society from within. One cannot accuse the dissidents of being an alien class, or of not accepting the Revolution, like those people who lost out in it. This is not a political opposition struggling for power. It is characteristic that the political accent of the dissident movement is generally low-key, while intellectual and moral questions come to the fore. This distinguishes the dissidents from the Russian revolutionaries of the past, and if they bring about some "revolution"—let us provisionally call it by that term—then it will be in the form of a reevaluation of values, which is the starting point for dissent.

Within each dissident this process of reevaluation takes its individual course under the influence of one or another of the contradictions in daily life. Each dissident encounters his or her own stumbling block, which serves as the catalyst of critical thought. For many dissidents this stumbling block, as we know, was the Twentieth Party Congress, in 1956, not only because their eyes were opened to the enormous crimes of the past, but also because, after having revealed to them some of these crimes, the Twentieth Party Congress and all of the subsequent Soviet ideology did not and could not give any sort of serious, historical explanation for these events. And although the regime has become more moderate since Stalin, this has not led to a more liberal and more democratic state system, which would provide some guarantee of human rights and human liberty. In the aftermath of the Twentieth Party Congress, the Soviet people were simply told, as before, to trust the party and the state in everything.

In the recent past, however, this faith has cost too much and has led us too far astray. As a consequence each dissident's ideological or childish faith in the justice of communism was replaced by individual reason and the voice of one's conscience. Thus the dissident movement is, in my opinion, primarily an intellectual movement; it is a process of independent and unintimidated thinking. At the same time these intellectual or spiritual aspirations are correlated to a feeling of moral responsibility, which is bestowed upon a man and forces him to think, speak, and write independently without regard for the norms and prescriptions of the state.

◆

I personally experienced this normative process of dissent a little bit differently. My period of reevaluating values and forming individual opinions was during the late 1940s and early '50s. That period of late, mature, and rampant Stalinism after the war coincided with the years of my studies, when I began to study the humanities at Moscow University, and the main stumbling blocks, which led to the collapse of revolutionary ideals, were problems of literature and art, which arose with particular poignancy in those days. After all, this was exactly the time when the frightful purges were carried out in the Soviet cultural world. To my misfortune, I loved modernism in art and everything that, as a result of the purges, was subject to destruction. I saw the purges as the death of culture and the end of any original thought in Russia.

In the internal conflict between politics and art I opted for art and rejected politics. At the same time I started to look closely at the nature of the Soviet state in general, in the light of the devastation that was visited on life and culture. Consequently I was exhilarated at Stalin's death. Having attempted to write "something original and artistic," I understood in advance that there would not be and could not be any place for it in Soviet literature. I never tried or even so much as dreamed of publishing it in my own country; so I simply sent the manuscripts abroad. This was nothing less than dropping out from the prevailing literary system and the literary environment. Sending works to the West was, however, the best means of "preserving the text" and did not represent a political action or a form of protest.

I did not therefore consider myself guilty of a political crime, when they arrested me and when the second period of my career as a writer began. Now, this was a natural form of behavior, and not a result of cunning on my part. Generally, a man who is thrown into prison should behave naturally—this is the only thing that helps. It is natural for the writer to affirm that literature neither is nor can serve the purpose of political agitation and propaganda, as is maintained by the Soviet government—which, by the way, conducts political agitation freely and incompetently in the West.

In this manner my friend Yuli Daniel and I managed to take the position of "pleading not guilty" despite the pressure of the court and the KGB. This rather strong pressure is exerted on your person and your family, and our denial of guilt played a specific role in the development of the dissident or, as it is called, the democratic movement, although we were not directly associated with this movement, but rather acted on our own.

The problem was that earlier on, in all public political trials in the Soviet Union, the "criminals" (in quotation marks and without quotation marks) confessed their guilt, repented, and publicly abased themselves before the Soviet court. Political justice in the Soviet Union was based on it. Of course, there had previously also been some people who repented and considered themselves not guilty, but no one ever heard about it. Outwardly everything went well: "the enemies of the people" confessed to being "enemies of the people" and asked for the chance to be good, honest Soviet citizens, or, even worse, not to be shot, so that they could improve, and by atoning for their crimes against the fatherland become good, honest Soviet citizens. For the state this meant reducing the people to a common denominator, to a "moral-political unity of the Soviet people and the party."

We, the dissidents, succeeded in breaking with this tradition. We succeeded in remaining ourselves and outside the Soviet "unity." In our court case (Yuli Daniel's and mine), this was made public, and it received support within the country and abroad, in the West, through "public opinion." All this happened without our willing it. Being in prison and being on trial, we did not presume that another process was beginning around our prosecution. We were isolated and could not imagine that it would lead to a chain reaction. We were simply writers and persisted in our own course.

At this point it is appropriate to remember that a dissident (I am using the expression now in its most general and broadest meaning) is not only a man who disagrees with the system and has the courage to express himself: he is also a man who does not consider himself guilty. This is, of course, a matter of personal choice, and nobody may impose upon anyone any "rules of behavior" before Soviet justice. This is a problem to be resolved by each individual. But the concept of the "dissident" presupposes a specific kind of moral resistance or force of conscience, which does not allow him to repent and turn into an ordinary Soviet citizen who speaks at the bidding of the state all his life. There are those who do not repent their words and their deeds, are consequently sent to labor camps, and remain dissidents. There are others who retract their dissent, repudiate themselves, get free, and become again "honest Soviet citizens." The warrant of dissidence is prison.

◆

I now turn to the third and last period of my experience as a dissident—the period from my emigration up to the present. I would like to dwell for a while on this point, since it is particularly complicated and, in my opinion, dramatic. I will hardly touch upon the West itself, because I am interested in the dissident-émigré environment and its press, in which I had occasion to get involved deeply enough to gain an exceedingly unsettling experience.

What has recently been going on with the dissidents who have come to the West should, in my opinion, be designated by the expression "dissident NEP." I am using this expression not as a scientific term but rather as an image, an analogy to that colorful period of Soviet history that began in the 1920s, after the Civil War, and continued for about five to seven years. In those days the government granted the country the so-called economic breather, with the purpose of adjusting an economy devastated by war and revolution. As we know, this was a comparatively peaceful and happy period, allowing the people to breathe relatively freely and grow fat a bit. Simultaneously, this was the time of crushing defeat for all opposition and the beginning of the powerful Stalinist consolidation. It was the time when the revolution degenerated into its opposite, a conservative, petty-bourgeois/bureaucratic system. It is amazing that, during the years of NEP (New Economic Policy), many heroes of the Revolution and the Civil War turned out to be cowards, opportunists, submissive executors of the new political system, veritable philistines and conformists. Does that mean that they had not been real heroes in the recent past? No, they were heroes, without any doubt; they had faced death and feared nothing. But the political climate had changed and they had entered a different environment, which demanded different human qualities. And yet it was also as if they had come into their own; they were the very medium of the triumphant Revolution. And so, if they had not fallen in battle, the heroes of yesterday turned into mediocre bureaucrats.

Now let us transfer some characteristics of NEP to our dissident experience. Having come to the West, we find ourselves not only in a different society but also in a different historical climate, at a different stage of its development. This is a peaceful and comparatively happy period in our personal histories. We have only to endure the test of prosperity, as well as the test of democracy and freedom, of which we had dreamed. As dissidents we are threatened by nothing except personal decadence. After all, it is very easy to be a dissident in the West (that is, a dissident with regard to the Soviet system). What threatened us with prison in the Soviet Union promises us here, with a certain effort, prestige and material prosperity.

Only the idea of "dissidence" itself fades somehow over here and loses its heroic, romantic, and moral aura. We essentially do not resist anything and risk nothing, but only shake our fists in the air in the belief that we are carrying on a battle for human rights. It is clear that we sincerely wish to help, and at times we actually do help those who are persecuted in the Soviet Union. But this has to be done: one has to think of those who are in prison over there. Only on our part (and this is worth remembering) all this is no longer a struggle, or a sacrifice, or an achievement; it is charity and philanthropy. It can even be an income, a living, and at times, unfortunately, a profitable enterprise. It is this last circumstance that sometimes adds a not altogether noble touch to the dissident cause in the West.

Everybody, of course, needs money, and if a dissident has no other specialty, he is forced to earn his living on this well-trodden path. Money is also necessary to publish books and journals, to organize conferences, and so on. And all these are useful and absolutely necessary things in Russia as well as in the West. As everyone already knows, however, money not only makes it possible to do good and permits one to live independently but, as it happens, it also corrupts and enslaves. And dissidents cannot escape this universal human law.

I do not mention any names, because it is not a question of names but of trends. And the trend, unfortunately, shows that there are cases when the dissident who comes to the West loses his distinguishing feature, his independence and his courage of mind, and enters the service of some dissident-émigré corporation, or the service of some dissident ideological boss. And he no longer speaks his mind but rather what is demanded of him. His adaptation is justified with the words, "You cannot survive here otherwise!" Moreover, this may be said by someone who only yesterday risked his life for his convictions.

And what are we to make of this? Was it the case that in the Soviet Union, in prison, he was spiritually free and could live in his own way, different from the majority, and without yielding to any son of pressure or bribery? And is it the case that here, in an environment of freedom, he adapts himself to the situation, because here, as it suddenly turns out, "you cannot survive otherwise"? Is freedom psychologically more dangerous for him, the dissident, than prison? Can it be that, given freedom, we become slaves? Or was Dostoevsky's Grand Inquisitor right when he said that people do not love freedom but fear it, and seek some support in life, in the form of bread, authority, and miracle? That people seek someone to worship and, "in order to do it surely together," look for a "community of worship" of some authority, to which they surrender their freedom? We are, however, not concerned here with the problems of human history and psychology in general but with a concrete phenomenon: the dissident movement. So, with reference to dissidents now in the West, the greatest danger of opportunism and conformism arises, as it seems to me, from the need for a general, communal worship of something or somebody.

Here it is necessary to take the specific character of émigré life into account. When coming to the West, we become very lonely, and we suffer from our loneliness. This affects us Russians in particular, for we are used to closer, more amicable contacts than we can notice in the West. Naturally, we look for our own people, for our environment, and we find it in the form of the dissident-émigré association. We easily make concessions to this environment and its authorities, insofar as we fear losing it; and the range of choices within the groups is extraordinarily limited. The community of thought that arises in this environment, the narrowness of the environment and its seclusion, and at times its conservatism and subordination to authority, sometimes even the émigré's material dependence on this authority and this environment—all these create the fertile soil to foster conformity.

We ourselves do not always realize how we turn from dissidents into conformists. After all, we do not commit treason, we do not leave one camp for the other. We only adjust ourselves subtly. But in exactly that way, the heroes of the Revolution did not realize their degeneration during the NEP period. After all, they did not betray the ideals of communism. The revolutionaries only turned into obedient party officials. This is why I am afraid that in our emigration, under the warm wings of the democratic West, we reproduce the archetype of the Soviet system without wishing it or being aware of it—only with a different, anti-Soviet valence. There is another essential difference: we do not have our police and we do not have those prisons. But there is already a censorship in its own right, and there are also informers. It is only that the Western police somehow do not accept our reports. Oh yes, we forgot: after all, this is a democracy!

◆

An outside observer interested in our problems does not always understand why and about what Soviet dissidents who have emigrated to the West argue so fervently among themselves. They do not understand why there is no agreement on opinions: after all, all of us are dissidents. I personally think that there is more agreement among us than is necessary. There is even an excess of agreement, to the detriment of our dissent. After all, the dissidents are by nature not a political party and do not even share an ideology. The repudiation of Soviet ideology presumes not only different thinking with regard to this ideology, but also diversity of thought within heterodoxy. If we are heretics, then there should be many heresies. This is, in my view, the value of dissent, which in its ideal form is not the nucleus of a new church or of a new, unified, anti-Soviet state, but rather a pluralistic community, even if only on paper.

I said before that the Soviet dissidents are by their nature an intellectual, spiritual, and moral opposition. The question is: opposition against what? Not simply against the Soviet system in general, but also opposition against the uniformity of ideas and their paralysis in Soviet society. And if we want a free Russian idea, a free Russian word and culture, to develop, we need diversity of thought. This is the most important precondition for the development of Russian culture. Why should diversity of thought be possible in the West, yet not for us dissidents? We are, after all, like anyone else, equipped with the rudiments of reason and a sense of justice.

Apart from this, there has recently been a clear split within the dissident movement, particularly on émigré soil. It is a split into two wings or directions; the first can provisionally be called the "authoritarian-nationalist" wing, and the second the "liberal-democratic" wing. By its nature, dissent is liberal and democratic, and that is the way it started. Therefore, the terms "Soviet dissidents" or "democratic movement" were and remain synonymous. The "national-authoritarian" wing appeared later and entered, as it seems to me, into a conflict with the main premises of the movement. It is understandable that, with the split now in process, serious and fundamental disagreements flare up. They form the basis of our quarrels.

I belong to the liberal-democratic wing—not because I believe in the imminent victory of freedom and democracy in Russia. On the contrary, I categorically do not believe in such a victory. At any rate, I do not see such prospects in the near, foreseeable future. But under the circumstances of Soviet despotism, it is correct for a Russian intellectual—in my opinion—to be a liberal and a democrat, and not to propose some other, new kind of despotism. Let us assume that democracy as a social and government system has no future in Russia. All the same, it is our vocation to remain proponents of freedom, because freedom, like some other "useless" concept—such as, for instance, art, goodness, or human thought—is an end in itself and does not depend on the historical or political trend.

This is why I cannot agree with those dissidents who propose to exchange communism for another variety of despotism under the banner of nationalism and religion, even though such changes are probably historically feasible. Although I personally belong to the Russian Orthodox Church and like the old Russian culture fully as

much as many writers and thinkers of the Slavophile circle, with regard to contemporary Russian nationalism I am extremely suspicious
of the idealization of the state order and the social customs of a Russia of the past. I am against the mixture of spiritual and material values, or of religious and political ones.

Let us say that many contemporary Russophiles tend to criticize the
West for the formalized way of life, for the fact that here judicial and
rationalistic categories of "law" and "justice" dominate, whereas the
ideas of Christian "love" and "goodness" were indigenous to Russia
from the very beginning. And " 'goodness' is higher than 'law.' " Yes, I
agree. Divine goodness and love are higher and greater than all human laws made on earth. But this theory seems to me dangerous and
insulting in reference to a government system—dangerous for the individual, and insulting to religion. After all, it is not God, not Christ,
who in reality rules a despotic state but the czar or the leader, who,
unfortunately, even if it is an Orthodox czar, frequently does not resemble God but rather the Devil. Of course, this czar has the opportunity to show "goodness" in circumvention of "law." But this
"goodness" itself, in order to be shown, requires unbelievable, uncon-
trollable, and autocratic power. And in practice such power does not
turn into love or goodness, but into executions. More precisely: many,
many executions, and a little bit of goodness. So, in my view, the formalized and rationalistic "law" is better than tsarist "goodness."

◆

Russian dissidents who have come to the West are sometimes afraid
of democracy here. They think that the West will gradually disinte-
grate under the pressure of the monolithic, totalitarian system of the
Soviet Union. They advise the West to turn to more authoritarian
principles. And, correspondingly, they want the Russia of the future
not to be a democracy but a more solid authoritarian-theocratic state.
In the end, the people who were, so it seems, saved from death by
Western democracy now would like to restrict it. Hence the moralistic
and didactic pronouncements to the West on the part of some Soviet
dissidents, who see this West for the first time and know it badly.

We should probably be more modest and, by transmitting our dis-
tressing experience to the West, be careful to teach the West how to
live and build its fundamental, Western society. We have already built
our society in the form of a communist state, from which we do not
know where to turn. The new Russian nationalists object to this argument by claiming that all our Russian misfortunes have come from

the West. Marxism came from the West. From the West came liberalism, undermining the autocratical-patriarchal foundation of Russia. All foreigners (Poles, Jews, Latvians, Hungarians) who brought about the October Revolution were Western intruders. Yet all this is but a search for a "scapegoat" somewhere from without. It is not we who are guilty but someone alien (the West, a world conspiracy, the Jews, and so on). In essence, this means casting off one's own sins and omissions. We are actually the good ones, we are clean, we are most fortunate, because we are Russians. And it is the "Devil" who interfered in our history.

What I am saying here is a sacrilege from the nationalists' point of view. For similar reasons, Russian nationalists call Russian liberals (and me, specifically) *Russophobes.* Like the decadent, liberal atheist in the West, we—in league with the Communists—hate the Russian people and Russia. It is difficult to defend oneself against such an accusation. After all, should one shout loudly that one loves Russia? That would be ridiculous. As far as I have observed, there are not that many Russophobes in the West. The converse, "Russophile" position would betray a lack of respect for the Russian people. If Russia could be conquered by a bunch of foreigners, how could this great by nation be so worthy? And if Russia is incompatible with democracy, would that not mean that, by this interpretation, the people itself is inclined to slavery? By the way, this fear of democracy, applied to the Russian people, has had bitter antecedents in our history. For the longest time the "Russian patriots" were afraid to abolish serfdom in Russia. Their concern: how could one grant freedom to a Russian peasant? After all, without the landowner's supervision he would immediately stop working and get drunk!

Such are our quarrels in the broadest and crassest outlines. These arguments are useful for the discovery of our different views on the matter, but in practice they are rather utopian. The Soviet system is extremely solid and does not promise any freedom (including freedom for the founding of an orthodox theocracy or autocracy). But we are always arguing: Do we need freedom? And we bring the needle of the compass, as has long been our custom, to the side of despotism. A very sad portent.

◆

How odd it is that in our Western environment the authoritarian-nationalist wing enjoys greater success and influence than the democratic one. This is so because, owing to its psychological makeup, the authoritarian direction is more party-oriented, more disciplined, more single-minded, and more obedient to the authority of the "leader" than the democrats, who lean by nature toward tolerance, pluralism, and diversity of thought. Moreover, nationalism and the proponents of the authoritarian system are supported by the largest part of the old émigrés, who make up the majority of the Russian public, and who are, so to speak, the Russian soil in the West. They support the authoritarian-nationalist wing by virtue of their inveterate, monarchist conservatism. For the old émigrés, prerevolutionary Russia is an indisputable ideal to which contemporary Russia—occupied by the Bolsheviks—dreams of returning. In Paris a nice elderly lady asked me, after she found out that I had recently come from Moscow, whether I had met *ours* there. "Which ours?" I asked timidly. She replied, "The Whites!" At this level of understanding the democratic dissidents who come to the West are something like "Soviet devils," who are specially sent here by the Bolsheviks, in order to disarm the last bulwark of the Fatherland.

It is interesting, however, that even Western circles sometimes tend to support the Russian nationalists and authoritarian representatives, even though the democratic dissidents are psychologically much closer to them. The logic here is as follows: freedom and democracy are good for the West, but for Russia something simpler and more reactionary is required—as for savages. Let me pose a purely rhetorical question: has democratic America not at times supported extremely reactionary, authoritarian, and totalitarian regimes in developing countries, hoping thereby to save these countries from the communist infection? And has it not lost with this policy? Yet I am not concerned with American politics, which I understand poorly, but with Russian culture. It is this difference of interests that keeps us sometimes from coming to a mutual understanding.

As an illustration I want to tell you of a private conversation I recently had with a very clever and perceptive Western Sovietologist. According to his personal convictions and tastes he is a liberal and a democrat, but politically he counts on Russian authoritarianism and nationalism. As a sophisticated man he is shocked by the rudeness of this direction, and if he were Russian, he would never become associated with it. But to him it seems a movement with more of a future and greater advantage to the West than that of the Russian democrats. I asked him, "Aren't you afraid that in the end, in succession to the Soviet system, or more likely, in the form of some kind of alliance with it, outright fascism will triumph in Russia?" It turns out that this does not upset him in any way. He regards Russian fascism as a realistic alternative to Soviet communism and hopes that Russian fascism may save the West from communism through its concern with nationalism.

I, personally, am not so optimistic; in my opinion, the West should save itself from communism by its own efforts, and not with the help of someone's fascism. But the greatest contradiction again consists in the fact that freedom is a necessity for Russian culture, whereas for my Western interlocutor Russian culture is of minor importance and not essential at all. To him it is important to save the world from a catastrophe. I personally do not undertake such great tasks as saving the world. My profession is narrower: I am a writer.

◆

In conclusion, I only want to confirm my "dissent." Under an avalanche of abuse, this is easy. As an émigré I began to understand that I am not an enemy of the Soviet government only, but generally: I am an enemy—an enemy as such—metaphysically, in principle. Not that I was someone's friend first and then became his enemy. I am not anyone's friend, but only an enemy.

The West, of course, only smiles gleefully at these "Russian specimens": exotics. After all, the West does not read Russian newspapers on this or that side of the ocean. But I do read them, and I can see. And this is my conclusion: there, in the Soviet Union, I was an "agent of Imperialism"; here, in exile, I am an "agent of Moscow."

Meanwhile, I have not changed my position, but have said the same thing: art is greater than reality. A threatening retribution is following me from various corners—for one and the same kind of books, for one and the same kind of statements, for one and the same style, for one and the same crime.

Psychologically, this somewhat resembles the sort of nightmare in one's sleep that does not come to an end. You know what happens in a dream: you seem to wake up, but only to find yourself in an even more intense continuation of your dream. Wherever you turn, you are an enemy of the people. No, even worse, even more horrible: you are Dante, who killed Pushkin; and you also killed Gogol. You hate culture. You hate "everything Russian" (earlier, in the first dream, it could be heard: "You hate everything Soviet," and incidentally, that too meant that you hate everything Russian). You hate your own mother, even your deceased mother. You are anti-Semitic. You are a misanthrope. You are a Judas who betrayed Christ in the

form of the new, communist, national-religious resurrection of Russia. I reason to myself that, despite all deficiencies, I am still not the
Antichrist. But what I think does not matter. It is all subjective. Objectively, that is, socially and publicly, I am the enemy of everything
that is fine in the world. What is more—of everything that is good,
everything that is human. What a horror!

I ask myself, how could I ever have sunk so low? After all, I was a
nice boy at some point, like all people. But apparently society knows
better than I what sort of man I am. After Soviet justice, if you will,
there is émigré justice—and the same evidence. Of course, they do
not throw you into a concentration camp. But a camp is not the most
frightful thing in the world. There it is even pleasant compared to
emigration, where they say that you have not been in any camp at all,
but that you are sent "on an assignment" to destroy Russian culture.

I am now interested in one question: why did Soviet, and anti-Soviet émigré, justice agree (agree literally) in their accusations of me,
a Russian dissident? Most likely, because both of these organs of justice are just and therefore so similar to each other. Who needs freedom? Freedom is a danger. Freedom is irresponsibility before the
authoritarian collective. Watch out for it—freedom!

But finally you awake in the morning after all these dreams and you
smile ironically at yourself: didn't you wish that? Yes, all that is true.
Freedom! Writing—this is freedom.

Translated from the Russian by Maria-Regina Kecht

To Cave Explorers from the West
1988

◆

GEORGE KONRÁD

George Konrád lives and works in Budapest, Hungary. His novels include *The Case Worker, The City Builder,* and *The Loser.* In 1974, when he and Ivan Szelenyi published their essay "The Intellectuals on the Road to Class Power," they were arrested and charged with subversive agitation. Konrád did not, however, accept the government's offer to emigrate. In 1990 he was elected president of International P.E.N., the first Central European to hold that position.

I have been living in Budapest for decades now, but I wouldn't dare to say that I know the city. Everyone there seems to know something that I don't. Simply looking at other people is enough to make me feel that I am just one of many passers-by.

The newcomer, who has spent less than a month in Budapest, and is already writing a book about it, may think that our city is an open-and-shut case. He hurries along to the next—to Prague, let's say, or Cracow—in order to dash off the same description there, so that the latest cliché about Central Europe may emerge.

But that quality that we generally call "Western" is, for all its advantages, the price we pay for the hasty cliché. Economical use of time carries with it a harmless superficiality. To create an "authentic account," all one need do is add a touch of local color to the stereotypes of journalism.

◆

The Westerner who travels in Eastern Central Europe also travels through his own wartime past. There are the shortages of wartime, there is the whiff of danger, the romantic accounts about how good people get into trouble because they are good.

But there is a longing, a bitter sense of deprivation, that the citizen of the West has never experienced. So too a sense of being subject to the powers-that-be which the writer in the West has never felt. There is a tight barrier that is all but impossible to break. Literature is one attempt at breaking out.

◆

For mutual understanding, tolerance is not enough; one also needs complicity. For an understanding of Central Europe, an excursion is not enough. We can share our experience only by living it together.

As a Hungarian, for whom life has been a little easier than for our neighbors, I have played the role of an "American uncle." After a short while, I realized that I was a caricature.

I do not assert that a person is better simply because his lot is hard. But neither do I believe that a person is better because his burden is light.

◆

Our burden is the state; the Westerner's is the voluntarily adopted cliché of majority rule. Our burden seems to us the more oppressive. There are those who console themselves with the idea that the palm tree grows taller under a weight. Who knows? In any case, all of us are deformed by our civilization.

◆

We do not live in the delirium of change. It is not our experience that everything has undergone a dizzying transformation. We find, instead, that the essentials are permanent: homes, friendships, the basic questions.

Much has changed in our lives, but many things on the surface. The deeper beneath the surface we go, the more illusory the change.

◆

We are the needy relatives, we are the aborigines, we are the ones left behind—the backward, the stunted, the misshapen, the down-and-out, the moochers, parasites, con-men, suckers. Sentimental, old-fashioned, childish, uninformed, troubled, melodramatic, devious, unpredictable, negligent. The ones who don't answer letters, the ones who miss the great opportunity, the hard drinkers, the babblers, the porch-sitters, the deadline-missers, the promise-breakers, the braggarts, the immature, the monstrous, the undisciplined, the easily offended, the ones who insult each other to death but cannot break off relations. We are the maladjusted, the complainers intoxicated by failure.

We are irritating, excessive, depressing, somehow unlucky. People are accustomed to slight us. We are cheap labor; merchandise may be had from us at a lower price; people bring us their old newspapers as a gift. Letters from us come sloppily typed, unnecessarily detailed. People smile at us, pityingly, as long as we do not suddenly become unpleasant.

As long as we do not say anything strange, sharp; as long as we do not stare at our nails and bare our teeth; as long as we do not become wild and cynical.

◆

We are sometimes more than normal, sometimes less. Not for us reliable, wise mediocrity, the clear-cut, consistent principles of life: prudence, thrift, attention to detail, precision, the painstaking accumulation of successes. For us, something else.

Come and visit, Western observer, but leave here in time. It may happen that you will become involved in something, and then it will be painful to tear yourself away if you wish to return to reality. This dream is oppressive and yet alluring. Everything in it is wretched, yes, but for some reason you feel at home here, and, what is more, there is food for thought if you make friends with the natives. Our life is crazier, more extravagant, but richer than the one from which you have come. Be careful, or you will become entangled here. The soil of this motherland, one can sink into it like mud.

◆

The nature of the writing profession is such that, before one sits down at one's desk, one must leave one's identity on the coat rack in the front hall. And one must slough off the stereotypes of one's environment. Above the clouds, the sun is always shining; that is where we meet.

Down here, this miserable self-pity—both individual and collective—interferes with thought, with our ability to see ourselves objectively. We are treated badly; we report this in various ways, or we report this in one voice. So we are treated badly. What can one conclude from this? History smiles on some and not on others. The fortunate sometimes feel an instinctive aversion to the unfortunate.

◆

In Central Europe, in the twentieth century—which began with World War I—it is not unimaginable, not even particularly surprising, for you to find, opening your eyes in bed one morning, as in a scene from a Kafka novel, that two strange men are standing next to your bed and telling you that you are under arrest.

It's no use resisting; you cannot avoid this persecution. They isolate you, bug your room, break you down, lock you in—and worse. The criminal trial is typical Central European theater. It shows that a person is helpless against others, against a faceless power. You assert your rights, but that only makes the situation worse. If you want to improve the system, you must accept with humility that you are guilty and that the authorities are right. It is wiser to throw yourself on their mercy than to insist with increasing desperation that you are innocent.

Seeing that a human being, from birth, is sentenced to death, it is not so difficult to accept that any misfortune is permanent and irrevocable. The blow falls, and it wears a human face.

◆

For the most part, Central European writers do battle, using words, with this powerful, incalculable force that dwells among us, a force that demands conformity and punishes truth-telling. There are those who hide their manuscripts; there are those who disguise their thoughts.

So that he will not be silenced, a writer remains silent—or he will be silent in many words, to avoid the unpleasantness writers face if they actually say something.

◆

The Western observer marvels how widespread ridicule of the state is here, although the ridiculers are all, in one way or another, people of the state, if for no other reason than that they are its hostages. In conducting their lives, they can never forget the presence of the state, its prying eye. Nor can they remove the state from their thoughts of the future.

We live in symbiosis with the state, by virtue of the fact that we live in Eastern Central Europe, where the majority of public people have taken a vow that they will neither speak nor write on certain subjects.

This vow demands the use of a special state language, a language designed to create a generation of writers who do not reach adulthood. By this I mean people who, while writing, keep an eye on what is permitted and what is not. The most advanced form of such obedience is when a subject, being forbidden, does not even enter the author's mind.

Such enforced adolescence produces resentment, the longing to retire into a cave, to make that cave a labyrinth.

◆

How would we view our literature if, by the touch of a magic wand, freedom of the press sprang from the soil? If suddenly no courage or morality was needed to write the truth?

A new era of history would dawn if the events in Hungary of 1956 could be called, in the press, a "revolution" by those who feel it was a revolution, and a "counterrevolution" by those who feel it was a counterrevolution.

In this improbable utopian situation, our present literature would seem unnecessarily subtle and windy. It would be like emerging from a communal neurosis. We would exclaim, amazed: What on earth was this complicated nonsense we were working on?

◆

But does not art benefit from subtlety and concealment? No doubt. The tension between speaking out and not speaking out is beneficial for art. One can jump heroically head-first from our world of cryptic language only into mere journalism.

Miracles in literature still happen. Success comes not to the majority but to a few. There is no formula for it. Even extraordinary talent cannot explain it; there are so many other factors. One genius goes to ruin, another does not.

It may be that our constant soul-searching is the most valuable thing. Daily, we tear apart and cross-examine our every belief and borrowed idea. Our obsession is to put everything into question. Since writing is a dangerous enterprise, and one pays a price for doing it, whoever writes what he thinks is an adventurer and must take into account every possibility, like a prisoner planning a jailbreak.

◆

As for values, we live in a no-man's-land. Neither the prewar values nor the contemporary Western values nor the contemporary Eastern values are applicable here. A liberal value system is fine, but the practice of it is a problem. The ideology of state socialism is on the decline, but the ideologies of democratic socialism or liberal democracy have not arrived yet. From the crow's nest the ship's boy does not cry, "Land ho!"

Even so, it is possible that interesting years are coming. If anything happens here, it will be because the Central Europeans do not acquiesce, convinced that they are destined for something more. That they deserve better. The resurrection of human dignity here occasionally assumes dramatic proportions. Although democratic experiments have been short-lived and unsuccessful, they have not been wasted. Their energy, conserved, repressed, will break out in a later generation, with greater force.

◆

People in this region must make dangerous decisions even when they are not looking for trouble. A friend of mine once said, in response to a rebuke, that he was not hitting the wall with his head, the wall was hitting him. There are unintentional heroes. Who chooses to be a hero? Normal Western people don't get into such situations.

Many interesting, intense people from here have wandered all over the world, and many have stayed put. We live in the vicinity of Western Europe, in roughly the same cultural sphere, among the monuments of Europe's past. We are Europe in the past tense, the exotic next door.

Relativism is our peculiarity. We can look at a thing one way and then another. With both cynicism and pathos, a combination unfamiliar in the West.

A few of our visitors have said that during their stay they found something warm, as if remembered from a previous life.

There is a lot of conversation, if you like conversation. From this oral literature, never printed, never recorded, something has settled into our books.

We are at the geographical center of Europe. On a sixteenth-century Spanish map, Europe is a reclining lady; her head is the Iberian Peninsula, and her navel is Buda. From Budapest one may look upon life no less effectively than from any other spot on earth.

◆

Here we are inbred. To our little world, its immediate family and its extended family, not only our relatives and friends belong, but our enemies as well. We have long known and kept an eye on each other. This intimacy is strange.

We have been pressed together into a small space; we are not empire-builders. From here we venture out into the larger world, then drift back, and cling together, nursing wounds of imagined offenses.

◆

We are not on the stage of world history; we do not brag about our power; people do not fear us. Our land is not as spacious, our spirit not as expansive as the Russians'; our mind understands the Western way of thinking better. We judge our circumstances, straitened by the East, from a point of view influenced by the West. Western ridicule counters Eastern inertia. Here one may learn how Eastern and Western mentalities contend—in our heads and in our beds.

Central European culture is both a half-breed and a cross-breed. It contains progress and fatalism. Premeditation and drunkenness. Time is not money here. We talk a lot, we sit at meetings. The trains run slower, the movies run slower.

◆

There are places we can go, people we can see, if we don't want to be alone. Sometimes there are violent, drunken brawls. An observer might think that such people are on bad terms, but no: they are merely getting things off their chests.

Our conversations branch like a luxuriantly leafy houseplant. Although our apartments are bugged, the talk flows in torrents. A new guest drops in, spends some time, and knows everybody—he knows even the people he does not know. There are moral judgments, cynical jokes. With such fairy tales we pass our history on to the younger generation. Paradoxes flower among the old pieces of furniture: threadbare, intricate, weatherbeaten relationships.

Translated by James A. Tucker

On Loss:
The Condition of Germany
1993

◆

GÜNTER GRASS

Günter Grass is Germany's most celebrated contemporary writer. He achieved worldwide recognition with the publication of *The Tin Drum,* his novel about Germany's World War II years. His other books include *Dog Years, The Flounder,* and, most recently, *Two States—One Nation?,* a collection of public addresses on the reunification of Germany.

Toward the end of last summer we went to a Danish island, as we have done for years now, looking to put some space between us and our "troublesome fatherland," yet mindful of how quickly and completely such small distance, a mere hop, skip, and jump, can be canceled out, especially in August, the traditional month for crises. The previous year it had been the failed putsch in the disintegrating Soviet Union that dominated our vacation and glued us to the radio. Two years earlier the island setting had been canceled out by the Persian Gulf crisis *qua* media event; we simply could not tune it out. And this year it was Germany that caught up with us.

Actually the island of Møn has plenty of homegrown excitement. From morning till night a sweeping meadow, rimmed by Baltic dunes, enjoys incessant air traffic. Wild geese by the thousands make a stopover there, practicing takeoffs and landings. Now and then a heron startles the gaggles of geese out of their languid rest. Constant racket, which eventually swallows itself up. And above the meadow, above the dunes, the skies are always filled with flight patterns, a writing which, when decoded, gives rise to legends. . . .

Last August, however, the sky was as good as empty—only gulls.

The dry summer had parched the meadow, closing the spacious airstrip to takeoffs and landings. But according to the radio, there was no lack of crises. As if the two events had been mischievously wired in parallel, the athletic triumphs and disappointments in Barcelona provided a running commentary on the daily dying in Sarajevo. The Olympic Games were taking place in Bosnia; the Olympic stadium lay within range of the Serbs' mortars. Reports overlapped. Simultaneous events appeared equally significant. Here medals were counted, there casualties. And the delights of the Olympics turned the horror into a mere subplot. A younger writer, always ready to pack up and go, would probably—or so I speculated—be able to cover both places, seizing control of the narrative situation with gripping words: snipers and female fencers, steroid scandals and blockade-runners, shortened national anthems and the seventeenth futile cease-fire, fireworks here, fireworks there. But all I could manage to get down in my notebook were scribblings on Germany. This damned inertia, like having lead weights in one's soles! On our wild-goose island, we did our best to put the alarming events of this month of crises out of our minds; blackberries were plentiful, after all, and we had fresh fish every day. But as we bundled the flounder heads in newspaper, from between their crossed eyes peeked yesterday's headlines. Later, under the Danish sky, we ate the headless flounder hot from the skillet. It was the beginning of August.

What makes sensitive people so insensitive? Though slightly irritable, we are nevertheless numbed. Even in church the minister remarks that too much is happening at once. Supposedly the glut of information is to blame for the general apathy. Because our society is overinformed, it behaves as if it were uninformed.

Or people ride their hobbyhorses: one person sees only the hole in the ozone layer, another is obsessed with health-care issues. If you grieve too much for the Bosnian refugees, you may neglect to include Somalia and the daily famine victims in your litany. Is the world out of joint, or is it only that the stock market is acting crazy, as it has so often recently?

◆

When the Olympic fireworks died away, for a while Sarajevo occupied center stage uncontested. This was painful, for the other hot spots could do no more than distract attention from this blatant failure of European politics. But even this disgraceful situation, in which the notion of "Europe" was revealed as a chimera, quickly became commonplace. Then news arrived from Germany, confirming once again that August was the month for crises.

Actually nothing new, just the same old stuff in a more extreme form. Over five hundred right-wing radicals repeatedly stormed a residence for asylum-seekers in Rostock-Lichtenhagen. From the windows of neighboring buildings Germans watched and cheered as stones and Molotov cocktails were thrown. That evening Germans saw them on television watching and cheering; some of them may even have recognized themselves.

Actually it was all familiar; this type of effectiveness had already been demonstrated in Hoyaswerda* and elsewhere. A routine had been worked out for transforming xenophobia into violence. This time, too, the police showed understanding for this terse expression of the people's will, and practiced restraint. A bit later the police were busy intercepting left-wing demonstrators. Here they showed greater zeal: this business could not be allowed to escalate. Our vacation radio carried the voices of politicians trying to outdo each other in displays of that easily mimed attitude known as bewilderment.

But then the rest of the world got involved, because, as more and more asylum-seekers' residences were set afire, there were witnesses abroad. Clips of howling mobs were disseminated worldwide. The "ugly German" was rearing his head again. Everywhere the headlines read "Rostock." So, sitting there on my Danish island, I jotted down notes for this address; my usual refuge, a manuscript, with its network of narrative escape routes, was blocked by a landslide. Something decisive had taken place.

Since then Germany has changed. Hoyaswerda could still be swept under the rug somehow, but since Rostock all the solemn declarations that accompanied the euphoria over unification have plummeted in value. Those whoops of triumph that greeted the end of the postwar period and hailed a new beginning, that festive mood that hoisted a unified Germany onto a pedestal—a dozen historians were already sharpening their pencils to write a new chapter in German history—that verbal prostitution so revolting even three years ago: all that has given way to a despondent meekness. Our past has tapped us on the shoulder, identifying us as perpetrators, fellow travelers, or members of the silent majority.

---

*In September 1991, in Hoyaswerda, neo-Nazis pelted a home for asylum-seekers with bricks as a crowd cheered. No arrests were made.

◆

Not that the shock silenced us. Protest was voiced, declarations and appeals gathered signatures. Recently huge rallies were organized to prove that we could still put up resistance. But the government policies of the last three years, which are to blame for this most recent relapse into German barbarity, have not been altered in the slightest, because none of their proponents see anything wrong with them. Meanwhile, the individual right to asylum—a jewel in our Constitution—is being put on the auction block to satisfy the instincts of the *Volk*, which the Nazis insisted on characterizing as "sound." Meanwhile, the policy of unity without unification is being pushed forward, bringing renewed division, this time based on socioeconomic inequality. And, meanwhile, neither the government nor the opposition seems willing or able to stop the shameless close-out sale being conducted with the assets of the bankrupt GDR and to take concrete steps to equalize the burden borne by the two parts of Germany.

Taking such steps was, and still is, the only right thing to do, for the East Germans spent forty years walled in, constantly spied on, and disenfranchised. They were never offered the option of Western freedom. In unfair measure they, not we, bore the burden for a war that was lost by all Germans. As soon as the Wall fell, this fact should have been acknowledged and acted upon as a matter of priority. We owed them that, not renewed disenfranchisement.

This question of the unfair distribution of the burden has troubled me and caused me to speak out since the early sixties; that is why I addressed the convention of the Social Democratic Party (SPD) on December 18, 1989, to call for a "far-reaching equalizing of the burden—due immediately and with no further preconditions." To finance it I suggested rigorous cuts in military expenditures and a graduated surtax. But at the time, my party comrades, who apparently believed in miracles, thought Willy Brandt's wonderful promise, "Now everything that belongs together will grow together," would come true without their lifting a finger. This even though it became apparent only weeks after the fall of the Wall that nothing worthwhile was ready to grow on its own, while profiteering was spreading like a cancer. After more than forty years of division, we Germans share only the burden of a guilty past; even our common language fails to produce understanding.

When I finished my speech, it was killed with faint applause, but at least it found its way into the written record of the meeting. A few weeks later, on February 2, 1990, at a congress in Tutzing on "New Answers to the German Question," I defended the proposition that "anyone thinking about Germany these days and looking for an answer to the German Question must include Auschwitz in his thoughts."

I also warned against creating German unity by slam-bang annexation, and suggested instead a confederation, at least for the present. These comments unleashed a storm of indignation. My speech had touched a raw nerve. I, the "self-appointed pessimist of the nation," the "notorious enemy of Germany unity," was accused of "instrumentalizing Auschwitz," of trying to abridge the Germans' right to self-determination by dredging up this old subject.

I would like to ask my critics, at the time so intoxicated with unity, whether they had any second thoughts when they learned recently that the so-called Jewish barracks at the Sachsenhausen concentration camp had been burned to the ground.

Back in 1990 they were all using the same demented railroad metaphor: "The train has left the station, and no one can stop it." Let me remind them today of the renewed barbarity for which their railroad imagery gave Germans the go-ahead.

Warnings against latent and overt anti-Semitism and about pogroms aimed at gypsies have been overtaken by events. Auschwitz and Auschwitz-Birkenau, where almost half a million Roma and Sinti were murdered, are very much with us again. In Germany today, gypsies are once more being classified as asocial elements. They have become regular targets of violence. Yet no political force seems willing or able to stop these repeated criminal acts.

On the contrary: it is not only, and not primarily, the skinheads who are shattering the democratic consensus of our society with their telegenic theatrics; rather, it was certain politicians whose verbal pyrotechnics ignited the subject of immigration and made the desperation of refugees and asylum-seekers a permanent campaign issue. By signaling the end of civilized behavior toward these people, they encouraged acts of violence and murder by right-wing radical groups then forming. Interior Minister Seiters recently negotiated an agreement with the Romanian government. If you read it carefully, you realize that it provides for deporting any Roma who seek asylum in Germany. This policy, and the steady stream of attacks on the asylum provisions in the Constitution, can be seen as more or less veiled preformulations of the slogan that is now unifying Germany: "Foreigners get out!"

One of these politicians, Volker Rühe, has in the meantime become minister of defense, and behaves as though he were single-handedly holding the nation together. When I described his activity as secretary general of the Christian Democratic Union as that of a "skinhead with a tie and hair," he dismissed this characterization as tiresome sniping. But I plan to continue pointing out the likeness, because terrorist behavior must not only be recognized for what it is, but also called by name—in the camp of the perpetrators. How can this government be expected to stop the double-dealing it initiated intentionally, and continues to pursue out of abject fear of the *Volk*, with its obstinately "sound" instincts?

The Federal Republic of Germany and its Constitution, the Basic Law, have been handed over to a demolition firm that claims to be engaged in conservation and preservation. The plan to celebrate the fiftieth anniversary of the first testing of the V-4 rocket in Peenemünde, called off only because of protests from abroad, is just one indication of how far things have gone. When the country's political center lurches to the right, and this development is laughed off instead of being recognized as an existential threat, we Germans had better consider ourselves dangerous—before our neighbors begin to view us as a threat. That is why I have chosen to denounce some of these solid citizens as arsonists, and to name them. That is why I point out that the present crisis in the country has its roots in government policy. That is why my "address on Germany" must avoid distracting details and excursions into superficial patriotism. Instead, I want to use the question mark to drill down to the deeper layers.

◆

Does no healing herb exist to cure this German tendency to regress? Do ancient runic inscriptions compel us to repeat the past? Must everything, even the miraculous gift of possible union, turn into something monstrous in our hands? Are we, still smarting from the wounds from our last excursion into the absolute, incapable of civil, humane dealings with each other and with foreigners? What do we Germans, in the midst of all our wealth, lack?

These questions I jotted down at the end of August in Denmark. This is a country not noted for excessive friendliness toward strangers. Yet in Denmark the kind of hatred that finds expression in a thirst for murder—such as we witnessed in Hoyaswerda, Rostock, and hundreds of other German towns—is unheard of, hardly thinkable, even under conditions of extreme stress.

In the spring of 1945, when the Soviet armies were pushing westward, many thousands of Germans fled over the Baltic to Denmark, which had been occupied by the Wehrmacht since April 1940. In May 1945 the Greater German Reich finally capitulated to the Allies. It never crossed the Danes' minds to vent their understandable anger or even hatred toward the country that had occupied them in violent acts against the German refugees. On the contrary: though suffering from shortages themselves, they provided for their enemies. The refugees' return to Germany had none of the earmarks of a brutal deportation. I could tell you about refugees from East and West Prussia who not once during their time in Denmark were reminded that they were refugees. By contrast, in the German towns to which they were assigned by the government they experienced persistent xenophobia. Even in those days people were saying, "Go back where you came from!"

The Danes take their high degree of civilized behavior for granted. They do not talk about it, or at most in ironic asides. We Germans, however, despite all our efforts, all our asseverations, have not succeeded in mending the crack in German society's civilized veneer that became visible in 1933.

In the early seventies it seemed reasonable to hope that we could at least fill this crack, if not obliterate it; a push for reform held out the promise that we would finally overcome our social backwardness. But before long extremists on the left were hurling their vituperative slogans against the vituperative tirades of Axel Springer's right-wing press conglomerate, and political murder came into style, starting with the attempt on Rudi Dutschke's life. Political opponents were quickly dubbed enemies. When Willy Brandt went to Poland and knelt before the Warsaw Ghetto monument, his act was greeted with scorn, even in the Bundestag. Starting with Konrad Adenauer's 1961 diatribe, intended to insult and injure the former émigré, Willy Brandt was treated as a stranger in Germany, and he remained a stranger until his death; no state memorial service could conceal that fact.

When the young man from Lübeck [Willy Brandt] fled from the Nazis to Norway, and later to Sweden, he requested and was granted asylum. The compromise adopted yesterday at the SPD convention*

*On November 17 the Social Democrats voted at a special meeting to accept changes to the constitutional provisions on asylum: applicants from countries considered free of political persecution would be sent home; persons denied asylum in another country would not be able to apply for asylum in Germany; applicants who falsified documents, suppressed records, applied under a false name, or were found guilty of a crime would be deported; and communities taking in asylum-seekers *(over)*

446 LEGACY OF DISSENT

does not allay my fears. I wish to put the Social Democrats on notice:
any SPD member of the Bundestag prepared in the near future to
limit the right to asylum that is guaranteed by our Constitution will,
by such an act, retroactively strike a blow against all emigrants, dead
as well as living—all those who were forced to leave Germany and
found a refuge in Scandinavia and Mexico, in Holland, England, the
United States. Any vote curtailing the right to asylum that receives a
majority in the Bundestag will mean a break with the history of German social democracy.

Some people might say, What difference can one more break
make? We Germans are used to breaks and splits. Being fragmented
has been normal for us—since the Thirty Years' War, at least. Ambivalence, duality, what one might call the Hamlet syndrome, is part of
us, which explains why we are constantly striving for unity, usually in
vain, or at too high a cost.

According to this interpretation, being German would mean being
split, in every aspect of our existence and consciousness. At the same
time, being German would mean suffering from the absence of unity,
which in turn explains why we are always preoccupied with ourselves.
For this we are ridiculed by our neighbors, who cultivate other, less
dangerous, forms of bad manners. But I have no patience with such
simplifications, handy though they may be. In point of fact the West
Germans hardly suffered from the division of their country. They actually made it worse, through indifference. Toward the end of the
two-state period, many even began to question the significance of
June 17—the national holiday instituted to commemorate a leader-
less workers' rebellion in East Berlin,** which West German politicians' rhetoric had transformed into a popular uprising. When the
prospect of unification suddenly appeared on the horizon, the West
Germans were terrified, for, in spite of the chancellor's lies, they had
a pretty good idea of what it would cost. No, we were not fixated on
unity. Perhaps we remembered vaguely from our history that unity
had brought us Germans nothing but misfortune.

◆

would dispense aid in kind rather than cash support. The SPD voted not to eliminate
the constitutional provision for asylum and the guarantee that individual cases would
be considered on their merit; but that merit was to be determined under the provisions of the 1951 Geneva Convention on political persecution.
  **Revolt of the workers of East Berlin, June 1953.

While preparing for this address last summer I made one note—Germans always go overboard!—that calls for amplification here, in the form of explanation or contradiction.

Do we, whom other countries admire for our earnest efforts to achieve security within our own four walls, really go overboard so badly? Contradictory evidence offers itself. Isn't it true that French and American political scientists and historians—Alfred Grosser and Fritz Stern, for instance—have, when asked, given us a satisfactory grade in political maturity?

Isn't it true that, as far as the western part of the country is concerned, forty years of continuing education in democracy have resulted in an exemplary degree of social consensus, which seemed to justify our ideological claim to a "social market economy"?

Isn't it true that up to the moment when we regained our national sovereignty we presented ourselves cautiously and modestly to the rest of the world? The economic giant as political dwarf—which explains why boasts like "We're somebody again" and similar posturing immediately brought placating rejoinders that everything was relative and that we should remember to be humble.

Isn't it true that we made every effort to comply promptly and obediently with any NATO directive, like good defensive players?

And up until the Historians' Debate*—which took place shortly before unification—didn't we bear patiently the burden of the past, the German guilt complex, the shame of a stigma that refused to fade, hoping, to be sure, that some day all that could be laid to rest?

And, altogether, don't we prefer to define phrases like "fond of order," "socially tolerant," "willing to compromise," "balanced," to arrogant demands of the "either-or" and "at any cost" variety?

It is certainly correct to say that the citizens of the Federal Republic of Germany seemed to have become civilized, on their own initiative and ahead of their political parties and special-interest groups. Even the harsh tone civil servants customarily employed toward citizens, based on mutual assumptions about governmental authority, had to yield in the face of the admonition "Be nice to one another." People were civil to each other. The past remained a compulsory topic for discussion in schools. To be sure, there were still old Nazis around, externally wedded to the past, in Nietzsche's phrase. But at the end of the sixties, when the NPD, a party of mostly older right-wing radicals, won seats in a number of local parliaments, the democratic left was

*The debate in the 1980s about the nature and sources of Nazism.

there, too, and succeeded in reducing the threat to insignificance by confronting, in an open, nonviolent way, the issues the NPD raised. The apparition vanished, the rightist camp fell apart.

At least that is how it appeared. The GDR, by definition avowedly antifascist, found itself deprived of a chance to gloat. In the West it seemed reasonable to hope that a last relapse had been survived. The younger generation had at its disposal a democratic preserve, generously equipped with discovery playgrounds, heated swimming pools, discotheques, and sociological expertise on tap. All this afforded the young folks ample comfort and freedom of movement, and held out the prospect of a peaceful, tolerant society based on heavy consumption of youth-oriented products. Styles changed innocuously, and the *Zeitgeist* was god.

◆

But even before the fall of the Wall and the slam-bang unification, the impression that Germany, at least its western part, had been cleansed turned out to be a delusion. Then the bankrupt GDR, with its entire inventory, animate and inanimate, was annexed by the Federal Republic's large chains and energy syndicates, banks and insurance companies. This annexation, cutely dubbed "united fatherland," did away with self-deception once and for all, uncovered the whole pan-German swindle, and—no sooner than we had achieved sovereignty—gave a powerful boost to our tendency to go overboard.

The social consensus, hammered together with such difficulty, at once began to crack at the joints. The modesty we had been trained to display was denounced as hidebound and provincial, and braggadocio became the order of the day. Influential newspapers urged us to jettison the burden of the German past, hitherto a painful component of our self-definition.

Meanwhile, the Soviet Union was collapsing, allowing the Western camp, and with it capitalism, to declare itself the winner over communism. As pan-Germans, we threw in our lot with the winning side, determined to set everything straight once and for all: there was to be no Third Way or even democratic socialism from now on. Renunciation of utopian ideals was prescribed like a cure for worms. Even where no real market existed, the free-market system was imposed with narrow-minded dogmatism. And the democratic left was to be removed from the picture entirely, for the sake of setting everything straight. This was the democratic left that had spoken out against communism, with clear arguments and free of blind hate; that had proved the most reliable bulwark against threats to the Federal Republic from the radical right; that despite internal dissension had shown itself stalwartly patriotic in defending the Constitution.

Germany has never suffered from a lack of cleaning men, but seldom has a clean-up been carried out so professionally. Those who initiated it, and are keeping it going, were primarily former communists and repentant Maoists. Adopting the style and methods of the Jacobins, they are already busy reintroducing load-bearing lampposts, as well as a relic from medieval times, the whipping-post. And because they have mastered the art of inducing public self-incrimination like no others, the German denunciation business will have plenty to do for the foreseeable future. God or whoever preserve us from the zeal of these converts!

Since this purge began, enlivening the editorial pages and providing some excitement at panel discussions, the democratic left can be found in only two forms: as a ghost one can conjure up, or as a few lone fossils. One of these fossils is speaking to you now. This is what I see when I look around me: the left has been ground down; the Third Way has been closed off. The last defenders of the Constitution will soon be on display at the zoo as an endangered species. The question must be asked: is there any political force currently in a position to fill this intentionally created gap and offer resistance to right-wing terror?

We cannot expect much from the middle-class moderates. They are vulnerable to the handwriting on the wall invoked by the likes of Stoiber, when he points to the "threat of the racial dilution of the German people"; to the moderates, any such thing is a fate worse than death, and they find themselves sympathizing with the right-wing terror, though it makes them uncomfortable: "What will people say abroad? It will scare off investors!" Streibl's allusions to a "multi-criminal society" and Minister of Finance Theodor Waigel's certainty that "future elections can only be won to the right of center" have not fallen on deaf ears.

On October 3, the Day of German Unity, right-wing radical hordes stormed through the streets of Dresden shouting the old Nazi cry, "*Juda verrecke*" ("Death to all Jews!"). The local police and reinforcements summoned from West Germany provided a protective escort. Meanwhile, in Schwerin, any protesters who turned out to demonstrate against the unity chancellor, who was celebrating his great role in history in the Schwerin Theater, were prudently removed from the scene. In Munich, where not long ago a few dozen leftist penny whistles evoked a massive police response, one can clearly perceive, even without referring to the precedent of the Weimar Republic, the right-leaning weakness of the enlarged Federal Republic.

Once again we seem to have gone overboard. The proposition I jotted down last August in Denmark in the form of a question could now be confirmed by further excesses over which the legislative branch of government has no control. Let me mention, as an all-too-compliant supplier of material to *Der Spiegel,* the agency set up to sift through the STASI's* files looking for informers. Ironically, the STASI's hard work is finally paying off; the slow-acting poison is taking effect. The civilized principle that used to obtain—"innocent until proven guilty"—has been reversed: now mere suspicion is considered evidence of guilt.

As a further example of going overboard let me mention the centralized nightmare known as the *Treuhandanstalt,* the agency charged with privatizing holdings in the former GDR. This agency has well-nigh unlimited power to decide people's fates. Nothing compelled us to create these monsters. Now they have taken on a life of their own. Whatever possessed us to behave so mercilessly toward battered, humiliated human beings? Did we West Germans secretly hope to prove ourselves at the "Ossis'" expense? Were they supposed to do penance for our permitting ourselves Chancellor Kurt Georg Kiesinger and thousands of lawyers and judges with Nazi credentials? Were they, our often invoked "poor brothers and sisters," supposed to indemnify us for the things that went wrong under the sun of the economic miracle? Apropos going overboard: how can one begin to measure the self-righteousness that finds expression in these actions?

◆

I said this at the beginning: during the summer, which was harsh and obstinately dry, the wild geese had halted their flights to our island. There were no distractions. I could not keep my writing paper from filling up with the accumulated bitterness of two years of unity. That is why my Danish notes now impel me to speak of myself, of Germany and myself. Of how I did not want to let go of this country. Of how I somehow mislaid this country. Of what I lack, and what I miss. Also of the things I am happy to be rid of. That is why I have titled my address "On Loss."

*The East German secret police.

The list is long; let me confine myself to a few telling examples. It began with the loss of my homeland. As painful as this loss remained, I could understand and accept the reasons for it. German guilt for wartime atrocities, for the genocide perpetrated on Jews and gypsies, for the murder of millions of prisoners of war and forced laborers, for the crime of euthanasia, and for the suffering we inflicted as occupying power on our neighbors, especially the Polish people—all this led to the loss of my homeland.

Compared with millions of refugees who had a difficult time coming to feel at home in the West, I was well off. With the help of language I managed, not to overcome the loss, but at least, by piecing words together like patchwork, to shape something from which the loss could be read.

Most of my books invoke the vanished city of Danzig, with its nearby hills and flatlands, with the dull pounding of the Baltic. As the years went by, Gdansk, too, became a topic that wanted to be written about. Loss made me eloquent. Only when you lose something entirely are you inspired with this passion for endless naming, this mania for calling the lost object by name until it finally answers. Loss as the prerequisite for literature. I am almost tempted to concoct a theory based on this experience.

In addition, the loss of my homeland has freed me up for other sorts of commitments. Having a real homeland carries a certain compulsion to stay put. That no longer applies. An almost frivolous pleasure in moving around indulges curiosity about the unfamiliar. A person without a homeland has wider horizons than people who inhabit small or even large inherited plots. Since no ideology artificially inflated the value of my loss—for nothing primally German was lost; nothing primally Polish was regained—I did not need the crutch of nationalism to understand myself as a German.

Different values became important to me. Losing them is more difficult to accept, because they do leave a gap that cannot be filled. I was accustomed to stirring up controversy with my written and spoken words. But during the last three years, that is, as long as I was criticizing German unification, misconceived from the outset, and making a litany of my warnings against the slam-bang process, I eventually had to recognize that I was speaking and writing into a void. My patriotism, which owes its allegiance not to the state but to the Constitution, was not welcome.

I was not alone. I would guess that the same loss has been experienced by Jürgen Habermas and Walter Jens, Christoph Hein and

Friedrich Schorlemmer, as well as by all those who, with Wolfgang Ullmann and the "Alliance for a Democratically Structured Federation of German Countries," tried in vain to carry out the obligation expressed in the last article of the Basic Law. This article 146, since deleted, directed that in case of unification the German people should be given a new Constitution to vote on.

The movement for that is past. Leading journalists supported the hasty annexation and dismissed article 146 as meaningless. They share the responsibility for the national catastrophe that unification has become. Yet to this day they refuse to admit that their misleading signals and the avoidance of a timely debate over the Constitution were mistakes that carry grave consequences.

Somewhere in secret a constitutional commission is in session. At the same time there is no lack of effort to place further restrictions on the already battered Basic Law.

Granted: speaking without an echo is new to me, and in the long run not very stimulating. Was the situation ever different? Certainly! There were a few years there, when Willy Brandt was chancellor, trying to make a reality of his first official exhortation, "Take a chance on more democracy!" Brandt and his wife, Rut, felt comfortable engaging in free-wheeling discussion with intellectuals. The bold concept of "political culture," now reduced to a mere rhetorical flourish, was actually lived for a while. That is to say, we listened to one another, a virtue that could be learned from Willy Brandt.

When Siegfried Lenz and I accompanied the chancellor to Warsaw in December 1970, we did not feel as though we had merely gone along for the ride. No, precisely because Lenz and I had both accepted the loss of our homeland, our presence implied recognition of Poland's western border. Proud of Germany? Yes, in retrospect I am proud of having been in Warsaw with Brandt.

By the way, it was not only Brandt and his inner circle who contributed to this form of political culture. There was Gustav Heinemann, too. Right after his election as federal president a journalist tried to trip him up with the question, "Do you love the state?" Heinemann responded with exemplary brevity, "I don't love the state, I love my wife." He, too, enjoyed the company of intellectuals, even for a game of cards.

◆

When I try to conjure up this period, so brief, yet of such lasting significance, I am speaking of something lost. Something that could have continued, but remained a one-time phenomenon. Willy Brandt's death made me feel this loss more acutely.

And other losses: Whatever became of the diversity of public opinion? What a rustling of leaves we had in the German journalistic forest when *Der Spiegel* was still true to its original promise, offering a clear alternative to the Springer press. Then there was the radical liberalism of the Hamburg weekly *Die Zeit,* which set it so clearly apart from the stodgy conservatism of the *Frankfürter Allgemeine,* even though their business sections took much the same tack. Now the editors of the cultural pages of these papers are interchangeable; they contradict each other only in coy asides. It has become fashionable to assume an air of superiority toward the democratic left. (There are exceptions to this unified editorial policy, of course. From the ashes of the once straitjacketed GDR press a few journals have managed to emerge in new forms. But, then, who in the West reads the eastern *Wochenpost?*) With public opinion already at risk from the galloping formation of press conglomerates, this trend to political conformity could be the death blow. That would mean a loss no democracy can survive.

To speak of these matters in Munich and not mention the *Süddeutsche Zeitung* would be impolite. Granted: it is still holding its own, at least for now. But although it is far more than a regional paper, it is certainly much better known in Bavaria than in Brandenburg.

Perhaps this last example makes it clear how estranged the Germans are from each other. They acknowledge each other's existence only reluctantly. With the differences between East and West hardening, Mecklenburgers and Saxons over there feel farther than ever from Rhinelanders and Swabians over here. Even North and South Germans remain strangers to each other, separated by the Main.

These distinctions result from our history, which promoted separatism and only rarely, and for the most part reluctantly, furthered unity. But perhaps our fear of strangers is the price we pay for the cultural multiplicity of the country, which often becomes apparent at state and athletic events.

Our federalist structure is appropriate. It guarantees not only the more disturbing but also the more stimulating differences, and safeguards, with the zeal of a cottage gardener maintaining his fences, our cultural riches, which can always count on those government subsidies that support everything from amateur theaters to archaeological sites.

Our Basic Law wants it this way. Yet federalism, a clever insurance the Germans took out against themselves, has suffered damage in the recent unification process. Not that the sovereignty of the individual provinces has been abrogated; no, the old German separatism, the accumulated self-centeredness of the provinces, their stubborn stewing in their own juice, their selfish scrabbling for subsidies and reparations, has robbed German federalism of that capacity to impose political structure that the federal government and the opposition have failed to manifest during the process of unification. But when federalism as a corrective fails, another loss must be added to the previous list.

I do not hesitate to call the Bundestag's decision to move the capital from Bonn to Berlin a farce. The president of the Bundestag has had to play the role of producer. The vote was taken, then essentially scuttled by business-as-usual in Bonn. The media are in on the act. The expensive set for future debates and window appearances has been dedicated. While everything continues in the same old groove, east of the Elbe the baby has fallen into the well and is screaming.

It's its own fault it fell in. Why all this blubbering? What do they want now? After a while you just stop listening.

Only Regine Hildebrandt, minister for social welfare of the state of Brandenburg, has enough voice left to get people to listen to the baby occasionally. She calls the continuing injustice by name. Whenever this woman makes an appearance, sparks fly from the television screen. She rejects the prevailing genteel tone. Her directness is refreshing; no one could accuse her of being slick. Who, if not Regine Hildebrandt, would be the ideal successor to President Richard von Weizsäcker!

But could we put up with this woman? Would her abrasive charm be compatible with our aesthetic of polish? Would we be brave enough to tolerate Regine Hildebrandt, the glowing passion of her demands, which would fuse the newly splintered country together again?

Or have we Germans become so estranged from one another that we can no longer see past our established property rights? And—the question has a certain urgency—is the inveterate foreignness that exists between Germans the source of the present hostility toward foreigners (whom we call "outlanders") that is covering our country with shame?

Rostock on the radio: the German Broadcasting System. On the Danish island I found an outlet for my rage; later I tried to transfer it with a cold needle to copper plates: punctuation as a last resort.

But even when the rage ebbed, it left sorrow and anger behind. Notes took the form of questions: What have you done to my country? What made this mess they call unity possible? What beer-induced enthusiasm persuaded the voting public to entrust this difficult task, which called for extraordinary political deftness, to a tax-cheat and a man who cooked the books? How were critical economic decisions left to that sinister trio, Bange-, Hauss-, and Möllemann?* What producer came up with the brilliant idea of smuggling the topic of dissension-ridden Germany into the blah-blah of the evening talk shows? What stupidity caused us to miscalculate what it meant to take in sixteen million Germans, so that we ended up saddling these people, who had already suffered the injustice of "real socialism," with capitalism's own brand of injustice? Why can't we Germans act humanely, if not toward foreigners at least toward our own people? What are we lacking?

Perhaps we are lacking those we fear—fear because they are strangers to us and look strange. We are suffering from too little exposure to those whom fear makes us hate. And perhaps we lack most acutely those found farthest down on the scale of contempt: the Roma and the Sinti, commonly known as gypsies. No one takes their side. No deputy in the European Parliament or in the Bundestag consistently represents their cause, calls attention to their desperate situation. There is no state to which they might appeal and which would be willing to support and embrace, as a matter of national policy, their claim, justified since Auschwitz, for what is pathetically termed reparation.

The Roma and the Sinti are the quintessential victims. "Deport them!" says Interior Minister Seiters, and gets Romania to cooperate. "Smoke them out!" bawl the skinheads, and provide Herr Seiters with a specific pretext for his deportation policy. But in Romania, too, and elsewhere the gypsies are the quintessential victims. Why should this be?

Because they are different, or worse still: different from different. Because they steal, and roam from one place to another, and have the evil eye, and also have that disturbing beauty that makes us look ugly. Because their very existence calls our value system into question. They are acknowledged to be useful for operas and operettas, but also seen—even if it sounds bad and reminds us of something bad—

*Martin Bangemann, Helmut Haussmann, and Jürgen Möllemann successively resigned as minister of economics because of scandal.

as asocial, degenerate, worthless. "Torch them!" the skinheads bawl.

Seven years ago Heinrich Böll was laid to rest. The coffin and the honorary pallbearers—Böll's sons, Lev Kopelev, Günter Wallraff, and I—were led by a gypsy band to the gravesite. That was what Böll had requested. For his final music he wanted these profoundly mournful, then suddenly desperately merry tunes. Not until today do I fully understand Böll's unspoken message.

Let them come and stay, if they wish. Let half a million and more Roma and Sinti be among us Germans; we need them desperately.

Look at little Portugal, where, in spite of all the refugees from the former colonies, thousands of gypsies have found a place, as if it were the most natural thing in the world.

You hard-bitten Germans, let your hearts be touched at last, and give the skinheads an answer dictated not by fear but by courage, a humane answer.

Stop pushing the gypsies out onto that old, well-trodden path.

They can help us, by providing an irritant to our rigid order. It would not hurt to have some aspects of their way of life rub off on us. They would be a gain, after so much loss. They could teach us how meaningless borders are; the Roma and Sinti do not recognize borders. The gypsies are at home everywhere in Europe. They truly are what we claim to be: born Europeans!

Translated from the German by Krishna Winston

Afterword

Two Cheers for Utopia
1993

◆

IRVING HOWE

We live in a time of diminished expectations. It's not exactly a time of conservative dominance, although the dominant politics in some countries is an unenthusiastic conservatism. Nor is it a time of liberal dominance, although in the United States the Clinton administration has given rise to some liberal hopes, by no means certain of realization. And it's certainly not a time of leftist domination, even though moderate social-democratic parties hold office in some European countries.

It's tempting to compare this post–cold-war moment to the postrevolutionary decades of early-nineteenth-century England. But the comparison is of slight value, since what we are experiencing might better be called a postcounterrevolutionary moment. Idealistic visions, utopian hopes, desires for social renovation are all out of fashion—indeed, are regarded as dangerous illusions that set off memories of totalitarian disasters. Leftist bashing, in both newspaper editorials and learned books, is very much in. The current catchword is sobriety, which sometimes looks like a cover for depression.

This is true of the intellectual world, with the exception of a few mavericks like Günter Grass. It is also true for what remains of the European left—either solid, decent social democrats with barely a touch of fire left in them or unrepentant communists masquerading as socialists in Eastern Europe.

There are, of course, many reasons for this mood indigo, only a few years after the enthusiasm raised by the "velvet revolution" in Czechoslovakia and the Gorbachev reforms in the former Soviet Union. But in this comment I want to focus on only one reason: the aftermath, or perhaps more accurately, the aftertaste of the collapse of communism.

Some years ago Theodore Draper made a remark in conversation that has stuck in my mind: the central experience of the twentieth century, he said, was communism, like it or hate it. To be sure, there was fascism and the end of colonialism, but fascism could be seen as essentially a ghastly reaction to the rise of radicalism and the end of colonialism as an all-but-inevitable cluster of events. In its years of influence and power, communism seized upon the imagination of millions of people throughout the world. Communist parties were powerful in most of the major European countries; a bit later, they appropriated the heritage of anticolonialism in Asian and African countries; and even in the United States, where the Communist Party was never a major force, it has been reliably estimated that nearly a million people passed through the Stalinist milieu (not the party) between, say, 1920 and 1950.

Declaring itself the legatee of humanism and the bearer of good news, communism inspired thousands—no, hundreds of thousands—of workers, students, intellectuals, to feats of devotion and, sometimes, heroism. Seldom have so many good people sacrificed themselves for so bad a cause. There were of course careerists, hacks, and thugs in the communist movement; but for many ordinary people "the movement" burned with flames of hope. Those of us who were longtime anti-Stalinists, enclosed in our little groups and sects, found it hard to acknowledge the idealism—twisted, distorted, corrupted yet idealism nonetheless—that went into the communist movement. To be sure, in the Eastern European countries the communist dictatorships attracted a large share of careerists (the kinds of people who in the United States might have been Republican officeholders). But there, too, the communists gained the support of decent, misguided followers. When the anti-Stalinist groups won over a handful of people from the Communist parties, it was almost always people who were intellectually and psychologically exhausted, their fanaticism burned out and their intellectual energies diminished.

The communist movement destroyed entire generations. The sheer waste of human resources, of the energies that might have been available for social renovation, is incalculable. With many rank-and-file militants, the sequel has been silence. With a good many former communist leaders, the sequel has been an ugly form of nationalism—as in Yugoslavia, where the leaders of both Serbia and Croatia are former prominent communists.

The results of this great historical disaster are staggering. Even those of us in the United States, insulated by our native mythologies, who were never tempted by communism, are experiencing the consequences. New generations, new energies do not arrive overnight.

There has first to be an interval of weariness, disillusionment, "pragmatism"—and diminished expectations.

◆

You can see the signs of this exhaustion if you pick up any of the leading intellectual journals. Some are sour (usually edited by ex-radicals) and others are timid (usually edited by quasiliberals). Some subsist by mocking the hopes of their youth. Others avoid any long-range expectations or desires. Still others narrow their focus of concern to the daily routines of politics, sometimes saying useful things, though not much more.

What I've been saying here holds, I'm afraid, for large segments of the European social democracy. Let me be clear: if I lived in any of the major European countries, I would belong to or support the social democratic party. I might be critical, I might tilt a little toward whatever left wing it had. But I would be part of it.

Yet the truth is that, except in one or two countries, social democracy today has become a decent and honorable party that (rhetoric apart—and that even less and less) does not really aspire to move beyond the status quo. Little of the spirit of socialism remains in these parties. That much said, it's only fair to add that this isn't entirely their fault. For one thing, the constituencies of these parties, the people who vote for them, also share in their spiritual hesitation, their intellectual skepticism and bewilderment. It's not as if "the masses" are pressing the social democrats for a more radical outlook. Nor is it as if there were a clear socialist idea or vision that the parties reject. For the truth—as every *Dissent* reader learns from every issue we publish, perhaps to excess—is that the socialist idea is as precarious as the ideas of the conservatives and liberals, though the latter have the advantage of being at ease with the existing social and political order, while the social democrats presumably desire some change. The difficulty of formulating an attractive program is far more serious for the social democrats than for their opponents. Devoted to decency and democracy—no small matters—the social democrats cannot evoke the idealism and selflessness of the socialist yesterday. The memories of yesterday grow dimmer; one of the last to embody these was Willy Brandt, and now he is gone.

So there really is no point in the old-style leftist denunciation of social democracy. What we can and should criticize the social democrats for is not that they have failed to come up with the "answers"; it is for having largely abandoned the questions.

Well, we *Dissent*ers, the handful of us, try to hold fast to the vision of social transformation, even as we have dropped many of the traditional proposals for how to reach it. Some of us call this belief socialism, out of a wish for historical continuity or for lack of a better label. It's not that we're smarter than most European social democrats; not at all. Our advantage, if that's what it is, consists in the fact that we are distant from power and therefore able or, indeed, driven to think in terms of long-range possibilities, the revival of the democratic left in what may turn out to be the not-very-near future. Of course we also respond to immediate issues, so that *Dissent* carries articles about taxes, health care, budget crises, and so on. But even if, at a given moment, the immediate issues loom large, at least some of us want to think in terms of long-range options. We want, that is, to avoid the provincialism of the immediate.

That's why in almost every issue of *Dissent* you'll find one or two articles about "market socialism" or allied topics. Some of our readers, I suspect, quietly skip past these articles. That's OK, as long as they see why we print them. Often enough, these articles are provisional, a little abstract, and inclined to disagreements with one another. They don't necessarily paint a picture of an actual future—who can? But they are efforts to indicate possibilities of renewal. They provide materials for developments some of us will never live to see. They are, if you please, sketches of utopia.

That word "utopia" has come into disrepute. In much intellectual discussion it tends to be used as a term of dismissal. And, of course, there are versions of utopia—based on force or terror or the will of a self-appointed "vanguard"—that are abhorrent. We have had enough of these.

But there are other utopias. There is the democratic utopianism that runs like a bright thread through American intellectual life—call it Emersonianism, call it republicanism, call it whatever you like. There is the utopia of community and egalitarianism.

In an essay Lewis Coser and I wrote some forty years ago in the second issue of *Dissent,* we quoted a passage from Ernst Cassirer that still speaks to our condition:

> A Utopia is not a portrait of the real world, of the actual political or social order. It exists at no moment of time and at no point in space; it is a "nowhere." But just such a conception of a nowhere has stood the test and proved its strength in the development of the modern world. It follows from the nature and character of ethical thought that it can never condescend to accept the "given." The ethical world is never given; it is forever in the making.

In the sense that Cassirer speaks of it, utopianism is a necessity of the moral imagination. It doesn't necessarily entail a particular politics; it doesn't ensure wisdom about current affairs. What it does provide is a guiding perspective, a belief or hope for the future, an understanding that nothing is more mistaken than the common notion that what exists today will continue to exist tomorrow. This kind of utopianism is really another way of appreciating the variety and surprise that history makes possible—possible, nothing more. It is a testimony to the resourcefulness that humanity now and then displays (together with other, far less attractive characteristics). It is a claim for the value of desire, the practicality of yearning—as against the deadliness of acquiescing in the "given" simply because it is here.

With all due modesty, I think this version of utopianism speaks for us. So, to friend and foe, at a moment when the embers of utopianism seem very low, I'd say: You want to call us utopians? That's fine with me.